T0320729

Teaching, Learning, and Leading With Computer Simulations

Yufeng Qian
Louisiana State University, USA

A volume in the Advances in
Educational Technologies and
Instructional Design (AETID) Book
Series

Published in the United States of America by
IGI Global
Information Science Reference (an imprint of IGI Global)
701 E. Chocolate Avenue
Hershey PA, USA 17033
Tel: 717-533-8845
Fax: 717-533-8661
E-mail: cust@igi-global.com
Web site: http://www.igi-global.com

Copyright © 2020 by IGI Global. All rights reserved. No part of this publication may be
reproduced, stored or distributed in any form or by any means, electronic or mechanical, including
photocopying, without written permission from the publisher.
Product or company names used in this set are for identification purposes only. Inclusion of the
names of the products or companies does not indicate a claim of ownership by IGI Global of the
trademark or registered trademark.

Library of Congress Cataloging-in-Publication Data

Names: Qian, Yufeng, 1967- editor.
Title: Teaching, learning, and leading with computer simulations / [edited
    by] Yufeng Qian.
Description: Hershey, PA : Information Sciences Reference, 2019. |
    Includes bibliographical references. | Summary: ""This book examines the
    recent advancement of simulation technology and explores the innovative
    ways that advanced simulation programs are used to enhance and transform
    teaching and learning"--Provided by publisher"-- Provided by publisher.
Identifiers: LCCN 2019015743 | ISBN 9781799800040 (hardcover) | ISBN
    9781799800057 (paperback) | ISBN 9781799800064 (ebook)
Subjects: LCSH: Education--Simulation methods. | Computer-assisted
    instruction.
Classification: LCC LB1029.S53 T43 2019 | DDC 371.39/7--dc23
LC record available at https://lccn.loc.gov/2019015743

This book is published in the IGI Global book series Advances in Educational Technologies and
Instructional Design (AETID) (ISSN: 2326-8905; eISSN: 2326-8913)

British Cataloguing in Publication Data
A Cataloguing in Publication record for this book is available from the British Library.

All work contributed to this book is new, previously-unpublished material.
The views expressed in this book are those of the authors, but not necessarily of the publisher.

For electronic access to this publication, please contact: eresources@igi-global.com.

Advances in Educational Technologies and Instructional Design (AETID) Book Series

ISSN:2326-8905
EISSN:2326-8913

Editor-in-Chief: Lawrence A. Tomei, Robert Morris University, USA

MISSION

Education has undergone, and continues to undergo, immense changes in the way it is enacted and distributed to both child and adult learners. In modern education, the traditional classroom learning experience has evolved to include technological resources and to provide online classroom opportunities to students of all ages regardless of their geographical locations. From distance education, Massive-Open-Online-Courses (MOOCs), and electronic tablets in the classroom, technology is now an integral part of learning and is also affecting the way educators communicate information to students.

The **Advances in Educational Technologies & Instructional Design (AETID) Book Series** explores new research and theories for facilitating learning and improving educational performance utilizing technological processes and resources. The series examines technologies that can be integrated into K-12 classrooms to improve skills and learning abilities in all subjects including STEM education and language learning. Additionally, it studies the emergence of fully online classrooms for young and adult learners alike, and the communication and accountability challenges that can arise. Trending topics that are covered include adaptive learning, game-based learning, virtual school environments, and social media effects. School administrators, educators, academicians, researchers, and students will find this series to be an excellent resource for the effective design and implementation of learning technologies in their classes.

COVERAGE

- Hybrid Learning
- Classroom Response Systems
- Virtual School Environments
- Bring-Your-Own-Device
- Curriculum Development
- Instructional Design Models
- Instructional Design
- Online Media in Classrooms
- Social Media Effects on Education
- Educational Telecommunications

IGI Global is currently accepting manuscripts for publication within this series. To submit a proposal for a volume in this series, please contact our Acquisition Editors at Acquisitions@igi-global.com or visit: http://www.igi-global.com/publish/.

The Advances in Educational Technologies and Instructional Design (AETID) Book Series (ISSN 2326-8905) is published by IGI Global, 701 E. Chocolate Avenue, Hershey, PA 17033-1240, USA, www.igi-global.com. This series is composed of titles available for purchase individually; each title is edited to be contextually exclusive from any other title within the series. For pricing and ordering information please visit http://www.igi-global.com/book-series/advances-educational-technologies-instructional-design/73678. Postmaster: Send all address changes to above address. ©© 2020 IGI Global. All rights, including translation in other languages reserved by the publisher. No part of this series may be reproduced or used in any form or by any means – graphics, electronic, or mechanical, including photocopying, recording, taping, or information and retrieval systems – without written permission from the publisher, except for non commercial, educational use, including classroom teaching purposes. The views expressed in this series are those of the authors, but not necessarily of IGI Global.

Titles in this Series

For a list of additional titles in this series, please visit:
https://www.igi-global.com/book-series/advances-educational-technologies-instructional-design/73678

For an entire list of titles in this series, please visit:
https://www.igi-global.com/book-series/advances-educational-technologies-instructional-design/73678

701 East Chocolate Avenue, Hershey, PA 17033, USA
Tel: 717-533-8845 x100 • Fax: 717-533-8661
E-Mail: cust@igi-global.com • www.igi-global.com

Editorial Advisory Board

Young Baek, *Boise State University, USA*
Emmanuel Fokides, *University of the Aegean, Greece*
Guiyou Huang, *Edinboro University, USA*

Table of Contents

Detailed Table of Contents

Chapter 1
A Strategic Overview and Vision of Simulation-Based Education in
Healthcare in England: Enhancing Patient Safety and Learner Development....... 1
Richard Price, NHS Health Education England, UK
Sukie Shinn, NHS Health Education England, UK

Simulation-based education (SBE) is an important modality for training a competent and safe healthcare workforce. It is also an important component of core training and continuing professional development for healthcare workers in the National Health Service (NHS) of the United Kingdom. A comprehensive review of SBE provision, led by NHS Health Education England (HEE), discovered many areas of good practice, but also identified inequalities in the access to and delivery of simulation. A framework was developed to help improve the quality, provision, and access to SBE. Case studies are provided in this chapter showcasing the different types of simulation which contributed to the good practice, how they are used in healthcare education, and how they link to the SBE framework. The chapter sets out some of the current challenges with equitable and high-quality provision, detailing plans to further enhance the education and training of the healthcare workforce through SBE through the delivery of a framework, strategic overview, and vision to support these plans.

Students in radiographic science education programs must master both the didactic education and psychomotor skills necessary to perform radiographic examinations on patients in a clinical setting. Simulation is the most common method of helping radiographic science students prepare to perform such examinations. Simulation can be performed either in live or virtual environments. Recently there has been a trend to adopt virtual simulation in medical education because of the reduced adverse effects virtual simulation provides as opposed to live simulation and real-world practice. Though there is a paucity of literature available discussing virtual simulation's use in radiographic science education, recent studies in this field and related medical imaging modalities have shown the benefits of using virtual simulation. The purpose of this chapter is to discuss the current use of virtual simulation in radiographic science education and characteristics to consider when implementing a simulation program.

Chapter 3

Orthodontic education, which currently emphasizes a didactic and apprenticeship approach, is facing numerous pedagogical challenges that affect knowledge delivery and instruction. This chapter discusses the challenges and limiting factors that affect orthodontic training and proposes the use of mobile augmented reality (MAR) to create a platform for effective learning, visualization, deliberate practice, effective feedback, and a personalized learning environment. MAR, with its visually enriched clinical simulations and ubiquitous learning, can effectively reduce cognitive dissonance and improve overall retention and skill gain by students. However, MAR has its limitations, as the technology is still new and limited evidence is available to back up the claims of knowledge and skill gain in the health professional's education. This chapter also provides future directions for exploring and enabling MAR so that it can become an efficient tool for learning and instruction across all faculties of education.

Chapter 4

Benjamin Just, University of Cincinnati, USA
Kay K. Seo, University of Cincinnati, USA

The purpose of this phenomenological study is to identify the types of ill-structured problems physical therapists face in the acute care setting for a computer simulation to train students in a professional physical therapist education program. Ten physical therapists who practiced in the acute care setting in four large urban Midwestern hospitals participated in semi-structured interviews. Results show that acute care physical therapists experience complex, ill-structured problems that encompass all direct and indirect patient care activities and are complicated by system factors outside of their control. Solving the problems described by the participants requires clear and accurate communication and an awareness of the role of physical therapy in the acute care setting. The use of these authentic challenges for a computer simulation can allow students in a professional physical therapist education program to develop better problem-solving skills.

Chapter 5

Andres Aguilera-Castillo, Universidad EAN, Colombia
Mauricio Guerrero-Cabarcas, Universidad EAN, Colombia
Camila Andrea Fúquene, Universidad de La Salle, Colombia
William Fernando Rios, Universidad de La Salle, Colombia

This chapter examines the experimental use of Cesim™ Global Challenge, a computer-based business simulation, in an undergraduate international business program in Bogota, Colombia. The authors analyzed the data from the simulation through the application of a nonparametric statistical analysis, in addition to the application of an ex-post survey instrument, in order to assess the relevance of using simulations in the acquisition of managerial skills among undergraduate students. Key findings include the observation of positive effects of computer simulations in learning environments, as they occur in the literature. The authors accepted the hypothesis that stated that more time spent in the simulation leads to better results in the default winning criteria. Finally, the survey instrument confirmed that the use of the simulation helped the students develop managerial soft skills.

A new teaching approach is presented which integrates observational learning through field teaching of business processes and simulation modeling in order to increase students' learning outcomes and acceptance of computer simulation technology. The teaching method, called LOSI (learning by observing, simulating, and improving), was conducted at a Croatian high education institution. The efficiency of the LOSI approach was investigated by conducting a survey based on the technology acceptance model (TAM). The indicators of ease of use, usefulness, and enjoyment in participating in LOSI were collected along with students' grades and their intention to use this technology in future work and education. The inter-relations among variables were analyzed by statistical tests. The results revealed that students find LOSI easy to use, useful in achieving learning outcomes, and highly enjoyable, while the ease of use and enjoyment is positively associated to usefulness (i.e., learning outcomes).

Chapter 7

The purpose of this chapter is to design a Minecraft simulation game where players can learn a language by communicating and negotiating meaning with other players. To achieve this, Gagné's events of instruction and Schmitt's strategic experience modules were adopted as a theoretical lens for simulation building. After the simulation game was designed, it was implemented to test its feasibility. The result shows that the simulation game has both the intended features of knowledge co-construction and the negotiation of meaning, as well as enjoyment of the game. The test result, however, also suggests that the simulation game needs more conditionals and loops in order for players to repeat their simulation game at any place and time.

The study presents results from the use of a 3D simulation for teaching functional skills to students with learning, attentional, behavioral, and emotional disabilities, attending regular schools. An A-B single-subject study design was applied. The participating students (eight eight-to-nine years old) explored the simulation (a virtual school), encountered situations in which they observed how they are expected to behave, and had to demonstrate what they have learned. Each student attended a total of four two-hour sessions. Data were collected by means of observations and semi-structured interviews. All students demonstrated improved functional skills both in terms of the number of behaviors they acquired and in terms of those that were retained and manifested in the real school environment. On the basis of the results, it can be argued that 3D simulations are a promising tool for teaching functional skills to students with disabilities.

Chapter 9

Creating positive learning outcomes regarding terrorism can be challenging. The nature of the topic offers several obstacles to learner understanding, not least of which is how to enable students to transcend their own cultural perspectives and develop deeper and more objective insights regarding the groups and causes that foster terrorism. Following an exploration of the growth in terrorism as an academic subject and the challenges posed to teaching in this area, this chapter presents a possible solution by describing an online role play exercise that has proven learning results over more than 25 years of usage. This tool, grounded in an experiential learning approach, can assist in easing some of the stresses faced by teachers and institutions, while also offering deeper and more insightful discoveries for participants.

This chapter presents a hypothesized evaluation framework for measuring the effectiveness of simulations for learning, while indirectly providing an instructional design framework. The proposed framework was formulated using course design concepts, a newly emerged purpose-based simulation taxonomy, and a frame using

Kolb's Experiential Learning Theory. To examine the untested taxonomy, which posited an alignment between purpose-based simulation categories to that of Bloom, an analysis reviewing literature within the last decade identified 80 articles. Correlation analysis indicated the area of application when compared to that of a modeling-based simulation type presented the strongest relationship. A summary section includes various domain examples to demonstrate an initial examination for fit to the newly proposed framework.

Preface

INTRODUCTION

The use of computer simulation has a long history in education and training. The root of this technology can be traced back to the mid-1940s during which the Monte Carlo method (a class of computational algorithms) was used on electronic computers to generate all possible outcomes to an event (Rubinstein & Kroese, 2007). The development of General Simulation Program (GSP)—the first general-purpose simulator that was created by Keith Douglas Tocher in the 1960s—marks the start of rapid growth of computer simulation in the subsequent decades (Goldsman, Nance, & Wilson, 2010). Since the late 1990s, with the advancement of computer, internet, and digital technologies, computer simulations have made momentous strides, especially in the early 2000s with the booming growth of visualization and 3D technologies (e.g., mixed reality, holographic imagery, 3D printing).

With the advance of simulation technology, computer simulation is becoming increasingly popular in education, especially in science, technology, engineering, mathematics, and healthcare and medical disciplines. There has also been growing interest in social sciences and humanities to use computer simulations to facilitate students' understanding and exploration of abstract and complex systems in social- and human-related disciplines.

Early research efforts on computer simulations started in the 1980s. Seminal works include Willis, Hovey, and Hovey's (1987) *Computer Simulations: A Source Book to Learning in an Electronic Environment*, and Whicker and Sigelman's (1991) *Computer Simulation Applications: An Introduction*. There was a surge of research interest in using computer simulation in online learning environments in the early 2000s; seminal works in this area include Aldrich's (2004) *Simulations and the Future of Learning: An Innovative (and Perhaps Revolutionary) Approach to e-Learning*, Gibson, Aldrich, and Prensky's (2007) *Games and Simulations in Online Learning: Research and Development Frameworks*, and Gibson and Baek's (2009) *Digital Simulations for Improving Education: Learning through Artificial Learning Environments*. Computer simulation, as a technology and a pedagogy, has also been examined in specific subject areas, including science (e.g., Honey & Hilton, 2011), mathematics (e.g., Röss, 2011), chemistry (e.g., Vanchiswaran, 2005), nursing education (e.g., Jeffries, 2012), and assessment (e.g., O'Neil, Baker, & Perez, 2016).

Decades of research on computer simulations have evidenced that computer simulation, as a powerful technological tool and research-proven pedagogical technique, holds great potential to enhance and transform teaching and learning in education and is therefore a viable tool to engage students in deep learning and higher-order thinking. With the advancement of simulation programs (e.g., mixed reality, artificial intelligence) and the expanded disciplines where computer simulation is being used (e.g., data science, cyber security), computer simulation is playing an increasingly significant role in leading the digital transformation in K-12 schools, higher education institutions, and training and professional development in corporate, government, and the military.

In the context outlined above, this book is intended to provide an updated examination of computer simulation technology and the ways that computer simulations are used to transform teaching and learning in both traditional and online learning environments across all subject areas. The editor and the contributors of the book aim to disseminate research-informed, evidence-based best practices and implementation recommendations in the use of computer simulations to better prepare students for the real world.

OVERVIEW

This book showcases recent development in and exemplary uses of computer simulation in various disciplines, including medical and healthcare training, business education, language learning, special education, and political science studies. What follows is a brief overview of each chapter.

In the opening chapter, Richard Price and Sukie Shinn present a comprehensive overview and strategic vision of simulation-based education in healthcare education in England. A categorization system of major uses of simulation in healthcare is developed and illustrated with simulation tools, including virtual-, augmented-, and mixed-reality technologies. The authors also identify five guiding principles to support the delivery of simulation-based education, along with specific key performance indicators. Although the context of the chapter is the United Kingdom, the categorization and implementation frameworks discussed provide the healthcare education professionals worldwide with practical guidance in the design and implementation of simulation-based education.

Focusing on radiographic science education, Chapter 2 explores the current use of virtual simulation in the field and things to consider when implementing a computer simulation program. Emphasizing the value of virtual simulation in radiographic science education, Christopher Ira Wertz, Jessyca Wagner, Trevor Mark Ward, and Wendy Mickelsen point out that virtual simulation and distributed practice are especially valuable tools and instructional techniques in helping students in radiographic science to practice and acquire both psychomotor skills and the competency in effective communication and interprofessional collaboration, which are essential to maintain high standards of healthcare.

Similarly, Chapter 3 discusses the current state and challenges in orthodontic education and identifies mobile augmented reality as a promising approach to overcoming the obstacles and moving orthodontics training forward. Gururajaprasad Kaggal Lakshmana Rao, Yulita Hanum P. Iskandar, and Norehan Mokhtar identify five major instructional uses of mobile augmented reality in orthodontics training, including deliberate practice, collaborative learning, personalized learning, ubiquitous learning, and feedback and formative assessment. Along with these opportunities, the authors also discuss the obstacles for mobile augmented reality integration and conclude that pedagogical transformation is deemed urgent in orthodontic education and mobile augmented reality holds great potential for the reform.

The use of ill-structured problems has long been recognized as an effective instructional approach to facilitating critical thinking and meaningful learning. Chapter 4 touches upon this topic by identifying specific types of ill-structured problems for simulation-enabled physical therapists training. In addition, Benjamin Just and Kay K. Seo describe the process of building an authentic case with ill-structured problems for computer simulation, illustrated with theoretical background and empirical evidence. As the authors suggest, the use of ill-structured problems in computer simulation is proven to be a promising approach to enhancing critical thinking and clinical reasoning of students in physical therapy education.

Following the four chapters on medical and healthcare education, Chapters 5 and 6 discuss two cutting-edge uses of computer simulation in business education. While the use of simulation is not new in the business education classroom, the adoption of computer simulation programs for acquiring both tangible and intangible business skills is still in its infancy. In Chapter 5, Andrés Aguilera, Mauricio Guerrero, Camila Andrea Fúquene, and William Fernando Ríos tested the use of Cesim™ Global Challenge, a computer-based simulation program that involves essential processes of a company's value chain and requires team-based problem-solving and decision-making skills, in an undergraduate international business program in Bogota, Colombia. The results of the study show that more time spent in the simulation leads to better performance in both subject content and managerial skills.

In a similar study, Marijana Zekić-Sušac, Adela Has, and Marinela Knežević examine the effect of a simulation-integrated approach on learning outcomes at a business school in a higher education institution in Croatia. Combining both fieldwork and computer simulation, this approach allows students to implement, observe, and improve a business process in a real company where students have the opportunity to experiment with the computer-simulation program and test the viability of ideas in reality. The results of the study reveal that the approach benefits both students and companies and points to a new direction in business education which makes the best use of both computer simulation and experiential learning.

With a focus on language learning, Chapter 7 depicts an instructional design process for building an online multi-user learning environment where knowledge co-construction and the negotiation of meaning play a pivotal role. Adopting Gagne's Nine Significant Events of Instruction and Schmitt's Strategic Experience Modules, Joeun Baek, Hyekyeong Park, and Ellen Min design and build several task-oriented virtual environments in Minecraft where English language learners can explore, interact, and collaborate to complete real-life tasks. While Minecraft is not a new platform with advanced simulation features, this study has proven that Minecraft is still a useful and viable virtual environment for learning tasks that require role-playing, knowledge co-construction, and the negotiation of meaning.

Chapter 8, written by Maria-Ioanna Chronopoulou and Emmanuel Fokides, examines the effect of a 3D simulation program for teaching functional living skills in the school environment to students with mild learning, attentional, behavioral, and emotional disabilities. The simulation was developed in OpenSimulator, an open source platform for developing online 3D virtual environments. The study results show that all students demonstrated improved functional skills in both virtual and real school environments. Literature on the use of computer simulation to special education students is scarce; Chronopoulou and Fokides' study contributes to the literature in this specific area with a well-designed quasi-experimental study, pedagogically sound and technologically appealing design of a simulation program, and a set of thoughtful and practical suggestions on the use of computer simulation to special education students.

Same as special education, teaching about terrorism through computer simulation is a less-touched-upon but much-needed research topic in extant simulation literature. In Chapter 9, Mat Hardy and Sally Totman detail the design and use of the Middle East Politics Simulation (MEPS), an online role-playing simulation program, for teaching Middle East studies at Deakin University, Australia. A principal gain for most participants in the MEPS is a greater understanding of the underlying causes of radicalisation - a desired sophisticated learning outcome in teaching complex academic topics such as terrorism. As the authors point out, the anonymity and asynchronicity of the MEPS program are two success factors that have contributed to helping students achieve learning outcomes at the deeper and more sophisticated level.

This book ends with a chapter on an evaluation framework for computer simulations. The majority of extant literature on computer simulation is largely discipline specific. To address the need for a comprehensive framework that guides the instructional design and measures the effectiveness of simulations for learning, Wendi M. Kappers develops such a framework that is built upon course design concepts, a purpose-based simulation taxonomy, and Kolb's Experiential Learning Theory. Kappers' framework sheds light on future research direction in cross-discipline framework development and validation in the design, development and evaluation of computer simulation in education.

CONCLUSION

Teaching, Learning, and Leading With Computer Simulations examines the recent advancement of simulation technology, including 3D MUVE, mobile augmented reality, explores the innovative ways that advanced simulation programs are used to enhance and transform teaching and learning, selects exemplary cases of digital learning by adopting simulation technology and pedagogy, and identifies challenges and future directions for practice, research, and theoretical development in using computer simulation in education and training. The 10 chapters together update the field with research-informed, evidence-based design and implementation recommendations in the use of computer simulation for higher levels of thinking and learning, which will better prepare students for real-world life, work, and challenges.

As seen in the chapters across the book, current research in computer simulations has heavily focused on "simulating" or "replicating" real-life tasks/challenges and environments/contexts in computer/online programs, as well as on whether and to what extent the knowledge, skills, competencies acquired from the simulation programs can be transferred into the real world. The "fidelity" of real world and desired learning outcomes are therefore the focal points of most current simulation research studies. As widely acknowledged by researchers, simulation-based approaches facilitate knowledge acquisition as well as promote higher levels of thinking and learning (e.g., reasoning, problem-solving, divergent thinking, decision-making, teamwork skills) which put high cognitive and metacognitive demands on students. The research on simulation-based learning environments, therefore, should also examine the learning "process" and "experience" of students (not only the "outcome"). How do students perceive and handle these challenging demands throughout the simulation process?

How do students eventually come up with discipline-specific and context-appropriate strategies to problem-solving and decision-making? What other areas in learning outcomes than performance that play significant roles thus should be considered in assessing in simulation-based learning? These are the research directions that future simulation research should look into. Results from such studies will benefit the design, development and assessment of computer simulation programs that will better facilitate students' learning in such learning environments.

This book is useful for educators, education leaders, education researchers, and stakeholders in both K-12 schools and higher education institutions. Its theoretical and pedagogical frameworks, trends and best practices in using computer simulations, and challenges and future directions identified by the studies in this book will help the target audience gain a comprehensive and deep understanding of computer simulation in education and training.

Yufeng Qian
Louisiana State University, USA

REFERENCES

Aldrich, C. (2004). *Simulations and the future of learning: An innovative (and perhaps revolutionary) approach to e-Learning*. San Francisco, CA: Pfeiffer.

Gibson, D., Aldrich, C., & Prensky, M. (Eds.). (2007). *Games and simulations in online learning: Research and development frameworks*. Hershey, PA: IGI Global. doi:10.4018/978-1-59904-304-3

Gibson, D., & Baek, Y. (Eds.). (2009). *Digital simulations for improving education: Learning through artificial learning environments*. Hershey, PA: IGI Global. doi:10.4018/978-1-60566-322-7

Goldsman, D., Nance, R. E., & Wilson, J. R. (2010). A brief history of simulation revisited. In B. Johansson, S. Jain, J. Montoya-Torres, J. Hugan, & E. Yücesan (Eds.), *Proceedings of the 2010 winter simulation conference* (pp. 567-574). Piscataway, NJ: IEEE. 10.1109/WSC.2010.5679129

Honey, M. A., & Hilton, M. (2011). *Learning science through computer games and simulations*. Washington, DC: National Research Council.

Jeffries, P. R. (2012). *Simulation in nursing education: From conceptualization to evaluation*. Washington, DC: National League for Nursing.

O'Neil, H. F., Baker, E. L., & Perez, R. S. (Eds.). (2016). *Using games and simulations for teaching and assessment: Key issues*. New York, NY: Routledge. doi:10.4324/9781315817767

Röss, D. (2011). *Learning and teaching mathematics using simulations: Plus 2000 examples from physics*. Berlin, Germany: De Gruyter. doi:10.1515/9783110250077

Rubinstein, R. Y., & Kroese, D. P. (2007). *Simulation and the Monte Carlo method* (2nd ed.). Hoboken, NJ: Wiley & Sons. doi:10.1002/9780470230381

Vanchiswaran, R. (2005). *Computer simulations in chemistry education*. Iowa, IL: Iowa State University Press.

Whicker, M. L., & Sigelman, L. (1991). *Computer simulation applications: An introduction*. Thousand Oaks, CA: SAGE.

Willis, J., Hovey, L., & Hovey, K. (1987). *Computer simulations: A source book to learning in an electronic environment*. New York, NY: Garland.

Chapter 1
A Strategic Overview and Vision of Simulation–Based Education in Healthcare in England:
Enhancing Patient Safety and Learner Development

Richard Price
NHS Health Education England, UK

Sukie Shinn
NHS Health Education England, UK

ABSTRACT

Simulation-based education (SBE) is an important modality for training a competent and safe healthcare workforce. It is also an important component of core training and continuing professional development for healthcare workers in the National Health Service (NHS) of the United Kingdom. A comprehensive review of SBE provision, led by NHS Health Education England (HEE), discovered many areas of good practice, but also identified inequalities in the access to and delivery of simulation. A framework was developed to help improve the quality, provision, and access to SBE. Case studies are provided in this chapter showcasing the different types of simulation which contributed to the good practice, how they are used in healthcare education, and how they link to the SBE framework. The chapter sets out some of the current challenges with equitable and high-quality provision, detailing plans to further enhance the education and training of the healthcare workforce through SBE through the delivery of a framework, strategic overview, and vision to support these plans.

DOI: 10.4018/978-1-7998-0004-0.ch001

Copyright © 2020, IGI Global. Copying or distributing in print or electronic forms without written permission of IGI Global is prohibited.

INTRODUCTION

The National Health Service (NHS) in the United Kingdom (UK) is one of the largest employers in the world, directly employing more than 1.5 million employees with diverse roles ranging from medical and nursing staff to allied health professionals and healthcare scientists. The NHS recently celebrated its 70th anniversary, being founded on 5 July 1948 on the premise that good healthcare should be available to all, regardless of wealth, and services should be provided for free at the point of delivery for all UK residents (NHS, 2016). The NHS serves a population of approximately 64.6 million with treatments ranging from emergency medicine and lifesaving operations to routine procedures, screening and public health interventions. The service is paid for out of general taxation which amounts to approximately £116.4 billion (approximately $148 billion dollars) annually.

The UK Department of Health and Social Care distributes the funding for the NHS to national and local commissioners such as NHS England, who then procure specific services from local bodies known as NHS Trusts, the voluntary sector and private providers who are responsible for the delivery of healthcare services as illustrated in Figure 1. These providers are regulated by the Care Quality Commission and NHS Improvement (Kings Fund, 2017). An NHS Trust is an organization serving either a specific function, or a targeted geographical area. Examples include:

- Hospital acute Trusts, providing secondary care services
- Mental health acute Trusts
- Ambulance service Trusts
- Community health Trusts, providing some primary care services.

To ensure the best possible care for patients, it is a requirement that the NHS workforce is sufficiently skilled and has the right abilities, attitudes and behaviors. In England, this task falls to Health Education England (HEE) which is an executive, non-departmental body of the UK Department of Health and Social Care, set up in 2012. It holds responsibility for the education and training of the entire healthcare workforce from undergraduate to postgraduate level and continuing professional development (CPD). The initial education of healthcare students is primarily provided through the funding of higher education placements within a healthcare setting. This involves healthcare students studying for extended periods of learning within a university, plus practical placements in a clinical environment, usually within an NHS Trust, working with patients and being mentored and supported by other healthcare professionals.

Figure 1. Simplified NHS structural diagram illustrating the relationship between the UK government bodies and the NHS healthcare provider services, with Health Education England being an executive, non-departmental body of the UK Department of Health and Social Care. Adapted from Kings Fund (2017)

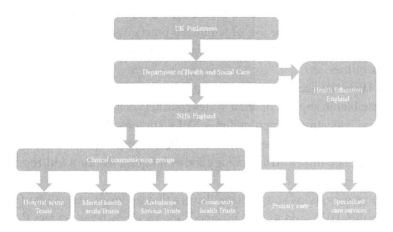

Once qualified, healthcare professionals join the NHS and enter the workplace, where there is a requirement of HEE and their NHS Trust to provide CPD and lifelong learning opportunities to ensure maintenance of professional registration and continuing delivery of outstanding care to patients. CPD is typically provided through a combination of traditional classroom training, online and digital learning and simulated practice or simulation-based education (SBE). Occupation-specific Royal Colleges support the professional registration of clinical professionals and represent their profession as well as providing additional education.

The funding for postgraduate medical and healthcare education is provided through a 'tariff' from the Department of Health and Social Care, delegated to HEE to manage. Funding is distributed to local education providers throughout England by HEE, through a Learning Development Agreement. Management of this funding is the responsibility of 13 local HEE office multi-professional Postgraduate Deans who hold responsibility for the commissioning of required services in their regions.

The increasing use of technology in healthcare delivery and changing patient and staff demographics have resulted in significant changes to the healthcare workforce in England. There are increased numbers of staff in some areas and decreased in others, as well as new roles emerging to meet some of the demands. As a result, online learning and simulation-based education (SBE) are increasingly being used to ensure high-quality learning takes place while reducing the risk of harm to patients and staff.

The Topol Review[1] (HEE, 2019), an independent report exploring the preparations required to deliver healthcare in a digital age, highlights the need for the healthcare workforce to be more adaptive to changes in practice and to increase their digital capabilities. Additionally, the NHS long-term plan[2] (NHS, 2019) highlights the changes taking place as a result of technology in the healthcare workplace. Both publications recommend the use of simulated practice to improve the clinical and non-clinical skills of the healthcare workforce in England, underpinned by excellent digital capabilities.

Within HEE, the Technology Enhanced Learning (TEL) program[3] (HEE, 2019b) is the key enabler in support of other system partners tasked to improve the delivery of healthcare education, which includes SBE. The program's aim is that patients and the public in England benefit from a healthcare workforce educated by the most effective, evidence-informed technology and techniques, working with regional TEL teams to deliver its objectives.

This section explains some of the drivers that underpin the work of the TEL program within HEE, and its role in supporting the high-level reviews that set out the recommendations around the strategic response to demand.

The TEL program has three core work streams outlined below. The first work stream is the largest and delivers two key services which support the other areas of the program, including SBE.

1. **Digital development and delivery:** The first of the services under this work stream is e-Learning for Healthcare (e-LfH). As one of the largest providers of e-learning in the world, e-LfH is managed by HEE on behalf of the NHS and the wider health and care system. It has an expending catalogue of digital educational resources covering broad areas of health and care. With a learning management system of over 1 million registered users, in 2018 there were over 7 million launches of e-learning (e-LfH, 2019). Learning resources are also accessed through another national learning management system via an interface, the Electronic Staff Record (ESR) and through several local learning management systems, meaning the educational reach of e-LfH content includes the entire 1.5 million workforce of the NHS.

The second element of this work stream relates to the development of the HEE Learning Hub, which is planned for launch in late 2019. It will be a powerful new digital platform that will provide easy access to a wide range of education and training resources for the health and care workforce in England. The premise behind The Learning Hub is that it will be the place to go to access and record learning from a broad range of shareable resources, including existing e-LfH courses and resources contributed and uploaded from the user community. The Learning Hub will also encourage discussions to take place around the uploaded learning content and networks to form around areas of shared interest to maximize the opportunities for collaboration and realize the potential of the resources. Learning content will range from digital courses and online resources to simulation scripts and the location of physical simulation equipment such as manikins.

2. **Horizon scanning, innovation and piloting:** This work stream supports work in the TEL program and more widely in healthcare education. The primary purpose of this work stream is to provide a research and development function in relation to new and emerging technologies to support education and training in healthcare and provide system leadership in the adoption of new and emerging educational technologies. It includes engaging with system partners in horizon scanning activities, looking at the potential for using emerging technologies in healthcare education; conducting prototyping of Artificial Intelligence driven tools by enhancing the learning experience and improving learning efficacy. There are inevitable crossovers into the other work streams with the various pilots and projects that are an ongoing part of the work of the TEL program, looking ahead at opportunities for using digital technology to enhance and improve learning opportunities.

3. **Simulation-based education, immersive technologies and video:** This work stream encourages the use of meaningful and cohesive SBE to support development of a well-trained and engaged multi-professional workforce that can deliver safe, effective care. Some of the work within this work stream is still in development, but the overall aims are that the vision for the delivery of SBE will be achieved through the publishing of a national framework and subsequent strategic overview. The role of this work stream is to support ongoing research to better understand the impact and applicability of SBE, immersive (virtual and augmented reality) technologies and video, and to provide a cohesive pathway with supplemented guidance that will aid delivery of SBE.

This chapter discusses the third TEL program work stream, exploring the use of SBE and technology-enabled simulation in healthcare. The chapter focuses primarily on SBE in England, not the whole of the UK, as Wales, Scotland and Northern Ireland have devolved responsibility for provision of their NHS services. The chapter aims to detail the current implementation of SBE including the modalities of delivery and sets out some of the current challenges with access to equitable and high-quality provision of SBE in England. It introduces the need for the development of a framework to support improvements to equitable and high-quality access to SBE before covering plans to further enhance the education and training of the healthcare workforce through SBE through the delivery of the framework, a strategic overview and vision to support these plans.

BACKGROUND

Simulation-Based Education (SBE) is a well-established technique for delivery of medical and healthcare education in the UK (Deshmukh, 2018). While there are differing definitions of what is meant by simulation and SBE, Gaba's definition (2004) is typically favored: "a technique – not a technology – to replace or amplify real experiences with guided experiences that evoke or replicate substantial aspects of the real world in a fully interactive manner" (p. i2).

Typically, SBE is designed to mimic clinical and medical techniques to provide healthcare professionals and trainees with a realistic experience of clinical practice in a safe environment where learning can take place. Increasingly, inter-disciplinary and multi-professional simulation is being used to simulate the human factors which can influence clinical outcomes in the healthcare workplace. Simulation, or 'synthetics', has been used effectively in the aeronautical industry and military to instill and reinforce human factor skills and as healthcare is usually delivered by teams, attention is increasingly being given to multi-professional patient care (CHFG, 2019).

The use of simulation in healthcare education is popular with students and teachers alike (Dickinson, Hopton, & Pilling, 2016; Lubbers & Rossman, 2017). As an experiential learning method, recreating a real-life clinical situation for learners to practice complex skills in the same manner as a professional environment is an attractive option, with a sound evidence base and clear rationale (Breymier et al., 2015; Jeffries, 2005; Kyle, & Murray, 2007; Yang et al., 2018), improving knowledge retention and learner confidence. The use of SBE enables the learner to reflect on their own and their team's performance and how they dealt with unexpected elements of a scenario (Schweller et al., 2018).

Use of clinical simulation as a learning tool can reduce student anxiety and increase confidence, enhancing the wellbeing of the caregiver (Alexander et al., 2018; Cowen, Hubbard, & Hancock, 2016). Additionally, the use of simulation can support 'doing the patient no harm' (Inman, 1860) as students can make mistakes without the consequences of these directly impacting a patient's health (Davis, Josephsen, & Macy, 2013; Kuehster & Hall, 2010). Issues related to reliability can also be improved, as situations can be better replicated for cohorts of students or modified to meet a learning outcome. This is especially important when simulation is used for assessment (Norcini & McKinley, 2007), such as during Objective Structured Clinical Examinations (Selim, Ramadan, El-Gueneidy, & Gaafer, 2012).

Advances in technology are helping to increase the use of SBE in healthcare, augmenting existing modalities or creating new modalities, driving adoption. For example, the use of manikins and standardized patients (clinical conditions described by actors) (Dearsley, 2013), can be complemented by the use of computer programs using scenarios that encourage critical thinking (Sousa Freire et al., 2018), and the provision of replica clinical records and other documents used to practice recording and reviewing of data (Clark, 2018).

The following sections provide a brief description of the primary modalities of simulation currently used in NHS workforce education and training, exploring how technology is being used to enhance each modality to improve educational outcomes.

Teamworking and Human Factors Simulation

Human factors (also known as ergonomics) is 'a discipline that considers both the physical and mental characteristics of people as well as the organizational factors or wider socio-technical system' (Ball et al., 2014). It describes the complex healthcare environment and the interactions between the people, equipment, systems and processes.

Many simulation programs in the NHS incorporate human factors and teamwork training to design systems that help teams to work effectively and safely. For example, human factors simulation is used to test and develop policies and optimize elements at new hospital sites prior to patients arriving in conjunction with computer modeling (Hellaby et al., 1997). Simulation scenarios are being developed not only with specific team learning outcomes but to embed the precursors for cognitive bias and other situations designed to specifically develop human factor skills.

In-Situ Simulation

In-situ simulation is SBE that is actively integrated into the physical environment, such as a hospital ward or a general practitioner's surgery as illustrated in Figure 2. This form of simulation enables multi-professional teams to practice a simulated scenario that reflects how it would be carried out, producing real-life scenarios to improve reliability and patient safety in high risk areas.

In the NHS, one example of in-situ simulation is a breached-delivery childbirth simulated on a maternity ward. This would see midwives, pediatricians and other maternity staff working through the problem in real-time on a manikin, building

Figure 2. In-situ simulation using actors in a mental health workshop for primary care front of house staff and administrators

team skills and trust in the team, as well as practicing the skills needed to deal with such as scenario. In-situ simulation has enabled the NHS to deliver higher fidelity experiences in a more diverse range of settings, some of which are technically challenging to reproduce in a simulation center (Fent et al., 2015). These include neonatal intensive care, pediatric operating theatres, patient transfers and multiple settings and multiple teams within a scenario. Increasingly, each scenario and associated learning outcomes are targeted at either system, process and resilience or clinical and human factors.

Cadaveric Dissection and Wet Tissue Simulation

Many of the practical skills that healthcare professionals perform require repeated practice. Although low fidelity simulations and advances in technology-based learning systems have helped to develop and improve skills, there remains a real need for deliberate practice using actual tissue, particularly in the sphere of surgical training. The use of live, anaesthetized animals in learning situations is forbidden by UK law but there are two alternative sources of tissue: human cadavers and dead animal tissue.

Cadaveric Dissection

The use of human cadavers – once the mainstay of medical anatomy teaching – has seen a resurgence in recent years in surgical training due to advancing surgical techniques and patient expectation. This has been helped by advances in preservation techniques such as fresh frozen and Theil embalmed cadavers (Hayashi et al., 2016). The use of cadavers offers several advantages, including offering a three-dimensional structural organization of the human body and its variations, an ability to perform complete surgical procedures and perhaps most importantly an appreciation of how tissues and structures feel. (Gelder, Paterson-Brown, 2015). Trainees and teachers report that they find cadaveric workshops beneficial, although the evidence that they are truly effective is hard to source (Gilbody et al., 2011). Indeed, Hamstra et al. (2006) claim that the learning process is more important than the physical substrate and that skills can be more effectively acquired on low fidelity models. Typically, undergraduate medical students are the main users of this form of simulation.

Wet Tissue

Dead animal tissue has been widely used in surgical training in so called 'wet-lab' settings. The major proponents of this approach have been cardiac surgeons both undergraduate and postgraduate, using primarily fresh pig hearts which have a close anatomical similarity to the human heart. Most heart operations can be practiced on pig hearts in a realistic and repeatable manner as demonstrated in Figure 3.

Several English hospitals have established permanent wet lab facilities to encourage self-directed opportunistic learning and many surgical disciplines have integrated wet labs into their training programs in the NHS. For example, the Royal College of Surgeons has developed a comprehensive integrated wet lab training program for cardiac surgery to support this (Nguyen et al., 2005).

Figure 3. Cardiac surgery being performed on dead animal tissue (a pig heart)

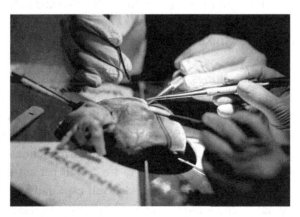

Simulation Manikins

The use of simulation manikins is widespread in healthcare education in both undergraduate taught programs and postgraduate in-situ and human factor simulation in the NHS (Ziv et al., 2003).

Early simulators offered a limited functional scope, with a focus on key anatomy and physiology (airway, respiratory and cardiovascular signs, circulatory access). These limitations were often mitigated by experienced faculty, using a range of techniques including; scenario design, 'stooge' faculty members within scenarios, scenario specific manikin selection and hybrid simulation (Lapkin et al., 2010).

As the use of manikins developed, so did their complexity, with simulators ranging from the hugely popular and familiar resuscitation manikins for performing cardio-pulmonary resuscitation (CPR) to specialist surgical simulators for simulating procedures such as an appendectomy, incorporating augmented reality and haptic feedback. Improvements in the design and use of manikins were largely driven by advances in technology, including smaller batteries and reduced duration of untethered function and lower power wireless aerials with reduced operating range.

Simulation manikins are classified by their levels of fidelity: low, medium and high. This relates to the degree of reality, or authenticity which ranges from completely artificial to an actual real-life situation. Suspension of disbelief is a core component of immersive simulation, contributing to learner engagement, fidelity and improved learning outcomes (Issenberg et al., 2005). The highest fidelity simulators employ various technologies to accurately mimic the clinical scenario and respond according to the clinical interventions performed on the manikin as illustrated in Figure 4. Nowhere is this more important than in pediatrics where the physical constraints of a pediatric manikin have historically placed limits on the range and effectiveness of technical function. The first high fidelity pediatric simulators were not developed until the 1990s when many of the technical limitations started to be bridged.

Pediatric Simulation Manikins

Training within pediatric settings has specific ethical considerations, including consent, psychological risk and reliability of communication. This has meant that pediatric simulators have found a significant role in the training of a diverse range of healthcare professionals. These professionals will be familiar with the importance of understanding a child's age-dependent perspective, varied modalities and preferences for communication, empathy and the need to treat both patient and family. The immersive nature of simulation therefore lends itself especially well to pediatrics, where more traditional teaching modalities may struggle to capture the essence of these complex interactions (Gamble et al., 2016).

Figure 4. Healthcare trainees practicing clinical observations on an adult simulation manikin connected to various monitoring devices. A member of simulation faculty can control the manikin remotely in response to trainee interventions

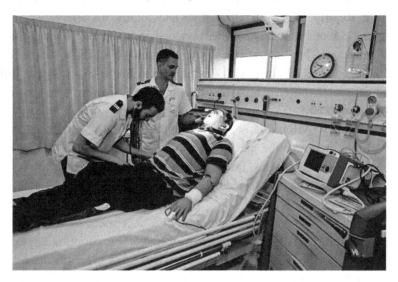

In contrast to adult healthcare, pediatrics requires a range of simulators to realistically simulate the natural age range of the pediatric population, including premature and term neonates, one-year-old and five-year-old manikins. Simulations are predominantly carried out in-situ with multi-disciplinary teams (nursing, allied health professional and non-registered staff) to simulate human factors as well as processes and systems.

Augmented, Virtual, and Mixed Reality Immersive Simulation

Advances in technology have made access to immersive virtual reality environments relatively affordable, generating significant interest in the potential role of immersive technologies in healthcare education in the NHS. The use of virtual, or augmented reality in simulation enables the learner to experience through the 'first-person' and to become part of the environment (Winn, 1993). This technology gives simulation faculty the potential to encourage learners to reflect on a deeper level and to therefore gain a much better understanding of the environment in which they work (Mantovani et al., 2003).

There are three types of immersive technology currently in use in healthcare education in England:

- **Augmented Reality (AR):** overlays additional digital display over real-world settings which can be viewed and manipulated through headpieces, smartphones, or glasses such as Google-Glass or Microsoft HoloLens.
- **Virtual Reality (VR):** an alternative and totally immersive environment which blocks out the real-world experience completely by filling the user's field of vision. This type of immersive technology typically makes use of a VR head mounted display (HMD) which are available in a range of different technical specifications, from the high-end HTC Vive Pro to the entry-level Google Cardboard.
- **Mixed Reality (MR):** this is a combination of the best aspects of both AR and VR and, requires the use of viewing equipment such as Magic Leap or Microsoft HoloLens. This immersive technology is often combined with simulation manikins to enhance the suspension of disbelief.

As interest in virtual and augmented reality has increased, so has access to the technology, resulting in a dramatic reduction in costs. This adoption has generated significant interest in the potential role of immersive reality in healthcare education. Though the NHS use of immersive reality as a training modality is still in its infancy, it is already being used to enable staff to experience a patient's perspective of care, allowing for reflection of humanistic skills in healthcare such as compassion and empathy, human factors and to reinforce clinical knowledge.

Many NHS organizations currently lack the required knowledge and experience in deploying VR for training; however, this is rapidly changing as the technology becomes more accessible and there is a growing recognition that the NHS needs the technical capacity and appropriately skilled faculty to effectively adopt VR in healthcare simulation.

Since 2018, HEE has sought to address this gap in knowledge by founding the VR Lab at Torbay and South Devon Hospitals NHS Foundation Trust to trial VR and immersive equipment and applications with public, patients and healthcare staff in clinical environments as demonstrated in Figure 5. South London and Maudsley NHS Foundation Trust have also been funded to develop a range of VR scenarios using standardized, or simulated patient experiences across a range of mental-health related conditions.

Haptic Simulation

Haptic simulation technologies recreate the sense of touch using forces, vibrations and motion. This allows the learner to feel the potential pressure, or resistance that would be experienced in a real-life situation, adding realism and promoting learner

Figure 5. Use of the Google Cardboard virtual reality equipment to train foundation doctors at Torbay and South Devon Hospitals NHS Foundation Trust

engagement while enabling assessment of skills (Reed et al., 2016). This form of simulation is particularly useful when combined with simulation manikins or immersive technologies to promote an increased sense of reality and a suspension of disbelief.

The primary focus of the current haptic simulations is the development of patient-specific treatment exercises to enhance patient safety and to support learners to practice in a safe environment. Emerging haptic technologies have an important role in the training and assessment of the healthcare workforce and there is widespread use within the early years of postgraduate medical and dental training programs in the NHS in England.

Haptic Simulation in Dental Education

Dentistry is a skills-based specialty which has traditionally focused on the acquisition of fine motor skills and development of hand-eye coordination through repetitive practice, similar to surgical disciplines which largely rely on cadaveric dissection and wet tissue simulation. These simulated tasks are reproduced on extracted or synthetic teeth, embedded within either plaster blocks or phantom head jigs. While this method reinforces learning of a defined task, it is not capable of reliably assessing problem-solving or action planning, which are essential components of safe clinical practice (Fugill, 2013). Haptic technology is bridging the gap between phantom head models and fully immersive VR environments to improve realism and accurately reproduce the clinical environment, an example of which is shown in Figure 6.

HEE has introduced haptic simulation into the early postgraduate years' programs for Foundation and Core dentistry students for both training and assessment. The simulated environment has reduced the cost of consumable materials, is readily accessible (as no technicians are required) and real-time feedback allows self-reflection and portfolio development. It also provides a baseline competency assessment of

Figure 6. Trainee dentist practicing on a haptic simulator of a human mouth

trainees entering the programs and is an early warning of specific learning needs. Emerging research from England is also enhancing the simulated experience through virtual dental caries, with the tactile sensation and disease pattern of natural pathology, replacing the phantom head simulations (Osnes & Keeling, 2017).

Simulated and Virtual Patients: Use of Actors and Virtual Scenarios

The use of simulated patients (professional actors or those with lived experienced behaving in role to replicate certain clinical conditions or situations) is a simulation technique in widespread use in the NHS, particularly in the field of mental health. Simulated patients are of great value in healthcare education and have proven to be more effective than manikins in providing simulated experiences requiring human interaction (Shin, Park, & Kim, 2015).

However, there are limitations with this modality as simulated patients need to be handled carefully, especially in the case of those with lived experience for whom performing as an actor may trigger or exacerbate previous trauma (Dudley, 2018). Use of simulated patients can also be resource intensive and relatively expensive compared to the use of manikins and other simulation methods (Bosse et al., 2015). The use of virtual patients, often in an immersive environment, increases reliability, as the responses of the patient can be replicated more exactly (Albright et al., 2018; MacLean et al., 2018), particularly when combined with immersive VR or AR (Booth et al., 2018).

In mental health education, the use of simulation has not been as widely adopted as in other areas of healthcare (Brown, 2008). However, the use of actors and virtual patients is increasing, where a real-life clinical setting is recreated for a trainee to practice their knowledge and skills (Patterson et al., 2018). As illustrated in Figure 7, simulated patients in mental health settings enable the environment to be controlled and modified based on the student's needs, encouraging deeper reflection and learning (Eppich & Cheng, 2015; Lendahls & Oscarsson, 2017).

This section of the chapter explained the background to the use of SBE in England using examples of the types of technology-enabled simulation in widespread use in healthcare education. The section also explored the increasing use of technology within healthcare education, such as the use of immersive technologies to create realistic scenarios in a virtual environment. In the next section, the chapter moves focus to some of the challenges of implementing SBE in a healthcare system as large as the NHS.

CURRENT CHALLENGES FACING THE ORGANIZATION

This section discusses some of the challenges that the NHS in England is currently facing, with particular emphasis on the role that SBE has to play in tackling these challenges.

Like many other public services and areas of government, demands are being made to provide a greater volume of training within the existing or a decreasing financial envelope while continuously improving the quality and standard of education. Alongside this demand, there is a greater emphasis on improving patient safety and ensuring a reduction in clinical incidents.

The NHS long-term plan highlighted the changing nature of healthcare, moving from a healthcare service to a wellbeing service, where patients are supported to maintain healthy lifestyles by clinicians rather than just being treated for specific

Figure 7. An actor playing an elderly patient in a simulated mental health scenario, attended by two healthcare trainees at South London and Maudsley NHS Trust

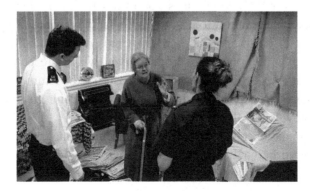

conditions as they arise. Additionally, the Topol Review highlighted the changing workforce profile that is required to deliver healthcare as emerging technologies are adopted in the NHS, suggesting new roles will be created while existing roles may change or disappear altogether.

The findings from both these reports suggest there is a need to train more staff and train them more rapidly so that they can enter the healthcare workforce more quickly. However, from other research, it is evident that many staff are resistant to these changes and there are differing attitudes and capabilities with respect to the emerging digital landscape. Indeed, HEE has developed a digital capabilities framework that highlights some of the key behaviors and abilities expected of NHS staff as new technologies and techniques emerge[4] (HEE, 2018).

As the use of simulation in healthcare education has developed and grown in England, it has proven difficult for HEE to be able to measure funding for SBE delivery or differentiate that which has been delivered through local providers and NHS Trusts. With this growth and development, pockets of excellence have emerged, with some of the adjacent geographical areas not having the same successes, or equity of access. This has resulted in a disproportionate delivery, which has not been conducive to innovation, or sharing of best practice and collaboration in SBE.

Part of the challenge for HEE has been the ability to gather information on the SBE that is currently being delivered throughout the country and measure funding for SBE delivery or differentiate that which has been delivered through local providers and NHS Trusts. There are different requirements according to geographical location, and these need to be addressed at the local level, rather than from a 'top-down' didactic approach. In addition, there are pockets of good practice in some areas, but not necessarily equity of access, and it is important that innovation be harnessed but simultaneously encouraged.

As highlighted in the previous section, there are a wide variety of different types of simulation in use in healthcare, ranging from physical manikins to professional actors, all supported through the use of technology. There continues to be a widely held perception of there being a necessity to invest in expensive equipment and technology to deliver SBE which does not always match the reality. Of course, simulation is only one solution to ensure high-quality learning takes place while reducing the risk of harm and there are numerous other modalities of learning in use such as e-learning and classroom training which are equally impactful. Differentiating the impact of simulation and measuring the return on investment of simulation versus other educational interventions is difficult given the volume of training being provided by the NHS.

Access to simulation regardless of where an individual works or studies in healthcare needs to be equitable and of sufficiently high quality that they gain maximum benefit from taking part in SBE.

The goal of HEE's work in simulation is to support the development of a well-trained and engaged multi-professional workforce that can deliver safe, effective care. To achieve this requires cooperation and collaboration to support adoption of good practice in SBE from regulatory bodies, higher education institutions (HEIs) and support across the four nations which constitute the UK (England, Wales, Scotland and Northern Ireland).

In this section, some of the key challenges facing the delivery of healthcare simulation were highlighted such as the need to train more people with fewer resources and the need to improve the equity of access to high-quality simulation and to provide a workforce responsive to technology changes. In the following section, the potential solution to these problems is introduced: the development of an SBE framework.

DEVELOPMENT OF A SIMULATION-BASED EDUCATION FRAMEWORK

In this section, the steps that were undertaken to agree and develop an SBE framework for healthcare educators in England are introduced, including the development of guiding principles and key performance indicators (KPIs). There is also discussion about some of the successes and challenges this work has highlighted as well as the steps taken to ensure successful adoption.

Due to the disparity in provision of SBE, HEE embarked on the development of a framework to support a national approach to the delivery of locally designed and delivered SBE. The approach was carefully considered to ensure engagement by enabling autonomy in delivery which would fit the needs of the specific area. It was hoped that this method would also ensure a more cohesive approach that would respond to and mitigate the barriers to success and to improve equity of access to SBE across England.

A report prepared jointly by an expert group from HEE and the Joint Royal Colleges of Physicians' Training Board in 2016 resulted in SBE being added to the curriculum for Core Medical Training (HEE, 2016). Similarly, in 2016, the Association of Simulated Practice in Healthcare (ASPiH) simulation standards were launched, with support from HEE (ASPiH, 2016). While accreditation against the ASPiH and Core Medical Training standards in the UK is optional, they provide the basis of a cohesive approach to the delivery of SBE.

It was agreed that for a strategic approach to the delivery of SBE to work, it needed to be developed afresh, which is why a wide engagement program was important to capture the views of the simulation and education communities. At each step of the framework's development, the various groups that would be instrumental in the delivery of the expectations within the SBE strategic overview and vision were consulted. This resulted in strong engagement and a desire to share and collaborate to help serve and deliver the key performance indicators as they and the strategic overview become embedded.

The initial investigatory work involved the gathering of information across all 13 local offices of HEE in order to inform the beginnings of a strategic approach to delivery. It was necessary to create and agree to a shared understanding of Simulation-Based Education (SBE), including the various elements, modalities and associated benefits. This was because of the differing perceptions noted during stakeholder engagement. This resulted in agreement of a shared purpose for the HEE SBE framework, to '...ensure development of a well-trained and engaged multi-professional workforce that is able to deliver safe, effective care by utilizing meaningful and cohesive simulation-based education'.

Five Guiding Principles of the SBE Framework

Five themes emerged upon analysis of the community responses, which formed the basis of the guiding principles of the framework for the delivery of SBE. These were tested within a Simulation Reference Group (SRG) before being launched in October 2018[5] (HEE, 2018b). The five guiding principles to support the delivery of SBE within provider training organizations are (as illustrated in Figure 8):

- **Principle One: Quality Outcomes.** Delivery of safe, effective care through workforce development. SBE investment is aligned with the delivery and continuing improvement of high quality, safe, effective care and enhancing the learner experience.
- **Principle Two: Leadership and Governance.** Simulation-based education and its leadership are clearly defined, and the appropriate governance model and processes are explicitly described.
- **Principle Three: Strategic Approach and Resource Allocation.** Each local area's strategic approach is aligned with the SBE national approach – connecting to Local Workforce and Action Boards – and there is consistency across the region. Where applicable, SBE is multi-professionally delivered and arrangements for resource allocation modelling are shared and understood.
- **Principle Four: Multi-Professional Faculty Development.** There is a clear and consistent approach to multi-professional faculty development across all local areas. There are clear mechanisms within multi-professional faculty development for sharing best practice and learning across the region.

Figure 8. HEE Simulation-based education framework five guiding principles

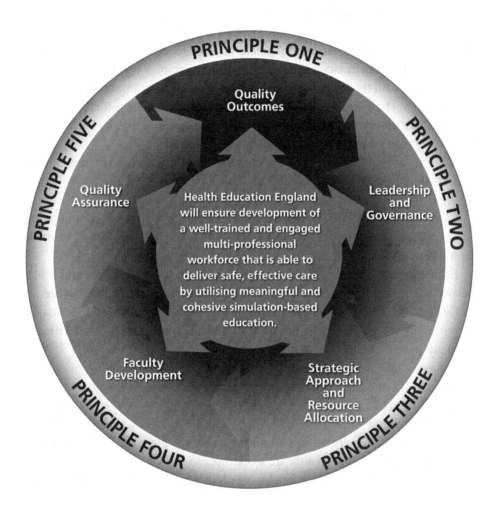

- **Principle Five: Quality Assurance.** There is a well-defined method for quality assuring the content and delivery of SBE using the HEE quality framework for education and training and other appropriate national standards, where necessary.

Each of the five guiding principles links back to the over-arching need for the delivery of safe, effective care through successful workforce education and development. While there is an inevitable overlap between the principles, there are common themes of quality, governance and accountability between the principles.

Key Performance Indicators of the SBE Framework

At the same time as the framework launch, a set of Key Performance Indicators (KPIs) to measure performance against the guiding principles was shared across all 13 local offices with the intention that they would regularly submit returns against these indicators. These 'light touch' KPIs helped to provide evidence for the adoption of the SBE framework and were intended to evolve in the future, in-line with the strategic overview and vision as it developed and evolved.

At the time of launch, there were 11 'light touch' KPIs identified to measure the spread of adoption of the framework:

- Evidence of evaluation frameworks for outcomes of SBE - e.g., a) improving quality and safety of patient care and b) developing a safe and capable workforce.
- Each local area office has clear processes for sharing of best practice and, when available, is raising awareness of e-LfH/The Learning Hub with providers.
- Evidence that lines of accountability, reporting mechanisms and escalation processes in the delivery of uni-professional and multi-professional SBE are in place, or that plans are in place if not.
- Evidence that documented approaches to the delivery of uni-professional and multi-professional SBE, including clarity on commissioning and refresh processes, are in place.
- Organizations who provide SBE through tariff, the LDA, or other resource allocations, are aware of opportunities and have plans in place to ensure uptake from the whole healthcare workforce.
- Evidence of or plans in place for sharing of SBE resources/facilities (including faculty).
- Evidence of or plans in place for educators to be able to access a faculty development program that aspires to a set of appropriate standards.
- Evidence of or plans in place for all faculty to receive feedback, guidance and support on professional development guidance.
- Evidence of or plans in place for faculty to have access to a community of practice/network to promote collaboration and sharing of best practice.

- Organizations receiving funding for the delivery of SBE – through Tariff, The Learning Development Agreement (LDA) or specific resource allocations – are working towards the application of ASPiH standards.
- Evidence of plans in place that will address any areas that have been highlighted as requiring improvement/support.

In the first-round light-touch KPIs, some of the key findings were that there is a need for a more cohesive approach to governance. This was shown through the planned engagement process with the local office Simulation Leads and also involved four regional TEL leads, with opportunities that developed as a result. This more cohesive approach to governance resulted in new processes for peer review and moderation, including an annual 'World Café' event, where there are opportunities to triangulate red, amber, green (RAG) ratings across the country.

Figure 9 illustrates the initial percentage of compliance of the 13 local offices against the 11 KPIs and the respective RAG ratings. The initial assessment of the overall compliance rate shows moderate compliance against the KPI criteria and

Figure 9. RAG ratings against the 11 SBE KPIs for the 13 HEE local offices

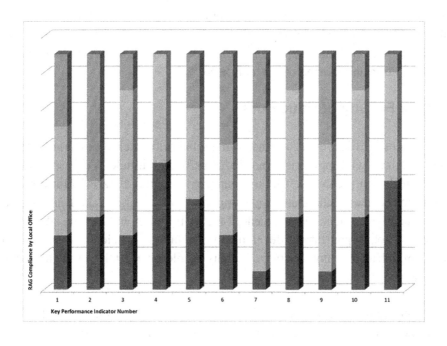

a moderate adoption of the SBE framework: red = 29%, amber = 47%, green = 24%. The 11 KPI's, their target audience and their associated RAG-rating criteria are presented in more detail in Appendix 1.

As the strategic overview becomes embedded, the wider workforce and HEE's Executive team will have a clear understanding about the delivery of SBE across England, providing clarity on where support might be needed to respond to the drivers for the implementation of the strategic overview. This clarity will be aided by the preparation of an annual report, which will be presented following receipt and analysis of the KPI responses.

SBE Toolkit to Support Adoption

To underpin the implementation of the SBE framework, HEE is developing a toolkit in support of each of the five guiding principles. This toolkit, which will be a living document that can be added to and amended over time, will take the form of guidance and advice to help the 13 local offices and NHS providers in their provision of SBE. It includes a suite of short films about SBE and its differing components, available on the SBE framework website[5].

In addition, a simulation community of practice is in development which will form part of HEE's new Learning Hub referenced earlier in this chapter, so that those already involved in the delivery of SBE can share their experiences and resources such as videos and scenario scripts. This community of practice will also be accessed by those with an interest in delivering SBE who are less experienced, thus enabling a forum where advice and support can be offered, as well as providing an avenue for collaboration and sharing of good practice.

Effective Faculty of Educators

The success of SBE delivery in healthcare in England ultimately relies on an effective faculty of trainers with appropriate knowledge, skills and attitudes. The responsibility for scenario design, pre-course briefing, management of the scenario and an effective de-brief, relies on a faculty that is well supported by their organisation and open to continuous improvement. One element of the SBE toolkit will include advice and resources to help organizations develop and maintain a proficient and sustainable faculty through an ongoing program of faculty development. It details the following faculty development recommendations:

1. **Provision of educational rigor:** A simulation faculty should be built on the foundation of sound educational principles if it is to meet the needs of its learners.

2. **Provision of faculty support and appropriate training:** Faculty should be trained to deliver high quality SBE. Investment in faculty development will enable faculty members to reach their full potential as educators. In addition, faculty members should be continually aware of their responsibilities to deliver high quality education with quantifiable learning outcomes to a diverse inter-professional group of learners.

3. **Enablement of a supportive and sustainable environment:** Powerful learning comes from becoming part of a 'community of practice' or learning through working together.

4. **Collaboration and sharing of best practice:** Working with other SBE providers is an important way to establish best practice, ensure parity of learning and to avoid unnecessary duplication. All simulation educators must be prepared to share their learning and learn from each other.

Stakeholder Involvement and Engagement

Creating a sense of ownership within the simulation community has also been a key success factor for the adoption of the SBE framework. The SRG was created to share knowledge and experience of simulation. Meeting twice a year, the SRG includes members from professional groups, the Royal Colleges and HEIs, who have been instrumental in project progress.

There is an active network of regional simulation groups across England, facilitated by HEE, in support of the SBE framework adoption. These SBE groups are where local organizations, NHS Trusts and SBE providers learn from each other's experiences and discuss and share good practice. For example, the initial response from the regional groups to the KPIs indicated mixed acceptance and understanding of the SBE framework. While some groups have clarity on the terms of reference and meet regularly, others meet less frequently. It is also not clear how organizations which are unaware of the network can become involved. Further work, through the HEE SBE Framework Quality Outcomes Task and Finish Group, is planned to develop some guidance on what makes a good and effective simulation network, and this will be shared with the other documents relating to advice and guidance within the SBE toolkit on the HEE website[5] and the new Learning Hub.

In addition, plans are underway for the preparation of a joint statement between HEE and the Academy of Medical Royal Colleges (AoMRC) to promote the SBE groups, as well as seeking a cohesive approach with regulatory bodies and associations, such as the Nursing and Midwifery Council (NMC), the General Medical and Dental Councils (GMC and GDC) and the Health and Care Professions Council (HCPC).

This section introduced the steps taken to implement the simulation-based education framework for healthcare educators in England, the guiding principles and the key performance indicators. This was followed by some of the steps taken to ensure successful adoption in the healthcare education community in England. In the proceeding section, recommendations for further research and development of the framework are discussed, including development of a National Strategic Overview and Vision on the delivery of SBE.

FUTURE RESEARCH DIRECTIONS

In the preceding sections, the challenges with access to equitable and high quality SBE were discussed along with the current modalities of SBE provision. To support addressing these inequalities, an SBE framework was developed and introduced across England which has so far enjoyed some success in its adoption. In this section, there is a discussion about the next steps with the development of the SBE framework and some proposed future work in this area.

The implementation of the SBE framework has been the first step of a process to influence the development and adoption of SBE in the NHS in England and to support HEE in its aim of ensuring the development of a well-trained and engaged multi-professional workforce that can deliver safe, effective care. Early indications suggest the framework has been well-received by the NHS and particularly the simulation community.

It is, however, important to note that such solutions will not be enough to ensure that the full potential for SBE is realized in the NHS. Healthcare professional bodies and regulatory bodies must adopt the SBE framework and subsequent strategic overview to inform their own strategic decisions on the matter. HEE local offices, NHS Trusts and other regional organizations in the NHS need to devise their own strategies building on this national work. In addition, the SBE community is recommended to use ASPiH standards or those of other accrediting bodies in order to ensure standards are met, whether that is to actively seek accreditation or not.

The four nations of the UK also need to ensure their support for the framework due to the amount of cross-border practice between the NHS in England and the rest of the UK, to provide a more cohesive approach to the adoption of the SBE framework. There are also opportunities to support adoption or development of similar SBE frameworks globally and in other industries to ensure global good practices are adopted around SBE in healthcare.

A National Strategic Overview and Vision on the Delivery of SBE

The next phase of this piece of work is to build on the SBE framework and develop a strategic overview and vision of the delivery of SBE for adoption across the NHS in England. Through the iterative approach and wider engagement, interest in this project has extended beyond HEE, with the result that the framework has influenced the development of HEI SBE strategies. There is also strong interest from the Royal Colleges and the Open University. This wider interest in the HEE SBE framework offers the opportunity for wider influence across HEI's, NHS Trusts and professional bodies, with the provision of a HEE strategic overview that will provide cohesion, as well as a vision for delivery, with HEE managing the workforce delivery.

However, for the development of a formal strategic overview to happen, a number of activities need to take place. Firstly, there needs to be a thorough understanding of the breadth of SBE, some of which has been outlined previously in this chapter, making sure all types of simulation from low to high fidelity are identified, with processes in place to identify new modalities as the field develops.

There needs to be a strong emphasis on building networks of SBE practitioners and educationalists, ensuring active channels of communication and the facilitation of opportunities for collaboration. In addition, there need to be effective mechanisms in place to ensure learners access the highest possible quality SBE and that this demonstrates an effective return on investment, with processes in place to measure these. The use of KPIs and the publication of the framework and guidance will be fundamental tools to support effective system leadership within SBE. The KPIs and any subsequent work on the strategic overview need to ensure that SBE, immersive technologies and video are being successfully operationalized and not just discussed.

Finally, there is a need to ensure that the discipline of devising and delivering SBE, irrespective of the modality being used, is founded on high quality, peer-reviewed published evidence. This is a broad discipline, with methods that are relatively nascent and as such, suffer in some areas from an undeveloped evidence base. It is recommended that there is active quality research conducted in the space, as well as encouragement on the use of evaluation in practice and the dissemination of findings. As the evidence base and delivery methodology for SBE grow, demand from professional groups and organizations are likely to increase. Such an increase is welcome; however, this will add greater impetus on the need for effective mechanisms of governance to support effective allocation of resources and return on investment.

As the SBE strategic overview moves towards implementation, some of the key elements of its delivery are going to be about how HEE and the TEL Programme can ensure that these KPIs are responding to the needs of other programs and pieces of work, not only within HEE, but across wider NHS organizations and regulatory bodies.

HEE is working with the Leeds Institute of Medical Education, a department in the faculty of medicine at the University of Leeds, on the development of a framework of standards for the delivery of VR and AR, building on the previous work which came from the VR Lab at Torbay and South Devon Hospitals NHS Foundation Trust. A second phase of work for the VR Lab is now planned, to include a new development of immersive video and VR content, developing a series of VR 360-degree experiences to be viewed on computers, laptops, mobile devices or VR headsets. Entitled 'A day in the life of…', each experience will take the viewer through the day of a colleague working in the NHS, showing expectations of the role, its diversity and the impact on patient care and safety. It is anticipated that these VR360 experiences will challenge some of the myths of healthcare roles within the NHS, resulting in increased recruitment and better understanding from the patient's perspective.

Similar work needs to take place across other modalities of simulation, including with manikins. Whilst there is likely to be steady progress on the fidelity and range of physiological functions across both adult and pediatric manikins, the unique qualities of pediatric healthcare will have an influence on developments. This is likely to include voice recognition, use of artificial intelligence software to simulate natural conversational speech and behavioral responses to environmental cues. Alongside this constant technological evolution, mature simulation programs are increasingly making rationalized purchase and deployment decisions, where manikin features are thoughtfully aligned with learning outcomes, cost implications and parallel fidelity strategies, to create targeted and effective simulation experiences.

The HEE national strategic overview and vision for the delivery of SBE must naturally be aligned to the recommendations highlighted in The Topol Review, the NHS Long Term Plan and HEE's wider national programs, including Cancer, Maternity and Public Health, Nursing, Urgent and Emergency Care and Primary Care. Once this alignment is in place, and the KPIs are fully embedded into the NHS workforce's approach to SBE, then the aspirational quality outcomes about delivery of educational excellence and enhanced patient care and safety will be delivered. The interim workflow for the next steps of the SBE framework is outlined in Table 1 below.

Table 1. Interim workflow for the next steps in the SBE framework development

Stage	Approximate Date
Preparation and release of individual KPI Reports per HEE local office	Early Summer 2019
Delivery of first tranche of guidance for SBE Toolkit	To be published in phases with the first delivery planned for Summer 2019. It will be a 'living' set of resources that will develop over time, to include digital and immersive technologies and will support the new HEE Learning Hub.
Preparation of the HEE Strategic Overview and Vision for the effective delivery of SBE	Ongoing work with first draft due in late Summer 2019
Release of refined and refreshed KPIs and plan for transition to business as usual (BAU)	Autumn 2019

There are many areas to explore in the further development of the SBE framework and to improve its spread of adoption. This section explored some of those opportunities for future enhancement, including the implementation of a formal strategic overview and vision. In the concluding section of this chapter, there will be a discussion of the overall coverage of the chapter and the conclusions reached from the work so far.

CONCLUSION

Advances in technology are beginning to have a profound impact on the way in which healthcare is delivered to patients, with seemingly endless improvements to diagnostic tools and to the treatments available. The healthcare workforce needs to be more adaptive to changes in practice as a result of emerging technologies. The Topol review and the NHS long-term plan both acknowledge these changes and note the requirement to adapt the way in which the NHS workforce is trained by increasing the use of technology in education, including through the increased use of technology in simulation and SBE.

However, there remains a challenge that not all staff and students working in healthcare have equitable access to high-quality SBE. While emerging simulation technologies can certainly address some of these challenges, there needs to be a recognition that investment in healthcare simulation needs to be equitable across England and that pockets of good practice should be communicated and spread widely to improve the overall quality of SBE provision.

At the start of this chapter, the work of the TEL program at HEE was highlighted as a key enabler in supporting the improvement of the delivery of healthcare education including SBE. The aim of the SBE work stream of the program is to ensure the development of a well-trained and engaged multi-professional workforce that can deliver safe, effective care.

The chapter then reflected on some of the existing simulation modalities and their current interfaces with technology to enhance their delivery and learner outcomes. These included: Teamworking and human factors, in-situ simulation, cadaveric dissection and wet tissue, use of manikins in pediatrics, immersive realities, haptic simulation in dentistry and the use of virtual patients.

The next section of the chapter reflected on the current challenges with a changing population demographic in England, putting increased demands on the healthcare system, with potentially fewer staff to deliver care. This likely will result in the need to provide a greater volume of training within the existing or a decreasing financial envelope while continuously improving the quality and standard of education. Inequalities in access to equitable and high-quality SBE were highlighted as a challenge, leading to the need for the development of a solution to address these problems.

To address these inequalities, an SBE framework was developed and introduced across England. The framework consists of five guiding principles, with success measured through a series of KPIs:

1. Quality Outcomes. Delivery of safe, effective care through workforce development.
2. Leadership and Governance.
3. Strategic Approach and Resource Allocation.
4. Multi-Professional Faculty Development.
5. Quality Assurance.

The framework has so far enjoyed some success in its adoption with the SBE community in healthcare but there is still much work to be done to improve the reach of the framework. Initiatives to increase adoption need to focus on stakeholder engagement, including engaging with simulation faculty and wider groups of stakeholders. One method of developing engagement includes the development of a toolkit to support the roll out of the framework and its guiding principles.

The final section of the chapter focused on the future development of the SBE framework to incorporate a National Strategic Overview and vision on its future delivery. This could include specific principles for the use of virtual and augmented reality or other forms of technology in simulation, expanding the reach to the four nations of the UK and beyond.

An ongoing challenge will be to ensure that the momentum gained through current engagement activities continues. This will mean that reporting on the delivery of SBE and sharing and collaboration becomes normal practice, resulting in reduction in duplication and silo working that will then enable true innovation.

The chapter reflected on the need for a national framework for SBE in England to improve overall access to simulation and to drive up the quality and consistency of training using simulation. The project outcome can conclude that the SBE framework has started being adopted and is a good model for improving educational standards, addressing inequalities, that could be rolled out more widely both in the UK and internationally.

ACKNOWLEDGMENT

This research received no specific grant from any funding agency in the public, commercial, or not-for-profit sectors. This chapter was supported through the work of the NHS Health Education England Technology Enhanced Learning program. The authors would like to acknowledge the following contributors with thanks:

Rebecca Burgess-Dawson, NHS Health Education England, United Kingdom
Andrew Dickenson, NHS Health Education England, United Kingdom
Alex Drinkall, NHS Health Education England, United Kingdom
Mark Hellaby, Manchester University NHS Foundation Trust, United Kingdom
Fleur Kellett, NHS Health Education England, United Kingdom
Chris Munsch, NHS Health Education England, United Kingdom
Nick Peres, Torbay and South Devon NHS Foundation Trust, United Kingdom
Neil Ralph, NHS Health Education England, United Kingdom
David Wright, Hull University Teaching Hospitals NHS Trust, United Kingdom

REFERENCES

Albright, G., Bryan, C., Adam, C., McMillan, J., & Shockley, K. (2018). Using virtual patient simulations to prepare primary health care professionals to conduct substance use and mental health screening and brief intervention. *Journal of the American Psychiatric Nurses Association*, 24(3), 247–259. doi:10.1177/1078390317719321 PMID:28754067

Alexander, L., Sheen, J., Rinehart, N., Hay, M., & Boyd, L. (2018). Mental health simulation with student nurses: A qualitative review. *Clinical Simulation in Nursing*, 14, 8–14. doi:10.1016/j.ecns.2017.09.003

ASPiH. (2016). *ASPiH Standards for Simulation-Based Education*. Retrieved from https://aspih.org.uk/standards-framework-for-sbe

Ball, J., Kumar Gunda, R., Awoseyila, A., & Sharma, A. (2014). Nuneosim survey - A triple blind study of nursing perception to simulation training in a tertiary neonatal intensive care setting. *BMJ Simulation, 1*(1). doi:10.1136/bmjstel-2014-000002.162

Booth, R., Sinclair, B., McMurray, J., Strudwick, G., Watson, G., Ladak, H., & Brennan, L. (2018). Evaluating a serious gaming electronic medication administration record system among nursing students: Protocol for a pragmatic randomized controlled trial. *JMIR Research Protocols, 7*(5), 138. doi:10.2196/resprot.9601 PMID:29807885

Bosse, H. M., Nickel, M., Huwendiek, S., Schultz, J. H., & Nikendei, C. (2015). Cost-effectiveness of peer role play and standardized patients in undergraduate communication training. *BMC Medical Education, 15*(1), 183. doi:10.118612909-015-0468-1 PMID:26498479

Breymier, T. L., Rutherford-Hemming, T., Horsley, T. L., Atz, T., Smith, L. G., Badowski, D., & Connor, K. (2015). Substitution of clinical experience with simulation in prelicensure nursing programs: A national survey in the United States. *Clinical Simulation in Nursing, 11*(11), 472–478. doi:10.1016/j.ecns.2015.09.004

Brown, J. (2008). Applications of simulation technology in psychiatric mental health nursing education. *Journal of Psychiatric and Mental Health Nursing, 15*(8), 638–644. doi:10.1111/j.1365-2850.2008.001281.x PMID:18803737

CHFG. (2019). *What are clinical human factors?* Retrieved from https://chfg.org/what-are-clinical-human-factors

Clark, J. (2018). New methods of documenting health visiting practice. In R. Michael (Ed.), *Vision and value in health information* (pp. 121–142). London, UK: CRC Press. doi:10.1201/9781315375380-10

Cowen, K. J., Hubbard, L. J., & Hancock, D. C. (2016). Concerns of nursing students beginning clinical courses: A descriptive study. *Nurse Education Today, 43*, 64–68. doi:10.1016/j.nedt.2016.05.001 PMID:27286947

CQC. (2018). *Opening the door to change. NHS safety culture and the need for transformation.* Retrieved from https://www.cqc.org.uk/sites/default/files/20181224_openingthedoor_report.pdf

Davis, S., Josephsen, J., & Macy, R. (2013). Implementation of mental health simulations: Challenges and lessons learned. *Clinical Simulation in Nursing, 9*(5), e157–e162. doi:10.1016/j.ecns.2011.11.011

Dearsley, A. (2013). Using standardized patients in an undergraduate mental health simulation AU - Alexander, Louise. *International Journal of Mental Health, 42*(2-3), 149–164. doi:10.2753/IMH0020-7411420209

Deshmukh, A. (2018). *Summary of health education England regional simulation strategies*. Unpublished manuscript.

Dickinson, T., Hopton, J., & Pilling, M. (2016). An evaluation of nursing students' perceptions on the efficacy of high-fidelity clinical simulation to enhance their confidence, understanding and competence in managing psychiatric emergencies. *Journal of Clinical Nursing, 25*(9-10), 1476–1478. doi:10.1111/jocn.13211 PMID:27001411

Dudley, F. (2018). *The simulated patient handbook: A comprehensive guide for facilitators and simulated patients*. London: CRC Press. doi:10.1201/9781315383774

e-LfH. (2019). *Health Education England e-LfH Hub Learner Analytics*. Unpublished manuscript.

Eppich, W., & Cheng, A. (2015). Promoting excellence and reflective learning in simulation (PEARLS): Development and rationale for a blended approach to health care simulation debriefing. *Simulation in Healthcare, 10*(2), 106–115. doi:10.1097/SIH.0000000000000072 PMID:25710312

Fent, G., Blythe, J., Farooq, O., & Purva, M. (2015). In-situ simulation as a tool for patient safety: A systematic review identifying how it is used and its effectiveness. *BMJ Simulation and Technology Enhanced Learning, 1*(3), 103–110. doi:10.1136/bmjstel-2015-000065

Fugill, M. (2013). Defining the purpose of phantom head. *European Journal of Dental Education, 17*(1), 1–4. doi:10.1111/eje.12008 PMID:23279394

Gaba, D. M. (2004). The future vision of simulation in healthcare. *BMJ Quality & Safety, 13*(suppl_1), 2–10. doi:10.1136/qshc.2004.009878

Gamble, A., Bearman, M., & Nestel, D. (2016). A systematic review: Children and adolescents as simulated patients in health professional education. *Advanced Simulation, 1*(1), 1. doi:10.118641077-015-0003-9 PMID:29449970

Geis, G. L., Pio, B., Pendergrass, T. L., Moyer, M. R., & Patterson, M. D. (2011). Simulation to assess the safety of new healthcare teams and new facilities. *Simulation in Healthcare, 6*(3), 125–133. doi:10.1097/SIH.0b013e31820dff30 PMID:21383646

Gelder, C. L., & Paterson-Brown, S. (2015). The role of anatomy in surgical training and the use of cadaveric training courses. *Bulletin of the Royal College of Surgeons of England*, *97*(3), 123–126. doi:10.1308/147363515X14134529301381

Gilbody, J., Prasthofer, A. W., Ho, K., & Costa, M. L. (2011). The use and effectiveness of cadaveric workshops in higher surgical training: A systematic review. *Bulletin of the Royal College of Surgeons of England*, *93*(5), 347–352. doi:10.1308/147870811X582954 PMID:21943455

Hamstra, S. J., Dubrowski, A., & Backstein, D. (2006). Teaching technical skills to surgical residents: A survey of empirical research. *Clinical Orthopaedics and Related Research*, *449*: 108–115. PMID:16760810

Hayashi, S., Munekazu, N., Shinichi, K., Ning, Q., Naoyuki, H., Shuichi, H., & Masahiro, I. (2016). History and future of human cadaver preservation for surgical training: From formalin to saturated salt solution method. *Anatomical Science*, *91*(1), 1–7. doi:10.100712565-015-0299-5 PMID:26670696

HEE. (2016). *Enhancing UK core medical training through simulation-based education: An evidence-based approach. A report from the joint JRCPTB/HEE Expert Group on Simulation in Core Medical Training*. Retrieved from https://www.jrcptb.org.uk/sites/default/files/HEE_Report_FINAL.pdf

HEE. (2018a). *A Health and Care Digital Capabilities Framework*. Retrieved from https://www.hee.nhs.uk/sites/default/files/documents/Digital%20Literacy%20Capability%20Framework%202018.pdf

HEE. (2018b). *National Framework for Simulation-Based Education*. Retrieved from https://www.hee.nhs.uk/our-work/technology-enhanced-learning/simulation-immersive-technologies

HEE. (2019a). *The Topol Review*. Retrieved from https://topol.hee.nhs.uk

HEE. (2019b). *Technology Enhanced Learning*. Retrieved from https://www.hee.nhs.uk/our-work/technology-enhanced-learning

Hellaby, M., Wood, S., & Herbert, N. (1997). Safely moving a hospital. *The Human Connection*, *2*, 18–19.

Inman, T. (1860). Foundation for a new theory and practice of medicine (book review). *Journal of Medical Science*, *40*, 450–458.

Issenberg, S. B., McGaghie, W. C., Petrusa, E. R., Lee Gordon, D., & Scalese, R. J. (2005). Features and uses of high-fidelity medical simulations that lead to effective learning: A BEME systematic review. *Medical Teacher*, *27*(1), 10–28. doi:10.1080/01421590500046924 PMID:16147767

Jeffries, P. (2005). A framework for designing, implementing, and evaluating: Simulations used as teaching strategies in nursing. *Nursing Education Perspectives*, *26*(2), 96–103. PMID:15921126

Kings Fund. (2017). *How is the NHS structured?* Retrieved from https://www.kingsfund.org.uk/audio-video/how-new-nhs-structured

Kuehster, C. R., & Hall, C. D. (2010). Simulation: Learning from mistakes while building communication and teamwork. *Journal for Nurses in Professional Development*, *26*(3), 123–127. doi:10.1097/NND.0b013e3181993a95 PMID:20508427

Kyle, R., & Murray, W. B. (2007). *Clinical simulation: Operations, engineering and management.* San Diego, CA: Elsevier Science & Technology.

Lapkin, S., Fernandez, R., Levett-Jones, T., & Bellchambers, H. (2010). The effectiveness of using human patient simulation manikins in the teaching of clinical reasoning skills to undergraduate nursing students: A systematic review. *JBI Library of Systematic Reviews*, *21*(6), 661–694. PMID:27820553

Lendahls, L., & Oscarsson, M. G. (2017). Midwifery students' experiences of simulation and skills training. *Nurse Education Today*, *50*, 12–16. doi:10.1016/j.nedt.2016.12.005 PMID:28006699

Lubbers, J., & Rossman, C. J. N. (2017). Satisfaction and self-confidence with nursing clinical simulation: Novice learners, medium-fidelity, and community settings. *Nurse Education Today*, *48*, 140–144. doi:10.1016/j.nedt.2016.10.010 PMID:27810632

MacLean, S., Geddes, F., Kelly, M., & Della, P. (2018). Simulated patient training: Using inter-rater reliability to evaluate simulated patient consistency in nursing education. *Nurse Education Today*, *62*, 85–90. doi:10.1016/j.nedt.2017.12.024 PMID:29306751

Mantovani, F., Castelnuovo, G., Gaggioli, A., & Riva, G. (2003). Virtual reality training for health-care professionals. *Cyberpsychology & Behavior*, *6*(4), 389–395. doi:10.1089/109493103322278772 PMID:14511451

Nguyen, P. K., Wasserman, S. M., Fann, J. I., & Giacomini, J. (2008). Successful lysis of an aortic prosthetic valve thrombosis with a dosing regimen for peripheral artery and bypass graft occlusions. *The Journal of Thoracic and Cardiovascular Surgery, 135*(3), 691–693. doi:10.1016/j.jtcvs.2007.11.012 PMID:18329497

NHS. (2016). *About the NHS*. Retrieved from https://www.nhs.uk/using-the-nhs/about-the-nhs/the-nhs

NHS. (2019). *The NHS Long Term Plan*. Retrieved from https://www.longtermplan.nhs.uk

Norcini, J. J., & McKinley, D. W. (2007). Assessment methods in medical education. *Teaching and Teacher Education, 23*(3), 239–250. doi:10.1016/j.tate.2006.12.021

Osnes, C., & Keeling, A. (2017). Development of haptic caries simulation for dental education. *Journal of Surgical Simulation, 4*, 29–34. doi:10.1102/2051-7726.2017.0006

Patterson, C., Perlman, D., Taylor, E. K., Moxham, L., Brighton, R., & Rath, J. (2018). Mental health nursing placement: A comparative study of non-traditional and traditional placement. *Nurse Education in Practice, 33*, 4–9. doi:10.1016/j.nepr.2018.08.010 PMID:30216804

Reed, T., Pirotte, M., McHugh, M., Oh, L., Lovett, S., Hoyt, A. E., ... McGaghie, W. C. (2016). Simulation-based mastery learning improves medical student performance and retention of core clinical skills. *Simulation in Healthcare, 11*(3), 173–180. doi:10.1097/SIH.0000000000000154 PMID:27093509

Schweller, M., Ribeiro, D. L., Passeri, S. R., Wanderley, J. S., & Carvalho-Filho, M. A. (2018). Simulated medical consultations with standardized patients: In-depth debriefing based on dealing with emotions. *Journal Revista Brasileira de Educação Médica, 42*(1), 84–93. doi:10.1590/1981-52712018v42n1rb20160089

Selim, A. A., Ramadan, F. H., El-Gueneidy, M. M., & Gaafer, M. M. (2012). Using objective structured clinical examination (OSCE) in undergraduate psychiatric nursing education: Is it reliable and valid? *Nurse Education Today, 32*(3), 283–288. doi:10.1016/j.nedt.2011.04.006 PMID:21555167

Shin, S., Park, J.-H., & Kim, J.-H. (2015). Effectiveness of patient simulation in nursing education: Meta-analysis. *Nurse Education Today, 35*(1), 176–182. doi:10.1016/j.nedt.2014.09.009 PMID:25459172

Sousa Freire, V. E. C., Lopes, M. V. O., Keenan, G. M., & Dunn Lopez, K. (2018). Nursing students' diagnostic accuracy using a computer-based clinical scenario simulation. *Nurse Education Today*, *71*, 240–246. doi:10.1016/j.nedt.2018.10.001 PMID:30340106

Winn, W. D. (1993). *A conceptual basis for educational applications of virtual reality. Human Interface Technology Laboratory Technical Report*. Seattle, WA: Human Interface Technology Laboratory. Retrieved from https://husily.ga/su1gsor63u.pdf

Yang, C.-W., Ku, S.-C., Ma, M. H.-M., Chu, T.-S., & Chang, S.-C. (2018). Application of high-fidelity simulation in critical care residency training as an effective learning, assessment, and prediction tool for clinical performance. *Journal of the Formosan Medical Association*. doi:10.1016/j.jfma.2018.12.003

Ziv, A., Wolpe, P. R., Small, S. D., & Glick, S. J. A. M. (2003). Simulation-based medical education: An ethical imperative. *Academic Medicine*, *78*(8), 783–788. doi:10.1097/00001888-200308000-00006 PMID:12915366

KEY TERMS AND DEFINITIONS

Framework: A set of guiding principles that are recommended but not mandated.

Human Factors: The interactions between the people, equipment, systems and processes in a complex healthcare environment.

In-Situ: Simulation conducted in the clinical environment rather than in a dedicated training center.

National Health Service: The statutory body responsible for providing healthcare to citizens of the United Kingdom.

Simulation: A technique for mimicking a real experience.

Simulation-Based Education: The application of simulation in an educational or learning environment.

Strategy: A solution to move from the current to a future position.

ENDNOTES

1   HEE Topol Review: https://topol.hee.nhs.uk
2   NHS Long Term Plan: https://www.longtermplan.nhs.uk
3   HEE TEL Program: https://hee.nhs.uk/tel
4   HEE Digital Capabilities Framework: https://www.hee.nhs.uk/our-work/
    digital-literacy
5   HEE Simulation Framework: https://www.hee.nhs.uk/our-work/technology-
    enhanced-learning/simulation-immersive-technologies

Chapter 2
Using Simulation in Radiographic Science Education

Christopher Ira Wertz
Idaho State University, USA & Boise State University, USA

Jessyca Wagner
Midwestern State University, USA & University of North Texas, USA

Trevor Mark Ward
Idaho State University, USA

Wendy Mickelsen
Idaho State University, USA

ABSTRACT

Students in radiographic science education programs must master both the didactic education and psychomotor skills necessary to perform radiographic examinations on patients in a clinical setting. Simulation is the most common method of helping radiographic science students prepare to perform such examinations. Simulation can be performed either in live or virtual environments. Recently there has been a trend to adopt virtual simulation in medical education because of the reduced adverse effects virtual simulation provides as opposed to live simulation and real-world practice. Though there is a paucity of literature available discussing virtual simulation's use in radiographic science education, recent studies in this field and related medical imaging modalities have shown the benefits of using virtual simulation. The purpose of this chapter is to discuss the current use of virtual simulation in radiographic science education and characteristics to consider when implementing a simulation program.

DOI: 10.4018/978-1-7998-0004-0.ch002

Copyright © 2020, IGI Global. Copying or distributing in print or electronic forms without written permission of IGI Global is prohibited.

INTRODUCTION

Radiographic Science (RS) education, like all healthcare education, is uniquely different from education in other professional fields. While education for other professional fields (e.g., engineering, history, English, education, biology, etc.) focus solely on didactic or schoolwork learning, healthcare education is dually split between didactic and clinical education (Densen, 2011; Scheckel, 2009). Students are not only expected to acquire the technical, cognitive learning required, but they must also master the psychomotor skills necessary to apply didactic knowledge to patients in a clinical setting.

Historically, for adult learners, pedagogical techniques (i.e., teacher-directed methods) are often preferred by those who have progressed the furthest in formal education, as is the case with students in higher education (Cross, 1982). This is not surprising as the majority of organized education is based on pedagogical principles, and those with more education have more experience with and feel comfortable in well-structured classes and lectures (Hulse, 1992).

In contrast, modern learning theories for adult learners include self-pacing and the ability for repetition, real-time and learner-controlled feedback, and on-demand accessibility to education at the convenience of the learner (Cook et al., 2012; Decker, Sportsman, Puetz, & Billings, 2008; Kong, Hodgson, & Druva, 2015; Olxaewski & Wolbrink, 2017). Traditional pedagogical techniques are not suited for modern adult learners in radiographic science education. There is a need for academic transformation and pedagogical innovation in RS education, because students are required to learn radiological and medical theory and technical information before being able to apply that knowledge to a clinical setting. Educators must find ways to adapt modern learning theories for adult learners to successfully educate the next generation of healthcare professionals. Simulation, both real-life and virtual simulation, has been found to be the most common educational tool used to train and prepare modern students in healthcare (Motola, Devine, Chung, Sullivan, & Issenberg, 2013; Shanahan, 2016).

Real-life simulation, a common practice in radiographic education, is the use of high-fidelity mannequins, disarticulated phantoms, and real-life people for the practice of radiographic positioning (Ahlqvist et al., 2013; Berry et al., 2007; Cook et al., 2012; Gordon, Oriol, & Cooper, 2004; Kasprzak, 2016; Kong et al., 2015; Wright et al., 2006). Virtual simulation, technology-enhanced simulation performed through the medium of a computer software program, offers the added benefits of self-paced learning, repetition, constant access, and instant feedback (Issenberg & Scalese, 2008; Kasprzak, 2016; Shanahan, 2016). This form of pedagogy is especially attractive to adult learners because they prefer interactive, hands-on learning with immediate feedback (Decker et al., 2008). More recent research is turning from traditional pedagogical models by identifying the uniqueness of educating adults, stating "Adults bring a plethora of knowledge and experience that can enhance their learning, as long as there is interactive, engaging, and collaborative instruction" (Whitney, 2014, p. 460).

Recently, the use of simulation has increased across the healthcare education continuum in such areas as patient safety, acquiring and honing clinical skills in a controlled environment, and promotion of individual and group learning (Monachino & Tuttle, 2015; Motola et al., 2013). In RS education, chief among these simulation trends is to improve psychomotor performance when preparing students to learn and practice in a clinical setting. The purpose of this chapter is to discuss the current use of simulation in radiographic science education and characteristics to consider when implementing a simulation program.

Clinical Requirements of Radiographic Science Programs

Students in RS education programs throughout the United States are required to learn and demonstrate the proper patient positions and radiation exposure factors for 37 mandatory exams and 34 elective exams in a clinical setting. Each exam is comprised of 2-6 images in differing patient positions, depending on the anatomy being imaged. Upon the successful completion of these exams, also known as "competencies", and the scholastic (didactic) components required by accredited RS programs, students are eligible to take a national registry exam given by the American Registry of Radiologic Technologists (ARRT). Successful completion of the ARRT exam allows students to become registered and certified radiologic technologists. This process of education and certification is similar to other medical professions such as doctors and nurses.

In RS education programs, program faculty teach students the technical and theoretical information necessary to perform all radiographic exams in classroom courses on campus. Clinical instructors (CIs) oversee, supervise, and evaluate students' competence as they perform these exams on patients in a clinical setting. The students start by learning the entry-level and most commonly performed exams, such as chest or hand exams. By the end of the educational program students must demonstrate competence in performing all required radiographic examinations in a safe and proficient manner. When students start the RS program, they have no previous experience with patient care and are often hesitant or unsure about positioning the patient and equipment to perform an x-ray examination. In medical imaging, when students are hesitant or lack knowledge and skills they are prone to produce images with decreased quality or expose patients to unnecessarily high amounts of radiation (Ortiz, 2015). Comfort, familiarity, and skills are acquired with time and practice, but these are experiences new RS students do not have.

To prepare students for the clinical setting, RS program faculty and CIs must find ways to develop student clinical competence. Competence is both a measurement of and indicator for student clinical preparedness; however, competence is not easily quantifiable (Williams & Berry, 1999), is ill-defined and subject to interpretation (Clarke & Holmes, 2007), and is vague (Castillo, Caruana, & Wainwright, 2011). The instructions given by the ARRT to educational radiography programs for determining student clinical competence are generalized and minimalistic:

Demonstration of clinical competence requires that the program director or the program director's designee has observed the candidate performing the procedure independently, consistently, and effectively during the course of the candidate's formal educational program. (ARRT, 2016)

Competencies are performed on real patients in the clinical setting under the supervision of designated representatives of the program director (e.g., CIs). Clinical instructors use the following criteria identified by the ARRT (2016) to evaluate clinical competence: patient identity verification; examination order verification; patient assessment; room preparation; patient management; equipment operation; technique selection; patient positioning; radiation safety; imaging processing; and image evaluation. Many of the preceding criteria are subjective to the evaluator and determining competence can vary greatly among different CIs.

The goal of radiography education programs is to prepare students to be clinically competent in the classroom and laboratory setting before demonstrating that competence on real patients in the clinical setting. Currently there is a paucity of literature available on preparing students to enter the clinical setting as it directly relates to RS. Though little information was found, literature reviews conducted by other researchers about the preparedness of RS students to enter the clinical setting found common pedagogical themes including active learning, motivation, case-based studies, reflection, situations which require critical-thinking skills, objective structured clinical examination, and engagement activities (Holmström & Ahonen, 2016; Marshall & Harris, 2000; Sedden & Clark, 2016). However, the most common theme among the articles reviewed was the use of simulation. These articles touted the benefits of simulation for RS students but cited little empirical evidence of their implementation. The research mainly pointed to the use of simulation in other allied health professions and advocated the implementation of such techniques in RS education. Research suggests RS students benefit from the opportunity to practice radiographic examinations in a simulated environment prior to demonstrating that competence on real patients in the clinical setting (Holmström & Ahonen, 2016; Marshall & Harris, 2000; Sedden & Clark, 2016; Shanahan, 2016).

Simulation

Simulation (both live and virtual) has been identified as the most common method of helping students prepare to perform radiographic examinations on real patients in hospitals and clinics (Ahlqvist et al., 2013; Berry et al., 2007; Cook et al., 2012; Gordon et al., 2004; Kasprzak, 2016; Kong et al., 2015; Shanahan, 2016; Wright et al., 2006). According to the Society for Simulation in Healthcare (n.d.), healthcare simulation "is a range of activities that share a broad, similar purpose – to improve the safety, effectiveness, and efficiency of healthcare services" (para. 1). This is often accomplished through various modalities within scenarios that seek to achieve a degree of realism to facilitate experiential learning (Cook et al., 2011; Issenberg, McGaghie, Petrusa, Gordon, & Scalese, 2005; McGaghie, Issenberg, Cohen, Barsuk, & Wayne, 2011). Real-life simulation in radiographic education is the use of high-fidelity mannequins, disarticulated phantoms, and real life people for the practice of radiographic positioning (Ahlqvist et al., 2013; Berry et al., 2007; Cook et al., 2012; Gordon et al., 2004; Kasprzak, 2016; Kong et al., 2015; Wright et al., 2006). This form of pedagogy is especially attractive to adult learners because they prefer interactive, hands-on learning with immediate feedback (Decker et al., 2008).

Simulations (a.k.a. real-life simulated learning scenarios) seek to "imitate real patients, anatomic regions or clinical tasks, or to mirror the real-life situations in which medical services are rendered" (Issenberg & Scalese, 2008, p. 33). The safe and risk-free environment offered through simulation gives students the ability to practice health care skills without endangering patients (Berry et al., 2007; Cook et al., 2012; Gordon et al., 2004; Kasprzak, 2016; Kong et al., 2015). For students who are training in healthcare related fields, simulation is an alternative educational method for situations when training in real-life scenarios is time consuming, expensive, or hazardous to themselves or to patients (Ahlqvist et al., 2013). Simulated learning scenarios also allow students to receive immediate and specific feedback about their performance from an evaluator (Cook et al., 2012; Kong et al., 2015; Wright et al., 2006). Multiple studies have shown medical simulation to be educationally effective (Ahlqvist et al., 2013; Gaba, 2004; Issenberg et al., 2005).

Virtual Simulation

While classroom and laboratory simulations have been a staple of medical education, recently there has been a migration of simulations into the virtual environment (Kasprzak, 2016). Virtual simulation generally falls under the broader category of serious games (i.e., games developed for a purpose other than entertainment) (Bauman & Ralston-Berg, 2015; Olxaewski & Wolbrink, 2017; Wang, DeMaria, Goldberg, & Katz, 2016). Virtual simulation is the use of technology-enhanced simulation for the same purpose as real-life simulation but performed through the medium of a computer software program (Issenberg & Scalese, 2008; Kasprzak, 2016; Shanahan, 2016). Examples may include the user manipulating a 3rd person avatar to accomplish tasks or spatially move through a virtual setting, or a 1st person setting where the user interacts with the virtual environment as they would on their own (i.e., instead of using and manipulating an avatar). Virtual simulation may also include real life instruments and tools used in combination with a virtual environment (Tjiam et al., 2014). A study by Tjiam et al (2014) had the user look at a computer screen which portrayed a virtual surgery simulation while the user manipulated real life surgical tools. The virtual simulation then portrayed the movement of the real life tools in virtual space displayed on the monitor. The goal of virtual simulation is to imitate a real-world process (Olxaewski & Wolbrink, 2017). This new form of simulation has been shown to increase student satisfaction and learning when compared to traditional teaching methods (Bauman & Ralston-Berg, 2015; Olxaewski & Wolbrink, 2017; Shanahan, 2016).

The benefits of real-life simulation are also found in virtual simulation with some additional advantages. Virtual simulations reduce the need for tangible products and physical space. Because of the virtual nature of the simulations, students can use the technology in any environment at any time. Virtual simulations can provide a scalable, convenient method for students to practice clinical skills in a safe environment while using interactivity and competition (Berry et al., 2007; Kasprzak, 2016; Olxaewski & Wolbrink, 2017). The gaming characteristics found in virtual simulation use motivational factors and cognitive scaffolding to promote learning and engagement (Bauman & Ralston-Berg, 2015; Olxaewski & Wolbrink, 2017). Learning theories for adult learners are applied through self-pacing and the ability for repetition, real-time and learner-controlled feedback, and on-demand accessibility to education at the convenience of the student (Cook et al., 2012; Decker et al., 2008; Kong et al., 2015; Olxaewski & Wolbrink, 2017).

Like real-world simulations, virtual simulations "allow students to develop their understanding and practise their skills, in a safe pre-clinical learning environment" (Shanahan, 2016, p. 218). Radiation therapy educational programs (which are similar but separate from RS) have found that the use of virtual simulation allowed students to practice technical skills which led to increased student confidence (Bridge, Appleyard, Ward, Phillips, & Beavis, 2007; Bridge et al., 2016; Green & Appleyard, 2011). Virtual simulation led to students being better prepared to perform in the clinical environment (Bridge et al., 2016). Students cited that the safe learning environment of virtual simulation allowed them to develop their skills without endangering patients, provided the ability to make and learn from mistakes, and decreased time pressure that occurs in the clinical environment as factors which lead to their increased performance (Bridge et al., 2007; Bridge et al., 2016; Green &

Appleyard, 2011; Shanahan, 2016). Similar benefits of narrowing the gap between psychomotor skills acquisition and clinical practice were found when using virtual simulation in certain surgical education trails (Berry et al., 2007; Densen, 2011; Gordon et al., 2004; Tjiam et al., 2014).

Virtual simulation, a method used for training in multiple industries, is increasingly being incorporated in health care education (Ghanbarzadeh, Ghapanchi, Blumenstein, & Talaei-Khoei, 2014; Ma, Jain, & Anderson, 2014). This educational method has been used to assess and support interdisciplinary learning and communication skill development (Lemheney et al, 2016; Shanahan, 2016). Virtual simulation holds promise for maximizing access and minimizing the cost of training simulation. Examples in health care include procedural simulation, objective structured clinical examinations, patient safety, patient education and engagement, teamwork, and replacing live patient encounters. The dynamic learning environment provided by virtual simulation is based in the theory of social participation: the concept of forming knowledge through interaction with other people (Berragan, 2011; Lemheney, et al, 2016). However, until recently, most virtual simulations have been designed for specific health care professions rather than interprofessional health care teams (Lemheney et al, 2016; Shanahan, 2016). Effective communication and interprofessional collaboration, generally considered as part of clinical competence, are essential to maintain high standards of health care.

Simulation can be used as a tool for assessing learning and skills rather than strictly for the teaching of skills. Assessing student learning and skills is an essential part of determining clinical readiness. A difficulty with real-life simulation is that the evaluator can be influenced by other factors outside of the simulation performance (i.e., personal relationships, individual preferences, sickness, mood, etc.) making their evaluation more subjective instead of strictly objective. However, unlike traditional simulation, assessments given through virtual simulations can offer an objective, standardized model for students to achieve metric benchmarks and immediate feedback without the bias of a human evaluator (Berry et al., 2015). Berry et al. (2007) found virtual simulations to be as effective as laboratory simulations in assessing technical skills in certain radiology procedures. Sabir, Aran, and Abujudeh (2014) agreed and additionally stated how simulations will be "more commonly used as an assessment tool as professional boards start to include simulation-based assessment in their certification and recertification procedures" (p. 513). However, these studies focus on the use of simulation as a method of assessment for doctors training to become radiologists (i.e., health care workers who specialize in the interpretation of radiographic images). On the other hand, radiographers, or radiologic technologists, are the medical professionals who perform medical imaging exams to acquire radiographic images. Currently the available literature about simulation's use in radiographic science focuses on its educational effectiveness and impact on clinical performance; little to no research has been performed on how simulation can be used as an assessment tool in the field of radiologic science.

Though virtual simulation offers many benefits to medical education, there are disadvantages. The introduction of new simulation software can cause technical difficulties which may diminish learning opportunities (Burden et al., 2012; James, Maude, Sim, & McDonald, 2012; St. John-Matthews, Gibbs, & Messer, 2013). Also, some studies have shown the ease of use and competence of using computers is associated with gender and age differences. Both Huffman, Whetten, and Huffman (2013) and Teo, Fan, and Du (2015) explored the relationship between technology self-efficacy and gender roles among university students. They found males report higher levels of self-efficacy in their own computing skills and competence than females. Helsper and Eynon (2010) reported in a study of United Kingdom citizens that those born with access to computers and the Internet (i.e., digital natives) have higher confidence in their computer abilities than those born before such technologies were available (i.e., digital immigrants); however, their findings did show digital immigrants can become as proficient with technology as digital natives through practice and acquiring skills. Based on these findings, student cohort differences as well as technological issues may impact the introduction of virtual simulation and its educational value. Despite the potential negative effects, virtual simulation can be used as a valuable educational tool when implemented properly (Shanahan, 2016). Based on the clinical education and competence requirements set by the ARRT, the attributes of virtual simulation are uniquely suited to fit the needs of educating and training RS students.

Virtual Simulation in Radiographic Science Education

Simulation in radiology has been used for many years in the form of "hot seat" conferences, case studies, and online teaching modules; however, truly immersive virtual simulations are new to the field (Desser, 2007). Primarily, virtual simulation has been used in healthcare to improve technical skill development. A summary of simulation options and uses in medical imaging education is shown in Table 1. With virtual simulation, the risk-free environment of simulated scenarios is combined with the freedom and versatility of the virtual world (Berry et al., 2007; Chetlen et al., 2015; Cook et al., 2012; Gordon et al., 2004; Kasprzak, 2016; Kong et al., 2015; Shanahan, 2016). Virtual simulation also provides a training scenario that is less awkward than students practicing on study participants or patients (Burden et al., 2012; Coline, Gihad, Philippe, & Yves, 2015; Desser, 2007; Lemheney, et al, 2016; Shanahan, 2016). For medical imaging specifically, there is an increasing

Table 1. Summary of simulation use in medical imaging education

Simulator Options	Procedural Skills Training	Non-Procedural Skills Training

Types of Simulators
• Part-task trainers
  o Head, neck, and torso mannequins
  o Practice ultrasound biopsy equipment
• Simulated patients
  o CPR dummies
  o Full body, computerized mannequins
• Immersive simulators
  o Computer programs
  o Virtual reality
Simulator Fidelity
• Low (least expensive and static)
• Medium
• High (most expensive and sophisticated
	Radiography
	• Virtual patients for positioning and image analysis
	• Simulated radiation dosages
	Sonography
	• Practice mannequins
	• Simulations of uncomfortable/ invasive exams
	• Part-task trainers
	Other Modalities
	• Radiation dose simulations in Nuclear Medicine
	• "Moving heart" thoracic studies in CT and MRI
	• Interpersonal skills
		Image Interpretation
		• Virtual workstation
		• Simulated DICOM and PACS training
		• ACR virtual teaching files
		Professionalism and Communication
		• Virtual patients for communication practice
		• Simulated interprofessional exams
		• Simulated exams to increase confidence

trend to use virtual simulation for medical doctors' training in radiology to increase interpretative skills. Other skills that can be acquired through virtual simulation include "management of contrast reactions, interpersonal and communication skills, professionalism, and team training" (Chetlen et al., 2015, p. 1253).

Simulator Options

Types of Simulators

There are various types of simulators used to train radiology professionals. Part-task trainers range from rudimentary to high-tech and represent one body part or a limited portion of reality so those trainings can focus on one particular skill (Chetlen et al., 2015; Desser, 2007; Klein & Neal, 2016). For example, there are head, neck, and torso mannequins for teaching venipuncture and line placement, and ultrasound simulators to hone scanning abilities or practice needle guided biopsies. Simulated and standardized patients are also a common simulator in radiology and are generally mechanical, virtual, and computer-enhanced mannequins. CPR dummies such as Resusci Anne and SimMan are used to simulate real patients and can be given symptoms and reactions through a computer to enhance the situation for the trainees (Chetlen et al., 2015; Desser, 2007; Klein & Neal, 2016). Finally, there are also virtual reality and immersive simulators. These use computer displays to simulate the physical world and use auditory, visual, and tactile feedback to guide the user through the scenario (Chetlen et al., 2015; Desser, 2007). The VIST-Lab in Sweden is a fully immersive interventional lab to teach endovascular procedures (Chetlen et al., 2015).

Simulator Fidelity

Fidelity describes the "degree to which the simulation matches the actual experience, as well as the level to which the skills in the real task are captured in the simulated task" (Klein & Neal, 2016, p. 909). Simulators are ranked as low-, medium-, or high-fidelity and range from inexpensive and static to sophisticated, computerized, and expensive (Wagner, 2017). Fidelity is measured in terms of equipment, environmental, and psychological realism. Most radiology procedures can be completed using low- or medium-fidelity equipment, decreasing the necessary cost required (Klein & Neal, 2016). No matter the fidelity of the simulator, the possibilities within radiology are growing and range from procedural skills training in multiple modalities to interpersonal skills for radiologists and technologists.

Procedural Skills Training

Radiography

A simulator was introduced in 2006 that utilizes a high-resolution computed tomography data set of the head and spine to create a virtual patient for technologists to practice positioning for cervical spine radiographs. Students manipulate a virtual tube and x-ray beam using computer animation and the resultant x-ray is produced using algorithms and no radiation. This allows students to evaluate their positioning performance without offering any radiation risk to patients (Desser et al., 2006). Pediatric radiography is another opportunity for virtual simulation. Pediatric patients require a change in radiation and contrast dosage and provide unique positioning and technique challenges. Virtual simulation has been used to estimate radiation dosages, present positioning challenges, mimic contrast reactions, and display pathology and anomalies specific to pediatric patients (Gaca et al., 2007; Stein-Wexler et al., 2010).

Interventional Radiology

Interventional radiology procedures are a highly utilized modality for virtual simulations. Ultrasound and computed tomography (CT) guided percutaneous procedures, neuroradiology, vascular interventional procedures, and catheter-based interventions, as well as training for acute radiologic emergencies, have all been practiced using virtual simulation (Chetlen et al., 2015; Desser, 2007). Using virtual simulation for these procedures has been shown to reduce fluoroscopy time, radiation dose, needle redirects, and overall procedure time (Chetlen et al., 2015). The establishment of virtual simulation in interventional radiology also sparked the use of these devices for competing departments, such as vascular surgery and cardiologists. Simulators such as the Procedicus VIST simulator, Angio Mentor, Simsuite, and CathLabVR system have all been developed and are undergoing validation studies (Desser, 2007).

Sonography

In the realm of medical imaging, sonography (a.k.a. ultrasound) imaging is a field similar to, but separate from RS, and is one such specialty benefitting from the use of virtual simulation. UltraSim, a sonographic simulation system, "consists of a full-size mannequin with realistic body contours and a soft torso surface, an ultrasound probe, and an ultrasound scanner console and monitor" (Desser, 2007, p. 820). This simulator was used in a study of 8 first-year residents for abdomen and pelvis scanning, where the investigators determined the simulator improved the residents' scanning abilities and interpretation skills (Monsky et al., 2002). Gynecological imaging exams are uncomfortable for both the patient and the inexperienced examiner, which can lead to increased stress and decreased image quality (Burden et al., 2012; Coline et al., 2015). Virtual simulation allows for the training of sonographers without the pressures of a live patient setting and possible repeat interventions, "thus accelerating the learning curve in a nonclinical environment" (Coline et al., 2015, p. 1663). Also, phantoms can be used to simulate patients for transthoracic and transesophageal echocardiography including 3D tracking (Chetlen et al., 2015).

Other Modalities

Virtual simulation can also be used in modalities such as nuclear medicine, CT, and magnetic resonance imaging (MRI). In nuclear medicine, training can be performed on the use of radiopharmaceuticals, including proper handling, dosage, and adverse reactions, as well as injections for difficult studies (Chetlen et al., 2015). Given the nature of CT and MRI, there are many computer-based simulators for these procedures, especially thoracic studies. "An anthropomorphic moving heart phantom is now available and has been used to assess functional cardiac parameters with MRI, multidetector, and dual-source CT" (Chetlen et al., 2015). Interpersonal skills can also be honed using virtual simulation for radiographic sciences.

Non-Procedural Skills Training

Image Interpretation

Virtual simulation is an exciting new tool for training medical students to interpret radiologic images. "The [virtual] workstation allows student manipulation and interpretation of entire imaging studies in a way that closely mirrors the clinical practice of radiology and supplements the educational approaches of didactic lectures and reading room observation" (Strickland, Lowry, Petersen, & Jesse, 2015, p. w290). Radiology simulators have been developed for residents prior to taking overnight call in the emergency department focused on DICOM and PACS training since radiologists are not generally on-campus during this shift (Ganguli et al., 2006; Towbin, Paterson, & Chang, 2008). Along these lines, the American College of Radiology (ACR) has created a cloud-based PACS called Radiology Content Management System providing virtual teaching files that can be used collaboratively throughout multiple institutions (Chetlen et al., 2015).

Professionalism and Communication

Communication is an important part of any healthcare department, but especially in radiology. Radiologists and technologists need to know how to communicate effectively, but most do not receive any formal training for this while in school (Chetlen et al., 2015; Klein & Neal, 2016). Virtual patients can be used to simulate situations for scenarios such as obtaining informed consent, discussing an error during a procedure, disclosing bad news, sharing results with an ordering physician, or determining the appropriate test to order. These patients can be programmed to experience various responses such as anger, disbelief, shock, guilt, and denial (Chetlen et al., 2015). This type of training can not only improve communication skills, but also increase empathy and attitudes toward patients and families. Simulation actives can be used to develop effective communication and collaboration in interprofessional health care teams (Shanahan, 2016; Lemheney, et al, 2016). Finally, the use of virtual simulation specific to RS education should be explored to help increase students' technical skills before interacting with patients.

Training for Radiographic Science Students

Studies have shown how using virtual simulated health care experiences can improve student performance in a clinical setting. Ahlqvist et al. (2013) developed a virtual simulator for radiographic examinations. The researchers compared student performance in the assessment of radiographic image quality after training with a convention manikin or with the virtual radiography simulator. Through a linear mixed-effect analysis, they found a statistically significant difference between the experimental and control groups regarding proficiency change and concluded, "there are indications that the virtual radiography simulator training can reduce tutor time and the time needed for training in the radiography [clinical setting]" (Ahlqvist et al., 2013, p. 387).

In a meta-analysis of articles which compared simulation versus other instructional methods, Cook et al. (2012) agreed with Ahlqvist et al. (2013), stating virtual simulation training is associated with higher learning outcomes. Cook et al. (2012) did caution, however, that their study could not address the costs, procedure of aligning simulation with educational objectives, or the method with which simulation is effectively integrated and that these factors would influence simulation's association with higher learning outcomes. Kong et al. (2015) studied students' knowledge acquisition after virtual simulation learning activities using pre- and post-tests. Their conclusions were similar to the previously mentioned studies, but had some additional conclusions which seemed to contradict some of their findings. While pre- and post-test indicated that both the students learned and the students perceived their confidence and positioning skills increased, the test results showed students perceived simulations did not help improve decision-making skills. Both Cook et al. (2012) and Kong et al. (2015) stated the need for future research to explore virtual simulation's role in developing critical-thinking skills and in the best methods of integrating simulation in established curriculum to align with educational objectives and goals.

Current Studies in Radiographic Science

Though there is currently a paucity of literature available on preparing students to enter the clinical setting as it directly relates to RS, some researchers have attempted to evaluate the effect of virtual simulation on students' clinical preparedness. Understanding the gaps in available empirical knowledge and assessing research attempts to fill that gap can help future researchers know what to study and how to better approach their research methods.

In an attempt to gather information about the use of virtual simulation in radiographic science, Thoirs, Giles, and Barber (2011) performed a literature review as well as surveyed and interviewed stakeholders of a medical radiation sciences program in Australia. They found Virtual Radiography™, a virtual radiography simulation system developed by Shaderware Ltd, was being used in the United Kingdom. Based on an interview of an academic using the virtual simulation program, student feedback was positive and the program supported acceleration of student skill level, better preparing them for clinical placement.

Encouraged by this information and two papers published by Shaderware (Cosson & Willis, 2012a; Cosson & Willis, 2012b), Shanahan (2016) developed a pilot study to use Projection VR™ (a simulation program within Virtual Radiography™ suite) as an educational tool in the laboratory component within an Australian RS program. The virtual simulation program was used in addition to traditional simulation practices. The researcher found an increase in students' self-efficacy scores and confidence level when setting up radiographic procedures. Increasing student confidence level in fundamental elements of radiography exams before students enter the clinical setting can make the transition from the university to the clinical practice less stressful for students (Mason, 2016; Shanahan, 2016). With these elements enhanced before students enter the clinical setting, students can use time in the clinical setting to focus on experiences and skills that can only be gained in the clinical setting, such as patient interaction skills (Bridge et al., 2016; Shanahan, 2016).

Another pilot study of an established software was conducted by Wagner (2017) using the program SIMTICS with a group of undergraduate radiographic science students in their final didactic semester before entering the clinical setting. SIMTICS is a computer software offering students an opportunity to practice positioning and all other elements of taking an x-ray using a virtual patient. Wagner (2017) wanted to use this to complement the limited hands-on lab time the students had to determine if it would increase their competence. The students that participated in the study did not complete the entire study as the investigator had hoped due to frustration with the program itself. While the program itself had potential and the students saw merit in it, there were many shortcomings, such as sensitivity of the program, inability to continue when mistakes were made, and limited study availability (Wagner, 2017).

Dikshit, Wu, Wu, and Zhao (2005) and Papamichail, Pantelis, Papgiannis, Karaiskos, and Georgiou (2014) developed their own simulation software to pilot with students. Dikshit et al. (2005) created a virtual simulation program using animated simulations for multiple modalities: x-ray, CT, MRI, ultrasound, and PET to fill a need for biomedical engineering students. In their program, students were provided with text information, web page links, animations, simulations, and online homework about imaging principles for each modality. The result was a diagnostic image where students could see the principles applied. At the time of publication, the program was being tested to determine if there was an increase in student comprehension of the concepts presented in the program, but no results were provided. Papamichail et al. (2014) developed an open access web-based educational platform with simulation and self-assessment features to teach medical students, radiology residents, physicists, and biomedical engineers about medical image reconstruction and processing. A preliminary evaluation of the program was performed by 46 medical students using a five-point Likert-type scale. Overall, the content of the course was considered effective, well structured, and relevant; however, the students found it would make a better supplement to lecture content rather than a stand-alone tool (Papamichail et al., 2014).

These current radiography simulation studies are pilot studies intended to demonstrate proof of concept for incorporating virtual simulation in RS education. Further, longitudinal research studies are needed to truly evaluate the use of virtual simulation in RS education, effective pedagogical characteristics of the simulation program, and the proper methods to implement such technologies in RS educational programs. Current research studies can help inform future researchers as to more effective methods of study and implementation techniques.

SOLUTIONS AND RECOMMENDATIONS

As previously identified, there is a need to transform pedagogical methods in RS education. Innovations in the use of simulation and the technological advances made to simulation technology call for transformation to previously established educational techniques. Educational programs must choose a virtual simulation technology that fits the standards of the profession as well as meets the unique needs of the program. Programs must also establish the validity and reliability of the simulation technology, curricular fit, and student motivation. One of the most popular and effective methods of implementing simulation in an RS program is through the principle of distributive practice, which is based in the educational theory of constructivism, the idea that learners build new knowledge based on knowledge they already have. If appropriately valid and reliable simulation programs match the educational curriculum and are implemented using the scaffolding of distributed practice and constructivism, these simulation technologies can offer educational programs the benefits of traditional simulation combined with the unique characteristics of virtual environments.

Choosing a Virtual Simulation Technology

Though there are only a limited number of virtual simulation programs dedicated to RS education, it is important to choose the best program when attempting to incorporate virtual simulation in RS education. The first step is to identify the specific needs of the RS program in a curriculum-based approach, a.k.a. "training needs analysis" (TNA) (Tjiam et al., 2014). TNA is the process of identifying the gap in training and related training needs. A TNA of RS students' preparedness to enter the clinical setting explores such questions as "Are students able to perform

RS exams?" "What prevents students from being prepared to perform RS exams in the clinical setting?" and "What can be done to better prepare students aside from giving them more clinical experience?". TNA is primarily conducted to determine in which areas training is needed, what needs to be taught, and what is the best method to teach (Tjiam et al., 2014). Outcomes of TNA include identification of training objectives, determining procedural proper steps, and analysis of pitfalls when designing training for RS students.

Simulation has already been identified as the most common and effective way for students to gain psychomotor skills in a pre-clinical setting. Since real life simulation is already a staple of RS programs, it is proposed to incorporate virtual simulation to help supplement real life simulation in preparing students to enter the clinical setting. Choosing a virtual simulation program should be based on the results of a programmatic TNA and the characteristics of the virtual simulation program best suited to fit the needs of the students. Following the model set by Tjiam et al. (2014), the procedural steps, technical and nontechnical pitfalls, and possible suitable simulator models for training RS students in radiographic exams may be determined by a representative panel using a questionnaire. The representative panel could be comprised of RS program faculty, recent graduates of the RS program, and entry-level RS students. The questionnaire should be centered on the steps necessary to complete radiographic exams via virtual simulation. The results of the questionnaire, in combination with the criteria identified by the ARRT (2016) to evaluate clinical competence, could then be used to develop outcome parameters (i.e., the desired results of using the virtual simulation program).

The next step is to determine the validity and reliability of the simulation program and to compare commercially available radiographic positioning virtual simulation programs. Currently there are only a small number of commercially produced radiographic positioning virtual simulation programs available. Narrowing the products available could be based on availability, cost, and compatibility with technology at the research location. The representative panel would be used to determine the validity of each program by using the virtual simulation to complete a series of radiographic exams and then evaluating each by answering Likert scale questions on a questionnaire. The panel will also be evaluated during each simulation by the researcher based on the outcome parameters identified in the TNA.

According to Schreuder, van Dongen, Roeleveld, Schijven, and Broeders (2009), validity is "defined as the property of being true, correct, and in conformity with reality" (p. 540.e1). Validity has three main components: face validity, content validity, and construct validity (Burden et al., 2012; Schreuder et al., 2009; Tjiam et al, 2014). Face validity measures to what degree the virtual simulation resembles a real life radiographic exam. This would be determined by the opinion of the experts (program faculty) and intermediates (recent graduates) on the representative panel through a Likert scale questionnaire and panel discussion group. The entry-level students (novice) should be excluded from establishing face validity because of their lack of knowledge about performing radiographic exams. Content validity is whether the simulator would be useful or appropriate in training RS students. Again, this would be determined by the representative panel via a questionnaire and discussion group. Because the novice group does not have the real world experience to establish content validity, they should be excluded from this portion of the study. Construct validity is the ability to differentiate between the skill levels of different users (e.g., novice vs intermediate vs expert). Construct validity could be measured using the outcome parameters identified by the TNA. Suspected outcome parameters include time to complete the exam, completing all portions of the radiographic exam, completing each step in the proper order, manually setting exposure factor techniques, the ability to adapt the exam to unique or difficult situations (i.e., trauma, pediatrics, geriatrics, patient ability level, etc.) and critique and evaluation of the images produced. Each group of the representative panel should be evaluated while using the virtual simulation based on TNA outcome parameters such as these.

Reliability is the ability to replicate results or confirm results over time. Golafshani (2003) states reliability is the extent to which results are consistent over time and an accurate representation of the phenomena as well as if the results of a study can be reproduced under a similar methodology. To ensure the reliability of this study the representative panel would perform the same radiographic exams using the virtual simulation programs at two different periods of time. The same questionnaires and evaluation administered by the researcher in the first phase of simulation testing should be used in the second phase of virtual simulation by the representative panel. Then the results from the two phases of simulation could be compared to determine reliability of the virtual simulation program.

Other factors must also be considered when choosing which virtual simulation program to incorporate into an established curriculum. The simulation must provide value in and of itself besides being used as an engaging activity (Bauman & Ralston-Berg, 2015). Intrinsic motivation drives students to "act freely" pursuing a particular activity for the sake of the pursuit, gaining satisfaction within themselves as opposed to reward from an outside source (Denis & Jouvelot, 2005). Some characteristics of intrinsic motivation in virtual simulations are similar to determining validity (Bauman & Ralston-Berg, 2015; Burden et al., 2012; Schreuder et al., 2009; Tjiam et al, 2014): the simulation representing real life practice (face validity); the simulation being appropriate, including opportunities for the learner to make decisions based on relevant situations; and providing training the student will use in real life (content validity), and the simulation having varied and appropriate consequences and outcomes (construct validity).

The simulation must also support or enhance the curricular and course objectives. Instructional designers refer to this "fit" as alignment (Bauman & Ralston-Berg, 2015). The primary objective of simulations should be to provide an educational activity which has directly translatable results to clinical readiness and performance by using intrinsic motivation. The goal of simulation should not be just to entertain or engage the student, though engagement and motivation are critical educational tools. Simulation should fill a need or gap in the current curriculum, perhaps one identified by a TNA, and be tied to learning objectives and outcomes.

Distributed Practice

The principle of repeating a learning experience or scenario over a period of time is called distributed practice (a.k.a. the spacing effect). Distributed practice is the "technique of distributing study or learning efforts over multiple short sessions, with each session focused on the subject matter to be learned" (Kapp, 2012, p. 65). Repeated learning or experience over time helps learned activities to transition from short-term to long-term memory. This long term learning helps learners retain access to memorized information over long periods of time (Kapp, 2012; Tshibwabaw et al., 2017). Distributed practice can help learners "retain access to memorized information over long periods of time because the spacing prompts deeper processing of the learned material" (Kapp, 2012, p. 65). Another, albeit counterintuitive, explanation is that allowing time for forgetting during the interval between successive learning experience promotes learning; the less accessible an item is in memory because of forgetting, the more memory of that item is strengthened when it is successfully retrieved (Slone & Sandhofer, 2017). Therefore, learning through distributed practice is a function of repetition and cognitive effort.

Studies indicate that distributed practice can speed learning and increase knowledge retention more so than massed practice (i.e., cramming) in medical education (Hulse, 1992; Nkenke et al., 2012; Robertson, Paige, & Bok, 2012). In repeatedly experiencing an educational scenario, learners can improve on past performance, sometimes seen in the form of additional score, a higher academic grade, or increased patient experience. Each iteration of a scenario leads to increased learning, but the effects are only seen after a period of time and not immediately. Educational experiences in medical education should be designed to be repeatable while still being engaging so as to keep learners involved when using the principle of distributed practice. Students engaged in repeated learning scenarios gain confidence through successful application of previously learned knowledge, reinforcing the transition of knowledge from short-term to long-term memory.

When confidence is gained and difficulty increases, the learner is drawn to reattempt the same or similar situations, analogous to the way healthcare workers apply the same principles and techniques to multiple, varying situations. In radiographic science education, distributed practice is a common method to teach students about medical imaging. Instruction is given over the broad topic of radiographic science, but in each class students are taught separate yet overlapping topics by various instructors through differing methods. The information is distributed and spaced over the duration of the educational program. Over the duration of the educational program, students incrementally increase in their skills, and consequently what is expected of them. Distributed practice is especially useful for medical educational programs, such as radiographic science, which require students to retain information gathered for over two years or more before taking a national certification exam. When simulation is incorporated in RS education, it allows students to practice and re-practice psychomotor skills and positioning techniques. Students use knowledge and experience gained in previous simulation sessions and apply it to new situations. Virtual simulation gives the added benefits of practice and learning in a safe environment without the need of physical space or time dedicated in a laboratory or clinical setting. The learning theory of students building new knowledge on preexisting knowledge is known as constructivism.

Constructivism

Constructivism is built on the idea that "knowledge resides in the learner and that learning is a social activity enhanced by reflection, metacognition and inquiry" (Dangel, Guyton, & McIntyre, 2004, p. 237). Epistemology for constructivism is based in the concept that the teacher and the learner are linked, constructing knowledge together (Guba & Lincoln, 1994). Instructional principles tied to constructivism require students to (a) solve realistic and complex problems; (b) collaborate with others to solve those problems; (c) use multiple perspectives to examine the problems; (d) take ownership of the learning process instead of being passive recipients; and (e) become aware of their own role in the knowledge construction process (Driscoll, 2000; Reiser, 2001). Learners actively create, interpret, and reorganize knowledge based on information gathered from their environment (Legg, Adelman, & Levitt, 2009). This means constructivism places emphasis on building knowledge when interacting with the environment to promote deep and lasting learning (Guba & Lincoln, 1994; Hoadley, 2004; Kolodner, 2004). Knowledge is then constructed when students reconcile formal instruction experiences with their existing knowledge, the cultural and social context in which ideas occur, and the environment created by the teacher. As students interact with the environment they create knowledge based on their interactions; this new knowledge is built on previously constructed knowledge. Students are involved in the learning process by means of understanding and reflecting on their environment. They learn through creating meaning based on real-life experiences, a key tenet of constructivism (Boger-Mehall, 1996; Reiser, 2001).

In recent years constructivism has been applied through an emphasis on authentic learning (Reiser, 2001). Authentic learning "is the idea that students should utilize their prior knowledge to engage with 'real' problems, tasks and challenges" (Splitter, 2009, p. 138). In radiographic science education, as with all health care education, all learning relates to authentic tasks. Authentic tasks include acquiring a diagnostic image, reducing patient exposure to radiation, caring for a patient, basic nursing duties, and similar activities. The entire radiographic science education curriculum is designed to support the transfer of knowledge to help the student become proficient in the clinical setting and develop as a professional in the field of radiology (Culp, 2015). As students use the knowledge they construct in the didactic and laboratory setting they are required to use this previously learned knowledge and apply it to new situations. New situations include recently learned radiographic positioning, patient type, and exam situation. Simulation, especially virtual simulation, offers educators an innovative way to transform current educational practices into more effective pedagogical techniques through the use of the constructivist model of learning and distributive practice. The principles of distributed practice and constructivism should provide scaffolding as educators seek to incorporate simulation in radiographic science education.

Radiography educators must determine the needs of their educational programs, if virtual simulation programs are valid and reliable, and if the virtual simulation programs match the educational curriculum. If structured in sound educational theories and implementation practices, empirical studies have shown virtual simulation to be a successful alternative or supplement to traditional simulation-based education.

FUTURE RESEARCH DIRECTIONS

As technology throughout the world continues to develop and advance, so too does innovation in simulation. The simulation methods discussed thus far, both real-life and virtual, are constantly being adapted to medical education. Since future students will have exposure to and experience with new and advancing technologies, these technologies should be adapted to educational use. Using these technologies in an educational setting is important because it uses tools and methods with which students are already familiar and have used in daily practice (Wertz, Hobbs, & Mickelsen, 2013). The challenge will be their proper implementation into radiologic science education. Few studies have specifically evaluated the role of simulation, specifically virtual simulation, in radiologic science education. Those which have addressed this specific challenge all identify proper adaptation and integration of simulation technologies into existing curriculum. These studies also express the importance of aligning such adaptations with measurable educational objectives, stating simulation should seek to support, not replace, current educational practices (Cook et al., 2012; Kong et al., 2015; Tjiam et al., 2014) Future research should seek to explore the best methods of integrating simulation in established curriculum to align with educational objectives and goals.

Though educational pedagogy and curricular adaptation are the most commonly identified areas for future research, the literature also identifies a number of other ideas. With the innovation and development of augmented and mixed reality technologies, more and unique opportunities are available in radiologic science education. Augmented reality overlays used during a patient exam can provide real-time information to the radiographer, such as body part thickness, skeletal anatomy, relative positioning, and patient motion (MacDougall, Scherrer, & Don, 2018). Simulation activities can be used to develop effective communication and collaboration in interprofessional health care teams (Shanahan, 2016; Lemheney, et al, 2016). In addition, this type of educational experience can be used to increased empathy and favorable attitudes towards patients and families (Chetlen et al., 2015). Varied and personalized simulation experience can help students develop critical thinking skills in a safe learning environment (Holmström & Ahonen, 2016; Marshall & Harris, 2000; Sedden & Clark, 2016). Virtual simulation offers a method of assessment free of personal bias or evaluator influence (Berry et al., 2015; Sabir et al., 2014). All these identified benefits of simulation lack sufficient empirical research, warranting future research to focus on these areas.

CONCULSION

RS students must complete a series of competence exams as part of their clinical education. They must meet ARRT criteria for these exams under the supervision of a registered radiologic technologist. Students must be prepared in the didactic and laboratory setting before they are ready to perform radiographic exams on real patients. Simulation is the most common practice for preparing RS students to enter the clinical setting. Studies have shown how psychomotor skills can be improved in a simulated environment and those skills can also translate to the clinical environment. Virtual simulation is a new educational tool which has the potential to help supplement deficiencies in traditional simulation such as demands for time, space, and equipment. Few studies have researched the effectiveness of implementing virtual simulation into an existing radiographic science positioning curriculum. Future research should evaluate virtual simulation programs for validity, reliability, and curricular fit.

REFERENCES

Ahlqvist, J. B., Nilsson, T. A., Hedman, L. R., Desser, T. S., Dev, P., Johansson, M., ... Gold, G. E. (2013). A randomized controlled trial on 2 simulation-based training methods in radiology: Effects on radiologic technology student skill in assessing image quality. *Simulation in Healthcare*, *8*(6), 382–387. doi:10.1097/SIH.0b013e3182a60a48 PMID:24096919

ARRT. (2016). *2017 radiography didactic and clinical competency requirements*. Retrieved from https://www.arrt.org/docs/default-source/discipline-documents/radiography/rad-competency-requirements.pdf?sfvrsn=20

Bauman, E. B., & Ralston-Berg, P. (2015). Virtual simulation. In J. Palagapas, J. Maxworthy, C. Epps, & M. Mancini (Eds.), *Defining excellence in simulation programs* (pp. 241–251). Philadelphia, PA: Lippincott Williams & Wilkins.

Berragan, L. (2011). Simulation: An effective pedagogical approach for nursing? *Nurse Education Today*, *37*(7), 660–663. doi:10.1016/j.nedt.2011.01.019 PMID:21334797

Berry, M., Lystig, T., Beard, J., Klingestierna, H., Reznick, R., & Lohn, L. (2007). Porcine transfer study: Virtual reality simulator training compared with porcine training in endovascular novices. *Cardiovascular and Interventional Radiology*, *30*(3), 455–461. doi:10.100700270-006-0161-1 PMID:17225971

Boger-Mehall, S. R. (1996). Cognitive flexibility theory: Implications for teaching and teacher education. In *Proceedings of Society for Information Technology & Teacher Education International Conference 1996* (pp. 991-993). Chesapeake, VA: Association for the Advancement of Computing in Education (AACE).

Bridge, P., Appleyard, R. M., Ward, J. W., Phillips, R., & Beavis, A. W. (2007). The development and evaluation of a virtual radiotherapy treatment machine using an immersive visualization environment. *Computers & Education*, *49*(2), 481–494. doi:10.1016/j.compedu.2005.10.006

Bridge, P., Crowe, S. B., Gibson, G., Ellemor, N. J., Hargrave, C., & Carmichael, M. A. (2016). A virtual radiation therapy workflow training simulation. *Radiography*, *22*(1), e59–e63. doi:10.1016/j.radi.2015.08.001

Burden, C., Preschaw, J., White, P., Draycott, T. J., Grant, S., & Fox, R. (2012). Validation of virtual reality simulation for obstetric ultrasonography: A prospective cross-sectional study. *Simulation in Healthcare*, *7*(5), 269–273. doi:10.1097/SIH.0b013e3182611844 PMID:22878584

Castillo, J., Caruana, C. J., & Wainwright, D. (2011). The changing concept of competence and categorisation of learning outcomes in Europe: Implications for the design of higher education radiography curricula at the European level. *Radiography*, *17*(3), 230–234. doi:10.1016/j.radi.2010.12.008

Chetlen, A. L., Mendiratta-Lala, M., Probyn, L., Auffermann, W. F., DeBenedectis, C. M., Marko, J., ... Gettle, L. M. (2015). Conventional medical education and the history of simulation in radiology. *Academic Radiology*, *22*(10), 1252–1267. doi:10.1016/j.acra.2015.07.003 PMID:26276167

Clarke, T., & Holmes, S. (2007). Fit for practice? An exploration of the development of newly qualified nurses using focus groups. *International Journal of Nursing Studies*, *44*(7), 1210–1220. doi:10.1016/j.ijnurstu.2006.05.010 PMID:16872614

Coline, C., Gihad, C., Philippe, B., & Yves, V. (2015). Randomized clinical trial of virtual reality simulation training for transvaginal gynecologic ultrasound skills. *Journal of Ultrasound in Medicine*, *34*(9), 1663–1667. doi:10.7863/ultra.15.14.09063 PMID:26283753

Cook, D. A., Brydges, R., Hamstra, S. J., Zendejas, B., Szostek, J. H., Wang, A. T., ... Hatala, R. (2012). Comparative effectiveness of technology-enhanced simulation versus other instructional methods: A systematic review and meta-analysis. *Simulation in Healthcare*, *7*(5), 308–320. doi:10.1097/SIH.0b013e3182614f95 PMID:23032751

Cook, D. A., Hatala, R., Brydges, R., Zendejas, B., Szostek, J. H., Wang, A. T., ... Hamstra, S. J. (2011). Technology-enhanced simulation for health professions education: A systematic review and meta-analysis. *Journal of the American Medical Association*, *306*(9), 978–988. doi:10.1001/jama.2011.1234 PMID:21900138

Cosson, P., & Willis, R. N. (2012a). *Comparison of student radiographers' performance in a real x-ray room after training with a screen based computer simulator*. Retrieved from Shaderware website: www.shaderware.com/distrib/etc/WhitePaper-ComparisonOfStudentRadiographersPerformanceInaRealXrayRoom AfterTrainingWithAScreenBasedComputerSimulator.pdf

Cosson, P., & Willis, R. N. (2012b). *Student radiographer perspectives on using a screen based computer simulator in diagnostic radiography*. Retrieved from Shaderware website: http://www.shaderware.com/distrib/etc/Whitepaper201211-St udentRadiographerPerspectivesOnUsingAScreenBasedComputerSimulatorInDiag nosticRadiography.pdf

Cross, K. P. (1982). *Adults as learners*. San Francisco, CA: Josey-Bass.

Culp, M. (2015). Constructivist learning theory and global health education for the radiologic sciences. *Radiologic Science & Education, 20*(2), 21–27. Retrieved from https://www.researchgate.net/publication/301543463_Constructivist_Learning_ Theory_and_Global_Health_Education_for_the_Radiologic_Sciences

Dangel, J. R., Guyton, E., & McIntyre, C. B. (2004). Constructivist pedagogy in primary classrooms: Learning from teachers and their classrooms. *Journal of Early Childhood Teacher Education, 24*(4), 237–245. doi:10.1080/1090102040240404

Decker, S. D., Sportsman, S., Puetz, L., & Billings, L. (2008). The evolution of simulation and its contribution to competency. *Journal of Continuing Education in Nursing, 39*(2), 74–80. doi:10.3928/00220124-20080201-06 PMID:18323144

Denis, G., & Jouvelot, P. (2005). Motivation-driven educational games design: Applying best practices to music education. In *Proceedings of the 2005 ACM SIGCHI international conference on advances in computer entertainment technology* (pp. 462-465. New York, NY: ACM. 10.1145/1178477.1178581

Densen, P. (2011). Challenges and opportunities facing medical education. *Transactions of the American Clinical and Climatological Association, 122*, 48–58. Retrieved from https://www.ncbi.nlm.nih.gov/pmc/articles/PMC3116346/ PMID:21686208

Desser, T. S. (2007). Simulation-based training: The next revolution in radiology education? *Journal of the American College of Radiology, 4*(11), 816–824. doi:10.1016/j.jacr.2007.07.013 PMID:17964504

Desser, T. S., Ahlqvist, J., Dev, P., Hedman, L., Nilsson, T., & Gold, G. E. (2006, November). *Learning radiology in simulated environments: Development of a simulator for teaching cervical spine radiography*. Paper presented at the Ninety-second International Conference of the Radiological Society of North America, Chicago, IL. Retrieved from https://www.researchgate.net/publication/266124016_ Learning_Radiology_in_Simulated_Environments_Development_of_a_Simulator_ for_Teaching_Cervical_Spine_Radiography

Dikshit, A., Wu, D., Wu, C., & Zhao, W. (2005). An online interactive simulation system for medical imaging education. *Computerized Medical Imaging and Graphics*, *29*(6), 395–404. doi:10.1016/j.compmedimag.2005.02.001 PMID:15996851

Driscoll, M. P. (2000). *Psychology of learning for instruction* (2nd ed.). Needham Heights, MA: Allyn & Bacon.

Gaba, D. M. (2004). The future vision of simulation in health care. *Quality & Safety in Health Care*, *13*(suppl_1), i2–i10. doi:10.1136/qshc.2004.009878 PMID:15465951

Gaca, A. M., Frush, D. P., Hohenhaus, S. M., Luo, X., Ancarana, A., & Frush, K. S. (2007). Enhancing pediatric safety: Using simulation to assess resident preparedness for anaphylaxis from intravenous contrast media. *Radiology*, *245*(1), 236–244. doi:10.1148/radiol.2451061381 PMID:17885191

Ganguli, S., Pedrosa, I., Yam, C. S., Appignani, B., Siewert, B., & Kressel, H. Y. (2006). Part I: Preparing first-year radiology residents and assessing their readiness for on-call responsibilities. *Academic Radiology*, *13*(6), 764–769. doi:10.1016/j.acra.2006.02.057 PMID:16679280

Ghanbarzadeh, R., Ghapanchi, A. H., Blumenstein, M., & Talaei-Khoei, A. (2014). A decade of research on the use of three-dimensional virtual worlds in health care: A systematic literature review. *Journal of Medical Internet Research*, *16*(2), e47. doi:10.2196/jmir.3097 PMID:24550130

Golafshani, N. (2003). Understanding reliability and validity in qualitative research. *Qualitative Report*, *8*(4), 597–606. Retrieved from http://nsuworks.nova.edu/tqr/vol8/iss4/6

Gordon, J., Oriol, N., & Cooper, J. (2004). Bringing good teaching cases "to life": A simulator-based medical education service. *Academic Medicine*, *79*(1), 23–27. doi:10.1097/00001888-200401000-00007 PMID:14690993

Green, D., & Appleyard, R. (2011). The influence of VERT™ characteristics on the development of skills in skill apposition techniques. *Radiography*, *17*(3), 178–182. doi:10.1016/j.radi.2011.04.002

Guba, E. G., & Lincoln, Y. S. (1994). Competing paradigms in qualitative research. In N. K. Denzin & Y. S. Lincoln (Eds.), *Handbook of qualitative research* (pp. 105–117). Thousand Oaks, CA: Sage.

Helsper, E. J., & Eynon, R. (2010). Digital natives: Where is the evidence? *British Educational Research Journal*, *36*(3), 503–520. doi:10.1080/01411920902989227

Hoadley, C. (2004). Learning and design: Why the learning sciences and instructional system need each other. *Educational Technology, 44*(3), 6–12. Retrieved from https://www.scribd.com/document/346368309/Learning-and-DesignL-Why-the-Learning-and-Instructional-Sciences-Need-Each-Other

Holmström, A., & Ahonen, S.-M. (2016). Radiography students' learning: A literature review. *Radiologic Technology, 87*(4), 371–379. Retrieved from http://www.radiologictechnology.org/content/87/4/371.full?sid=1a3efa4a-7651-43f5-8b7d-7bc217953a25 PMID:26952061

Huffman, A. H., Whetten, J., & Huffman, W. H. (2013). Using technology in higher education: The influence of gender roles on technology self-efficacy. *Computers in Human Behavior, 29*(4), 1779–1786. doi:10.1016/j.chb.2013.02.012

Hulse, S. F. (1992). Learning theories: Something for everyone. *Radiologic Technology, 63*(3), 198–202. PMID:1736320

Issenberg, S., & Scalese, R. (2008). Simulation in health care education. *Perspectives in Biology and Medicine, 51*(1), 31–46. doi:10.1353/pbm.2008.0004 PMID:18192764

Issenberg, S. B., McGaghie, W. C., Petrusa, E. R., Gordon, D. L., & Scalese, R. J. (2005). Features and uses of high-fidelity medical simulation that lead to effective learning: A BEME systematic review. *Medical Teacher, 27*(1), 10–28. doi:10.1080/01421590500046924 PMID:16147767

James, J., Maude, P., Sim, J., & McDonald, M. (2012). Using Second Life for health professional learning: Informing multidisciplinary understanding. *International Journal of Modern Education Forum, 1*(1), 24–30.

Kapp, K. M. (2012). *The gamification of learning and instruction: Game-based methods and strategies for training and education.* San Francisco, CA: Pfeiffer.

Kasprzak, T. (2016). Technology and radiology education – Meeting the needs of millennial learners. *Academic Radiology, 23*(7), 844–847. doi:10.1016/j.acra.2016.03.003 PMID:27118526

Klein, K. A., & Neal, C. H. (2016). Simulation in radiology education: Thinking outside the phantom. *Academic Radiology, 23*(7), 908–910. doi:10.1016/j.acra.2016.02.013 PMID:27052525

Kolodner, J. L., Dorn, B., Thomas, J. O., & Guzdial, M. (2012). In D. Jonassen & S. Land (Eds.), *Theoretical foundations of learning environments* (pp. 142–170). New York, NY: Routledge.

Kong, A., Hodgson, Y., & Druva, R. (2015). The role of simulation in developing clinical knowledge and increasing clinical confidence in first-year radiography students. *Focus on Health Professional Education: A Multi-Disciplinary Journal, 16*(3), 29-44. doi:10.11157/fohpe.v16i3.83

Legg, T. J., Adelman, D., & Levitt, C. (2009). Constructivist strategies in online distance education in nursing. *The Journal of Nursing Education, 48*(2), 64–69. doi:10.3928/01484834-20090201-08 PMID:19260397

Lemheney, A. J., Bond, W. F., Padon, J. C., Leclair, M. W., Miller, J. N., & Susko, M. T. (2016). Developing virtual reality simulations for office-based medical emergencies. *Journal of Virtual Worlds Research, 9*(6), 1–18. doi:10.4101/jvwr.v9i1.7184

Ma, M., Jain, L. C., & Anderson, P. (2014). Future trends of virtual, augmented reality, and games for health. In *Virtual, Augmented Reality and Serious Games for Healthcare 1* (pp. 1–6). Heidelberg, Germany: Springer Berlin Heidelberg. doi:10.1007/978-3-642-54816-1_1

MacDougall, R. D., Scherrer, B., & Don, S. (2018). Development of a tool to aid the radiologic technologist using augmented reality and computer vision. *Pediatric Radiology, 48*(1), 141–145. doi:10.100700247-017-3968-9 PMID:28866805

Marshall, G., & Harris, P. (2000). A study of the role of an objective structured clinical examination (OSCE) in assessing clinical competence in third year student radiographers. *Radiography, 6*(2), 117–122. doi:10.1053/radi.1999.0229

Mason, S. L. (2016). Radiography student perception of clinical stressors. *Radiologic Technology, 77*(6), 437–450. Retrieved from http://www.radiologictechnology.org/content/77/6/437.long PMID:16864623

McGaghie, W. C., Issenberg, S. B., Cohen, E. R., Barsuk, J. H., & Wayne, D. B. (2011). Does simulation-based medical education with deliberate practice yield better results than traditional clinical education? A meta-analytic comparative review of the evidence. *Academic Medicine, 86*(6), 706–711. doi:10.1097/ACM.0b013e318217e119 PMID:21512370

Monachino, A. M., & Tuttle, S. A. (2015). Just-in-time training programs. In J. Palagapas, J. Maxworthy, C. Epps, & M. Mancini (Eds.), *Defining excellence in simulation programs* (pp. 127–134). Philadelphia, PA: Lippincott Williams & Wilkins.

Monsky, W. L., Levine, D., Mehta, T. S., Kane, R. A., Ziv, A., Kennedy, B., & Nisenbaum, H. (2002). Using a sonographic simulator to assess residents before overnight call. *AJR. American Journal of Roentgenology*, *178*(1), 35–39. doi:10.2214/ajr.178.1.1780035 PMID:11756082

Motola, I., Devine, L. A., Chung, H. S., Sullivan, J. E., & Issenberg, S. B. (2013). Simulation in healthcare education: A best evidence practical guide. AMEE Guide No. 82. *Medical Teacher*, *35*(10), e1511e–1530. doi:10.3109/0142159X.2013.818632 PMID:23941678

Nkenke, E., Vairaktaris, E., Bauersachs, A., Eitner, S., Budach, A., Knipfer, C., & Stelzle, F. (2012). Spaced education activates students in a theoretical radiological science course: A pilot study. *BMC Medical Education*, *12*(1), 32. doi:10.1186/1472-6920-12-32 PMID:22621409

Olxaewski, A. E., & Wolbrink, T. A. (2017). Serious gaming in medical education: A proposed structured framework for game development. *Simulation in Healthcare*, *12*(4), 240–253. doi:10.1097/SIH.0000000000000212 PMID:28027076

Ortiz, A. (2015). Staff technologist to clinical instructor: Using the Clinical Instructor Academy. *Radiologic Technology*, *87*(1), 112–113. Retrieved from http://www.radiologictechnology.org/content/87/1/112.full?sid=872cc3bc-eaea-4a8f-bdc4-1a55c7f75830 PMID:26377276

Papamichail, D., Pantelis, E., Papagiannis, P., Karaiskos, P., & Georgiou, E. (2014). A web simulation of medical image reconstruction and processing as an educational tool. *Journal of Digital Imaging*, *28*(1), 24–31. doi:10.100710278-014-9689-9 PMID:25000920

Reiser, R. A. (2001). A history of instructional design and technology: Part II: A history of instructional design. *Educational Technology Research and Development*, *49*(2), 57–67. doi:10.1007/BF02504928

Robertson, H. J. F., Paige, J. T., & Bok, L. R. (2012). *Simulation in radiology*. New York, NY: Oxford University Press. doi:10.1093/med/9780199764624.001.0001

Sabir, S. H., Aran, S., & Abujudeh, H. (2014). Simulation-based training in radiology. *Journal of the American College of Radiology*, *11*(5), 512–517. doi:10.1016/j.jacr.2013.02.008 PMID:23770063

Scheckel, M. (2009). Nursing education: Past, present, future. In G. Roux & J. A. Halstead (Eds.), *Issues and Trends in Nursing: Essential Knowledge for Today and Tomorrow* (pp. 27–61). Burlington, MA: Jones & Bartlett Learning.

Schreuder, H. W. R., van Dongen, K. W., Roeleveld, S. J., Schijven, M. P., & Broeders, I. A. M. J. (2009). Face and construct validity of virtual reality simulation of laparoscopic gynecologic surgery. *American Journal of Obstetrics and Gynecology*, *200*(5), 540.e1–540.e8. doi:10.1016/j.ajog.2008.12.030 PMID:19285646

Sedden, M. L., & Clark, K. R. (2016). Motivating students in the 21st century. *Radiologic Technology*, *87*(6), 609–616. Retrieved from http://www.radiologictechnology.org/content/87/6/609.full?sid=1a3efa4a-7651-43f5-8b7d-7bc217953a25 PMID:27390228

Shanahan, M. (2016). Student perspective on using a virtual radiography simulation. *Radiography*, *22*(3), 217–222. doi:10.1016/j.radi.2016.02.004

Slone, L. K., & Sandhofer, C. M. (2017). Consider the category: The effect of spacing depends on individual learning histories. *Journal of Experimental Child Psychology*, *159*, 34–49. doi:10.1016/j.jecp.2017.01.010 PMID:28266333

Society for Simulation in Healthcare. (n.d.) *What is simulation?* Retrieved from http://www.ssih.org/About-SSH/About-Simulation

Splitter, L. J. (2009). Authenticity and constructivism in education. *Studies in Philosophy and Education*, *28*(2), 135–151. doi:10.100711217-008-9105-3

St. John-Matthews, J., Gibbs, V., & Messer, S. (2013). Extending the role of technology enhanced learning within an undergraduate radiography programme. *Radiography*, *19*(1), 67–72. doi:10.1016/j.radi.2012.10.003

Stein-Wexler, R., Sanches, T., Roper, G. E., Wexler, A. S., Arieli, R. P., Ho, C., ... Soosman, S. K. (2010). An interactive teaching device simulating intussusception reduction. *Pediatric Radiology*, *40*(11), 1810–1815. doi:10.100700247-010-1764-x PMID:20652235

Strickland, C. D., Lowry, P. A., Petersen, B. D., & Jesse, M. K. (2015). Introduction of a virtual workstation into radiology medical student education. *AJR. American Journal of Roentgenology*, *204*(3), W289–W292. doi:10.2214/AJR.14.13180 PMID:25714314

Teo, T., Fan, X., & Du, J. (2015). Technology acceptance among pre-service teachers: Does gender matter? *Australasian Journal of Educational Technology*, *31*(3), 235–251. doi:10.14742/ajet.1672

Thoirs, K., Giles, E., & Barber, W. (2011). The use and perceptions of simulation in medical radiation science education. *The Radiographer*, *58*(3), 5–11. doi:10.1002/j.2051-3909.2011.tb00149.x

Tjiam, I. M., Berkers, C. H., Shout, B. M., Brinkman, W. M., Witjes, J. A., Scherpbier, A. J., ... Koldewijn, E. L. (2014). Evaluation of the educational value of a virtual reality TURP simulator according to a curriculum-based approach. *Simulation in Healthcare, 9*(5), 288–294. doi:10.1097/SIH.0000000000000041 PMID:25275719

Towbin, A. J., Paterson, B. E., & Chang, P. J. (2008). Computer-based simulator for radiology: An educational tool. *Radiographics, 28*(1), 309–316. doi:10.1148/rg.281075051 PMID:18203945

Tshibwabwa, E., Mallin, R., Fraser, M., Tshibwaba, M., Sanii, R., Rice, J., & Cannon, J. (2017). An integrated interactive–spaced education radiology curriculum for preclinical students. *Journal of Clinical Imaging Science, 7*(1), 22. doi:10.4103/jcis.JCIS_1_17 PMID:28584689

Wagner, J. B. (2017). Online simulation in an undergraduate radiologic technology program. *Proceedings of the University of North Texas College of Information Research Exchange Conference, USA*, 51-55.

Wang, R., DeMaria, S. Jr, Goldberg, A., & Katz, D. (2016). A systematic review of serious games in training health care professionals. *Simulation in Healthcare, 11*(1), 41–51. doi:10.1097/SIH.0000000000000118 PMID:26536340

Wertz, C. I., Hobbs, D. L., & Mickelsen, W. (2013). Integrating technology into radiology science education. *Radiologic Technology, 86*(1), 23–31. Retrieved from http://www.radiologictechnology.org/content/86/1/23.full PMID:25224084

Whitney, R. R. (2014). Differentiating instruction in postsecondary education. *Radiologic Technology, 85*(4), 458–462. Retrieved from http://www.radiologictechnology.org/content/85/4/458.full?sid=1a50e948-f86a-4c41-b3a2-c17bdaa24ebb PMID:24614440

Williams, P. L., & Berry, J. S. (1999). What is competence? A new model for diagnostic radiographers: Part 1. *Radiography, 5*(4), 221–235. doi:10.1016/S1078-8174(99)90055-X

Wright, S. W., Lindsell, C. J., Hinckley, W. R., Williams, A., Holland, C., Lewis, C. H., & Heimburger, G. (2006). High fidelity medical simulation in the difficult environment of a helicopter: Feasibility, self-efficacy and cost. *BMC Medical Education, 6*(49), 1–9. doi:10.1186/1472-6920-6-49 PMID:17020624

KEY TERMS AND DEFINITIONS

Clinical Education: Hospital or healthcare facility environment where a learner applies didactic education to a real-life setting under the supervision of medical professionals, a.k.a. internship or practicum.

Constructivism: The educational theory that learning occurs when new knowledge acquired when new information is associated with or reconciled to the individuals existing knowledge.

Didactic Education: traditional environment of education occurring in a classroom or online where a learner is given information by the educator, a.k.a. schoolwork.

Distributed Practice: The educational technique of repeating a learning experience or scenario over time which helps learned activities transition from short-term to long-term memory, a.k.a. the spacing effect.

Radiographic Science: The science of using medical imaging technologies (e.g., x-ray, computed tomography [CT], magnetic resonance imaging [MRI], sonography [ultrasound], etc.) and positioning techniques to acquire medical images which aid in the diagnosis and treatment of medical pathologies and conditions.

Self-Efficacy: One's own self perception of one's ability or skill level.

Simulation: The use of a mock or training scenario to practice a real-live situation in a safe and repeatable environment without endangering participant safety.

Virtual Simulation: The use of technology to enhance, augment, or replace real-life simulation.

Chapter 3
Enabling Training in Orthodontics Through Mobile Augmented Reality:
A Novel Perspective

Gururajaprasad Kaggal Lakshmana Rao
Universiti Sains Malaysia, Malaysia

Yulita Hanum P. Iskandar
ⓘ https://orcid.org/0000-0002-8037-5800
Universiti Sains Malaysia, Malaysia

Norehan Mokhtar
Universiti Sains Malaysia, Malaysia

ABSTRACT

Orthodontic education, which currently emphasizes a didactic and apprenticeship approach, is facing numerous pedagogical challenges that affect knowledge delivery and instruction. This chapter discusses the challenges and limiting factors that affect orthodontic training and proposes the use of mobile augmented reality (MAR) to create a platform for effective learning, visualization, deliberate practice, effective feedback, and a personalized learning environment. MAR, with its visually enriched clinical simulations and ubiquitous learning, can effectively reduce cognitive dissonance and improve overall retention and skill gain by students. However, MAR has its limitations, as the technology is still new and limited evidence is available to back up the claims of knowledge and skill gain in the health professional's education. This chapter also provides future directions for exploring and enabling MAR so that it can become an efficient tool for learning and instruction across all faculties of education.

DOI: 10.4018/978-1-7998-0004-0.ch003

Copyright © 2020, IGI Global. Copying or distributing in print or electronic forms without written permission of IGI Global is prohibited.

INTRODUCTION

Clinical education using computer-based simulation training has served as an adjunct approach in health profession education (Katoue, Iblagh, Somerville, & Ker, 2015). The advances in technology combined with enhanced applicability have yielded various learning elements, including real-life clinical training in a variety of disciplines (Harder, 2018). Factors such as deliberate practice, student-centred learning, safe and ethical learning, and the learning happening at the student's desired pace make simulation-based training promising. Simulation-based training, with its variations in presentation, can be either human-based or computer-based. Computer-based simulation, specifically mobile augmented reality (MAR), is the scope of this chapter.

MAR research shows that its development and usage will increase greatly with the education and healthcare sectors becoming the huge benefactors of this progression. The education sector is estimated to have around 7 million users of AR and MAR by 2020 (Statista, The Statistics Portal, 2018). The same trend is predicted for MAR technology, which is currently one of the most explosive of AR applications. MAR is predicted to transform educational practices by opening new pathways that involve interactive and intelligent systems. MAR can function ubiquitously as the hardware required to implement an application is available in the form of either a smartphone or a tablet computer. The ability to experience MAR is becoming more common, as the sensors, processing, and display features necessary for AR applications are already widely available and form the core of mobile devices. These gains in power and features enable learning to become cost-effective. MAR applications already have been integrated into the fields of engineering (Bazarov, Kholodilin, Nesterov, & Sokhina, 2017), tourism (Tussyadiah, Jung, & tom Dieck, 2018), marketing and advertising (Scholz & Smith, 2016), navigation (Houser, 2019), medicine (Hamza-Lup, Rolland, & Hughes, 2018; Jung, Lee, Biocca & Kim, 2019), and dentistry (Kwon, Park, & Han, 2018; Llena, Folguera, Forner, & Rodríguez-Lozano, 2018; Milovanovic, Moreau, Siret, & Miguet, 2017).

In education, MAR has been found to have several advantages over conventional methods of training. It supports millennial students' needs for knowledge assimilation, dissemination, and retention through three dimensional (3D) real-world visualisation and haptic sensing. MAR also provides a suitable platform for building enhanced learning systems for orthodontic training. The platform helps educators create a scenario for any learning task by providing a learning mechanism for excellent visualisation and psychomotor skill acquisition. In addition, MAR's ability to deliver learning content in an effective and easy-to-use format overcomes the challenges of ineffective visual cognition, the dissonance phase in learning transition, lack of assessment of student engagement and motivation, ineffective feedback, lack of an effective technology-supported learning environment, and lack of personalisation, all of which affect both knowledge and skill acquisition in orthodontic education.

The creation of mobile learning has thus opened new pathways for delivering content in a multitude of ways. The applications of MAR in orthodontics are opening a pathway for other dental specialities to incorporate similar ways to train students and improve skill acquisition. Thus, the applications of MAR in orthodontics provide scope and an impetus for detailed deliberation. The goal of this chapter is to explore and address the implications of MAR in orthodontic training.

BACKGROUND

An Overview of Orthodontic Education

The model of orthodontic education follows an apprenticeship approach in which the knowledge exchange remains hugely didactic and controlled. Clinical competence is learnt under the direct and close supervision of a tutor (Horst, Clark & Lee, 2009). Clinical skills are typically transferred from the teacher to the student via demonstrations either in a simulated environment and or on a patient. These demonstrations include practical exercises, such as model analysis, cephalometric analysis, and wire bending and appliance construction. The demonstrations also teach skills related to patient assessment and clinical examination essential for formulating a diagnosis and treatment plan based on the individual traits of the patient.

Practical exercises are demonstrated by a tutor, and subsequently the tasks are repeated by the student in the laboratory. The skills necessary to gain competence include close observation, motor coordination, and a desire to progress (Horst et al., 2009). Practical exercises are usually repeated to reach a certain level of mastery, which varies among students because not all have the same hands-on competence. The tasks have to be accepted and appreciated by the tutor before the student can progress to the next task. In the simulation laboratory, the student needs to constantly reflect and receive feedback on their work (Alqahtani, Al-Jewair, AL-Moammar, Albarakati, & ALkofide, 2015). Feedback is usually provided by the tutor at the completion of the task before proceeding to the next task (Icopino, 2007). The student relies heavily on the tutor's evaluation rather than on his/her own motivation and understanding of the task. Face-to-face discussion with the instructor usually occurs after the procedure (Garrison & Vaughan, 2008). Thus, the student may focus more on pleasing the tutor than on in-depth learning. This approach is beneficial to the student because it increases progression forward, which has the psychological advantage of improving well-being and the perception of gaining competence faster than his/her peers. This type of learning creates a stressful situation for the student, who want to progress quickly to avoid peer pressure and the feeling of underachievement. The goal of progressing to the next task, which is an extrinsic factor of motivation, creates superficial learning and results in limited retention. The motivation to complete a task overtakes the motivation to learn, thereby preventing deeper learning (Howe, 1988). Preclinical and clinical training takes place in a controlled, safe, and simulated environment in the absence of patients. On achieving competence in preclinical orthodontics, the student progresses towards clinical orthodontics, which involves active interaction with patients. Exposure to and interaction with patients are what shapes the student into becoming a fully-fledged clinician.

Current Technologies in Orthodontic Education

Orthodontic education has been meeting students' requirements by adopting computer-assisted learning (CAL) in its curriculum for the last two decades (Ludwig, Bister, Schott, Lisson, & Hourfar 2016; Schorn-Borgmann, Lippold, Wiechmann, & Stamm, 2015). CAL has gained momentum as a means of knowledge delivery in several dental schools as a direct impact of the availability of e-learning resources. The ease of access has made e-learning a popular choice amongst orthodontic students. The higher acceptability of e-learning content is particularly associated with the surge of smart devices. Current CAL techniques used in orthodontics provide resources on-the-go, which matches the needs of millennial students. CAL resources have influenced learning about a range of topics, and CAL packages with didactic, interactive, simple animation, and self-assessment components have been used (Miller, Hannum, Morley, & Proffit, 2007).

The School of Dentistry at Birmingham University in the United Kingdom was one of the front runners in implementing an online orthodontic e-course (Ireland, Smith, Alder, Sandy, & Chadwick, 2005). The virtual learning environment supports both the didactic and clinical components of the undergraduate orthodontic curriculum (Linjawi, Hamdan, Perryer, Walmsley, & Hill, 2009). A simulation-based interactive treatment planning system was developed for training orthodontic students (Rodrigues, Silva, Neto, Gillies, & Ribeiro, 2007), and live participation in seminars via video conferencing has been used for a live demonstration of techniques (Bednar et al., 2007). Additionally, Acuscape International, Inc. (Glendora, CA, USA) developed a 3D virtual patient. The method combines standard cephalometric radiographs and routine photographs to create a 3D digital patient, which allows computer-assisted identification of anatomy and anatomic landmarks in a web-based environment

(Harrell, Hatcher, & Bolt, 2002). A visual hypertext system is another technology-supported learning approach that has been studied. The system allows students to have an interactive experience with text linked to numerous graphic images. The system utilises case-based situations for learning clinical problems in the orthodontic setting. The system also allows self-assessment and automatic evaluation (Aly, Willems, Carels, & Elen, 2003).

SureSmile (OraMetrix, Richardson, TX, USA) is an all-digital system for orthodontic diagnostics, treatment planning, and fabrication of customized arch wires. The system helps students to develop a virtual treatment plan that can be further used to customise and fabricate archwires with the help of wire-bending robots (Larson, Vaubel, & Grünheid, 2013). SBLi for Orthodontics - Scenario-Based Learning interactive SBLi® software developed by the University of Queensland, was used to develop modules on clinical and procedural parts of orthodontics (Naser-ud-din, 2015). Additionally, a computed tomography (CT) scan of the jaw using a video image for tracking teeth for guided bracket placement has been reported (Aichert, Wein, Ladikos, Reichl, & Navab, 2012). AR visual and haptic cues can be embedded in a system for learning the significant skill of bracket positioning on teeth, thereby enhancing the psychomotor and cognitive skill development of students (Rao, Mokhtar & Iskandar, 2017). Another study proposed AR-based bracket placement without the need for a CT image (Rao et al., 2017), and yet another suggested learning orthodontic cephalometry using AR and machine learning (Rao, Mokhtar, Iskandar & Srinivasa, 2018). Implementing AR for surgical navigation and simulation may also prove useful for orthognathic surgery training. For example, AR has been used as a learning aid for 3D virtual planning for mandibular reconstruction and fracture reduction simulations (Badial et al., 2014). However, the technologies currently available are very limited in their functionalities and cater only to certain student needs.

Global Challenges in Current Orthodontic Education

Speciality orthodontic training utilises current technological advances for diagnosis and treatment planning, with the vast majority specifically oriented towards improving treatment outcomes. Technology has led to shortened treatment times and more effective treatment procedures. However, this phenomenon of swiftness and enthusiasm for technological acceptance and adoption currently is limited and poorly conceived in orthodontic student education. The teaching and learning cycles continue to follow the didactic approach using two-dimensional (2D) learning resources in a fixed preclinical laboratory setting. To highlight the current pedagogical challenges facing orthodontic education, the discussion is divided into six sections.

Ineffective Visual Cognition

In studies of orthodontic students, most were categorized as visual learners. Application of Felder and Soloman's Index of Learning Styles demonstrated that most residents (72.4%) chose visual learning aids to understand the subject matter (Hughes, Fallis, Peel, & Murchison, 2009; Murphy, Gray, Straja & Bogert, 2004). The students preferred to see how information connects to the world and were oriented towards facts and procedures. Thus, visual cognition is an important aspect of learning.

However, the procedural tasks in preclinical and clinical orthodontic training lack visual clarity of techniques and concepts. When a technique is demonstrated by a faculty member, the students tend to crowd around the demonstrator and have limited scope for proper observation. This kind of teaching ensures patient safety, but student learning is not efficient (Frey & Gerry, 2006). The complex biological interactions among teeth movement, force application and force generation for tooth movement, force distribution, and torque are a few examples for which the student must rely on his/her imaginative skills to grasp the concept. For teeth to be moved orthodontically, the force systems acting on the teeth, bracket slot, and wire must be mentally visualised. Once the force systems have been visualised and understood, actual application of these forces to the teeth can take effect. The dynamics of tooth movement thus requires higher order thinking to choose the right amount of force and the direction of force application. The lack of visualisation of these biological and physiological systems working together dynamically and specifically makes it difficult for students to understand (Victoroff & Hogan, 2006). This creates ineffective cognition of the underlying principles of orthodontic science, thereby leading to the use of improper treatment mechanics.

Demonstrations further prevent the development of visual-spatial ability, which is an important trait for health professionals because body structures are three-dimensional. The lack of a conducive visual-spatial learning tool means that students must imagine different scenarios and techniques within an ineffective mental model (Vuchkova, Maybury, Camile, & Farah, 2011). Ineffective visual cognition affects motor skill development (Sanders et al., 2008). It has been demonstrated that premotor and motor neural cortices show significantly increased activity when observing tasks with the intention of subsequent reproduction, as compared to passive observation (Frey, & Gerry, 2006). The orthodontic speciality involves an immense amount of hands-on exercises with varying amounts of motor learning (Ben-Gal, Katorza, Weiss, & Ziv 2017). These exercises are necessary for gaining the fine motor skills that are a prerequisite for constructing intra-oral appliances (removable and fixed). Hands-on exercises are demonstrated as a group activity with the tutor performing a task, which is observed and followed in a sequential manner. Demonstrations also lack an inadequate field of view and do not permit repeatability of sessions, making it difficult for students to gain knowledge and skill. However, effective understanding of the tasks is dependent on the factors of group size, observation skills of the student, specificity, ease of seeing, briefness in content, and pace of demonstration (Victoroff & Hogan, 2006).

The ability to grasp and work on preconceived ideas about various techniques, such as appliance construction, is thus affected by improper visual cognition. The failure to identify and correct these misjudgements early in a student's learning progression will have an adverse impact on the treatment principles adopted by the student.

Dissonance Phase in Learning Transition

Orthodontic training happens in two phases: preclinical and clinical. The preclinical phase follows the apprenticeship approach, wherein the student learns the procedural tasks under the close observation of a tutor. The knowledge and skill gained in these preclinical training sessions are expected to reach a certain proficiency level before the student can progress to the clinical phase (Qutieshat, 2018). Preclinical training takes place in a controlled environment with the use of simulations of varying kinds. Current training uses deliberate practice as a method of gaining competency. The simulated procedural tasks provide the basic infrastructure of a manikin with a set of teeth. These lifeless, stationary replicas of patients provide limited real-world experience. Following this phase, the student is exposed to live patients in a real-world clinical environment. Students who lack prior clinical experience find the concepts of preclinical education inaccessible and find it difficult to transition into the clinic (Horst et al., 2009). The effect of the transition between simulated and real-world environments on learning is unclear (Serrano, Botelho, Wesselink, & Vervoorn, 2018). There is a lack of understanding of the challenges faced and methods used to eliminate the dissonance phase in learning and transferring the procedural tasks from the preclinical to the clinical setting.

Lack of Assessment of Student Engagement and Motivation

The preclinical and clinical training phases combine various levels of subjective and objective evaluation to assess a student's knowledge and skill gain. The assessment, however, has a very limited scope in understanding student engagement, mood, and motivation (Suksudaj, Townsend, Kaidonis, Lekkas, & Winning, 2012). A closer examination and understanding of student engagement would allow for the provision of appropriate instructional interventions. Self-motivation in preclinical and clinical training has been poorly researched. The motivational factors that affect learning in an orthodontic environment require further study, as not all students have similar motivational triggers and motivating factors. Motivation and inquisitiveness to learn and acquire practical and clinical skills in the absence of a goal need to be assessed as well (Orsini et al., 2015). This highlights the need for assessment of the psychological parameters affecting orthodontic students.

Ineffective Feedback

Preclinical and clinical training lacks an effective feedback mechanism (Mitchell, Gillies, Mackert, 2017; Rountree & Adam, 2014). The feedback provided by the tutor is subjective in nature. In orthodontic training, procedural tasks do not include immediate feedback, yet the timing of the feedback received by the student is important because a time lapse creates learning dissonance. Instead, students receive comprehensive feedback and evaluation at the task completion stage (Victoroff & Hogan, 2006). A delay prevents simultaneous error identification, adding to the latency in procedural learning. The feedback mechanism currently employed in orthodontic student training needs revision, which should also incorporate objective assessment.

Lack of an Effective Technology-Supported Learning Environment

Technological integration into the educational sphere is not to the same extent as seen in clinical orthodontics. The orthodontic training that occurs over several years is limited to the hours of practice in dental school laboratories and dental hospital clinics. The exchange of knowledge outside the learning centres is limited to e-learning. The lack of enthusiasm for adopting technology-enabled learning has resulted in a deficient learning environment (Dragan, Dalessandri, Johnson, Tucker, & Walmsley, 2018). Students do not have access to procedural tasks, simulations, and patient exposure outside working hours at the dental school and hospital. For deliberate practice to take place, the student must rely heavily on the physical locations of the dental school. This is a serious issue, as education and training have to be ubiquitous and student-centric. The restrictions on the student in accessing and learning anywhere and anytime reflect on the ineffectiveness of the current orthodontic learning systems. Conventional learning resources should not limit the scope of learning. The lack of a learning environment that caters to the needs of millennial students is a necessity that cannot be ignored. The students' need for interaction, engagement, knowledge sharing, and collaborative qualities have to be integrated in the orthodontic curriculum. Fortunately, several universities around the world have acknowledged this need and have included technology-supported learning in their strategic plan (University of Toronto, Achieving Impact through Excellence,

Strategic Plan, 2014–2019, University of Iowa College of Dentistry Strategic Plan 2015–2020, UK College of Dentistry Strategic Plan 2016–2020, University of Florida College of Dentistry, Strategic Plan 2019–2024, University of Louisville School of Dentistry (ULSD), Strategic Plan, 2017–2020, The University of Sydney School of Dentistry Overarching Strategic Goals and Objectives 2018–2022).

Lack of Personalisation

Orthodontic training following the apprenticeship and deliberate practice approach has failed to incorporate a diverse learning structure. The learning structures or styles currently employed are something of a 'one size fits all situations' method (Rao et al., 2018a). This method does not consider the individual learning styles and preferences of students. The failure to include diverse strategies for learning can have negative outcomes or even demotivate students from learning further. This issue has received very little attention in the literature (Al Hamdan, Tulbah, Al Duhayan, & Al Bedaiwi, 2016). The personalisation of learning, which is still considered to be a new concept, needs to evolve into a strategy for effective knowledge delivery.

PRESENTING A NOVEL PERSPECTIVE FOR ORTHODONTIC EDUCATION USING MAR

The inadequacies in orthodontic education and training require a careful analysis of the factors that control effective content delivery. The six deficiencies discussed above have partly crippled content dissemination and knowledge exchange in orthodontic training. To overcome these issues, we suggest a technology-assisted learning system using MAR. The applications of MAR have shown promise for enhancing learning in complex scenarios and contexts such as in language learning (Godwin-Jones, 2016), history (Efstathiou, Kyza & Georgiou, 2018), museums (Hsiao, Chang, Lin, & Wang, 2016), marine education (Lu & Liu, 2015), interior design (Milovanovic et al., 2017), teleplanning and surgical navigation techniques, and implant placement and orthognathic surgeries (Fushima, & Kobayashi, 2016; Katic et al., 2015; Wang, Suenaga, Yang, Kobayashi, & Sakuma, 2017). The development of intelligent learning systems with 3D visualisations and human-computer interaction can bring about a tremendous change in the cognition of complex concepts. The unseen can be seen through MAR.

AR is a feature-rich interface that adds 3D, textual, and haptic sensing abilities to any learning content. MAR applications have been shown to enhance motivation and learning in various faculties of education (Khan, Johnston, & Ophoff, 2019). The orthodontic student's learning assessment involves knowledge and skill evaluation, and it identifies competency and proficiencies in task performance for a range of topics from anatomy to complex treatment mechanics. Hands-on practical training is assessed against the required norms of task execution.

MAR provides a suitable platform for the creation of a technology-supported learning environment for orthodontic education. Our proposed system includes a learning environment for making orthodontic training effective and engaging, and it provides an intelligent support system for orthodontic students. The system can assess the competence of the student and provide tasks based on his/her individual competence. The system can also adapt content based on the student's physical location to enhance learning. The learning system can provide real-time assessment through error identification and feedback. These features, in addition to haptic sensing, constitute a powerful learning resource for orthodontic students. The tasks can be accessed anywhere, anytime, and as many times as needed. MAR allows students to learn from misjudgements and errors and see the results immediately. Seeing the errors will help develop reasoning skills and contingency plans for avoiding the same in a clinical environment. MAR also can train the student to work better clinically with increased confidence (Khan et al., 2019). The complex pedagogies of orthodontic education and training can be simplified and delivered to students in an easy-to-use and easy-to-understand format using MAR.

The core components of deliberate practice, collaborative learning, personalisation, ubiquitous learning, effective feedback, and formative assessment will be discussed and summarised with examples drawn from other fields to provide an idea of how the MAR orthodontic learning system will enhance learning. The reason for utilising non-orthodontic examples is because such learning systems currently are lacking in orthodontics. However, Table 1 lists the components and their MAR practicalities and shows how different components will work as a system to deliver MAR learning content.

The proposed system will provide the student with the tools to help learn an orthodontic technique or a procedure with ease. With features of 3D rendering, the complex concepts of orthodontic teeth movement as well as biological and physiological interactions can be easily recreated to function as a feature-rich 3D object (Bergeron & Cline, 2011). The 3D object is rendered in scale, colour, and texture. The procedural tasks can be taught in an AR format accessible through a mobile device. The tasks have textual, audio, and video output to engage the learner. The haptic sensors interacting with specific content can make learning realistic. MAR will enable clarity of procedural tasks, as each student controls what they see and interact with (Dutã et al., 2011). With 3D modelling and inbuilt tactile feedback, the system heightens the learning experience (Nara, Beppu, Tohda, Suzuki, 2009).

Table 1. Core components of the proposed orthodontic learning system and their MAR practicalities

Core components	MAR practicality
Deliberate practice	Access to preclinical and clinical orthodontic task repetitions delivered as MAR content Access to MAR learning content to reach competence in any learning task (e.g., impression recording, model analysis, cephalometric analysis, bracket positioning, etc.)
Collaborative learning	Access to MAR learning content individually, as a pair, or as part of a group Access to MAR learning content through multiple devices for collective reasoning and problem-solving
Personalisation	Access to individualised MAR learning content based on student learning preferences and styles Access to MAR learning content delivered through visual, audio, textual, and kinaesthetic modes
Ubiquitous learning	Access to MAR learning content beyond conventional learning spaces (anywhere) Access to MAR learning content for extended duration beyond the scheduled duration and hours of learning (anytime)
Feedback and formative assessment	Ability to provide instant feedback on any given task through various hints using on-screen display, haptic feedback to convey errors, and colour changes to depict positive outcomes Ability to access student learning and task performance by the tutor, thereby assessing the student on the content learnt, time spent on a task and competence reached in task execution

The skills to be mastered in a health profession setting require repeated task performance to reach a certain acceptable level of proficiency (Lyon, Hoover, Giusti, Booth, & Mahdavi, 2016). The same principle applies to orthodontic training, as techniques such as wire bending, cephalometric analysis, and bracket positioning require numerous repetitions. This is an area that can be supported by MAR, as it allows the student to perform the learning tasks as many times as needed in a simulated environment. Figure 1 shows a non-orthodontic example (placing a nasogastric tube) to highlight the process of deliberate practice; it is an example of how a complex clinical learning task can be visualised and learnt through MAR.

The deliberate practice can be performed by two students to learn a complex scenario by utilising the MAR system. MAR can provide the students with the ability to learn as a pair or collaborate with another learner through accessing the same content from different devices. The collaborative interaction to learn a complex theoretical or clinical task enables easier visualisation of the same task in an engaging manner with the added advantage of solving the complex task with collective reasoning. The interaction is not limited to just two users but can be

Figure 1. MAR approach to learning the complex clinical skill of placing a nasogastric tube in a patient (adapted from Aebersold et al., 2018)

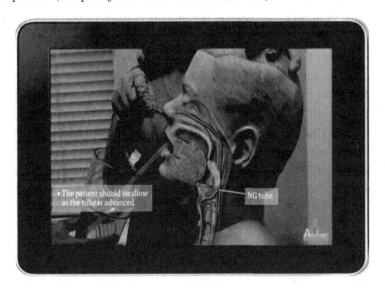

extended to multiple users accessing the same learning content simultaneously. This team-based learning approach can enhance problem-solving (Burgess et al., 2017). Deliberate practice for gaining competence can be performed using MAR without the need to be present at the physical location of a dental school or hospital. Thus, the student is in a better position to handle deliberate practice methods, as MAR lets task performance take place at his/her convenience (Bernie, Anthony, & Cathryn, 2018). In addition, tutors have a wider understanding of individual student needs, as students can express their needs better when enabling modifications and task corrections. MAR also can enhance knowledge acquisition (Llena et al., 2018), as the AR systems work ubiquitously without the constraints of time and place (Bernie et al., 2018). The pace of performing a task can be on par with the student's learning pace, thus bolstering skill retention and recall. Moreover, MAR experience can be enhanced by learning in conjunction with a tutor or clinician for a much more interactive and personal learning experience.

Personalisation is another feature that can be easily and effectively embedded into the MAR system. Students can choose various interactive interfaces based on their learning styles of visual, auditory, read/write, or kinaesthetic modes. The system will support each of these styles by adapting the content to the appropriate needs of an individual student. It also provides visual learning aids through 3D recreation of complex interactions for easier visual cognition and deep learning (Limbu, Jarodzka,

Klemke, & Specht, 2018). The areas of developmental anatomy, cephalometrics, and biomechanics can be learnt and supplemented with interactive personalized in situ 3D visualisation. MAR can create the illusion of looking inside the anatomical structures and seeing mechanical and physical interactions of orthodontic treatment mechanics. Audio-enabled MAR, via voice over functions, can provide a richer experience for the students and allow them to interact with the learning content. Textual illustrations for meanings, definitions, and classifications can be presented through MAR as factual information, which still forms a major part of the theoretical learning in orthodontic education. Figure 2 shows the AR screenshot of a MAR medical education app with voice guidance.

Furthermore, the learning objectives can all be adapted to provide content with textual, voice over, and interactive MAR orthodontic scenarios. MAR can make the personalised learning system more relevant by allowing students to visualise and interact with different concepts in real time and in the digital world. Through personalised learning, MAR can make orthodontic knowledge more accessible through experiential learning opportunities. Kinaesthetic training, which is an essential skill for orthodontic treatment, can be effectively created using MAR. Figure 3 shows the clinical scenario of cavity preparation as seen in an oral cavity. The use of instruments and position of the teeth and instruments can all be visualised in a safe environment. This provides students with an extended interaction with the learning content beyond the preclinical hours.

Figure 2. MAR medical education app using voice guidance (adapted from Augmented Reality in Medical Education - Harmony Studios)

Figure 3. Dental cavity preparation as seen through a MAR approach (adapted from Rhienmora, Gajananan, Haddawy, Dailey, & Suebnukarn, 2010)

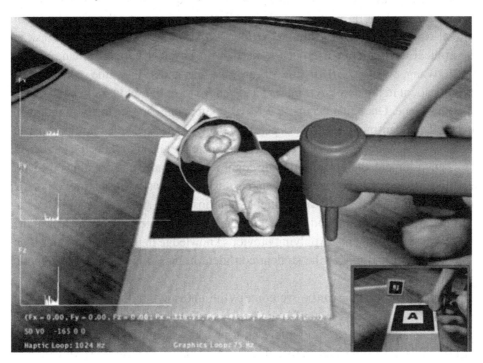

The MAR system will assist the student by providing effective feedback during the learning process through tactile, auditory, and visual cues. The feedback will be task-oriented and immediate, thereby preventing any lag in feedback provision. The system will support ubiquitous learning. The ability to generate content, adapt content, and provide feedback anywhere and anytime will break the restrictions of learning in fixed physical laboratories and clinical environments. This will foster continuation of learning outside the traditional settings. The system also will support a formative assessment of students during the entire interaction. The system can assess the progress, the hints utilised, and the time spent on learning tasks to assess student competence.

The dissonance phase occurs when the student is experiencing a learning event in a new environment. Upon progressing to the clinical phase from the preclinical phase, students often find it difficult to adapt to the new environment and new scenarios. This dissonance creates anxiety and underachievement, leading to de-motivation. However, the problems in this transitioning phase can be solved by AR (Serrano et al., 2018). A student who has the requisite knowledge can be exposed to clinical scenarios and simulations in the clinical setting without a patient being present. Students can learn, understand, and perform the required orthodontic diagnostic and treatment planning tasks in MAR. MAR allows overlaying the digital content on real-world surroundings (clinical setting). MAR can recreate a clinical task in the clinical environment without the need for a physical patient (Huang, Yang, Hsieh, Wang, & Hung, 2018). Students are able to visualise the same scenario for a virtual patient in the new environment and can perform the set tasks to gain a level of competence. Once this occurs, the MAR component can be slowly withdrawn, and students can move on to real patients. Thus, MAR provides an appropriate medium for students with varying levels of competence and apprehension to learn in a safe environment, thereby eliminating cognitive dissonance and creating powerful learning. Students can be exposed to increasing levels of task complexities on MAR before transitioning to real-world patient scenarios (Juan, Alexandrescu, Folguera, García-G, 2016). This method of transition can help alleviate anxiety and fear of the unknown among students. Applying previous knowledge in new surroundings then becomes easier and makes the student confident in handling real-life orthodontic case scenarios.

Discontinued learning can be overcome by the innovative and smart MAR learning system through its ability to work ubiquitously and on demand (Bernie et al., 2018). The millennial student who seeks information instantly and through multiple channels will find MAR extremely attractive and engaging. Thus, the use of MAR can help support student engagement. The MAR tasks can be designed to include multiple formats and multiple sensory stimuli to captivate the student's attention. Each MAR task can be followed by a short survey or questionnaire to determine the responses of students. Through tracking algorithms, the MAR system can provide valuable data about student interaction with the system. The dwell time, task repetitions, and student contexts can help identify how well the system motivates the student. These assessments can enable instructional designers to adapt orthodontic content to match student preferences.

FEATURES OF MAR

MAR is a technology that provides a new paradigm for human-computer interaction to enable the integration of real-world experience with digital world content (Barab, Hay, Barnett, & Squire, 2001; Kroeker, 2010). By providing an experience superior to conventional systems, MAR is making the conventional pedagogies exciting and interactive (Noll, von Jan, Raap, & Albrecht, 2017). The ease of use and the interactive interface provide cognitive stimuli and realistic feelings. MAR technology has seen increased usage and adaptation in education (Bernie et al., 2018). MAR delivers learning content in an observable format that is seldom possible in traditional 2D modes. This has the potential to help students link their prior knowledge with the real world. The MAR tasks and applications have a strong impact on students' learning perceptions, as they allow students to interact in challenging scenarios. AR creates a diverse and intuitive human-computer interaction by immersing the user in a real-world setting with virtual elements (Huang et al., 2019). The non-intrusive interaction aids medical and dental education immensely, as real experiments on patients are strictly regulated, with competency dictating the level of patient exposure (Kuehn, 2018).

MAR usually incorporates three main technologies. Image recognition, interactive controls, and computer graphics form the core of the AR system, irrespective of the field of application. The context awareness and context sensitive features of MAR increase its functionality and application for education (Noll, Häussermann, von Jan, Raap, & Albrecht, 2014). Context awareness depends on two factors: static content and dynamic rendering. Static content consists of a combination of virtual objects with descriptions with an intuitive, symbolic, or textual presentation. Dynamic rendering allows the description of virtual objects in relation to a context through format and registration. The format provides visual properties of colour and transparency parameters, whereas registration provides control of the 3D registration with scale, rotation, and translation parameters. The next significant aspect of a MAR is a trigger mechanism that can initiate and launch an AR experience. The triggers can be marker-based or markerless (Bacca, Baldiris, Fabregat, Graf, & Kinshuk, 2014). Marker-based or tangible AR requires a preidentified marker determined by the designers. In contrast, markerless or gesture-based AR recognises different gestures trained and incorporated by the developers. The move towards markerless AR is on the rise, as this method does not require pretrained markers for the AR experience and can be used ubiquitously.

Tracking techniques are the next requirement for an AR experience. The three kinds of tracking methods are sensor-based, vision-based, and hybrid tracking (Zhou, Duh, & Billinghurst, 2008). Sensor-based tracking can be divided into inertial, magnetic, electromagnetic, and ultrasonic categories. Vision-based tracking can be classified as marker-based or feature-based (markerless/gesture-based) methods (Kolivand, Rhalibi, Tajdini, Abdulazeez, & Praiwattana, 2018) while hybrid tracking combines vision-based tracking with magnetic tracking, or with inertial tracking (Pinz et al., 2002). Optical tracking handheld devices (mobile devices, optical see-through glasses), head-mounted displays (video-see-through glasses, holographic projector, anaglyph glasses, alternate frame sequencing, and polarization displays), and spatial projection (LCD display or autostereoscopic display) are the types of hardware currently in use. To summarize, MAR combines real and virtual objects in a real environment in real time using one of the tracking methods to register and align real and virtual objects together, thereby augmenting the object through the display of a mobile device (Nincarean, Alia, Halim, Rahman, 2013).

MAR has promising benefits for various applications in education (Sural, 2017). MAR technology has been applied to various fields ranging from primary education (Parhizkar et al., 2012) to military education (Livingston et al., 2011). Figure 4 depicts a surgical application (Vávra et al., 2017) of MAR currently used in orthognathic surgery training.

The applications cater to the diverse needs of students, professionals, industrial workers, and general public. Use of MAR has been increasing in this decade, with the field of education benefitting the most (Aleksandrova, 2018). Students benefit most, as implementation is happening at a rapid pace globally and is covering the entire range of subjects and disciplines in higher education including language learning (Santos et al., 2016), art history and museums (Chang et al., 2014), interior design (Siltanen, 2017), and several others. Wider integration is also beginning to occur in medical, surgical, and clinical care applications, as MAR meets the demand for visualisation without the need for invasive procedures. AR has been integrated into the fields of neurosurgery, spine surgery, laparoscopic surgery, endoscopic surgery, pancreatic surgery, and cancer surgeries, which collectively are called AR-aided surgeries (Vávra et al., 2017). The speciality of oral and maxillofacial surgery has been using AR for teleplanning and surgical navigation techniques, implant placement, and orthognathic surgeries (Badial et al., 2014). Nevertheless, dental applications

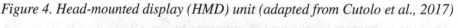

Figure 4. Head-mounted display (HMD) unit (adapted from Cutolo et al., 2017)

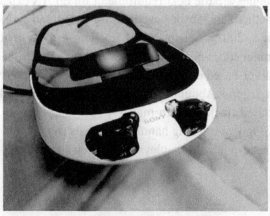

are less common than in the medical field, and incorporation of AR technology in dental education is occurring at a sluggish pace and is used primarily for preparing cavities and crowns (Kwon et al., 2018).

USE OF MAR IN ORTHODONTIC EDUCATION

In recent years, a number of possible applications of MAR in the educational setting have been identified (Zhu, Lilienthal, Shluzas, Masiello, & Zary, 2015). These applications have provided an effective learning environment with positive outcomes, as indicated throughout the literature (Küçük, Kapakin, & Göktaş, 2016). The use of MAR in orthodontic education is non-existent and is reflected by the lack of studies, except for two that used AR for bracket placement (Aichert et al., 2012). That study utilised a light-weight AR system guided through a video image based on a CT image. The study attempted to position brackets on the CT image of a patient's maxilla and mandible through a monocular AR system (Figure 5).

The other study that provided a conceptual framework for bracket positioning using AR did not use CT images. Instead, the AR model for simulating bracket positioning using a guidance system divided the teeth into gridlines in both horizontal and transverse planes, with the centre/midlines of the teeth serving as the ideal position for a bracket. The bracket, when placed on the tooth model, guided the user by showing colour changing areas, with red highlighting the wrong position and green highlighting the correct or ideal position (Rao et al., 2017). The use of AR-based cephalometric analysis along with validation from machine learning was proposed in another study (Rao et al., 2018b). However, the field of orthodontics

Figure 5. A monocular AR system using a CT scan to help position brackets (the grey areas on the surface of teeth) on maxillary and mandibular teeth (adapted from Aichert et al., 2012)

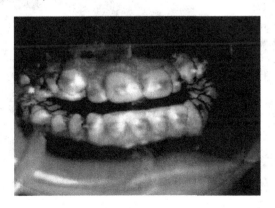

has used AR in only a few surgical scenarios, with AR functioning as part of a navigation system for orthognathic surgeries (Fushima & Kobayashi, 2016; Woo et al., 2015). Figure 6 shows a haptic controlled AR system used in jaw surgeries. A haptic cursor is used to highlight the bone fragment, which can then be grasped and manipulated. The haptic forces guide the user during manipulation.

The AR systems assist surgeons and surgical residents in determining the best ways to traverse anatomical structures in complex surgeries. Most of the current systems use a head-mounted display (HMD) unit for visualisation (Figure 4).

Strong evidence proving the effectiveness of MAR will be required before orthodontic educators will accept and implement a technologically supported pedagogy. This situation is evident in the lack of studies utilising MAR as a teaching aid for orthodontic students. Thus, we need to explore the gaps and suggest potential applications of MAR for orthodontic education.

OBSTACLES AND LIMITATIONS FOR INTEGRATION OF MAR IN ORTHODONTIC EDUCATION

The current systems utilised in clinical orthodontics do not fully use the functionalities of MAR. The primary role of an AR system has been to provide a real-world simulated surgical field for surgeons to navigate anatomical structures and plan complex jaw surgeries using an HMD (Figure 4). The HMD is in itself a limitation for educational use. The costs of purchasing and maintaining such units might prevent wider acceptance from an educational perspective. How to handle such units

Figure 6. The AR system used in 3D reconstruction in orthognathic surgeries (adapted from Olsson, Nysjö, Hirsch, & Carlbom, 2013)

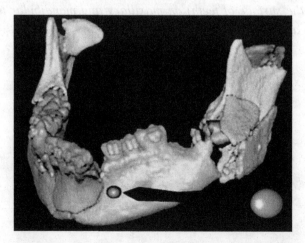

is another area of expertise currently lacking amongst orthodontists and orthodontic educators. The systems are extremely complex and require several hours of technical training to learn to run the system smoothly. The educational applications and scope of MAR have not been reported, as the current research focuses on treatment and clinical applications but not on education. The following discussion provides a detailed explanation of the limitations and reasons for a lack of understanding and enthusiasm for incorporating MAR into orthodontic education.

Lack of a Strong Theoretical Foundation

The lack of evidence to support the benefits of MAR in the learning environment has resulted in a poor understanding of technology-assisted learning in orthodontic education. Existing studies have only described MAR from the perspective of a conceptual framework for certain aspects of orthodontic training (Rao et al., 2017; Rao et al., 2018b). None of the studies has assessed learning theories and how MAR can effect changes. Thus, educational designers continue to underutilise MAR technology. MAR technology has not yet been used by instructional designers to test learning theories and their implications in orthodontic education (Juan et al., 2016), and technological advances continue to be resisted by the faculty (Brownstein, Murad, & Hunt, 2015; Dragan et al., 2018).

Lack of Knowledge about Creating MAR Content for Orthodontic Education

The lack of technical knowledge about creating MAR content also has prevented its wider acceptance (Dutã et al., 2011). Orthodontic content, which is rich in illustrations, has not been connected with technology for content creation. The complexities of 3D modelling, rendering, and interface design have remained a challenge for orthodontic educators. Although AR has been tremendously efficient in other fields, orthodontic education has been slow to implement AR functionalities in its training and student education. The theoretical foundations for AR and its significance in learning and retention have been poorly researched. Moreover, cognitive development following exposure to AR learning systems has yet to be understood.

Lack of Research on AR and MAR in Orthodontics and Orthodontic Education

Studies of technological advances and their effects on orthodontics are hard to find. Orthodontic science, which depends on evidence-based methods, has failed to provide resources for AR integration. The field concentrates hugely on the treatment aspects of orthodontic science, with little or no attention paid to addressing pedagogical questions. This lack of enthusiasm from the orthodontic community has proved counterproductive for the incorporation of new technologies such as AR and MAR (Schönwetter, Reynolds, Eaton, De Vries, 2010). Orthodontic education is still a stronghold of the apprenticeship approach. This traditional didactic method is preventing integration of advances in technology. The tutor-controlled environment suffers from subjective assessments (Victoroff & Hogan, 2006). This type of learning inhibits the integration of technology, as tutors are unwilling to accept newer technology and its pedagogical benefits (Dragan et al., 2018). This is a major impediment to the integration of MAR technology into orthodontic education.

Lack of an Effective Learning Environment Incorporating MAR

Current learning in orthodontics relies greatly on tutors and their evaluations (Dutã et al., 2011) of the students' progress through different levels of knowledge and capabilities to reach a competent level. The lack of a learning environment specifically designed for orthodontic training and education has tremendous implications for the way knowledge is disseminated (Dragan et al., 2018). This lack further limits the integration of MAR into orthodontic education.

The points highlighted above provide readers with a better understanding of what is currently hindering implementation of MAR on a wider basis among orthodontic training institutions. However, the limitations highlighted herein can be overcome by creating mechanisms for exploration and development through research.

FUTURE DIRECTIONS

MAR, with its 3D visualisations, ubiquitous access, and personalised learning, still has limitations in terms of 3D recreation and rendering, limited haptic feedback, and dependence on markers. These limitations together with the unenthusiastic academic world and inconclusive pedagogical benefits mean that MAR is a distant reality. However, certain pathways to overcoming these constraints seem viable.

For 3D recreation and rendering, new guidelines for app development can be established to cater to the specific needs of orthodontic learning content. The creation of specific medical education platforms will certainly pave the way for more content development. Easier access to CT 3D images/video can enhance the creation of 3D content. These images can be unified for the purposes of educational content development, thereby increasing their usage by non-medical teams. The focus should be on creating apps rather than learning app development. Educators with special interests in technology can be trained to create and maintain such MAR learning content. For the haptic feedback to be improved, focussed research on this aspect is crucial. The various forms of haptic stimuli, the duration, and the intervals of these stimuli require a deeper understanding by developers. In addition, correlations between haptic feedback and learning will need to be studied and analysed. The MAR content works via exposure to a predefined marker, but these markers limit the usability of the MAR application. Marker-less MAR using different gestures or real people to launch MAR learning content will be a boon for clinical training. For instance, users can launch a learning experience just by pointing the phone's camera at their hands or their friends' heads or at a patient. This non-invasive learning approach can be a huge benefit, as learning can happen either in a real clinical environment or outside the clinic. This approach can be validated by incorporating machine learning as a tool for effective assessment. The machine learning approach with ambient validation support can provide meaningful assessment faster and without the need for a physical tutor (Rao et al., 2018b). Machine learning also can eliminate subjective assessment, thereby reducing bias in student assessment. The other factors affecting faculty acceptance of MAR implementation require their own solutions, such as Education 4.0, which is aimed at educating clinicians and academicians about the tremendous potential of MAR by establishing channels for collaboration across different fields. The scope of integration can be enhanced once teachers and clinicians use the technology on a day-to-day basis and begin to understand the implications of such interactive education. This should foster acceptance and indirectly motivate them to use MAR technologies as interventional approaches.

The behavioural aspects of student engagement and motivation to use the learning content in MAR require extended research, which will allow fine tuning of the MAR interfaces. Learning content retention following exposure to MAR content is another challenging area that requires extensive analysis. Orthodontic research must become inclusive of educational research and must eliminate its microscopic view. Educational research, which is treated less enthusiastically by the orthodontics field, must be revived through interaction and collaboration with professionals from different backgrounds. For future applications and integration of advances in technology such as MAR, strong evidence linking the pedagogical benefits provided by these technologies and technology-assisted learning systems must be clearly presented. In order to change the learning pathways of orthodontic students, MAR, which is at its infancy stage, needs a boost in the number of clinical trials devoted to understanding how it affects knowledge exchange, skill acquisition, and avoidance of dissonance specific to orthodontic education and training. Clinical research alone cannot effect changes in pedagogy, nor can it provide the necessary impetus for realising the educational guidelines and theoretical foundations of learning. The inclusion of educational research must be undertaken as an agenda and implemented to reap the benefits of technology.

CONCLUSION

The current chapter has described the speciality field of orthodontics, the specifics of orthodontic education, and an overview of technologies currently employed in the educational sphere. It has highlighted the limitations and challenges currently affecting orthodontic education. The limitations pose a serious challenge for educators and instructional designers, as there is a lack of understanding, research, and integration of technology-assisted learning and technology-enabled learning (Dragan et al., 2018). The lack of full-scale research and the presence of a learning environment suitable for orthodontic students have left pedagogical concepts unchanged. The effectiveness of technology-enabled learning has not been utilised, as implementation of new methods for knowledge exchange has not been explored and have been resisted by faculties of education (Schönwetter et al., 2010; Dragan et al., 2018). The benefits of smart learning through MAR have remained conceptual and at best a prototype (Juan et al., 2016). However, MAR and its features provide a rich learning experience that would be extremely valuable to both students and tutors. Orthodontic education should be redefined to incorporate the MAR technology in order to overcome the deficiencies of traditional learning methods. These limitations make orthodontic training and science ineffective and dated. Student preferences and personalisation, which have been addressed effectively in several other domains, are not yet recognized as important attributes in orthodontic education. The failure to identify pedagogical issues stems from the unenthusiastic attitude of teachers, educators, and clinicians. The negative factors need to be identified and addressed for the betterment of the orthodontic students and the orthodontic community at large. Research inclusiveness is another factor that requires policy changes and allocation of funding, as they drive interest in carrying out research activities. The orthodontic fraternity should establish support systems for educational researchers to implement technology-assisted learning as a fundamental necessity for millennial students' learning and training. Students should be supported in developing a positive attitude and understanding of these concepts with the wider ambition of creating future educational researchers and scientists.

REFERENCES

Abdul-Muhsin, H. M., & Humphreys, M. R. (2016). Advances in laparoscopic urologic surgery techniques. *F1000Res, 21*(5), 716. doi:10.12688/f1000research.7660.1

Aebersold, M., Voepel-Lewis, T., Cherara, L., Weber, M., Khouri, C., Levine, R., & Tait, A. R. (2018). Interactive anatomy-augmented virtual simulation training. *Clinical Simulation in Nursing, 15*, 34–41. doi:10.1016/j.ecns.2017.09.008 PMID:29861797

Aichert, A., Wein, W., Ladikos, A., Reichl, T., & Navab, N. (2012). Image-based tracking of the teeth for orthodontic augmented reality. *Medical image computing and computer-assisted intervention: MICCAI 2012 International Conference on Medical Image Computing and Computer-Assisted Intervention, 15*(2), 601-8.

Al Hamdan, E. M., Tulbah, H. I., Al Duhayan, G. A., & Al Bedaiwi, L. S. (2016). Preferences of dental students towards teaching strategies in two major dental colleges in Riyadh, Saudi Arabia. *Education Research International, 2016*, 1–9. doi:10.1155/2016/4178471

Aleksandrova, M. (2018). *Augmented reality in education: The hottest EdTech trend 2018 and how to apply it to your business*. Eastern Peak 2019. Retrieved from https://easternpeak.com/blog/augmented-reality-in-education-the-hottest-edtech-trend-2018-and-how-to-apply-it-to-your-business

Alqahtani, N. D., Al-Jewair, T., AL-Moammar, K., Albarakati, S. F., & ALkofide, E. A. (2015). Live demonstration versus procedural video: A comparison of two methods for teaching an orthodontic laboratory procedure. *BMC Medical Education, 15*(1), 199. doi:10.118612909-015-0479-y PMID:26537393

Aly, M., Willems, G., Carels, C., & Elen, J. (2003). Instructional multimedia programs for self-directed learning in undergraduate and postgraduate training in orthodontics. *European Journal of Dental Education, 7*(1), 20–26. doi:10.1034/j.1600-0579.2003.00263.x PMID:12542685

Anatomage. (2018). Retrieved from https://www.anatomage.com/anatomage-dental

Assis, G. A., Corrêa, A. G., Martins, M. B., Pedrozo, W. G., & Lopes Rde, D. (2016). An augmented reality system for upper-limb post-stroke motor rehabilitation: A feasibility study. *Disability and Rehabilitation. Assistive Technology, 11*(6), 521–528. PMID:25367103

Augmented Reality in Medical Education - Harmony Studios. (2017). Retrieved from https://www.youtube.com/watch?v=9XGsebK0TPI

Azuma, R., Baillot, Y., Behringer, R., Feiner, S., Julier, S., & MacIntyre, B. (2001). Recent advances in augmented reality. *IEEE Computer Graphics and Applications, 21*(6), 34–47. doi:10.1109/38.963459

Bacca, J., Baldiris, S., Fabregat, R., & Graf, S., & Kinshuk. (2014). Augmented reality trends in Education: A systematic review of research and applications. *Journal of Educational Technology & Society, 17*(4), 133–149.

Badial, G., Ferrari, V., Cutolo, F., Freschi, C., Caramella, D., Bianchi, A., & Marchetti, C. (2014). Augmented reality as an aid in maxillofacial surgery: Validation of a wearable system allowing maxillary repositioning. *Journal of Cranio-Maxillo-Facial Surgery, 42*(8), 1970–1976. doi:10.1016/j.jcms.2014.09.001 PMID:25441867

Barab, S. A., Hay, K. E., Barnett, M. G., & Squire, K. (2001). Constructing virtual worlds: Tracing the historical development of learner practices/understandings. *Cognition and Instruction, 19*(1), 47–94. doi:10.1207/S1532690XCI1901_2

Bazarov, S. E., Kholodilin, I. Y., Nesterov, A. S., & Sokhina, A. V. (2017). Applying augmented reality in practical classes for engineering students. *IOP Conference Series: Earth and Environmental Science, 87*. Retrieved from https://iopscience.iop.org/article/10.1088/1755-1315/87/3/032004/pdf

Bednar, E. D., Hannum, W. M., Firestone, A., Silveira, A. M., Cox, T. D., & Proffit, W. R. (2007). Application of distance learning to interactive seminar instruction in orthodontic residency programs. *American Journal of Orthodontics and Dentofacial Orthopedics, 132*(5), 586–594. doi:10.1016/j.ajodo.2007.06.008 PMID:18005831

Ben-Gal, G., Katorza, L., Weiss, E. I., & Ziv, A. (2017). Testing motor learning curves among dental students. *Journal of Dental Education, 81*(10), 1171–1178. doi:10.21815/JDE.017.076 PMID:28966181

Bergeron, B., & Cline, A. (2011). An adaptive signal-processing approach to online adaptive tutoring. *Studies in Health Technology and Informatics, 163*, 60–64. PMID:21335759

Bernie M. G., Joseph, A., & Cathryn, J. (2018). Using mobile augmented reality to enhance health professional practice education. *Current Issues in Emerging eLearning, 4*(1), 224-247.

Brownstein, S. A., Murad, A., & Hunt, R. J. (2015). Implementation of new technologies in U.S. dental school curricula. *Journal of Dental Education, 79*(3), 259–264. PMID:25729019

Burgess, A., Bleasel, J., Haq, I., Roberts, C., Garsia, R., Robertson, T., & Mellis, C. (2017). Team-based learning (TBL) in the medical curriculum: Better than PBL? *BMC Medical Education, 17*(1), 243. doi:10.118612909-017-1068-z PMID:29221459

Chang, K.-E., Chang, C.-T., Hou, H.-T., Sung, Y.-T., Chao, H.-L., & Lee, C. M. (2014). Development and behavioral pattern analysis of a mobile guide system with augmented reality for painting appreciation instruction in an art museum. *Computers & Education, 71*, 185–197. doi:10.1016/j.compedu.2013.09.022

Cutolo, F., Meola, A., Carbone, M., Sinceri, S., Cagnazzo, F., Denaro, E., & Ferrari, V. (2017). A new head-mounted display-based augmented reality system in neurosurgical oncology: A study on phantom. *Computer Assisted Surgery, 22*(1), 39–53. doi:10.1080/24699322.2017.1358400 PMID:28754068

Dolphin. (2019). *Dolphin Ceph Tracing*. Retrieved from https://www.dolphinimaging. com/product/Imaging?Subcategory_OS_Safe_Name=Imaging_Plus#Ceph_Tracing

Dragan, I. F., Dalessandri, D., Johnson, L. A., Tucker, A., & Walmsley, A. D. (2018). Impact of scientific and technological advances. *European Journal of Dental Education, 22*(Suppl. 1), 17–20. doi:10.1111/eje.12342 PMID:29601675

Dutã, M., Amariei, C. I., Bogdan, C. M., Popovici, D. M., Ionescu, N., & Nuca, C. I. (2011). An overview of virtual and augmented reality in dental education. *Oral Health and Dental Management, 10*(1), 42–49.

Efstathiou, I., Kyza, E. A., & Georgiou, Y. (2018). An inquiry based augmented reality mobile learning approach to fostering primary school students' historical reasoning in non-formal settings. *Interactive Learning Environments, 26*(1), 22–41. doi:10.1080/10494820.2016.1276076

Eliades, T., & Athanasiou, A. E. (2015). *Orthodontic postgraduate education: A global perspective.* New York, NY: Thieme.

Frey, S. H., & Gerry, V. E. (2006). Modulation of neural activity during observational learning of actions and their sequential orders. *The Journal of Neuroscience, 26*(51), 13194–13201. doi:10.1523/JNEUROSCI.3914-06.2006 PMID:17182769

Fushima, K., & Kobayashi, M. (2016). Mixed-reality simulation for orthognathic surgery. *Maxillofacial Plastic and Reconstructive Surgery, 38*(1), 13. doi:10.118640902-016-0059-z PMID:27014664

Garrison, D. R., & Vaughan, N. D. (2008). *Blended learning in higher education: Framework, principles, and guidelines.* San Francisco, CA: Jossey-Bass.

Godwin-Jones, R. (2016). Augmented reality and language learning: From annotated vocabulary to place-based mobile games. *Language Learning & Technology, 20*(3), 9–19.

Hamza-Lup, F. G., Rolland, J. P., & Hughes, C. (2018). *A distributed augmented reality system for medical training and simulation.* Retrieved from https://www.researchgate.net/publication/329362500_A_Distributed_Augmented_Reality_System_for_Medical_Training_and_Simulation

Harder, N. (2018). The value of simulation in healthcare: The obvious, the tangential, and the obscure. *Clinical Simulation in Nursing, 15*, 73–74. doi:10.1016/j.ecns.2017.12.004

Harrell, W. E. Jr, Hatcher, D. C., & Bolt, R. L. (2002). In search of anatomic truth: 3-dimensional digital modeling and the future of orthodontics. *American Journal of Orthodontics and Dentofacial Orthopedics, 122*(3), 325–330. doi:10.1067/mod.2002.126147 PMID:12226616

Horst, J. A., Clark, M. D., & Lee, A. H. (2009). Observation, assisting, apprenticeship: cycles of visual and kinesthetic learning in dental education. *Journal of Dental Education, 73*(8), 919–933. PMID:19648563

Houser, K. (2019, February 11). *Google is rolling out AR navigation for its map app.* Retrieved from https://futurism.com/the-byte/ar-navigation-google-maps-app

Howe, K. (1988). Against the quantitative-qualitative incompatibility thesis or dogmas die hard. *Education Research, 17*(8), 10-16.

Hsiao, H.-S., Chang, C.-S., Lin, C.-Y., & Wang, Y.-Z. (2016). Weather observers: A manipulative augmented reality system for weather simulations at home, in the classroom, and at a museum. *Interactive Learning Environments, 24*(1), 205–223. doi:10.1080/10494820.2013.834829

Huang, K. T., Ball, C., Francis, J., Ratan, R., Boumis, J., & Fordham, J. (2019). Augmented versus virtual reality in education: An exploratory study examining science knowledge retention when using augmented reality/virtual reality mobile applications. *Cyberpsychology, Behavior, and Social Networking*, 22(2), 105–110. doi:10.1089/cyber.2018.0150 PMID:30657334

Huang, T.-K., Yang, C.-H., Hsieh, Y.-H., Wang, J.-C., & Hung, C.-C. (2018). Augmented reality (AR) and virtual reality (VR) applied in dentistry. *The Kaohsiung Journal of Medical Sciences*, 34(4), 243–248. doi:10.1016/j.kjms.2018.01.009 PMID:29655414

Hughes, J. M., Fallis, D. W., Peel, J. L., & Murchison, D. F. (2009). Learning styles of orthodontic residents. *Journal of Dental Education*, 73(3), 309–327. PMID:19289721

Iacopino, A. M. (2007). The influence of "new science" on dental education: Current concepts, trends, and models for the future. *Journal of Dental Education*, 71(4), 450–462. PMID:17468305

Ireland, A. J., Smith, A. S. A., Alder, D. M., Sandy, J. R., & Chadwick, S. M. (2005). Building a learning community on-line: The first step towards a national virtual learning environment in orthodontics. *Journal of Orthodontics*, 32(3), 214–219. doi:10.1179/146531205225021141 PMID:16170064

Jasinevicius, T. R., Landers, M., Nelson, S., & Urbankova, A. (2004). An evaluation of two dental simulation systems: Virtual reality versus contemporary non-computer-assisted. *Journal of Dental Education*, 68(11), 1151–1162. PMID:15520234

Juan, M. C., Alexandrescu, L., Folguera, F., & García-G, I. (2016). A mobile augmented reality system for the learning of dental morphology. *Digital Education Review*, 30, 234–247.

Jung, S., Lee, J., Biocca, F., & Kim, J. W. (2019). Augmented reality in the health domain: Projecting spatial augmented reality visualizations on a perceiver's body for health communication effects. *Cyberpsychology, Behavior, and Social Networking*, 22(2), 142–150. doi:10.1089/cyber.2018.0028 PMID:30668138

Katic, D., Spengler, P., Bodenstedt, S., Castrillon-Oberndorfer, G., Seeberger, R., Hoffmann, J., & Speidel, S. (2015). A system for context-aware intraoperative augmented reality in dental implant surgery. *International Journal of Computer Assisted Radiology and Surgery*, 10(1), 101–108. doi:10.100711548-014-1005-0 PMID:24771315

Katoue, M. G., Iblagh, N., Somerville, S., & Ker, J. (2015). Introducing simulation-based education to healthcare professionals: Exploring the challenge of integrating theory into educational practice. *Scottish Medical Journal, 60*(4), 176–181. doi:10.1177/0036933015607272 PMID:26403571

Khan, T., Johnston, K., & Ophoff, J. (2019). The impact of an augmented reality application on learning motivation of students. *Advances in Human-Computer Interaction, 1*, 14. Retrieved from https://www.hindawi.com/journals/ahci/2019/7208494

Kim, Y., Kim, H., & Kim, Y. O. (2017). Virtual reality and augmented reality in plastic surgery: A review. *Archives of Plastic Surgery, 44*(3), 179–187. doi:10.5999/aps.2017.44.3.179 PMID:28573091

Kolivand, H., Rhalibi, A. E., Tajdini, M., Abdulazeez, S., & Praiwattana, P. (2018). *Cultural heritage in marker-less augmented reality: A survey.* Retrieved from https://www.intechopen.com/books/advanced-methods-and-new-materials-for-cultural-heritage-preservation/cultural-heritage-in-marker-less-augmented-reality-a-survey

Kroeker, K. (2010). Mainstreaming augmented reality. *Communications of the ACM, 53*(7), 19–21. doi:10.1145/1785414.1785422

Küçük, S., Kapakin, S., & Göktaş, Y. (2016). Learning anatomy via mobile augmented reality: Effects on achievement and cognitive load. *American Association of Anatomists, 9*(5), 411–421. doi:10.1002/ase.1603 PMID:26950521

Kuehn, B. M. (2018). Virtual and augmented reality put a twist on medical education. *Journal of the American Medical Association, 319*(8), 756–758. doi:10.1001/jama.2017.20800 PMID:29417140

Kumar, A. (2017). E-learning and blended learning in orthodontic education. *APOS Trends Orthod, 7*(4), 188–198. doi:10.4103/apos.apos_49_17

Kwon, H. B., Park, Y. S., & Han, J. S. (2018). Augmented reality in dentistry: A current perspective. *Acta Odontologica Scandinavica, 76*(7), 497–503. doi:10.1080/00016357.2018.1441437 PMID:29465283

Larson, B. E., Vaubel, C. J., & Grünheid, T. (2013). Effectiveness of computer-assisted orthodontic treatment technology to achieve predicted outcomes. *The Angle Orthodontist, 83*(4), 557–562. doi:10.2319/080612-635.1 PMID:23181776

Limbu, B. H., Jarodzka, H., Klemke, R., & Specht, M. (2018). Using sensors and augmented reality to train apprentices using recorded expert performance: A systematic literature review. *Educational Research Review*, *25*, 1–22. doi:10.1016/j.edurev.2018.07.001

Linjawi, A. L., Hamdan, A. M., Perryer, D. G., Walmsley, A. D., & Hill, K. B. (2009). Students' attitudes towards an on-line orthodontic learning resource. *European Journal of Dental Education*, *13*(2), 87–92. doi:10.1111/j.1600-0579.2008.00545.x PMID:19368551

Livingston, M. A., Rosenblum, L. J., Brown, D. G., Schmidt, G. S., Julier, S. J., Baillot, Y., ... Maassel, P. (2011). Military applications of augmented reality. In B. Furht (Ed.), *Handbook of augmented reality*. New York, NY: Springer. doi:10.1007/978-1-4614-0064-6_31

Llena, C., Folguera, S., Forner, L., & Rodríguez-Lozano, F. J. (2018). Implementation of augmented reality in operative dentistry learning. *European Journal of Dental Education*, *22*(1), e122–e130. doi:10.1111/eje.12269 PMID:28370970

Lu, S.-J., & Liu, Y.-C. (2015). Integrating augmented reality technology to enhance children's learning in marine education. *Environmental Education Research*, *21*(4), 525–541. doi:10.1080/13504622.2014.911247

Ludwig, B., Bister, D., Schott, T. C., Lisson, J. A., & Hourfar, J. (2016). Assessment of two e-learning methods teaching undergraduate students cephalometry in orthodontics. *European Journal of Dental Education*, *20*(1), 20–25. doi:10.1111/eje.12135 PMID:25560366

Lyon, L. J., Hoover, T. E., Giusti, L., Booth, M. T., & Mahdavi, E. (2016). Teaching skill acquisition and development in dental education. *Journal of Dental Education*, *80*(8), 983–993. PMID:27480710

Ma, M., Fallavollita, P., Seelbach, I., Von Der Heide, A. M., Euler, E., Waschke, J., & Navab, N. (2016). Personalized augmented reality for anatomy education. *Clinical Anatomy (New York, N.Y.)*, *29*(4), 446–453. doi:10.1002/ca.22675 PMID:26646315

Miller, K. T., Hannum, W. M., Morley, T., & Proffit, W. R. (2007). Use of recorded interactive seminars in orthodontic distance education. *American Journal of Orthodontics and Dentofacial Orthopedics*, *132*(3), 408–414. doi:10.1016/j.ajodo.2007.03.015 PMID:17826612

Milovanovic, J., Moreau, G., Siret, D., & Miguet, F. (2017). Virtual and augmented reality in architectural design and education: An immersive multimodal platform to support architectural pedagogy. *Proceedings from 17th International Conference, CAAD Futures*.

Mitchell, J. K., Gillies, R. A., & Mackert, R. (2017). Setting expectations about feedback in dental education. *MedEdPORTAL, 13*, 10580. Retrieved from https://www.mededportal.org/publication/10580

Murphy, R. J., Gray, S. A., Straja, S. R., & Bogert, M. C. (2004). Student learning preferences and teaching implications. *Journal of Dental Education, 68*(8), 859–866. PMID:15286109

Nara, N., Beppu, M., Tohda, S., & Suzuki, T. (2009). The introduction and effectiveness of simulation-based learning in medical education. *Internal Medicine (Tokyo, Japan), 48*(17), 1515–1519. doi:10.2169/internalmedicine.48.2373 PMID:19721295

Naser-ud-Din, S. (2015). Introducing Scenario Based Learning interactive to postgraduates in UQ Orthodontic Program. *European Journal of Dental Education, 19*(3), 169–176. doi:10.1111/eje.12118 PMID:25212808

Nifakos, S., Tomson, T., & Zary, N. (2014). *Combining physical and virtual contexts through augmented reality: Design and evaluation of a prototype using a drug box as a marker for antibiotic training*. Retrieved from https://peerj.com/articles/697

Nincarean, D., Alia, M. B., Halim, N. D. A., & Rahman, M. H. A. (2013). Mobile augmented reality: The potential for education. *Procedia: Social and Behavioral Sciences, 103*(26), 657–664. doi:10.1016/j.sbspro.2013.10.385

Noll, C., Häussermann, B., von Jan, U., Raap, U., & Albrecht, U. (2014). Mobile augmented reality in medical education: An application for dermatology. In *Proceedings of the 2014 workshop on Mobile augmented reality and robotic technology-based systems*. Bretton Woods, NH: ACM.

Noll, C., von Jan, U., Raap, U., & Albrecht, U. V. (2017). *Mobile augmented reality as a feature for self-oriented, blended learning in medicine: Randomized controlled trial*. Retrieved from https://www.ncbi.nlm.nih.gov/pubmed/28912113

O'Brien, K., & Spencer, J. (2015). A viewpoint on the current status of UK orthodontic education and the challenges for the future. *British Dental Journal, 218*(3), 181–183. doi:10.1038j.bdj.2015.50 PMID:25686440

Olsson, P., Nysjö, F., Hirsch, J.-M., & Carlbom, I. B. (2013). A haptics-assisted cranio-maxillofacial surgery planning system for restoring skeletal anatomy in complex trauma cases. *International Journal of Computer Assisted Radiology and Surgery, 8*(6), 887–894. doi:10.100711548-013-0827-5 PMID:23605116

OnyxCeph. (n.d.). Retrieved from, http://www.onyxceph.de

Orsini, C., Binnie, V., Evans, P., Ledezma, P., Fuentes, F., & Villegas, M. J. (2015). Psychometric validation of the academic motivation scale in a dental student sample. *Journal of Dental Education, 79*(8), 971–981. PMID:26246537

Parhizkar, B., Obeidy, W. K., Chowdhury, S. A., Gebril, Z. M., Ngan, M. N. A., & Lashkari, A. H. (2012). *Android mobile augmented reality application based on different learning theories for primary school children.* Paper presented at 2012 International Conference on Multimedia Computing and Systems. 10.1109/ICMCS.2012.6320114

Pinz, A., Brandner, M., Ganster, H., Kusej, A., Lang, P., & Ribo, M (2002). Hybrid tracking for augmented reality. *ÖGAI Journal, 21*(1), 17-24.

Qutieshat, A. S. (2018). Assessment of dental clinical simulation skills: Recommendations for implementation. *Journal of Dental Research and Review, 5*(116), 23. Retrieved from http://www.jdrr.org/text.asp?2018/5/4/116/250788

Rao, G. K. L., Iskandar, Y. H. P., & Mokhtar, N. (2018a). A review of learning styles in orthodontic education. *Education in Medicine Journal, 10*(3), 1–13. doi:10.21315/eimj2018.10.3.1

Rao, G. K. L., Mokhtar, N., Iskandar, Y. H. P., & Srinivasa, A. C. (2018b). Learning orthodontic cephalometry through augmented reality: A conceptual machine learning validation approach. *Proceedings of 2018 International Conference on Electrical Engineering and Informatics (ICELTICs)*, 133-138.

Rao, G. K. L., Mokhtar, N. B., & Iskandar, Y. H. P. (2017). An integration of augmented reality technology for orthodontic education: Case of bracket positioning. *Proceedings of 2017 IEEE Conference on e-Learning, e-Management and e-Services (IC3e)*, 7-11.

Rhienmora, P., Gajananan, K., Haddawy, P., Dailey, M. N., & Suebnukarn, S. (2010). Augmented reality haptics system for dental surgical skills training. *Proceedings of the 17th ACM Symposium on Virtual Reality Software and Technology*, 97-98. 10.1145/1889863.1889883

Rodrigues, M. A. F., Silva, W. B., Neto, M. E. B., Gillies, D. F., & Ribeiro, I. M. M. P. (2007). An interactive simulation system for training and treatment planning in orthodontics. *Computers & Graphics, 31*(5), 688–697. doi:10.1016/j.cag.2007.04.010

Rountree, J., & Adam, L. (2014). *BDS clinical tutor evaluation results*. Dunedin, New Zealand: University of Otago Faculty of Dentistry.

Sanders, C. W., Sadoski, M., van Walsum, K., Bramson, R., Wiprud, R., & Fossum, T. W. (2008). Learning basic surgical skills with mental imagery: Using the simulation centre in the mind. *Medical Education, 42*(6), 607–612. doi:10.1111/j.1365-2923.2007.02964.x PMID:18435713

Santos, M. E. C., Lübke, A. W., Taketomi, T., Yamamoto, G., Rodrigo, Ma. M. T., Sandor, C., & Kato, H. (2016). Augmented reality as multimedia: the case for situated vocabulary learning. *Research and Practice in Technology Enhanced Learning, 11*(1), 4. Retrieved from https://www.ncbi.nlm.nih.gov/pubmed/30613237

Scholz, J., & Smith, A. N. (2016). Augmented reality: Designing immersive experiences that maximize consumer engagement. *Business Horizons, 59*(2), 149–161. doi:10.1016/j.bushor.2015.10.003

Schönwetter, D. J., Reynolds, P. A., Eaton, K. A., & De Vries, J. (2010). Online learning in dentistry: An overview of the future direction for dental education. *Journal of Oral Rehabilitation, 37*(12), 927–940. doi:10.1111/j.1365-2842.2010.02122.x PMID:20726942

Schorn-Borgmann, S., Lippold, C., Wiechmann, D., & Stamm, T. (2015). The effect of e-learning on the quality of orthodontic appliances. *Advances in Medical Education and Practice, 6*, 545–552. PMID:26346485

Serrano, C. M., Botelho, M. G., Wesselink, P. R., & Vervoorn, J. M. (2018). Challenges in the transition to clinical training in dentistry: An ADEE special interest group initial report. *European Journal of Dental Education*. Retrieved from https://onlinelibrary.wiley.com/doi/full/10.1111/eje.12324

Siltanen, S. (2017). Diminished reality for augmented reality interior design. *The Visual Computer, 33*(2), 193–208. doi:10.100700371-015-1174-z

Statista, The Statistics Portal. (2018). *Statista dossier about Augmented Reality (AR)*. Retrieved from https://www.statista.com/study/38227/augmented-reality-ar-statista-dossier

Suenaga, H., Tran, H. H., Liao, H., Masamune, K., Dohi, T., Hoshi, K., & Takato, T. (2015). Vision-based markerless registration using stereo vision and an augmented reality surgical navigation system: A pilot study. *BMC Medical Imaging, 15*(1), 51. doi:10.118612880-015-0089-5 PMID:26525142

Suksudaj, N., Townsend, G. C., Kaidonis, J., Lekkas, D., & Winning, T. A. (2012). Acquiring psychomotor skills in operative dentistry: Do innate ability and motivation matter? *European Journal of Dental Education, 16*(1), e187–e194. doi:10.1111/j.1600-0579.2011.00696.x PMID:22251344

Sural, I. (2017). Mobile augmented reality applications in education. In G. Kurubacak & H. Altinpulluk (Eds.), *Mobile technologies and augmented reality in open education* (pp. 200–214). Hershey, PA: IGI Global. doi:10.4018/978-1-5225-2110-5.ch010

The University of Sydney School of Dentistry Overarching Strategic Goals and Objectives. 2018-22. (n.d.). Retrieved from, https://sydney.edu.au/content/dam/corporate/documents/faculty-of-medicine-and-health/dentistry/sydney-dental-school-strategic-plan.pdf

Tussyadiah, I. P., Jung, T. H., & tom Dieck, M. C. (2018). Embodiment of wearable augmented reality technology in tourism experiences. *Journal of Travel Research, 57*(5), 597–611. doi:10.1177/0047287517709090

UK College of Dentistry Strategic Plan 2016-2020. (n.d.). Retrieved from https://dentistry.uky.edu/sites/default/files/UKCDStrategicPlan2016.pdf

University of Florida College of Dentistry. Strategic Plan 2019-2024. (n.d.). Retrieved from https://cod-strategic-plan.sites.medinfo.ufl.edu/files/2018/07/18-UFCD-Strategic-Plan-FINAL.pdf

University of Iowa College of Dentistry Strategic Plan 2015-2020. (n.d.). Retrieved from https://www.dentistry.uiowa.edu/sites/default/files/docs/admin/COD_Strategic_Plan_2015-20.pdf

University of Louisville School of Dentistry (ULSD). Strategic Plan, 2017 – 2020. (n.d.). Retrieved from http://louisville.edu/dentistry/about/strategic-plan 2017-2020

University of Toronto. Achieving Impact through Excellence, Strategic Plan, 2014-2019. (n.d.). Retrieved from https://www.dentistry.utoronto.ca/sites/default/files/2016-06/strategic_plan_2014-2019.pdf

Vávra, J. P., Zonča, R. P., Ihnát, P., Němec, M., Kumar, J., Habib, N., & Gendi, A. E. (2017). Recent development of augmented reality in surgery: A review. *Journal of Healthcare Engineering, 9*. doi:10.1155/2017/4574172 PMID:29065604

Victoroff, K. Z., & Hogan, S. (2006). Students' perceptions of effective learning experiences in dental school: A qualitative study using a critical incident technique. *Journal of Dental Education, 70*(2), 124–132. PMID:16478926

Vuchkova, J., Maybury, T. S., Camile, S., & Farah, C. S. (2011). Testing the educational potential of 3D visualization software in oral radiographic interpretation. *Journal of Dental Education, 75*(11), 1417–1425. PMID:22058390

Wang, J., Suenaga, H., Yang, L., Kobayashi, E., & Sakuma, I. (2017). Video see-through augmented reality for oral and maxillofacial surgery. *International Journal of Medical Robotics and Computer Assisted Surgery, 13*(2), e1754. doi:10.1002/rcs.1754 PMID:27283505

Won, Y. J., & Kang, S. H. (2017). Application of augmented reality for inferior alveolar nerve block anesthesia: A technical note. *Journal of Dental Anesthesia and Pain Medicine, 17*(2), 129–134. doi:10.17245/jdapm.2017.17.2.129 PMID:28879340

Woo, T., Kraeima, J., Kim, Y. O., Kim, Y. S., Roh, T. S., Lew, D. H., & Yun, I. S. (2015). Mandible reconstruction with 3D virtual planning. *Journal of International Society for Simulation Surgery, 2*(2), 90–93. doi:10.18204/JISSiS.2015.2.2.090

Zhao, M. Y., Ong, S. K., & Nee, A. Y. C. (2016). An augmented reality-assisted therapeutic healthcare exercise system based on bare-hand interaction. *International Journal of Human-Computer Interaction, 32*(9), 708–721. doi:10.1080/10447318.2016.1191263

Zhou, F., Duh, H. B.-L., & Billinghurst, M. (2008). Trends in augmented reality tracking, interaction and display: A review of ten years of ISMAR. *IEEE International Symposium on Mixed and Augmented Reality 2008*, 193-202. 10.1109/ISMAR.2008.4637362

Zhu, E., Lilienthal, A., Shluzas, L. A., Masiello, I., & Zary, N. (2015). Design of mobile augmented reality in healthcare education: A theory-driven framework. *JMIR Medical Education, 1*(2), e10. doi:10.2196/mededu.4443 PMID:27731839

KEY TERMS AND DEFINITIONS

Cognitive Dissonance: Feelings of discomfort when a person's beliefs run counter to his/her behaviors and/or new information that is presented to him/her.

Learning Environment: The diverse physical locations, contexts, and cultures in which students learn.

Mobile Augmented Reality: A type of mobile application that incorporates and complements built-in components in a mobile phone and provides a specialized application to deliver reality-based services and functions.

Orthodontic Education: A specialty training in dentistry that includes a comprehensive course of study in clinical and didactic orthodontics for a period of 2–4 years. The orthodontic postgraduate training program is designed to train clinical specialists to include extensive didactic, clinical, and research experience.

Orthodontics: The dental specialty that is concerned with the diagnosis and treatment of dental deformities as well as irregularity in the relationship of the lower to the upper jaw.

Personalization: The action of designing or producing something to meet someone's individual requirements.

Technology-Supported Learning Environment: An environment in which appropriate technology is integrated to support learners and teachers.

Visual Cognition: The branch of psychology that is concerned with combining visual data with prior knowledge to construct high-level representations and make unconscious decisions about scene content.

Chapter 4
Creating a Computer Simulation with Ill-Structured Problems for Physical Therapists in the Acute Care Setting

Benjamin Just

(iD) https://orcid.org/0000-0001-5011-9024
University of Cincinnati, USA

Kay K. Seo
University of Cincinnati, USA

ABSTRACT

The purpose of this phenomenological study is to identify the types of ill-structured problems physical therapists face in the acute care setting for a computer simulation to train students in a professional physical therapist education program. Ten physical therapists who practiced in the acute care setting in four large urban Midwestern hospitals participated in semi-structured interviews. Results show that acute care physical therapists experience complex, ill-structured problems that encompass all direct and indirect patient care activities and are complicated by system factors outside of their control. Solving the problems described by the participants requires clear and accurate communication and an awareness of the role of physical therapy in the acute care setting. The use of these authentic challenges for a computer simulation can allow students in a professional physical therapist education program to develop better problem-solving skills.

DOI: 10.4018/978-1-7998-0004-0.ch004

Copyright © 2020, IGI Global. Copying or distributing in print or electronic forms without written permission of IGI Global is prohibited.

INTRODUCTION

As healthcare reform is realized, the responsibilities for entry-level physical therapists (PTs) have expanded (Plack, 2002). In the acute care setting, improvements in the understanding of the benefits of early rehabilitation in the intensive care unit and access to electronic medical records (EMR) have provided PTs the opportunity to have a greater impact, but decreasing lengths of stay and increasing levels of acuity have made providing excellent care more challenging. PTs in the 21st century work as consultants who are tasked with using their unique education and professional perspectives to solve ill-structured problems (ISP) in challenging, fast-paced environments (Dean, 2009).

Educating students in a professional physical therapist education program to be successful in the acute care setting can be challenging. This difficulty is not due to the fundamental nature of physical therapy practice in the acute care setting, but rather because the didactic coursework must help students develop the cognitive processes that are needed to assimilate and synthesize the vast amounts of information from a multitude of sources including physicians on the care team, the EMR, the patient, and his or her family members. This requires a student to organize the information, evaluate its relevance to a particular patient case, and then make appropriate clinical decisions.

These complex skills can be effectively taught in a computer simulation that is highly structured to promote critical thinking or clinical reasoning. This chapter focuses on identifying the types of ISPs physical therapists face in the acute care setting, which can be used for a computer simulation for PT students. The central research question pursued is: What types of ISPs should be included in a computer simulation to train PTs in the acute setting? To shed light on this, the study explores the components of a typical, ill-structured patient scenario as well as the ill-structured challenges an acute care PT encounters.

CRITICAL THINKING AND ILL-STRUCTURED PROBLEMS

The most recent studies in the field of physical therapy education are focused on improving and measuring critical thinking or clinical reasoning skills (Brudvig, Mattson, & Guarino, 2015 & 2016; Fu, 2015; Furze, Black, Hoffman, Barr, Cochran, & Jensen, 2015; Furze, Gale, Black, Cochran, & Jensen, 2015). There is a robust history of researching the means of improving the critical thinking ability of allied health students, but the results have been mixed (Coker, 2010; Hunter, Pitt, Croce, & Roche, 2014; Kantar, 2014; O'Dell, Mai, Thiele, Priest, & Salamon, 2009; Vendrely, 2005).

This is likely due to the lack of a gold standard to measure critical thinking or clinical reasoning ability. More importantly, the definition of critical thinking changes in each study. In the physical therapy education literature, there is no agreement on the definition of critical thinking or clinical reasoning, which makes the design of courses or curricula to improve these abilities difficult. An examination of the scenarios that require critical thinking or clinical reasoning will find the fundamental cognitive ability needed is actually problem solving.

Problems

In order to understand the theories and strategies of problem solving, one must have an understanding of problems. At a basic level, a problem is the difference between a defined current state and a goal state wherein there is value to achieving the goal state (Jonassen 1997). Throughout the extant literature on problems, there are two general categories to describe problems. The first of these is the well-structured problem (WSP). Jonassen (1997) describes WSPs as "constrained problems with convergent solutions that engage a limited number of rules and principles within well-defined parameters" (p. 65). The second category is the ISPs which "include greater complexity, less definite criteria for deciding if a solution has been reached, lack of complete information, absence of a 'legal move generator,' and no convenient list of accepted procedures" (Nagy, 1990, p. 3). ISP may have several solutions or methods to find a solution, and lack clarity in regards to the rules or principles that should be used for problem-solving (Jonassen, 1997).

Not all problems fit neatly into one of the aforementioned categories. There are three elements that determine the structuredness of a problem on a spectrum from a WSP to an ISP. The first of these is structuredness, which describes how many elements of a problem are known, how many rules or principles must be applied, and the number of possible solutions that exist (Jonassen, 2000). The second of these elements is the complexity of the problem. More complex problems have more variables that are less connected, and those connections are less stable over time (Jonassen, 2000). Increasing the complexity of a problem is perceived by the problem solver as an increase in difficulty, but this is not the only element that can be manipulated to change the difficulty of a problem. The last element is the characteristic of abstractness, which can also be described as the domain-specificity of the problem (Jonassen, 2000). Depending on the type of problem, and whether or not it is situated, more domain-specific knowledge may be required to identify a solution.

Problem Solving

All problems have a desired goal state or solution. The process of finding or deciding on a solution is problem solving. WSPs have clear, expected solutions while ISPs are more likely to have a range of possible solutions. Conceptually, these two categories require different processes to arrive at a solution. Although it is common to qualify a problem as "easy" or "hard," these descriptors have very little intrinsic value in regards to the problem-solving process. But it is important to consider the number of solutions and the myriad of pathways to find each solution.

Solving WSPs tends to be less challenging because there are very few solutions, and in many cases only one solution. In order to find the correct solutions, a specific rule or formula is applied based on the information provided. The solution that is generated is then compared to the expected solution and evaluated dichotomously. The solution can be obtained even if the solver does not have the necessary prerequisite knowledge by using a "guess and check" or means-end strategy. To this end, strategies to solve WSPs are grounded in understanding concepts, identifying relevant information, and selecting the appropriate rule or formula.

The problem-solving process for ISPs is more challenging because there are often multiple correct solutions, or in some cases no correct solutions. There are also multiple domain-specific pathways to arrive at each solution and no clear way to determine which is the "most correct" solution. It is quixotically impractical to attempt to identify domain-specific strategies for all of the types of ISPs, but it is possible to teach general strategies to solve ISPs (Jozwiak, 2004).

Cognitive Information Processing

ISPs "possess problem elements that are unknown or not known with any degree of confidence" and "multiple solutions, solution paths, or no solutions at all" (Jonassen, 2000, p. 67). These characteristics require problem solvers to cognitively manage the known and unknown elements, attempt to uncover domain-specific relationships between elements, and choose and apply appropriate evaluative criteria throughout the problem-solving process. When considering that working memory "not only holds information for a limited amount of time, but also holds a limited amount of information" (Driscoll, 2005, p. 75), it is evident that working memory is a limiting factor to ISP solving. Cognitive information processing theory includes the concept of automaticity, which suggests that concepts and skills can be practiced until they become habitual (Driscoll, 2005). This concept applies directly to problem solving when non-routine problems become routine with practice, and routine problems will often appear more well-structured (Jonassen, 2000). Frederickson (1984) identified the benefits of solving routine problems as "a gradual increase in speed because a reduction in the load on working memory making possible a unitary rather than a piecemeal operation" (p. 371).

Schema

The transformation from non-routine problems to routine problems is also supported by schema theory. Schema was defined by Rumelhart (1980) as "a data structure for representing the generic concepts stored in memory" (p. 34). As previously reported, one of the characteristics of ISPs is the complexity, which is the number of interconnected relationships between the components of the problem. Experts in a given domain are assumed to have a more developed understanding of the relationships in the domain due to their experience with the domain specific concepts and knowledge. By comparison, Glaser (1984) found that novices organize their knowledge "around the literal objects explicitly given in a problem statement" (p. 98). Ertmer et al. (2008) observed similar findings, noting that novices did not think much beyond the written description of the problem, but experts created robust mental models. Therefore, in order to solve ISPs, "knowledge organization and schema acquisition are more important for the development of expertise than the use of particular methods of problem solving" (Kirschner, Sweller, & Clark, 2006, p. 83).

Case-Based Reasoning

Using schemata from prior experiences and applying them to solve new problems is at the heart of case-based reasoning (CBR; Koldner, 1992). Pattern recognition within a domain is one of the hallmarks of expert problem solvers. CBR leverages an increased number of opportunities to gain experience which leads to a deeper and more diverse set of prior experiences (Choi & Lee, 2009). Problem solving strategies that employ CBR prevent the need to break all of the concepts presented in the problem into their component parts in order to define a problem space, thus decreasing demands on working memory and increasing efficiency. (Frederickson, 1984; Koldner, 1992)

Cognitive Requirements

Problem solving is a cognitive task that results in a measurable or actionable solution. Problem solving is more than an abstract intellectual ability or thinking skill: It is a task with teachable strategies and procedures that consistently lead to solutions.

The cognitive requirements for ISP solving include cognitive skills, domain-specific knowledge, and the ability to reflect on each stage of the ISP solving process.

Choi and Lee (2009) described the cognitive skills for ISP solving in two categories. The first category includes skills used for identifying a problem or creating a mental representation of a problem, and the second category includes the skills for creating solutions. Almost all of the skills are found in both categories and include considering multiple perspectives, justifying an argument, critically assessing solutions, and incorporating domain-specific theory (Choi & Lee, 2009). The ability to consider multiple perspectives is important because ISPs often have multiple solution paths which must be assessed in order to select the most appropriate or correct solution. Problem solvers who can view a problem from multiple perspectives create more robust problem representations (Choi & Lee, 2009).

It follows that each solution path and pathway must be justified and assessed critically. Novices may follow each solution path to its end and then assess the associated solution. This means-end approach is inefficient and impractical given the number of ISP solutions that exists for any given problem. The complementary skills of justification and critical assessment applied to a particular solution pathway can improve the efficiency and accuracy of the ISP-solving process by eliminating unlikely candidates.

The last cognitive skill for problem identification is incorporating domain-specific theory and knowledge. Choi and Lee (2009) suggest "domain-specific knowledge plays an important role in solving…ill-structured problems," but "it is more important for problem solvers to understand what they read (theories, principles, etc.) and apply the knowledge to particular problems" (p. 109).

Domain-specific knowledge was found to be highly indicative of success when solving ISPs. Shin, Jonassen, and McGee (2003) reported that structural knowledge, justification skills, and the problem solver's attitude towards the domain predicted the success of solving ISPs in familiar contexts. When solving problems in unfamiliar contexts, structural knowledge, justification skills, and the regulation of cognition were found to be significant predictors (Shin et al., 2003). The highly-situated contexts of ISPs make it difficult to transfer problem-solving skills to unfamiliar contexts (Jonassen, 2000). Ge (2003) suggests that when domain specific knowledge is not available, "metacognitive awareness leads to reorganizing areas of limited understanding, adopting working hypotheses, asking questions," and reflecting on the process (p. 22).

In order for a solver to be successful, he or she must have the ability to reflect on the process and outcomes of ISP solving (Tawfik, Rong, & Choi, 2015). By reflecting on outcomes of any given solution pathway or solution, a solver can continue to build more robust schema needed to solve ISP's. This concept is consistent with the schema related assimilation and accommodation changes described in Piaget's (1977) theory of cognitive development. When novices build new schema by reflecting on the processes and solutions, they transition away from the means-end approach described above and begin to become more efficient at solving ISPs (Furze, Black, Hoffman, Barr, Cochran, & Jensen, 2015).

SOLVING III-STRUCTURED PROBLEMS IN A COMPUTER SIMULATION

Steps to ISPS

There continues to be debate regarding the efficacy of improving the abstract cognitive skills (Vendrely, 2005; Vogel, Geelhoed, Grice, Murphy, 2009), but the assertion that problem solving can be taught is supported in the extant literature (Jonassen, 2000; Jozwiak, 2004). The procedures or steps of ISP solving are the focus of problem-solving instruction.

There are five common steps among the problem-solving procedures in the literature. These are 1) problem representation, 2) solution development, 3) solution justification, 4) solution selection, and 5) solution evaluation. The steps are presented in the order they would be used from the time the problem is introduced and continues until the problem is solved. Choi and Lee (2009) suggest that models for problem solving are presented linearly, but all "models...consider ill-structured problem solving as a dialectic and recursive process" (p. 103).

The first step is problem representation, which includes defining the problem and creating a mental representation of the problem. The scope of ISPs often appears boundless, and in order to begin to solve a problem, the information must be organized. This can be achieved by applying schemata from previous experiences, or organizing the information using social, historical, and cultural contexts (Jonassen, 2000). This is the step of the process that is the most taxing on working memory, and performance is most reliant on the problem solver's personal experiences. Novice and expert performance during this step is more divergent than any other step. Jonassen and Ionas (2008) reported that "although expert problem solvers index their knowledge more by experiences, novices and advanced beginners must develop understanding of the causal relationships that compromise the problem space for virtually any kind of problem" (p. 291). Domain-specific knowledge is also an important component of problem representation, but is most valuable when paired with understanding of domain-specific theories and prior experiences (Choi & Lee, 2009).

The second step in problem solving is solution development, which is "a creative process that relies not only on prior experiences but also unrelated thoughts and emotions" (Jonassen, 1997, p. 81). Structural and procedural knowledge improve the efficiency and accuracy of solution development (Shin et al., 2003). Solution justification, which is the third step, is fundamentally intertwined with solution development. Information about potential solutions must be obtained and evaluated by domain-specific knowledge and personal beliefs (Jonassen, 1997). Problem solvers must be able to create cogent arguments to justify the most promising solutions (Jonassen & Kim, 2010). The process of solution development and justification is recursive and will lead to selecting a solution.

The final steps of problem solving are selecting a solution and then monitoring and evaluating the solution. It should be evident that the problem-solving process ends with choosing and acting on a solution, but this can be challenging when solving ISPs. When faced with multiple correct solutions, or no correct solution in some types for problems, deciding on a single solution should be a hard stop in the process. Evaluating a solution is important because "the effectiveness of any solution can be determined only by how it performs" (Jonassen, 1997, p. 82). The additional benefit of evaluation as a discrete step is the opportunity for the learner to process the information so that the experiences can be applied to future problem-solving efforts. Ertemr et al. (2008) argue that solving ISPs is a taxing cognitive task that distracts problem solvers from internalizing the experiences.

Tools to Enhance Problem Solving

Teaching people to solve problems is not as simple as providing a list of steps and a few practice problems. As the complexity of a problem increases and the structuredness decreases, problem solvers benefit from external tools to help organize information and apply expert strategies. The literature supports the use of question prompts and scaffolds as tools to assist with ISP solving and teaching others to solve problems. Many of the successful examples augment these tools with the use of technology, especially in asynchronous learning environments.

Scaffolds

A scaffold is a "process that enables a...novice to solve a problem, carry out a task or achieve a goal which would be beyond his unassisted efforts" (Wood, Bruner, & Ross, 1976, p. 90). Jonassen (1997) suggested that adding scaffolds may reduce the cognitive load of solving ISPs. Scaffolds are most successful when provided to assist with problem representation (NG, Cheung, & Hew, 2010) and solution justification (Ertmer et al., 2008). As previously discussed, novices approach ISP solving by identifying discrete components (problem representation) and using a means-end approach to "guess and check" (justify) possible solutions. Experts identify patterns or themes within the ISP to create a mental representation and integrate their theoretical, structural, and contextual knowledge to select and justify a solution.

Scaffolds were found to increase the number of perspectives identified during problem representation (Zydney, 2010) and provide a more robust understanding of the problem (Zydney, 2008). Ertmer et al. (2008) compared the problem-solving performance of novice problem solvers with and without scaffolds to experts in the same field. The authors found that the both treatment and control groups spent the same amount of time solving the problem, but the treatment groups performance was not significantly different from the experts. Choi and Lee (2009) also reported on the benefits of using scaffolds and found that the use of scaffolds helped with the transfer of the problem-solving skills when solving ISPs in different domains.

Prompts

Prompts can be considered a specific type of scaffold that are used to help solve ISPs (Chen, 2010). Fundamentally, prompts are statements or questions that guide the problem-solving process. Prompts can help organize information, focus on particular components of a problem, create robust mental models of the problems, and realize the relationships between problem components (Chen, 2010; Lee & Spector, 2012). Manipulating prompts is one way to provide the appropriate level of guidance for the problem solver's experience. Lee and Spector (2012) suggest novices need more guidance to provide structure than experts, and providing experts too much structure can have a negative effect on their performance and efficiency. It is also necessary to provide specific prompts for a particular outcome. Chen (2010) found that "integration prompts helped the development and integration of cognitive schema," and "procedure prompts helped directing students' attention to specific features of the problem in order to arrive at the solutions and complete the problem-solving task" (p. 300). As with other types of scaffolds, prompts may help the transfer of problem-solving skills to a "contextually dissimilar problem" (Ge & Land, 2003, p. 23).

Ill-STRUCTURED PROBLEMS AND PHYSICAL THERAPY

Cognitive abilities are a popular trend in the PT literature, in part because the role and responsibilities of physical therapists continue to grow. As state and federal laws change to make it easier to visit a PT for the primary care of musculoskeletal injuries and impairments, the problems that physical therapists must solve are becoming more complex and less structured. The focus in the literature ten years ago was *critical thinking*, but much of the research was inconclusive because it is difficult to define and measure abstract cognitive processes. In the past three years, the focus has turned to *clinical reasoning*, and the most current publications are reporting about the development of instruments to measure clinical reasoning within the domain of physical therapy.

When considering the definitions of the different types of problems and the experiences of novices who are solving ISPs, the applications for PT education were blatant. For example, Jonassen and Hung (2006) described the division of troubleshooting hypotheses into four levels – system, sub-system, device, and component. This is the same process that physical therapists use for differential diagnosis when completing an initial evaluation. An example of this is a patient who is complaining of fatigue during exercise. The physical therapist would use structural and domain-specific knowledge to assess the cardiopulmonary system (system level), the heart (sub-system level), the left side of the heart, (component level), and find an abnormal rhythm causing decreased cardiac output. For a novice clinician, the process of identifying relationships and complementary functions of the systems in the body, and integrating the expectations for a system at rest compared to a system under stress in healthy and diseased patients can feel overwhelming. Additionally, one consequence of selecting a poor solution is the death of the patient, it is easy to see how the strategies for solving ISPs apply to PT intervention.

The other aspect of ISPs that could be beneficial to the field of PT is the concept of metaproblems (Jonassen, 2000). During the initial evaluation of the patient, a physical therapist will usually have to solve more than ten problems from six different classifications of problems. The current trend in education is to use interventions to apply *clinical reasoning* with the goal of efficient, safe, evidence-based practice. If the initial evaluation was approached as an ISP, and students were taught to use appropriate strategies, PT education could be even more successful.

In the field of PT, ISPs are consistent with intervention in the acute medical setting. Patients with numerous comorbidities or a labile medical stability require an increased awareness of the signs and symptoms of intolerance to activity. This could include changes to cardiac output, acute hypoxemia, and syncope, which require disease specific monitoring and an immediate response from the physical therapist.

The ISPs faced by PTs fit well into the problem typology described by Jonassen (2000). Physical therapy evaluations and treatments could be categorized as decision making problems, troubleshooting problems, strategic performance problems, and dilemmas. All of these are complex, dynamic ISPs that can be challenging, even to master clinicians. The important difference between critical thinking or clinical reasoning and problem solving is that learning to solve ISPs is a skill that can be taught.

There is a gap in the extant research regarding improving ill-structured problem-solving skills in physical therapy education. However, there is a large volume of research regarding the development of ISPs (Jonassen, 1997) and the techniques for teaching problem-solving skills in other fields (Jonassen, 2006) that could be transformative for physical therapy education. The first step in developing ISPs is to determine the types and components of authentic physical therapy problems. To this end, the purpose of this phenomenological study is to examine the perceptions of acute care PTs in order to identify the types of ISPs they face.

IDENTIFYING TYPES OF ILL-STRUCTURED PROBLEMS FOR A COMPUTER

SIMULATION FOR PHYSICAL THERAPY EDUCATION

Methodologists suggest a sample size of up to ten participants in a phenomenological study (Crewswell, 1994). Prior research suggests that ideal candidates would have either more than ten years of experience or a graduate degree in physical therapy and are working in the acute care setting (Costello, Elrod, & Teppers, 2011). Interviews were completed with a convenience sample of ten participants. The participants represented four urban hospitals in a large Midwestern city. Eight females and two males agreed to be interviewed, and all participants were practicing in the acute care setting and had earned graduate degrees in physical therapy. All of the participants had more than four years of experience; five participants have between five and ten years, and three had been practicing for more than ten years. Data was collected by completing interviews with semi-structured and open-ended questions.

The data was analyzed in the manner suggested by Moustakas (1994) for a phenomenological study. Before beginning the analysis, the primary researcher bracketed his experiences and expectations. Initially, the interviews were transcribed and significant statements about the participants' experiences with ISPs were identified. These statements were categorized to create a list of non-repetitive themes, which was then used to write textural descriptions of the participants' experiences and structural descriptions of the settings and contexts of the experiences. In the final step in the analysis, the primary researcher composed a composite description of the textural and structural descriptions in order to capture a holistic description and understanding of the participant's experience of the ISPs.

Findings

Acute care physical therapists experience ISPs with almost every patient intervention. The typical problem begins when the order to initiate physical therapy services is received, and it is not resolved until all of the necessary communication about the intervention is complete. Some components of the problem include challenges that arise during indirect patient care activities such as patient prioritization, patient rounding, and participating with internal quality improvement projects. Additional components are seen during direct patient care activities, such as the challenges that are consistent with the role of a physical therapist in the acute care setting including completing physical assessments and gait training.

Direct Patient Care

Demographics

Patients under the care of acute care physical therapists are typically elderly and admitted to the hospital due to illness, injury, or elective procedure. They are often ill, having a high level of acuity requiring multiple tests and procedures. Those patients that are injured are admitted to the hospital due to a trauma such as a fall or a progressive disease process such as dementia or Parkinson's disease. Many patients are admitted after elective procedures such as total hip arthroplasty, total knee arthroplasty, or back surgery.

Acuity

The patient's level of acuity is a challenge in the acute care setting because the patient may not be medically stable for aggressive intervention. This could result in the patient not being able to tolerate physical therapy intervention or demonstrating a labile response. Some of the markers of acuity that PTs evaluate are lab values, the presence of invasive lines, imaging results, location in the hospital, medical procedures, current medications, and the patient's comorbidities. PTs must first determine if the patient is safe to participate with therapy by reviewing the chart and communicating with staff members, and continuously evaluates the patient's stability throughout treatment. Several participants reported the trend that patients who are acutely ill tend to decline therapy intervention more often.

Motivation

The patients' willingness to participate is a challenge that was reported by all of the participants. Each of the clinicians used the term "refuse" to describe a patient's unwillingness to participate. For example, one participant reported, "Refusals would probably be the biggest one that is most typical. The patient refuses because they don't feel well. They're sick here in the hospital and they don't want to do it." Patients refusals can occur prior to initiating therapy intervention and during the course of intervention. When patients refuse prior to the initiation of therapy, the primary reason they provide is not feeling well due to feeling sick, being in pain, or complaining of nausea and vomiting. PTs must make decisions regarding how to encourage a patient that has refused to participate and when to accept a refusal. This decision is made more difficult when differentiating between patients who chronically refuse to participate and those who provide a rational and legitimate reason for refusing. For example, patients may decline therapy until pain medication has been administered.

The participants asserted that patients may refuse because they do not understand the role of therapy in discharge planning or have unrealistic expectations for when physical therapy will be initiated in the acute care setting. In order to be successful in the acute care setting, physical therapists must be able to communicate their role and the goals of therapy clearly. One participant suggested, "On refusals I try to really explain what I'm here, what my role is in the hospital. I try my best to pose it as, 'If you work with me, you have a better shot of getting out of here sooner than just lying in bed and doing nothing.' Getting out of the hospital quicker."

Discharge Planning

Discharge planning is one of the most important and most complicated problems that PTs face in the acute care setting. The basic components of this problem are determining the safest discharge location; how much assistance will the patient need after discharge; and the equipment the patient requires. Discharge planning is challenging, especially for students and novice clinicians because the solution is rarely simple. One of the clinicians reported, "I feel the most... frustrated because most of the time, people want a black and white answer, and there's a lot of gray." Patients and staff members expect discharge planning decisions to be prompt, formulaic, and fixed. Unfortunately, there are multiple points of information that go into the decision including the patient's mobility, balance, cognition, comorbidities, level of assistance, acuity, and restrictions ordered by the physician.

Discharge decisions are made more complicated when a patient or family member provides incomplete or incorrect information about the patient's prior level of function, level of assistance at home, and home environment. Poor communication about the role of physical therapy and the PT's decision-making process can decrease a patient's motivation and satisfaction, especially if the discharge recommendation is different than a patient's expectations. The challenge was described as, "I think a big problem is just trying to figure out what the best discharge plan is, but the patient may not agree...trying to convince the patient what is in their best interest as far as ongoing therapy and supervision needed at discharge."

Indirect Patient Care

Communication

The most frequently discussed component of the problems faced in acute care is communication. Participants reported this is often due to charting errors leading to a variety of incorrect orders including a weight bearing status or activity level that is not consistent with the patient's diagnosis or medical status. A student or novice clinician may not have the experience necessary to determine the appropriateness of an order. One clinician reported, "There is a big learning curve that you don't really realize. There is so much medical stuff that you need to know."

Communication challenges effect the PT's ability to be efficient due to scheduling the patient for therapy. One participant described the challenge as, "Communication with nursing staff to set schedules up. Chart reviews. Documentation. Communication between coworkers about the patient. Kind of things that revolve around planning the day around the patient." This included a lack of communication about the tests and procedures which resulted in the PT attempting to provide intervention when the patient was off of the nursing unit.

Communication challenges are not limited to inter-professional communications. Two types of problems regarding communication about expectations were reported. The first is when the patient's expectations are incongruous with the reality of being admitted to the hospital. This was generalized by one participant who observed, "Being in the hospital is usually not the brightest point in peoples' lives. Usually speaking, they are still sick. Even when they leave they're still not where they exactly want to be." This is typical when the physician does not explain all of the aspects of recovering from surgery, or when it takes longer to meet a patient's needs than expected.

The second problem with poorly communicated expectations occurs when staff expectations are not met. An example of this is when a physician plans a patient discharge location and level of care based on a procedure or diagnosis and not the patient's mobility and safety. Another example that occurs during the patient's admission is when a physician or nurse expects therapy to perform a certain mobility task that is not appropriate due to the patient's level of acuity. The challenge was described by one participant as, "The expectation that the doctor has, that the patient has, and that the nurse has might not all match up to what the patient's able to do. Getting everybody on board with that."

Often, PT's rely on a patient's family members to divulge pertinent information when the patient is unable to communicate. This typically includes information about a patient's prior level of function and the preadmission environment. The information that family members provide can be beneficial in helping to answer questions and clarify information during the evaluation, but can be problematic when the family does not have the correct information. This can impair communication with discharge planning and communicating with the patient and family.

Availability

In the acute hospital setting, patients are admitted for medical reasons and not for physical therapy services, which can make it difficult to fit physical therapy into a patient's schedule. Medical procedures and tests such as dialysis, surgery, imaging, and the placement of an invasive line take precedence over physical therapy services. "There are always the issues of patients being gone all day for tests, or they're gone five hours for dialysis. Or we are waiting for an orthopedic consult about a patient who had a fall, and they don't come till 24 or 36 hours later." Patients may also be unavailable when they are receiving care from other staff members. This can include nursing care, respiratory therapy treatments, pharmacist education, physician rounding, occupational and speech therapy treatments, or visits with chaplain services. Patient availability is also limited when family or visitors are present due to the patient wanting to spend time with them, or the family declining therapy services.

Productivity

One of the external challenges to direct patient care is the hospital's productivity requirements. Meeting productivity expectations can be challenging when a PT is required to attend department staff meetings, rehab staff meetings, unit-based council meetings, round with physician teams, and participate with other hospital committees because this non-patient care time is not considered productive time.

Patient availability and willingness to participate can also make meeting productivity more challenging. One participant described the challenge as, "You spend so much time running around and just trying to find a patient that's in the room and willing to participate, that you ate up half of your day with non-patient care responsibilities, and you still need to make your visits." Preparing for therapeutic intervention often requires the PT to obtain equipment that the patient requires or wait for post-surgical bracing to be delivered.

Public Relations

When asked about the challenges that are faced by acute care PT's, one participant responded "I think I learned in the real world it's a lot more PR (public relations) than it is PT, in the acute setting I think. A lot more PR." With the advent of the Hospital Consumer Assessment of Healthcare Providers and Systems survey affecting Medicare reimbursement, PTs have become more aware of their role in improving patients' satisfaction. Due to the increased amount of time that PTs provide direct patient care, they regularly receive patient complaints about his or her hospital admission. The complaints that were reported most frequently include long wait times for a call light, personality conflicts with nursing staff, and concerns about their personal needs being met. Receiving this information and addressing the patient's concerns can interfere with a PTs ability to complete therapeutic interventions, and may require the PT to alter the patient's plan of care. One example reported by a clinician was, "They are preoccupied with some other aspect of their health care. Sometimes they want to make sure that they don't miss the doctor, or they know they have food coming up in ten minutes."

ISP COMPUTER SIMULATION

Computer simulation for ISP solving offers numerous benefits. The primary benefit is to provide students with the opportunity to practice solving ill-structured cases allowing them to build more robust schemas and become more efficient at using case-based reasoning. This use of computer simulation makes this possible through self-paced repetition and the ability to offer multiple levels of difficulty.

Repetition

One hallmark of ISPs is that there are multiple solution paths to a problem. The traditional model for introducing ISPs in physical therapy education is through the "paper cases" delivered with a fixed amount of limited information in a text format. This model provides students with the opportunity to follow only a single solution path. If a student is successful, it could be difficult to determine if his or her success is due to "blind luck," the "prepared mind," or the student's actual ability (Makri & Blanford, 2012). Alternatively, if the student is not successful, he or she cannot attempt a different solution path.

Using a computer simulation instead of the traditional model allows students to repeat a scenario with a varying amount of information allowing them to attempt multiple solution pathways. Additionally, this repetition can be self-paced. Unlike the traditional model students' choices can be recorded at each decision point so that they can reflect on the effectiveness of the chosen solution path. The iterative cycle of following a solution path and reflecting of the decisions made on that path build the type of robust schema needed to improve the ISP-solving process.

Level Of Difficulty

Another benefit of using a computer simulation instead of the traditional case presentation method is the ability to modify the level of difficulty of the case. The difficulty of an ISP is dependent on how structured the problem is, the amount of information and relationship between data points, and the amount of domain specific knowledge needed to solve the problem. As previously described, the "paper case" method offers a limited amount of fixed information, while a computer simulated case can be designed to present a more dynamic learning experience. Increasing the level of difficulty can be as simple and profound as changing the delivery of domain specific content or limiting the amount of time available to make a decision.

Case Authenticity

The data described above will be used in a computer simulation for students in a case-based course in an entry-level, doctorate of physical therapy program in a large public university in the Midwest. The main thrust of the course content is the assessment and treatment of patients admitted in an acute care hospital who have cardiopulmonary disease. The most common ISP faced by physical therapists working in the hospital setting is discharge planning. As the findings suggest, discharge planning decisions include information from multiple, sometimes competing, sources, and can be solved with multiple solutions.

None of the clinicians that participated in this study reported the completion of physical therapy interventions as challenging. This was not surprising given the inclusion criteria for this study because experienced clinicians should have a more developed ability to solve problems than novice clinicians or students. Regardless of their level of experience, they will all face the same challenges in the clinical setting.

There was a pattern in the types of problems observed that was dependent on the number of years of experience of the participant. Those having more than six years of experience identified challenges related to operations at the facility level such as communication and availability. In contrast, participants with less than six years of experience focus on challenges in the room such as with the patient motivation and level of acuity. This pattern supports the need for more attention on solving ISPs that contain too much or too little information available. In this regard, a simulation should include the types of distractions that PTs face in the clinic and contain scenarios focused on evaluating and treating acute care patients with the added challenges to communication, patient availability, and complicated discharge planning. Problem solving, like any skill, should be introduced and included throughout acute care courses and should be commensurate with students' progression in the program.

The simulation is designed in a branching scenario format and will allow students to review a patient's medical chart, interview hospital staff members (physician, nurse, social workers), and gather pertinent components of the physical exam. The simulation ends with the student making the discharge planning decision and completing a reflection on their decision-making process. Students are given the option of completing the simulation on different levels of difficulty in order to practice the case with decreasing levels of structuredness.

Future research should focus on the novice clinicians' perceptions of ISPs in order to identify challenges that contain the appropriate level of complexity for students in professional physical therapist education programs. Definitely there is a need to include ill-structured problem-solving in the discussion about improving the critical thinking and clinical reasoning of students in physical therapy education. There is also an opportunity for more research on which ill-structured problem-solving strategies are most successful in physical therapy education and how those strategies can be better realized in a computer simulation.

CONCLUSION

Computer simulations offer multiple benefits for preparing students to solve ISPs. This chapter presents the philosophical framework for teaching ISP solving using a computer simulation and describes the process of building an authentic case for the simulation. Physical therapy education makes prolific use of written case studies created by instructors or provided in textbooks. These cases allow students to be presented with scenarios that are timely for classroom instruction and easily manipulated to focus on a specific topic. The limitation of these case studies is that they can be solved through memorization or a thorough research of course materials. They can be solved with well-structured problem-solving strategies without challenging the cognitive abilities that are needed when in the clinic. By comparison, the dynamic interaction of a live-action case study in a computer simulation is able to create a more authentic experience for students while requiring them to solve problems in real time.

In order to create authentic cases, designers should focus on collecting data that describe realistic scenarios. The research conducted for the simulation in this chapter found that acute care PTs experience complex ISPs that encompass all direct and indirect patient care activities and are complicated by system factors outside of their control. Solving the problems described by the participants requires clear and accurate communication and an awareness of the role of physical therapy in the acute care setting.

Future iterations of the simulation will allow students to choose from multiple cases, include time sensitive / time limited decisions, and allow catastrophic failures during the scenarios. Additionally, a guided reflection which is focused on the steps to ISPs solving, will be built into the end of each simulation. This will promote reflection on the students' decision-making process and improve the building of efficient schema.

REFERENCES

Brudvig, T., Mattson, D., & Guarino, A. (2015). Critical thinking skills and learning styles in physical therapists trained in India enrolled in a master's program. *Journal, Physical Therapy Education, 29*(4), 5–13. doi:10.1097/00001416-201529040-00003

Brudvig, T., Mattson, D., & Guarino, A. (2016). Critical thinking skill and learning styles in entry-level doctor of physical therapy students. *Journal, Physical Therapy Education, 30*(4), 3–10. doi:10.1097/00001416-201630040-00002

Choi, I., & Lee, K. (2009). Designing and implementing a case-based learning environment for enhancing ill-structured problem solving: Classroom management problems for prospective teachers. *Educational Technology Research and Development, 57*(1), 99–129. doi:10.100711423-008-9089-2

Coker, P. (2010). Effects of an experiential learning program on the clinical reasoning and critical thinking skill of occupational therapy students. *Journal of Allied Health, 39*(4), 281–286. PMID:21184024

Costello, E., Elrod, C., & Teppers, S. (2011). Clinical decision making in the acute care environment: A survey of practicing clinicians. *Journal of Acute Care Physical Therapy, 2*(2), 46–54. doi:10.1097/01592394-201102020-00001

Crewswell, J. (1994). *Qualitative inquiry and research design: Choosing among the five approaches*. Thousand Oaks, CA: SAGE.

Dean, E. (2009). Physical therapy in the 21st century (part II): Evidence-based practice within the context of evidence-informed practice. *Physiotherapy Theory and Practice, 25*(5), 354–368. doi:10.1080/09593980902813416 PMID:19842863

Driscoll, M. P. (2005). *Psychology of learning for instruction* (3rd ed.). Boston, MA: Pearson.

Ertmer, P. A., Stepich, D. A., Flanagan, S., Kocaman, A., Christian, R., Reyes, L., . . . Ushigusa, S. (2008). Ill-structured problem solving: Helping instructional design novices perform like experts. *Annual meeting of the American Educational Research Association*. Retrieved from http://ertmer_AERA2008_ExpertNovice.pdf

Frederiksen, N. (1984). Implications of cognitive theory for instruction in problem solving. *Review of Educational Research, 54*(3), 363–407. doi:10.3102/00346543054003363

Fu, W. (2015). Development of an innovative tool to assess student physical therapists' clinical reasoning competency. *Journal, Physical Therapy Education, 29*(4), 14–26. doi:10.1097/00001416-201529040-00004

Furze, J., Black, L., Hoffman, J., Barr, J., Cochran, T., & Jensen, G. (2015). Exploration of students' clinical reasoning development in professional physical therapy education. *Journal, Physical Therapy Education, 29*(3), 22–33. doi:10.1097/00001416-201529030-00005

Furze, J., Gale, J., Black, L., Cochran, T., & Jensen, M. (2015). Clinical reasoning: Development of a grading rubric for student assessment. *Journal, Physical Therapy Education, 29*(3), 34–45. doi:10.1097/00001416-201529030-00006

Ge, X., & Land, S. M. (2003). Scaffolding students' problem-solving processes in an ill-structured task using question prompts and peer interactions. *Educational Technology Research and Development, 51*(1), 21–38. doi:10.1007/BF02504515

Glaser, R. (1984). Education and thinking: The role of knowledge. *The American Psychologist, 39*(2), 93–104. doi:10.1037/0003-066X.39.2.93

Hunter, S., Pitt, V., Croce, N., & Roche, J. (2014). Critical thinking skills of undergraduate nursing students: Description and demographic predictors. *Nurse Education Today, 34*(5), 809–814. doi:10.1016/j.nedt.2013.08.005 PMID:24018356

Jonassen, D. (1997). Instructional design models for well-structured and ill-structured problem-solving learning outcomes. *Educational Technology Research and Development, 45*(1), 64–94. doi:10.1007/BF02299613

Jonassen, D. (2000). Toward a design theory of problem solving. *Educational Technology Research and Development, 48*(4), 63–85. doi:10.1007/BF02300500

Jonassen, D., Strobel, J., & Lee, C. (2006). Everyday problem solving in engineering: Lessons for engineering educators. *Journal of Engineering Education, 95*(2), 139–151. doi:10.1002/j.2168-9830.2006.tb00885.x

Jozwiak, J. (2004). Teaching problem-solving skills to adults. *MPAEA Journal of Adult Education, 33*(1), 19–34.

Kantar, L. (2014). Assessment and instruction to promote higher order thinking in nursing students. *Nurse Education Today, 34*(5), 789–794. doi:10.1016/j.nedt.2013.08.013 PMID:24035312

Kirschner, P. A., Sweller, J., & Clark, R. (2006). Why minimal guidance during instruction does not work: An analysis of the failure of constructivist, discovery, problem-based, experiential, and inquiry based learning. *Educational Psychologist, 41*(2), 75–86. doi:10.120715326985ep4102_1

Koldner, J. L. (1992). An introduction to case-based reasoning. *Artificial Intelligence Review, 6*(1), 3–34. doi:10.1007/BF00155578

Makri, S., & Blandford, A. (2012). Coming across information serendipitously – part 2: A classification framework. *The Journal of Documentation, 68*(5), 706–724. doi:10.1108/00220411211256049

Moustakas, C. (1994). *Phenomenological research methods.* Thousand Oaks, CA: SAGE. doi:10.4135/9781412995658

Nagy, P. (1990). *Modelling ill-structured problem solving with schema theory.* Paper presented at the annual conference of the Midwestern Educational Research Association, Chicago, IL.

O'Dell, B., Mai, J., Thiele, A., Priest, A., & Salamon, K. (2009). The hot seat: Challenging critical thinking and problem solving skills in physical therapist students. *The Internet Journal of Allied Health Sciences and Practice, 7*(1), 1–10.

Piaget, J. (1977). *The development of thought: Equilibration of cognitive structures.* Oxford, UK: Viking Press.

Plack, M., & Wong, C. K. (2002). The evolution of the doctorate of physical therapy: Moving beyond the controversy. *Journal, Physical Therapy Education, 16*(1), 48–59. doi:10.1097/00001416-200201000-00008

Rumelhart, D. (1980). Schemata: The building blocks of cognition. In R. J. Spiro, B. C. Bruce, & W. F. Brewer (Eds.), *Theoretical issues in reading comprehension* (pp. 33–58). Hillsdale, NJ: Erlbaum.

Shin, N., Jonassen, D. H., & McGee, S. (2003). Predictors of well-structured and ill-structured problem solving in an astronomy simulation. *Journal of Research in Science Teaching, 40*(1), 6–33. doi:10.1002/tea.10058

Tawfik, A. A., Rong, H., & Choit, I. (2015). Failure to learn: Towards a unified design approach for failure-based learning. *Educational Technology Research and Development, 63*(6), 975–994. doi:10.100711423-015-9399-0

Vendrely, A. (2005). Critical thinking skills during a physical therapist professional education program. *Journal, Physical Therapy Education, 19*(1), 55–59. doi:10.1097/00001416-200501000-00007

Wood, P. (1983). Inquiring systems and problem structure: Implication for cognitive development. *Human Development, 26*(5), 249–265. doi:10.1159/000272887

ADDITIONAL READING

Chen, C. (2010). Promoting college students' knowledge acquisition and ill-structured problem solving: Web-based integration and procedure prompts. *Computers & Education, 55*(1), 292–303. doi:10.1016/j.compedu.2010.01.015

Hung, W. (2011). Theory to reality: A few issues in implementing problem-based learning. *Educational Technology Research and Development, 59*(4), 529–552. doi:10.100711423-011-9198-1

Jonassen, D. H., & Hung, W. (2006). Learning to troubleshoot: A new theory-based design architecture. *Educational Psychology Review, 18*(1), 77–114. doi:10.100710648-006-9001-8

Jonassen, D. H., & Kim, B. (2010). Arguing to learn and learning to argue: Design justifications and guidelines. *Educational Technology Research and Development, 58*(4), 439–457. doi:10.100711423-009-9143-8

Lee, J., & Spector, J. M. (2012). Effects of model-centered instruction on effectiveness, efficiency, and engagement with ill-structured problem solving. *Instructional Science, 40*(3), 537–557. doi:10.100711251-011-9189-y

Ng, C. S. L., Cheung, W. S., & Hew, K. F. (2010). Solving ill-structured problems in asynchronous online discussions: Built-in scaffolds vs. no scaffolds. *Interactive Learning Environments, 18*(2), 115–134. doi:10.1080/10494820802337629

Purtilo, R. B., & Doherty, R. F. (2011). *Ethical dimensions in the health professions* (5th ed.). St. Louis, MO: Elsevier.

Vogel, K. A., Geelhoed, M., Grice, K. O., & Murphy, D. (2009). Do occupational therapy and physical therapy curricula teach critical thinking skills? *Journal of Allied Health, 38*(3), 152–157. PMID:19753426

Zydney, J. M. (2008). Cognitive tools for scaffolding students defining an ill-structured problem. *Journal of Educational Computing Research*, *38*(4), 353–385. doi:10.2190/EC.38.4.a

Zydney, J. M. (2010). The effect of multiple scaffolding tools on students' understanding, consideration on different perspectives, and misconceptions of a complex problem. *Computers & Education*, *54*(2), 360–370. doi:10.1016/j. compedu.2009.08.017

KEY TERMS AND DEFINITIONS

Acuity: A description of the severity of a patient's medical status. This can include the primary diagnosis and prognosis, comorbidities, and baseline measures of health.

Acute Care Setting: Physical therapy practice in a traditional hospital where patients are admitted for emergency medical, surgical, and obstetric services. This is different from an acute rehab setting where patients are admitted for high intensity rehabilitation services.

Discharge Planning: An interdisciplinary process with the goal of transitioning a patient from the hospital to the next level of care.

Ill-Structured Problem: A problem with multiple solution pathways and multiple solutions, in which the solver is provided with too much or too little information.

Inter-Professional Communication: Synchronous and asynchronous communication among the various healthcare professionals with the goal of making medical decisions.

Productivity: This is typically a measure of time spent on patient care that is considered billable. This includes assessment and intervention activities when a health care professional is in direct contact with the patient. This does not include interprofessional communication and consultation time.

Well-Structured Problem: A problem with a single solution that can be solved by applying a specific rule or using the correct tool. Solvers are presented with the information need to solve the problem.

Chapter 5
Simulations in Business Education:
A Case Study of Cesim™ Global Challenge

Andres Aguilera-Castillo
https://orcid.org/0000-0002-9484-7047
Universidad EAN, Colombia

Mauricio Guerrero-Cabarcas
Universidad EAN, Colombia

Camila Andrea Fúquene
Universidad de La Salle, Colombia

William Fernando Rios
Universidad de La Salle, Colombia

ABSTRACT

This chapter examines the experimental use of Cesim™ Global Challenge, a computer-based business simulation, in an undergraduate international business program in Bogota, Colombia. The authors analyzed the data from the simulation through the application of a nonparametric statistical analysis, in addition to the application of an ex-post survey instrument, in order to assess the relevance of using simulations in the acquisition of managerial skills among undergraduate students. Key findings include the observation of positive effects of computer simulations in learning environments, as they occur in the literature. The authors accepted the hypothesis that stated that more time spent in the simulation leads to better results in the default winning criteria. Finally, the survey instrument confirmed that the use of the simulation helped the students develop managerial soft skills.

DOI: 10.4018/978-1-7998-0004-0.ch005

Copyright © 2020, IGI Global. Copying or distributing in print or electronic forms without written permission of IGI Global is prohibited.

INTRODUCTION

The rapid changes and developments in telecommunication and information technologies have affected many aspects of modern life. For instance, the pervasive use of technology is having a strong impact on the labor market and its economic development demands, and hence on educational strategies aiming to adapt complex communications to transform them into new problem-solving skills (Bogers & Sproedt, 2012; McClarty et al., 2012). Thus, a common concern for educational programs, professors, and students is to cope in a more competitive and technology-driven world.

Scholars have emphasized the importance of transforming mainstream educational practices into technology-based approaches, considering the new learning generation demands. For example, Prensky (2001) introduced one of the most interesting concepts regarding the effects of technology on the *digital natives* (i.e., new generations of learners):

Today's students - K through college - represent the first generations to grow up with this new technology. They have spent their entire lives surrounded by and using computers, videogames, digital music players, video cams, cell phones, and all the other toys and tools of the digital age. Today's average college grads have spent less than 5,000 hours of their lives reading, but over 10,000 hours playing video games (not to mention 20,000 hours watching TV). Computer games, email, the Internet, cell phones and instant messaging are integral parts of their lives. (p.1)

In order to address the educational needs of the digital natives, motivation, engagement and flow are elements that play a fundamental role in the learning process of newer generations (among them, *millennials, and Generation Z*). In the last decades, a growing body of research has found games and simulations to be integral tools to reach out to a younger generation of students with particular learning styles and a unique relation with technology (Csikszentmihalyi, 1990; Fasli & Michalakopoulos, 2006; Gundala & Singh, 2016; Shea, Sherer, Quilling, & Blewett, 2011; Tennyson, 2011). Moreover, the benefits of adapting elements from games and simulations in educational strategies include the improvement of students' decision-making skills, critical and complex thinking, and a major proclivity for teamwork, among others (Tanner, Stewart, Totaro, & Hargrave, 2012; Yang & Yi, 2010).

For the purposes of this chapter, simulations are found to be a more suitable tool in business education, considering they build a link between abstract concepts and real-world outcomes, unlike games, which do not necessarily introduce real-world scenarios in their design (Ben-Zvi, 2010). Nonetheless, this chapter briefly reviews the elements and aesthetics of games in order to discuss a feature which is applied in education technology: gamification. This feature adapts elements and rationale of games into serious activities or simulations; thus, gamification is a key attribute of Cesim™ Global Challenge.

The use of simulations in education has been well documented in fields such as physics, engineering, medicine or business (Bizelli, Fiscarelli, & Fiscarelli, 2013; Eisenhardt & Ninassi, 2016; Peterková, 2014; Ruiz, Castiblanco, Cruz, Pedraza, & Londoño, 2018). However, this research found that, even though empirical evidence or case studies of simulations in business education are abundant, especially on topics related to management, supply chain, accounting, and marketing, they mainly implement traditional simulations, while case studies on digital or computer-based simulations are found in a lesser extent (Gundala & Singh, 2016; Sánchez, Mota, Hernández, García, & Tlapa, 2016; Van der Merwe, 2013). Consequently, this study aims to test a computer-based and gamified simulation as Cesim™ Global Challenge and assess its results in accordance to what has been found in the literature.

Cesim™ Global Challenge is a simulation that leads students to work in teams to manage a simulated company that manufactures and commercializes mobile phones. In order to achieve this, team members had to solve problems and make decisions in essential processes of the company's value chain, such as production, demand, logistics, finance, human resources, taxes, and research and development. Teams had to compete against each other to achieve the highest cumulative total shareholder return (CTSR), which is the default winning criteria within the simulation. This experiment took place in the Business and International Relations undergraduate program at Universidad de La Salle in Bogotá (Colombia), where a total of 222 students took part of the simulation during three academic semesters.

In order to contrast the outcomes and dynamics the authors found in the literature against the empirical results of Cesim™ Global Challenge simulation, this chapter includes a literature review describing the evolution of experiential learning theories and its influence on simulations for business education, followed by a broad description of the simulation (market conditions) and changes the authors implemented in each semester. The next section discusses the analysis of the data resulting from the simulations, where the researchers formulated three hypotheses: 1) More time in the simulation leads to better results in the winning criteria; 2) adding complexity to the simulation results in a worse performance in the winning criteria; 3) more practice rounds in the simulation imply better results in the winning criteria. Two different statistical tests (i.e., Spearman's rank correlation coefficient and median test for K samples) were used to understand the relationship between different variables and the CTSR. The study also included an ex post survey, which had a 65.7% response rate and was designed to capture demographic, cohort, and students' perception of the simulation. Finally, the research closes with a discussion on the potential gains of simulation use in business education and in corporate training.

LITERATURE REVIEW

In the last 50 years, there has been an increasing research interest regarding the impact and benefits of using game elements and simulations in educational strategies, with the refinement of them being improved with computational capabilities, in order to more efficiently enhance creativity, social competences, innovation, among other skills necessary in a work environment (Csikszentmihalyi, 1990; Fasli & Michalakopoulos, 2006; Gundala & Singh, 2016; Shea et al., 2011; Tennyson, 2011). For instance, Shea et al. (2011) emphasized the importance for organizations to have employees who are able to be avid team players, and capable of accomplishing projects that require online interaction and understanding of the new geographic and time boundaries.

The experiential benefits of using games and simulations in the formation and transmission of knowledge have also been previously documented. On one hand, researchers have concluded that the use of these strategies creates greater student engagement, improves skill acquisition in corporate training, enables a complex experience of social dynamics, allows the formation of entrepreneurial values and principles, and provides an increased sense of the "real world" by playing a game or running a simulation. Thus, schools, universities and corporations are progressively including experiential approaches in their curriculum and training programs (Burke, 2012; Gentry, 1990; McClarty et al., 2012; Onofrei & Stephens, 2014; Shea et al., 2011; Wawer, Milosz, Muryjas, & Rzemieniak, 2010). Relatedly, Ma, Oikonomou, and Jain (2011) state that the implementation of tools such as serious games and - as the authors argue in this chapter - simulations in classrooms and training are considered cost-efficient and can be used along with traditional learning methods to enhance knowledge acquisition.

Learning Theories and Models

Several authors argue that experiential learning theories and models offer an accurate methodological framework to understand how games and simulations provide an active learning experience due to their practical and result-oriented methods (Birknerová, 2010; Garris, Ahlers, & Driskell, 2002; Gentry, 1990; Williams, 2011). As Williams (2011) affirmed, the success of these tools "can be attributed to the extent in which they address the shifting focus of educational process toward experiential learning, development of decision-making skills, promoting teamwork, motivating students, applying theory" (p. 2). Thus, the following theories and models will provide important elements and processes that will help understand the role of simulations in educational environments.

First of all, Bloom's (1984) taxonomy model of educational objectives aimed to explain the progression of a cognitive operation understanding and subsequent application in six levels, starting with a basic stage of recognizing information to an advanced stage of application and deconstruction of concepts: 1) Basic knowledge, 2) comprehension, 3) application, 4) analysis, 5) objective synthesis, and 6) objective evaluation. These six levels have four transversal dimensions: Factual (introducing concepts), conceptual (synthesis of factual knowledge), procedural (subject-specific techniques), and metacognitive (summarize experience and theory) (Anderson & Lawton, 1988).

Similarly, the structure of observed learning outcomes (SOLO) taxonomy Biggs and Collis introduced in 1982 was also formulated as a methodology of learning through the application of concepts. However, its authors proposed that the criteria for categorizing the cognitive learning performance should be measured in terms of complexity (Biggs & Collis, 1982). The SOLO approach describes five levels of performance development, ranging from a basic stage of defining and identifying a simple procedure to an advanced stage of predicting, evaluating, creating, prioritizing, analyzing, and applying abstract concepts (Biggs & Tang, 2007).

Ultimately, in 1984, Kolb introduced the experiential learning theory. In addition to the approaches, Kolb (1984) suggested that life experience was a fundamental mechanism to transmit concepts that would be later applied into active experimentation. This theory described four main stages of the active learning experience: 1) Concrete experience (perception and feelings), 2) reflection (theoretical insights of the experience), 3) abstract conceptualization (thinking and categorizing information), and 4) active experimentation (application of knowledge and conclusions). As William's (2011) research found, business simulations "recreate a Kolb's experiential learning model, where a business game generates a series of micro-experiences, followed by instant feedback and reflection and the application of the reflective to a new situation as the game develops" (p. 15).

These theories have evolved with the progressive integration of technology in educational environments. For instance, technology has changed from being an information/knowledge transmission vehicle towards an applicable, interactive, and collaborative tool for modern pedagogic and didactic approaches (Anderson & Dron, 2011; Kapp, Blair, & Mesch, 2014; Lave & Wenger, 1991). Novel approaches such as e-learning mantain the active practical-theoretical learning experience within an Internet-based environment, where both online education and in-class teaching are applied (Berge & Collins, 1995; Connolly & Stansfield, 2006).

Before understanding the definition and characteristics of games and simulations, this study will briefly introduce the logics of play. According to Bogers and Sproedt (2012), play is a free and adaptive activity in a "state of mind of conductive learning through exploration" (p. 7), which is characterized by being iterative, temporal, uncertain, free (as opposed to ordered), goal-oriented, and limited/closed (Huizinga, 1950). Thus, play is the primary drive of games, which shape and route the activity of playing into a purpose and goal-oriented activity (Bogers & Sproedt, 2012).

Games

Games are defined as a structured activity whereby two or more participants compete to reach a certain goal, while a set of rules and challenges are encountered and completed (Birknerová, 2010). They are structured by a set of specific characteristics and elements, such as the possibility of interaction through fantasy, sensory stimuli, control, mystery, dynamic visuals, and elements as a narrative, rules, goals, challenges, and feedback (Garris et al., 2002; McClarty et al., 2012; Prensky, 2001; Thornton & Cleveland, 1990).

In addition, from a new generation's perpective, millennials have demonstrated more engagement with challenging activities with rich graphics and multitasking interfaces. Also, the fun element of playing drives participants to a state of intensity and absorption that can lead to what Csikszentmihalyi (1990) called a state of flow, where participants are so immersed and focused in their environment that the challenges and motivations converge (Huizinga, 1950; Klopfer, Osterweil, Groff, & Haas, 2009; Pintrich & Schrauben, 1992).

Zichermann and Cunningham (2011) describe gamification as the inclusion of game elements and mechanics to increase engagement in a serious activity such as learning. This concept has been a recent matter of study due to the positive outcomes in a student's learning experience. The authors developed the mechanics, dynamics, and aesthetics (MDA) framework for the design of game elements, such as points (score keeping), levels (rounds), leaderboards, rewards, feedback, and achievements (Aguilera, Fúquene, & Ríos, 2014).

Simulations

A simulation can be defined as a model of the real world where participants have the opportunity of learning by doing, reaching specific goals, creating opportunities, and assessing strategies (Birknerová, 2010; Crookall, Oxford, & Saunders, 1987; Greenblat, 1981; Shannon, 1988). The basic elements of simulations include a realistic environment, a script, and defined roles (Birknerová, 2010; Garris et al., 2002). Simulations can be classified as linear, systemic or cyclical, depending on the complexity of the decision-making process (Aldrich, n.d.; Kapp et al., 2014).

According to Chou and Liu (2015), simulations have four main objectives: a) To create a linkage between the skills learned in the theoretical world and their practice in the professional world; b) to increase students' analytical and problem solving skills, due to the multiplicity of scenarios; c) to refine students' decision-making abilities through an active leaning experience; d) to provide the necessary tools for learners to transit from an information-taking to a self-leaning stage, which is compatible with the SOLO taxonomy learning model.

The Cesim experience is significant. Given the reality-based assumptions of the simulation, students are required to develop decision-making competency by exploring and creating their own understandings of the competitive environment. The Cesim experience allows the creation of interactive scenarios that let the students build a sense of memory through iteration until the decision-making process becomes optimal (Kapp et al., 2014; Vos, 2015). Simulations can be found in a wide variety of educational fields, such as science, business, math, and military gaming (Tsai, Yu, & Hsiao, 2012).

Simulations in Business Education

Business simulations aim to provide an interdependent real-world business environment where parameters, metrics, and conditions are set for trainees to interact with and apply their knowledge (Garris et al., 2002; Peterková, 2014; Seethamraju, 2006). The parameters of the simulation are understood as macrometrics revenue, cost of goods sold, stock price, market share and micrometrics sales, employee retention, and job satisfaction, among others (Kapp et al., 2014). On the other hand, economic conditions are set with information from markets, financial data, and customer behavior trends (Vos, 2015).

There is consensus over the learning phases of business simulations. The authors have identified four stages in the literature, from the concepts in the works of Aldrich (2002), Birknerová (2010), and Riley, Cadotte, Bonney, and MacGuire (2013):

1.   **Startup Phase:** The first approach to the simulation is characterized by the identification of the objectives, classroom discussion of the assumptions, and the narrative or script. Tutorials and trials are needed, before starting the simulation formally.
2.   **Transition Phase:** The students have the basic information, assumptions, and goals of the simulation to begin playing and devising individual and team strategies.

3. **Growth Phase:** Iteration is critical to reach the goals and to understand the narrative and team behavior in the simulation. In the growth phase, iterations help trainees to develop and strengthen the skills the participants need to acquire. Accordingly, the level of the challenge can be adjusted to match team performance.

4. **Accountability Phase:** The evaluation and assessment of participants' performance is pivotal to the goal of the simulation. Feedback on the metrics, winning criteria, key performance indicators, and other metrics of performance are essential to the next iteration to achieve better results.

In addition, the positive outcomes of using business simulations include the following skill/ability/competency areas: strategic thinking, planning, communication, application of numbers, negotiating skills, group decision-making, data handling, tendency to take more risks, leadership, creativity, innovation, cooperation and competition, problem solving, responsibility, and being able to connect knowledge from diverse areas of business (Bogers & Sproedt, 2012; Kirriemuir & McFarlane, 2004; Mendoza, 2017).

The role of the instructor in business simulations is of major concern. Her/his ability, experience, and cognition (i.e., perception, reasoning, and judgment of the simulation) are important for the development of pedagogic and didactic strategies, where teachers are not only meant to impart information, but to guide students towards meaningful learning (Kikot, Fernandes, & Costa, 2014). The instructor has three main functions during the simulation: First, plan and execute teaching strategies; second, guide students' learning process throughout the simulation; third, design suitable feedback and assessment tools (Vos, 2015).

SIMULATION DESCRIPTION

Cesim™ Global Challenge is a licensed business simulation which is used for educational purposes. It is focused on developing skills in areas such as strategic management, international business, global operations, and business policy. The main goal, or winning criteria, in this case, is to achieve the highest CTSR of a fictional company. The narrative of the simulation presents this fictional company that manufactures and commercializes mobile phones in three main markets: The United States, Asia, and Europe (Cesim, 2014). The simulation is gamified and computer-based; it enables team members to work virtually, allowing participants to develop abilities such as leadership, communication, problem solving, teamwork, and other skills encountered in a real work environment (Ferrazzi, n.d.).

The simulation allows students to work in teams of maximum five people, and the unit of time to measure performance is one round (equivalent to a fiscal year). The instructor has the control to "pace" the simulation, and, after the round closes, the simulation retrieves with a feedback of each team's performance followed by a class discussion. An interval of around 4-5 days among rounds takes place to review the results of the "fiscal year" and extrapolate relevant concepts of the syllabus with the simulation.

The maximum number of rounds in trial mode is three, while in competition mode the maximum is 12. All teams start the simulation with the same market conditions (i.e., revenue, market share, and production costs, among others), and, as the simulation advances, challenges increase. The result of each team depends on the decisions made and the team's ability to adapt to the changing environment of the market. However, team performance in the simulation has a pattern of path dependency starting from the first competitive round.

Every round presents changing market conditions, such as diplomatic tensions and international geopolitical crises, volatility in exchange rates, changes in tariff policy, labor market policy, and other variables that impact estimated sales, costs, and revenue. Team performance is evaluated through the CTSR and the valuation of the shares that each company had issued.

The simulation aims to develop both tangible and intangible knowledge. Tangible knowledge is related to theoretical and management concepts that are used within the simulation, whereas intangible knowledge consists in the abilities the participants acquire through the experience of the simulation by applying the concepts they have learned during the experience (Cesim, n.d.).

The simulation has the following modules: Production, demand (which includes network coverage and elasticity), technology attractiveness, human resources, R&D, marketing, logistics, finance, and decision checklist.

Production

In the simulation, decision making starts with production (Figure 1). There are two basic production locations, United States and Asia, which can be used to cover the demand in the three markets of the simulation: United States, Asia, and Europe. Initially, every team starts with the same amount of production facilities in the United States, then each team decides what would be the production strategy, and prioritizes either Asia or United States for production. This is supposed to be according to each team's demand forecast and strategy for the next rounds.

Figure 1. Production dashboard in Cesim™ Global Challenge
Source: Cesim, n.d.

The production analysis and strategy are linked to the learning curve. Students have to find an optimal production point to minimize the costs they are facing when producing a new technology, because production cost is also shown as the result of a function of cumulative production by technology (e.g., innovation, R&D, and licensing).

The main parameter of the production module is the basic in-house production unit cost, which considers variables (e.g., economies of scale, planning penalty, and learning curve multipliers) that will reflect on other variables related to production costs (e.g., the basic outsourcing costs, the initial number of own facilities, the production plant capacity, and inventory costs). Students ought to strategically plan whether these costs should be set higher or not, and their progressive impact in the overall production development during the rounds (Cesim, 2014).

Demand

As the production module, the basic demand has a starting point for all teams (between 0 and 2.000 K of units). Basic demand is shown in percentage, and each team can decide a higher or lower demand, depending on their strategies towards pricing, number of features, and advertising (company advertising and technology advertising), among others. Therefore, the total demand considers the team's strategy towards the variables, and will reflect on the market size throughout the simulation, as Figure 2 shows (Cesim, 2014).

Network Coverage

One of the main assumptions in the simulation is technological innovation. The simulation starts with a 100% network coverage for Technology 1, with a transition

Figure 2. Demand dashboard in Cesim™ Global Challenge
Source: Cesim, n.d.

towards Technology 4. There are four available technologies in the simulation, each has up to 10 additional features that can be included in each marketing mix. This submodule, which is presented as an index, is of pivotal education importance, given the dynamic nature of technology development or evolutionary trends and production, which is directly linked to other sections of the simulation (e.g., licensing, human resources management, and R&D investments). All these sections have a direct impact on the team's performance and on the winning criteria (Cesim, 2014).

Elasticity

This submodule illustrates the impact of price elasticity, advertisement elasticity, corporate social responsibility elasticity and elasticity in the number of features in the quantity demanded. Students are encouraged to learn through the rounds about the effects of their estimated demand and the actual results in parameters such as cumulative part of advertising, technology market share elasticity, technology advertising elasticity, and the cross-elasticity multiplier:

- **Price Elasticity:** The platform accepts negative values for the estimated price elasticity, and, for the absolute value, a range from 1 to 6, thus, the higher the absolute value, the more sensitive will be the price of the product in the market. The simulation also prompts the students to be aware of changes in the general price levels, which, if not considered, may lead to a decreased demand.
- **Advertising Elasticity:** Higher levels of elasticity in advertising are translated into a higher demand. Hence, students should understand when they should overspend (or not) on advertisement.
- **Social Responsibility Elasticity:** For this category, the simulation sets 0 as default, and students are intended to understand that customers' perception of ethic suppliers reflects on a gradual increase in elasticity.
- **Elasticity in the Number of Features:** As for advertising elasticity, the number of features of elasticity should be high. This is understood as a better appreciation from customers for the additional features of the product.

Technology Attractiveness

This submodule allows for comparison of the behavior of the same product in two markets. Attractiveness will differentiate each technology and the perception of customers towards the product's appeal (Cesim, 2014).

Human Resources

Human resources are a key but optional module in the simulation. The instructor can enable it and inventory management voluntarily. Given the learning curve for the instructor leading the simulation, the authors decided to include the human resources and inventory management modules only in the last cohort of this analysis. The teams' decisions include hiring workers, defining salaries, assigning working hours, and preparing training budgets directly related to the company's R&D process (Cesim, 2014).

Research and Development

In the R&D module, students choose to either develop an in-house R&D program or license the technology they need to produce better mobile equipment, thus considering R&D costs vis-à-vis the cost of licensing (Cesim, n.d.). In the simulation, investments in R&D would take effect in two rounds (i.e., two fiscal years) to achieve production capabilities; on the other hand, licensing has immediate effects in the production process. It is up to each team to decide which strategy to pursue between these two possible options to reach the strategic objectives of each team (Cesim, 2014).

Marketing

This module of the simulation presents three main challenges to the students: a) Additional features of the phones by technology; b) pricing; c) the amount of money dedicated to promotion in each geographical area. In the first place, phones' additional features can be applied if the company has invested enough in R&D or in licensed products. Promotion is fundamental to allow the consumer to achieve awareness and recognition in each of the three markets of the simulation (i.e., United States, Europe, and Asia) (Cesim, 2014).

Logistics

Prioritizing markets and selecting the right location for production facilities is one of the main issues in managing a global business. The logistics module provides the students with the challenge of handling logistics in an optimal way, according to the team's strategy. Teams should allocate the production capacity in the right places and in the right time, according to the changing market environment and their own demand expectations, also keeping in mind to avoid inventory excess (Cesim, n.d.).

Finance

The objective in this module is to manage the company's finance and to maximize the capital return to the equity holders. The finance module in Figure 3 includes treasury management, management of long-term loans, share issues, buy backs, and dividend payments. Treasury management helps the students to manage international money transaction among the served markets. Transfers can be used to build new factories, to finance new technology development, and to reduce accumulated debt (Cesim, 2014).

Figure 3. Finance dashboard in Cesim™ Global Challenge
Source: Cesim, n.d.

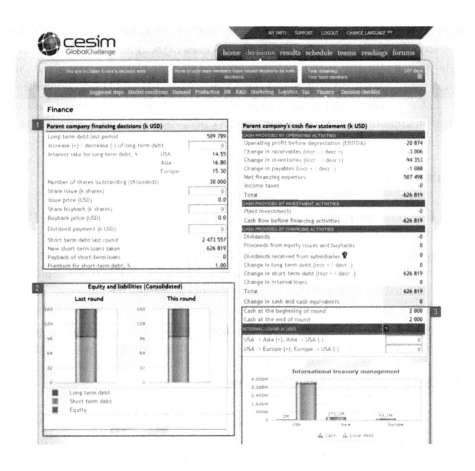

Decision Checklist

The decision checklist module allows the students to see the individual decisions of each team member. The teams have to decide which of the members' decisions (or combination of them) should be saved to close the round and start the next round. When the round is closed, the teams are able to review their decisions against their rival teams' decisions (Cesim, 2014).

FROM THEORY TO PRACTICE: THE APPLICATION OF A BUSINESS SIMULATION

The simulation was used for three consecutive semesters in the undergraduate class Internationalization Strategies at La Salle University in Bogota, Colombia. A total of seven classes used the simulation as an integral part of their classroom experience. Two classes participated in the first semester, two additional classes in the second semester, and three additional classes in the third semester. Students self-organized into teams, and then they registered in the platform, picked a name for their team, and had up to three practice rounds before the simulation competition started. The practice and competitive rounds were supplemented with traditional in-class instruction, during which instructors addressed students' questions and held discussion.

Simulation Debut: First Semester

In the first controlled scenario, two classes participated in the simulation. Both had the benefit of two practice rounds to become familiar with the simulation, its tools, and the dynamics of the challenge. After the practice rounds, six competitive rounds took place, and each was equivalent to a fiscal year. As this was a debut, the authors decided to adopt the default setting and not to include the human resources and inventory modules in the simulation. According to the data from the simulation, nearly one out of four students was identified as not actively participating in the simulation and contributed poorly to the overall time their team spent working online.

Adjusting Features: Second Semester

During the implementation of the simulation's second phase, a total of 19 teams participated from two classes. In order to address the free-riding question the instructors and the students identified in the previous semester, the instructors included the time spent in the simulation in the grading criteria for the semester. As a result, the percentage of students that were considered free riders dropped from 23.66% to 16.71%. Another significant adjustment was to extend the number of practice rounds to three (the maximum the simulation permitted) and competitive rounds to seven.

Implementation of New Features: Third Semester

For the final semester of this study, the instructors enabled human resources and inventory modules in the simulation to add some complexity to the decision making. Three classes participated, for a total of 28 competing teams. The number of practice and competitive rounds remained the same as the preceding semester. The grading criteria were unchanged for both teams and individual performance.

Measuring the Simulation's Impact: Metrics and Results

The dataset the authors collected from the simulation were used to evaluate the findings in their literature review, and to understand how the amount of participant-time in the simulation affected the CTSR performance, and the effects after adding complexity to the simulation outcome.

The researchers tested the dataset using two nonparametric tests: Spearman's rank correlation coefficient, which is also known as Spearman's Rho, and the median test for K samples. They used two criteria to choose these tests over the parametric kind: 1) The median of the sample better represented the central tendency of the data; 2) each sample ranged from 6 to 10 data points, and was not big enough to ascertain it was normally distributed.

On one hand, the research intended to assess if a correlation existed between the amount of time spent in the simulation and the results of the CTSR as the default winning criteria. As Table 1 highlights, the study applied Spearman's rank correlation coefficient test which confirmed that the hypothesis "the amount of time is directly proportional to CTSR performance" was correct. It showed a strong link between results of the starting and final rounds of the simulation in all seven classes the researchers observed. Introducing a minimum time required for each player helped to reduce free riding to improve participants' experience throughout the simulation.

On the other hand, as Table 2 shows, the authors utilized different variables throughout the conducted periods of time, adding more complexity to the simulation. As a result, they employed the median test for K samples to find discrepancies along the winning criteria (CTSR) of the different groups in all the cohorts they observed. They formulated the null hypothesis to show that both samples (i.e., the default version and the complexity added version) were to show the same median. However, the alternative hypothesis wanted to confirm if there were differences regarding the median of the samples due to a change on the results among the groups.

Table 1. Spearman's Rho correlations for CTSR and time

			CTSR (p.a.)	Total Registered Time per Team (s)
Spearman's Rho	CTSR (p.a.)	Correlation Coefficient	1,000	,486**
		Sig. (bilateral)	.	,000
		N	169	169
	Total registered time per team (s)	Correlation Coefficient	,486**	1,000
		Sig. (bilateral)	,000	.
		N	169	169

Note: **Correlation is significant at the level 0,01 (bilateral). *Calculations were obtained by using IBM SPSS 2018.*

Source: Authors' design; data from Global Challenge (Cesim, n.d.)

Table 2. Summary of hypotheses tests: complexity added

	Null Hypothesis	Test	Sig.	Decision
1	CTSR median (p.a.), % 2014 are the same among return range's categories.	Median test for independent samples.	,389	Keep null hypothesis.
2	CTSR median (p.a.), % 2015 are the same among return range's categories.	Median test for independent samples.	,389	Keep null hypothesis.

Note: Asymptotic significances are shown. Significance level is, 05

Source: Authors' calculations by using IBM SPSS 2018

After running the test, the null hypothesis was accepted. Introducing both the human resources and the inventory modules to add complexity to the simulation did not skew the results for the last cohort and it was not a hindrance to understanding, adapting, and getting similar profitability during the simulation, when compared to the groups that played the standard version.

Additionally, when it comes to the practice rounds and their influence on the simulation performance, the findings are widely conclusive. As Table 3 shows, students prefer as many practice rounds as possible in order to try alternative strategies to obtain better results. Nevertheless, after applying the same method of median test for K samples, the authors found that an additional practice round is not definitive, when it comes to CTSR increase or better simulation performance, as it happens with the amount of time which is invested in the simulation. Finally, there is not a

Table 3. Summary of hypotheses tests: Practice rounds

	Null Hypothesis	Test	Sig.	Decision
1	2Practice's median are the same among RangeReturn categories.	Median test for independent samples.	,261	Keep null hypothesis.
2	3Practice's 2Practice's median are the same among RangeReturn categories.	Median test for independent samples.	,261	Keep null hypothesis.

Note: Asymptotic significances are shown. Significance level is, 05
Source: Authors' calculations by using IBM SPSS 2018

direct relation among the CTSR performance in the simulation and the amount of practice rounds, which also implies how skills can be modeled and adapted by the simulation environment.

EX-POST SURVEY

The authors designed a survey instrument to capture information on the students' perception regarding the use of simulation. The survey captured demographics, cohort, and students' perceptions. One hundred forty-six out of 222 participants responded for a 65.7% response rate.

The authors found that 68.5% of the participants were female, and the median age was 20.5 years, which hints at the idea of a digital native population. For 88.4% of the respondents, Global Challenge was their first experience with a business simulation in a formal educational setting; 11.6% had limited previous simulation experience. Relatedly, 17.8% of the respondents were from the first semester, with 34.9% from the second, and 45.3% from the third. The survey was sent out to all the students who had participated in the simulation at the end of the third semester, and reflects the importance of obtaining immediate feedback as the response rates by semester show.

The survey asked students about the ease of using the simulation's platform, the usefulness of concepts they learned in other classes, and their perception towards the relevance of the simulation. A Likert scale was used to rate the statements from one to five, from strongly disagree to strongly agree. Students were asked to grade the following statement: "Practice rounds allow students to become familiarized with the different variables and let them formulate and develop different strategies for the simulation challenge."

Most respondents considered practice rounds to be beneficial, and allowed them to become acquainted with the simulation and to begin the process of formulating strategies. The following statement was: "The simulation platform is easy to use, login, simulation rules, game features, and the winning criteria is clear." A little over two-thirds (68.8%) of the survey respondents either agreed or strongly agreed with the statement that the rules, goals, and objectives were easy to understand.

The next two statements of the survey inquired if the simulation was useful to their understanding of concepts from other related subjects in their undergraduate program (Figure 4), and if the simulation provided utility and tools in strengthening their knowledge in other relevant subject areas.

There was overwhelming agreement, with over 90% of the respondents strongly agreeing and agreeing to both statements. The simulation proved itself as a bridge to integrate the traditional classroom setting with a real-world business simulation. The students found the simulation useful in providing tools to deepen their understanding and knowledge from other subjects.

The following questions from the survey (Figures 5 and 6) addressed whether the simulation experience was pertinent and useful to the academic goals of the Business and International Relations program at La Salle University, and whether the skills acquired by playing the simulation were deemed useful in their professional field.

The consensus was that the simulation experience was pertinent and relevant to the goals of the University program, and that it provided useful real-world tools relevant to their professional careers. From team formation, decision making, responsibility,

Figure 4. Simulation utility in strengthening knowledge

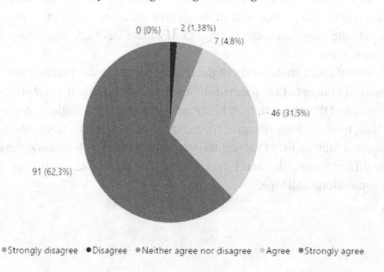

● Strongly disagree   ● Disagree   ● Neither agree nor disagree   ● Agree   ● Strongly agree

Figure 5. Simulation usefulness to the goals of undergraduate program

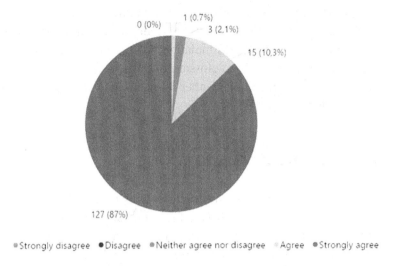

Figure 6. Skills acquired by playing the simulation deemed useful in the professional field

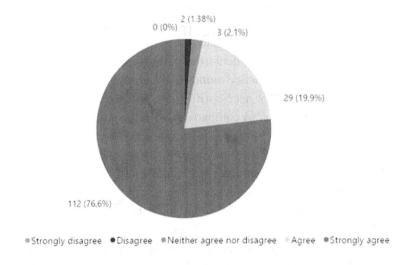

and strategic thinking, among others, the students/players valued the simulation experience as a remarkable tool to enhance their future professional development.

At the end of the survey, the respondents were asked for their recommendations, in order to improve the experience with the use of Global Challenge in a university setting. Almost a third (32%) recommended improvements in terms of better explanation of rules, items, platform, and winning criteria. In addition, 21% felt that there was no need to make changes to the simulation, while 10% thought that more practice rounds would be useful. Nine percent of the participants suggested to have more competitive rounds in simulation. On the other hand, 8% felt that it would be useful to have a simplified glossary of terms to increase clarity, and 5% asked for the usage of the simulation in other courses. Up to 15% of the respondents chose not to provide feedback.

SOLUTIONS AND RECOMMENDATIONS

In terms of specific implications for instructors, which derived from the authors' internal process of adjusting at each stage of the simulation, teachers will find this study helpful to avoid issues that are not explicitly described in most of the existing literature on simulations in business education. More in detail:

- Instructors are encouraged to understand the importance of the time variable for a student's better planning, understanding, analysis, and decision making in the simulation. As these research findings indicate, time was found to be not only a standard variable, but an important factor that can make the difference in a student's learning outcomes.
- Even though some of the students the authors surveyed affirmed that the implementation of more practice rounds in the simulation was necessary, this study showed that it is not necessarily true. Instructors should analyze the difficulty of the simulation in comparison with the students' learning stage, in order to decide the best way to approach practice rounds.
- The inclusion of a glossary of terms is also recommended when implementing simulations that require students to understand complex or numerous concepts, measures, and dynamics.
- The dynamics could be improved by allotting more time to read and understand the material related to the simulation, in terms of description, key performance drivers, and relations among variables. Depending on the design of the course, it would be convenient to hand out the material a week or two in advance to actually study the main issues and think about how to approach them when the environment changes during the simulation.
- It would be helpful to explain to the students the authenticity of the task and the skills to be acquired. In undertaking the task, they learned a process, so some time should be used to justify how the simulation is going to benefit them in improving their profile.

- Instructors should have control before each round over the level of satisfaction and the level of challenge for each group, in order to certify that the simulation is still interesting and a fun activity for every student. If this is not the case, they should provide specific tasks that make the simulation compelling again.

- Instructors should provide additional resources to those students that get high marks in every round. This can make the activity more challenging and interesting for those who excel in this kind of environments.

- The use of self-, peer-, and co-assessment should be formally implemented, so the teamwork performance could be fine-tuned, and those students who are not completely engaged would have to change their attitude during the activity.

Based on these research findings, it is worth highlighting that Cesim™ Global Challenge is not the only licensed computer-based simulation. Simulations such as CompanyGame, LABSAG, Business Global, SimVenture or InQba were found to have similar features and similar winning criteria. This confirms the importance of implementing simulations for business education, due to the need of applying tools that allow an adequate transfer of knowledge. However, importantly, unlike other simulators, Cesim™ is a gamified platform. This feature was expected to increase students' engagement with the simulation and its learning outcomes.

In addition, the literature the authors reviewed evidenced that, on one hand, very few of the existing computer-based simulations for business (self-developed or licensed) were tested and assessed beyond the theoretical considerations. Also, computer-based simulators, especially self-developed ones, tend to focus on specific components of the business value chain in a separate way. Thus, this study helps academic research by providing an empirical study of the experience, problems, successes, and opportunities of implementing tools such as simulations inside a classroom.

In terms of limitations, this study implemented both qualitative and quantitative approaches to minimize the impact of biased results from the ex-post-survey, which the authors carried out in a short-termed scope. However, in order to assess the validity of a simulation in terms of long-term impact, this type of studies requires constant follow up.

FUTURE RESEARCH DIRECTIONS

This chapter considers both quantitative and qualitative results, based on data from the software and perceptions from the ex-post survey. This approach includes a number of limitations that highlight opportunities for future research. First, a second phase might take into account objective performance indicators of learning gains that complement students' viewpoints regarding their skills improvement. Second, the study was based on a small sample of students and a few cohorts using the same business simulation. It is important to validate the results across multiple cohorts of students studying in different institutional contexts, and, if possible, use similar tools to Cesim. In this regard, the methodological approach was therefore not designed to analyze or control for differences between cohorts, but rather to identify consistent patterns and relationships that can be generalized across all cohorts. Furthermore, student heterogeneity, teaching approaches or didactic methodologies may impact final results. It would be necessary to ratify the connection among these variables and their role on simulation learning outcomes.

Future research might focus on the repercussions simulations have on learning outcomes by measuring and analyzing the evolution of students using simulations across several years of study. This study focused on the students' perspective. It would be helpful to include graduates and alumni, in order to compare and understand whether active engagement in business simulations leads to better employment opportunities or promotion outcomes. Likewise, future studies might explore instructors' outlook regarding the value of implementing business simulations in different courses. This line of inquiry might focus on training, methodologies, and supporting strategies instructors used to optimize learning outcomes.

Finally, gamification tools as the simulation the authors implemented through this research will be used to engage students with more attractive schemes of learning and skills attainment. However, due to the recent technological advances, such as virtual reality and artificial intelligence, organizations will look after methods to alternatively develop skills and competences among its employees (Burke, 2012).

This will bring the need to study the current transformation of educational and training strategies and the implementation of features virtual reality and artificial intelligence provide, such as the possibility of predicting/improving performance, identifying learning paths, personalizing experiences or even the adaptation of sociocultural and gender perspectives in games and simulations.

CONCLUSION

In contemporary life, business education is just one of the many aspects which are affected by the use of information and telecommunication technologies. These technologies are almost pervasive in a university setting, thus becoming both an opportunity and a challenge for educators. The challenge is to compete for students' attention, as they are lured by their diverse screens and attractive user interfaces. However, the almost pervasive availability of mobile devices and Internet access are also an opportunity to use these technologies as a new vehicle to reach educational goals.

As the literature review and the described experience showed, the use of simulations and games has a positive impact on knowledge acquisition. Gamification is still a novel tool for educators. Indeed, its full potential is still to be seen, as the technique is increasingly being used in educational and corporate settings. Among the benefits of the use of simulations are the development and enhancement of relevant skills and increased engagement, which may lead to a higher performance inside the organization applying gamified tools.

The authors formulated and tested three hypotheses using statistical analysis. The first hypothesis (i.e., more time in the simulation leads to better results in the winning criteria) was accepted. The statistical analysis confirmed the need of encouraging students to spend plenty of time developing their game strategy and their plan for the whole simulation. Otherwise, the possibilities to outplay the competition significantly diminish.

The second hypothesis (i.e., adding complexity to the simulation results in a worse performance in the winning criteria) was rejected. The median test for K samples helped to invalidate the idea that added complexity could lead to poor results, when compared to the default settings in the simulation (without human resources and inventory modules). Students adapted to such intricacies and responded positively to the challenges of the enabled features.

The third hypothesis (i.e., more practice rounds in the simulation implies better results in the winning criteria) was rejected. Furthermore, the findings were useful to reject the common assumption that the more practice rounds one plays, the better the results at the end of the simulation. The data show that the learning process is reinforced through the interaction in the competitive rounds.

Additionally, combining the resulting data from the simulation and the ex-post survey, the authors benefited from both quantitative and qualitative data for a more comprehensive analysis and comparison with other experiences. This method helped to develop an analytical approach that showed how important and effective the simulation was during the students' learning process. Moreover, it helped to determine the relevance of applying gamified tools to enhance and enrich students' managerial soft skills; in this research, leadership, decision-making, teamwork, effective communication and other relevant skills needed in a real business environment.

The diffusion and adoption of new technologies such as virtual reality may contribute to the need of a robust body of research regarding the use of games and simulations in business education. This is a promising field for research, as more data are gathered, and more experiences using simulations are recorded, compared, and analyzed. Iteration in this field is pivotal to refine assumptions, corroborate hypothesis, and discover new and valuable findings in business education.

REFERENCES

Aguilera, A., Fúquene, C. A., & Ríos, W. F. (2014). Aprende jugando: El uso de técnicas de gamificación en entornos de aprendizaje. *IM-Pertinente*, 2(1), 125–143.

Aldrich, C. (2002). *A field guide to educational simulations*. Alexandria, VA: ASTD.

Aldrich, C. (n.d.). *Six criteria of an educational simulation*. Retrieved from https://goo.gl/LoUFrU

Anderson, P. H., & Lawton, L. (1988). Assessing student performance on a business simulation exercise. *Developments in Business Simulation & Experiential Exercises*, *15*, 241–245.

Anderson, T., & Dron, J. (2011). Three generations of distance education pedagogy. *International Review of Research in Open and Distance Learning*, *12*(3), 80–97. doi:10.19173/irrodl.v12i3.890

Ben-Zvi, T. (2010). The efficacy of business simulation games in creating decision support systems: An experimental investigation. *Decision Support Systems*, *49*(1), 61–69. doi:10.1016/j.dss.2010.01.002

Berge, Z., & Collins, M. (1995). *Computer-mediated communication and the online classroom in distance learning*. Retrieved from https://www.december.com/cmc/mag/1995/apr/berge.html

Biggs, J., & Tang, C. (Eds.). (2007). *Teaching for quality learning at university*. Belkshire, UK: Open University Press.

Biggs, J. B., & Collis, K. F. (1982). *Evaluating the quality of learning – the SOLO taxonomy*. New York, NY: Academic Press.

Birknerová, Z. (2010). The use of simulation business games in university education. *Bulgarian Journal of Science and Education Policy*, *4*(2), 202–215.

Bizelli, M. H., Fiscarelli, P. E., & Fiscarelli, S. H. (2013). Interactive simulations to physics teaching: A case study in Brazilian high school. *International Journal of Learning and Teaching*, *5*(1), 18–23.

Bloom, B. S. (1984). *Taxonomy of educational objectives: The classification of educational goals*. New York, NY: Longman.

Bogers, M., & Sproedt, H. (2012). Playful collaboration (or not): Using a game to grasp the social dynamics of open innovation in innovation and business education. *Journal of Teaching in International Business*, *23*(2), 1–32. doi:10.1080/0897593 0.2012.718702

Burke, B. (2012, November 5). *Gamification 2020: What is the future of gamification?* Retrieved from https://goo.gl/lQrJxo

Cesim. (2014). *Manual del usuario*. Helsinki: Cesim Global Challenge.

Cesim. (n.d.). *Cesim global challenge introduction*. Helsinki: Cesim Global Challenge.

Chou, C. H., & Liu, H. C. (2015). The effectiveness of web-based foreign exchange trading simulation in an international finance course. *Journal of Teaching in International Business*, *24*(1), 4–20. doi:10.1080/08975930.2013.810047

Connolly, T., & Stansfield, M. (2006). Using games-based elearning technologies in overcoming difficulties in teaching information systems. *Journal of Information Technology Education*, *5*(1), 450–476.

Crookall, D., Oxford, R., & Saunders, D. (1987). Towards a reconceptualization of simulation: From representation to reality. *Simulation/Games for Learning, 17*(4), 147-171.

Csikszentmihalyi, M. (1990). *Flow: The psychology of optimal experience*. New York, NY: Harper Collins.

Eisenhardt, A., & Ninassi, S. B. (2016). The use of simulation and cases to teach real world decision making: Applied example for health care management graduate programs. *Journal of Learning in Higher Education*, *12*(1), 71–75.

Fasli, M., & Michalakopoulos, M. (2006). Learning through game-like simulations. *Innovation in Teaching and Learning in Information and Computer Sciences*, *5*(2), 1–11. doi:10.11120/ital.2006.05020005

Ferrazzi, K. (n.d.). *Getting virtual teams right*. Retrieved from https://goo.gl/byiOjF

Garris, R., Ahlers, R., & Driskell, J. E. (2002). Games, motivation, and learning: A research and practice model. *Simulation & Gaming, 3*(4), 441–467. doi:10.1177/1046878102238607

Gentry, J. W. (1990). What is experiential learning? In J. W. Gentry (Ed.), *Guide to business gaming and experiential learning* (pp. 9–20). Asbury, IA: Nichols Publishing.

Greenblat, C. (1981). Teaching with simulation games: A review of claims and evidence. In R. E. Duke & C. Greenblat (Eds.), *Principles of practice of gaming-simulation* (pp. 62–83). London, UK: Sage.

Gundala, R. R., & Singh, M. (2016). Role of simulations in student learning: A case study using marketing simulation. *Journal of Educational Research and Innovation, 5*(2), 1–14.

Huizinga, J. (1950). *Homo ludens: A study of the play-element in culture.* Boston, MA: Beacon.

Kapp, K. M., Blair, L., & Mesch, R. (2014). *The gamification of learning and instruction fieldbook: Ideas into practice.* San Francisco, CA: Wiley.

Kikot, T., Fernandes, S., & Costa, G. (2014). Business simulators and lecturer's perception! The case of University of Algarve. In *ETHICOMP 2014* (pp. 1–12). Paris, France: University of Pierre and Marie Currie.

Kirriemuir, J., & McFarlane, A. (2004). *Report 8: Literature review in games and learning.* Bristol: FutureLab.

Klopfer, E., Osterweil, S., Groff, J., & Haas, J. (2009). The instructional power of: Digital games, social networking, simulations and how teachers can leverage them. *The Education Arcade, 1*(1), 1–20.

Kolb, D. A. (1984). The process of experiential learning. In D. A. Kolb (Ed.), *Experiential learning* (pp. 20–38). Upper Saddle River, NJ: Prentice-Hall.

Lave, J., & Wenger, E. (1991). Legitimate peripheral participation. In J. Lave & E. Wenger (Eds.), *Situated learning: Legitimate peripheral participation* (pp. 27–44). Cambridge, UK: Cambridge University Press. doi:10.1017/CBO9780511815355.003

Ma, M., Oikonomou, A., & Jain, L. C. (2011). *Serious games and edutainment applications.* London, UK: Springer. doi:10.1007/978-1-4471-2161-9

McClarty, K., Orr, A., Frey, P., Dolan, R., Vassileva, V., & McVay, A. (2012). *A literature review of gaming in education.* Upper Saddle River, NJ: Pearson.

Mendoza, F. D. (2017). Uso de simuladores de negocio como estrategia de aprendizaje adaptativo: Una experiencia en el aula. *Revista Virtu@lmente, 5*(2), 26-44.

Onofrei, G., & Stephens, S. (2014). Simulation games in operations management: The importance of immediate post game analysis. *Global Management Journal, 6*(1-2), 61–64.

Peterková, J. (2014). Evaluation of managerial simulation games benefit in teaching process. In M. Zięba, & K. Zięba (Eds.), Innovative approaches to business education-selected issues (pp. 31- 42). Horsens.

Pintrich, P. R., & Schrauben, B. (1992). Students' motivational beliefs and their cognitive engagement in classroom academic tasks. In D. H. Schunk & J. L. Meece (Eds.), *Student perceptions in the classroom* (pp. 149–183). Hillsdale, NJ: Lawrence Erlbaum Associates.

Prensky, M. (2001). *Digital game-based learning.* New York, NY: McGraw-Hill.

Riley, R. A. Jr, Cadotte, E. E., Bonney, L., & MacGuire, C. (2013). Using a business simulation to enhance accounting education. *Issues in Accounting Education, 28*(4), 801–822. doi:10.2308/iace-50512

Ruiz, C. R., Castiblanco, I. A., Cruz, J. P., Pedraza, L., & Londoño, D. C. (2018). Juegos de simulación en la enseñanza de la Ingeniería Industrial: Caso de estudio en la Escuela Colombiana de Ingeniería Julio Garavito. *Entre Ciencia e Ingenieria, 12*(23), 48–57. doi:10.31908/19098367.3702

Sánchez, C., Mota, D. R., Hernández, G., García, J. L., & Tlapa, D. A. (2016). Simulation software as a tool for supply chain analysis and improvement. *Computer Science and Information Systems, 13*(3), 983–998. doi:10.2298/CSIS160803039S

Seethamraju, R. (2006). Enhancing student learning of enterprise integration and business process orientation through an ERP business simulation game. *Journal of Information Systems Education, 22*(1), 19–29.

Shannon, R. E. (1988). *Simulación de sistemas diseño, desarrollo e implementación.* Editorial Trillas.

Shea, T. P., Sherer, P. D., Quilling, R. D., & Blewett, C. N. (2011). Managing global virtual teams across classrooms, students, and faculty. *Journal of Teaching in International Business, 22*(4), 300–313. doi:10.1080/08975930.2011.653911

Tanner, J. R., Stewart, G., Totaro, M. W., & Hargrave, M. (2012). Business simulation games: Effective teaching tools or window dressing? *American Journal of Business Education*, 5(2), 115–128. doi:10.19030/ajbe.v5i2.6814

Tennyson, R. D. (2011). Simulation technologies in global learning. In P. Ordoñez de Pablos, M. Lytras, W. Karwowski, & R. W. Lee (Eds.), *Electronic globalized business and sustainable development through IT management: Strategies and perspectives* (pp. 1–16). Hershey, PA: Business Science Reference. doi:10.4018/978-1-61520-623-0.ch001

Thornton, G. C., & Cleveland, J. N. (1990). Developing managerial talent through simulation. *The American Psychologist*, 45(2), 190–199. doi:10.1037/0003-066X.45.2.190

Tsai, F. H., Yu, K. C., & Hsiao, H. S. (2012). Exploring the factors influencing learning effectiveness in digital game-based learning. *Journal of Educational Technology & Society*, 15(3), 240–250.

Van der Merwe, N. (2013). An evaluation of an integrated case study and business simulation to develop professional skills in South African accountancy students. *International Business & Economics Research Journal*, 12(10), 1137–1155.

Vos, L. (2015). Simulation games in business and marketing education: How educators assess student learning from simulations. *International Journal of Management Education*, 13(1), 57–74. doi:10.1016/j.ijme.2015.01.001

Wawer, M., Milosz, M., Muryjas, P., & Rzemieniak, M. (2010). Business simulation games in forming of students' entrepreneurship. *International Journal of Euro-Mediterranean Studies*, 3(1), 49–71.

Williams, D. (2011). *Impact of business simulation games in enterprise education.* Paper Presented at *2010 University of Huddersfield Annual Learning and Teaching Conference*, University of Huddersfield.

Yang, X., & Yi, Y. (2010). Student learning in business simulation: An empirical investigation. *Journal of Education for Business*, 85(4), 223–228. doi:10.1080/08832320903449469

Zichermann, G., & Cunningham, C. (2011). *Gamification by design: Implementing game mechanics in web and mobile apps.* Sebastopol, CA: O'Reilly Media.

ADDITIONAL READING

Cohen, D. (2006). *The development of play*. East Sussex, UK: Taylor & Francis.

Guy, R. S., & Lownes-Jackson, M. (2015). The use of computer simulation to compare student performance in traditional versus distance learning environments. *Issues in Informing Science and Information Technology, 12*, 95–109. doi:10.28945/2254

Hoover, J. D., & Whitehead, C. J. (1975). An experiential-cognitive methodology in the first course in management: Some preliminary results. *Simulation Games and Experiential Learning in Action, 2*, 25–30.

Jacobs, R., & Baum, M. (1987). Simulation and games in training and development. *Simulation & Games, 18*(3), 385–394. doi:10.1177/104687818701800305

Krathwhol, D. R. (2002). A revision of Bloom's taxonomy: An overview. *Theory into Practice, 41*(4), 212–264. doi:10.120715430421tip4104_2

Ordoñez de Pablos, P., Lytras, M., Karwowski, W., & Lee, R. W. (2011). *Electronic globalized business and sustainable development through IT management: Strategies and perspectives*. Hershey, PA: Business Science Reference. doi:10.4018/978-1-61520-623-0

Springer, C. W., & Borthick, A. F. (2004). Business simulation to stage critical thinking in introductory accounting: Rationale, design, and implementation. *Issues in Accounting Education, 19*(3), 277–303. doi:10.2308/iace.2004.19.3.277

Vlachopoulos, D., & Makri, A. (2017). The effect of games and simulations on higher education: A systematic literature review. *International Journal of Educational Technology in Higher Education, 14*(1), 14–22. doi:10.118641239-017-0062-1

KEY TERMS AND DEFINITIONS

Computer-Based Simulation: The adaptation of simulation models into a digital or web-based platform.

Cumulative Total Shareholder Return (CTSR): The method of measuring a company's performance by dividing its market value into the number of shares at the end and the beginning.

Experiential Learning: A set of academic theories, models, and approaches that keep as fundamental the real-life experience as a mechanism to understand, adapt, and replicate a certain learning objective.

Games: An activity driven by the logics of play where two or more participants compete to reach a specific goal while being framed by a set of rules and challenges.

Gamification: The application of game elements and mechanics in other activities with the purpose of increasing engagement.

Play: A fun, spontaneous, and adaptive activity whereby a subject learns by exploring and experiencing.

Simulation: The modeling of real-world and controlled scenarios where subjects must reach reaching specific goals.

Chapter 6

The Use of Discrete-Event Simulation for Business Education:
Learning by Observing, Simulating and Improving

Marijana Zekić-Sušac
ⓘ https://orcid.org/0000-0001-6322-1917
University of Osijek, Croatia

Adela Has
University of Osijek, Croatia

Marinela Knežević
University of Osijek, Croatia

ABSTRACT

A new teaching approach is presented which integrates observational learning through field teaching of business processes and simulation modeling in order to increase students' learning outcomes and acceptance of computer simulation technology. The teaching method, called LOSI (learning by observing, simulating, and improving), was conducted at a Croatian high education institution. The efficiency of the LOSI approach was investigated by conducting a survey based on the technology acceptance model (TAM). The indicators of ease of use, usefulness, and enjoyment in participating in LOSI were collected along with students' grades and their intention to use this technology in future work and education. The inter-relations among variables were analyzed by statistical tests. The results revealed that students find LOSI easy to use, useful in achieving learning outcomes, and highly enjoyable, while the ease of use and enjoyment is positively associated to usefulness (i.e., learning outcomes).

DOI: 10.4018/978-1-7998-0004-0.ch006

Copyright © 2020, IGI Global. Copying or distributing in print or electronic forms without written permission of IGI Global is prohibited.

INTRODUCTION

Computer simulation modeling is included in university curricula worldwide due to its many benefits. Qian (2016) observes that computer simulations in higher education include three main components: technical affordances, learning opportunities, and learning outcomes. Simulations improve students' analytical thinking ability, problem solving, and creativity (Jadrić et al., 2014). However, using computer simulation tools in business classes can be problematic if the students do not have enough prior knowledge of the business processes they must simulate. This chapter presents a new teaching approach that integrates observational learning through field teaching and simulation tools at a Croatian institution of higher education, to increase students' acceptance of computer-simulation technology and learning outcomes. Called LOSI (Learning by Observing, Simulating, and Improving), the approach was implemented with real business processes. At the beginning of the course, students were taken to field teaching in three different companies where the company managers introduced them to the business processes on site: (1) a natural-gas-distribution company, (2) a food-production factory (bakery products), and (3) a winery. The students were able to see the processes, ask questions, take notes on the process entities, duration, dynamics, and costs, and even try to assist in some processes. After the field teaching, their assignment was to create simulation models of the business processes they had witnessed by using one Arena Simulation tool. In the final stage of the LOSI approach, the students were asked to propose improvements to the business processes they had modeled. At the end of the course, survey was conducted to gather information on students' intentions to use this technology in the future. The chapter provides an overview of previous research in the area of computer-simulation tools and Technology Acceptance Model (TAM) theory used in this research, followed by the methodology description, results, and discussion of benefits and limitations of the suggested teaching method for business schools.

BACKGROUND: THEORY AND PREVIOUS RESEARCH

All simulation models are simplifications of reality (Zeigler, 1976). According to Greasley (2003), simulation provides a way of experimenting with a model of an organizational system in the attempt to understand its behavior under several scenarios. Borshchev and Filippov (2004) defined the simulation model as a set of rules that describe how the system being modeled will change in the future, given its present state. Van der Aalst (2010) described the computer simulations as attempts to imitate real life or hypothetical behavior on a computer, in order to explore how to improve processes or systems and to predict their performance under different circumstances.

Simulation models are based on mathematical models that can be divided into static and dynamic simulation models (Greasley, 2017). Static simulation models are the representation of the system at a certain time, while dynamic simulation models represent system changes over time (Law & Kelton, 1991). The dynamic simulation model can be divided into continuous and discrete simulation model types. In this chapter, the discrete simulation is used to model a system that can be represented by a series of events (Greasley, 2017). According to Law and Kelton (1991), discrete-event simulation refers to modeling of a system as it evolves over time by a representation in which the state variables change instantaneously at separate points in time. Borshchev and Filippov (2004) define discrete-event modeling as the approach based on the concept of entities, resources, and block charts describing entity flow and resource sharing. The basic elements of discrete simulations are entity, event, activity, and process. The main objects of the system are entities that usually represent, for example, people, documents, parts, and machines, and can be permanent or temporary. Entities move through processes, e.g., the blocks of the flowchart (Borshchev & Filippov, 2004). In other words, entities pass through a set of logically related, sequential events. The events represent an instantaneous occurrence that may change the system state at some point in time (Law & Kelton, 1991), while the interaction between entities is represented through activities. Discrete-event simulations are valuable in understanding business processes, providing insight into the processes and a better understanding of the consequences of different operational and strategic decisions, which ultimately lead to better decision making. Analyzing production and service processes, allocation of resources, the optimal number of employees, and reduction of queues are some of the problems to which simulation modeling can be applied (Majić et al., 2015). The development of high computer power and speed contribute to the appearance of a variety of simulation tools and applications. Computer-simulation software is useful as a teaching tool; much research indicates positive relationships between scenario-based simulation games and learning output, effective learning, student satisfaction, perceived usefulness, and intentions to use computer-simulation methods (Chapman & Sorge, 1999; Pasin & Giroux, 2011; Tao et al., 2009; Tiwari et al., 2014).

However, there is a lack of research that deals with discrete-event simulations as a teaching tool and its impact on learning outcomes, and student intentions to use simulation tools. Researchers have mostly focused on the comparison of different discrete-event simulation tools in education (Jadrić et al., 2014; Pereira et al., 2011), rather than on their influence on further usage and usefulness in relation to learning outcomes. Grusec (1992) discusses the benefits of social learning theory suggested by Robert Sears and Albert Bandura (Bandura, 1971) which proves that people learn from one another, via observation, imitation and modeling.

The well-known technology acceptance model (TAM) is a theoretical background suggested by Davis in 1986, and later expanded by several authors (van der Heijden, 2004), extending the theory of reasoned action (TRA) by Ajzen and Fishbein (1980). Several studies prove the efficiency of TAM as a theoretical model for explaining and predicting the intention of users to continue to use a technology or a system (Legris, Ingham, & Collerette, 2003; Park, 2009). The model consists of two basic components proven to influence technology acceptance—perceived ease of use and perceived usefulness—as well as possible external factors that influence those two components. Van der Heijden (2004) suggests an additional component, enjoyment, which was also used in the current research. Figure 1 shows the structure of the TAM model with the added enjoyment factor.

As Figure 1 shows, the survey examined a total of 15 indicators grouped into four latent variables (constructs): perceived ease of use, perceived usefulness, perceived enjoyment, and intention to use. The Methods section describes each indicator and the latent variables. It is important to emphasize that the indicators for ease of use and enjoyment were determined on the basis of validated instruments suggested in previous research (van der Heijden, 2004), while the perceived usefulness was defined

Figure 1. The structure of TAM model used (van der Heijden, 2004, modified)

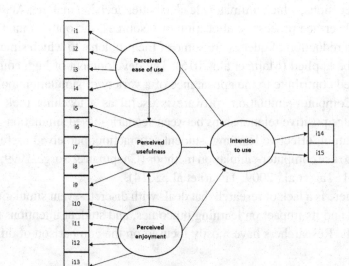

specifically for this research by using the perceived level of learning outcomes for the course as indicators of technology usefulness. Such modification of TAM enables a specific approach to measuring the impact on learning outcomes of a technology and the intention to use the technology in the future.

THE ISSUES AND THE APPROACH

The main issues of teaching methodology observed in previous generations of students that are tackled in this research are: (a) poor student interest in doing simulation modeling of the imaginary processes that they had not observed previously in real life, and (b) a lack of intention to use simulation tools in their future education and work. Therefore, the learning outcomes of the Business Simulations course could not have been satisfactorily realized in the past. In order to overcome these issues, the LOSI approach is suggested based on the observational learning theory (Bandura, 1971; Grusec, 1992) with the addition of simulation learning, while the TAM model is used to test its efficiency.

The following steps of the **LOSI** approach were constructed and implemented with the 2018-2019 class:

Step 1: Preparation phase (preparing students for simulations and field teaching)

Students were theoretically prepared in class on the simulation-modeling topics, and instructed by teachers on how to gather information during field teaching: to take notes on business processes (input entities, resources, duration of processes, dynamics, workflow, output, and costs), to ask questions of practitioners, and to actively participate in some parts of processes (e.g., pushing trolleys of dough from one part of the food-production company facility to another, wine tasting)

Step 2: Field-teaching phase (active observing of real-life processes)

Teachers organized field teaching with companies that were willing to accept a group of students on a guided tour throughout the company, where the hosts were instructed to show and describe their business processes to students (three separate one-day trips organized in three companies in the region).

Step 3: Simulation-modeling phase

Teachers assisted students in computer labs to use the acquired knowledge on business processes to design simulation models using the Arena Simulation tool for discrete-event simulations. Students were divided into four-member teams and each team selected a business process to model. The graphical flowchart was created on the dashboard, the distributions for arrival time of entities and duration of processes were determined, the simulation parameters were set, and the simulation run and the outputs were observed.

Step 4:   Improvements to business processes

After observing simulation results in multiple scenarios (e.g., by changing the distribution functions of arrival time and process duration, changing the number of engaged resources), the students were asked to write down their suggestions for improving business processes that would decrease waiting time, idle time, number of entities in queue, and total cost, as well as increase resource utilization.

Two main research questions were the focus: (1) How does the LOSI approach to field teaching and simulation modeling influence learning outcomes (and student grades)? and (2) How do students accept the field teaching and simulation modeling (LOSI approach) with respect to their intention to use this approach in their future work or study? In order to answer these questions, a survey was conducted at the end of the semester with the cohort of students participating in the course and using the LOSI approach.

METHODS

Teaching business-simulation modeling without understanding business processes often results in a lack of student motivation, low quality of created simulation models, and poor performance of learning outcomes. To increase all of these, the group of 32 students that attended the Business Simulation course at a Croatian higher-education institution were taught using the LOSI teaching method, which integrates field teaching and computer simulation tools to achieve the learning outcomes. After completing the course, the students were asked to fill out a questionnaire that consisted of 16 questions organized in the following way: four questions were related to the ease of use of business-simulation tools with field teaching (LOSI approach); five questions to its usefulness; four questions to enjoyment during use; two questions to intention to use the tools in the future; and the student's final grade. Usefulness is described in this research by the way the students perceive the usefulness of the teaching approach for achieving the four learning outcomes of the course. Each learning outcome was represented by one question (indicators $i5$ to $i9$). The learning outcomes of the course were:

- To adopt basic terms in simulations;
- To describe the basic steps in the simulation-modeling process;
- To choose suitable methods for simulation modeling of a business process;
- To create a simulation model and explain the results;
- To understand how to apply simulation modeling in practice.

The structure of the questionnaire was as follows:

- **i1** - The use of business simulation tools in combination with field teaching was clear and understandable.
  Response: 10-point interval scale: 1 – I completely disagree, 10 – I completely agree.
- **i2** - The use of business simulation tools in combination with field teaching did not require much mental effort.
  Response: 10-point interval scale: 1 – I completely disagree, 10 – I completely agree.
- **i3** – The use of business simulation tools in combination with field teaching was easy to use.
  Response: 10-point interval scale: 1 – I completely disagree, 10 – I completely agree.
- **i4** - With field training and business simulation tools you can easily create a simulation model.
  Response: 10-point interval scale: 1 – I completely disagree, 10 – I completely agree.
- **i5** – With field training and business simulation tools I could better adopt basic terms in simulations.
  Response: 10-point interval scale: 1 – I completely disagree, 10 – I completely agree.
- **i6** – With field training and business simulation tools I could have learned better to describe the basic steps in the simulation modeling process.
  Response: 10-point interval scale: 1 – I completely disagree, 10 – I completely agree.
- **i7** – With field training and business simulation tools I could better choose which methods are suitable for simulation modeling of a business process.
  Response: 10-point interval scale: 1 – I completely disagree, 10 – I completely agree.
- **i8** – With field teaching and business simulation tools I could better learn to create a simulation model and explain the results.
  Response: 10-point interval scale: 1 – I completely disagree, 10 – I completely agree.
- **i9** – With field teaching and business simulation tools I could better understand how to apply simulation modeling in practice.
  Response: 10-point interval scale: 1 – I completely disagree, 10 – I completely agree.
- **i10** – The level of enjoyment while using business simulation tools combined with field teaching (from terrible to enjoyable).

Response: 10-point interval scale: 1 – terrible, 10 – enjoyable.

- **i11** – The level of enjoyment while using business simulation tools combined with field teaching (from monotonous to exciting).
  Response: 10-point interval scale: 1 – monotonous, 10 – exciting.
- **i12** – The level of enjoyment while using business simulation tools combined with field teaching (from uncomfortable to comfortable).
  Response: 10-point interval scale: 1 – uncomfortable, 10 – comfortable.
- **i13** – The level of enjoyment while using business simulation tools combined with field teaching (from boring to interesting).
  Response: 10-point interval scale: 1 – boring, 10 – interesting.
- **i14** – I intend to use business simulation tools combined with gathering knowledge of the field in the near future for practical purposes.
  Response: 10-point interval scale: 1 – I completely disagree, 10 – I completely agree.
- **i15** - I intend to deepen the use of business simulation tools and gathering knowledge of the field in the near future to improve my knowledge and skills.
  Response: 10-point interval scale: 1 – I completely disagree, 10 – I completely agree.
- **Grade** – final grade
  Response: ordinal scale of grades: 1, 2, 3, 4, 5.

Table 1 presents the numerical characteristics of responses. The indicators of the constructs Ease of Use and Enjoyment were designed to follow the research of van der Heijden (2004). All calculations were conducted in R studio software.

The survey was conducted after the end of the winter semester 2018-2019. To generate the results, in addition to descriptive statistics, several statistical tests were performed, such as the Shapiro-Wilk test of normality, Spearman's rank order coefficient as a nonparametric measure of correlation, one-sided test of significance of positive correlation for each pair of variables, one-sided test of significance of negative correlation, and two-sided Mann-Whitney-Wilcoxon test to examine the difference between the two sample medians (Sheskin, 1997). In all tests, the 0.05 level of significance was used. Due to the limitation of sample size, the structural equation modeling (SEM) is not used here, but its use is planned in future research, when new cohorts complete the course and join the survey.

RESULTS

In this chapter the model components and their associations were analyzed, and then the results for each research question were shown.

Table 1. The main numerical characteristics of responses

Question code	Numerical characteristics	Group of questions (construct) and average numerical characteristics of the construct
i1	Min.: 5; 1st Qu.: 8; Median: 9; Mean: 8.69; 3rd Qu.: 10; Max.: 10; St. dev.: 1.47	Ease of use Min.:3.75; 1st Qu.: 7.19; Median: 8.13; Mean: 7.97; 3rd Qu.: 9.06; Max.: 10; St. dev.: 1.47
i2	Min.: 2; 1st Qu.: 6; Median: 7.5; Mean: 7.25; 3rd Qu.: 9; Max.: 10; St. dev.: 2.17	
i3	Min.: 4; 1st Qu.: 6; Median: 8; Mean: 7.78; 3rd Qu.: 9; Max.: 10; St. dev.: 1.79	
i4	Min.: 3; 1st Qu.: 7.75; Median: 8.5; Mean: 8.16; 3rd Qu.: 9.25; Max.: 10;St. dev.: 1.76	
i5	Min.: 1; 1st Qu.: 8; Median: 9; Mean: 8.53; 3rd Qu.: 10; Max.: 10; St. dev.: 2.08	Usefulness Min.: 1.2; 1st Qu.: 7.95; Median: 9; Mean: 8.42; 3rd Qu.: 9.6; Max.: 10; St. dev.: 1.95
i6	Min.: 1; 1st Qu.: 7.75; Median: 9; Mean: 8.38; 3rd Qu.: 10; Max.: 10; St. dev.: 1.95	
i7	Min.: 1; 1st Qu.: 7.75; Median: 9; Mean: 8.03; 3rd Qu.: 9; Max.: 10; St. dev.: 2.08.	
i8	Min.: 1; 1st Qu.: 8; Median: 9; Mean: 8.47; 3rd Qu.: 10; Max.: 10; St. dev.: 1.95	
i9	Min.: 2; 1st Qu.: 8.58; Median: 9.5; Mean: 8.77; 3rd Qu.: 10; Max.: 10;St. dev.: 1.96	
i10	Min.: 2; 1st Qu.: 7; Median: 8;Mean: 8.06; 3rd Qu.: 10; Max.: 10; St. dev.: 1.92	Enjoyment Min.: 2.5; 1st Qu.: 7.38; Median: 8.38; Mean: 8.09; 3rd Qu.: 9.5; Max.: 10; St. dev.: 1.83
i11	Min.: 2; 1st Qu.: 7; Median: 8; Mean: 7.97; 3rd Qu.: 10; Max.: 10; St. dev.: 2.06	
i12	Min.: 3; 1st Qu.: 7.75; Median: 9; Mean: 8.22; 3rd Qu.: 10; Max.: 10; St. dev.: 1.86	
i13	Min.: 3; 1st Qu.: 7; Median: 9; Mean: 8.13; 3rd Qu.: 10; Max.: 10; St. dev.: 1.91	
i14	Min.: 1; 1st Qu.: 3; Median: 4; Mean: 3.75; 3rd Qu.: 4.25; Max.: 5; St. dev.: 1.05	Intention to use in the future Min.: 1.5; 1st Qu.: 3; Median: 4; Mean: 3.7; 3rd Qu.: 4.5; Max.: 5; St. dev.: 0.94
i15	Min.: 1; 1st Qu.: 3; Median: 4; Mean: 3.66; 3rd Qu.: 4; Max.: 5; St. dev.: 0.97	
Grade	Min.: 3; 1st Qu.: 4; Median: 4.69; Mean: 4.39; 3rd Qu.: 5; Max.: 5; St. dev.: 0.72	Grade

Model Components

Components of the used TAM model were the following constructs – perceived ease of use, usefulness, enjoyment and intention to use. Figure 2 shows line plots of average values of each construct variable and of the variable that represents student grades, while Figure 3 shows the boxplots of the same variables.

Figure 2. Line plots of average values of construct variables and student grades

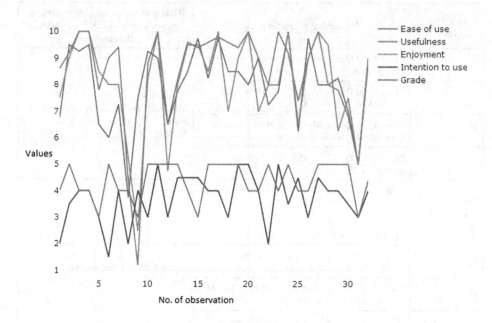

Figure 3. Boxplots of average values of construct variables and student grades

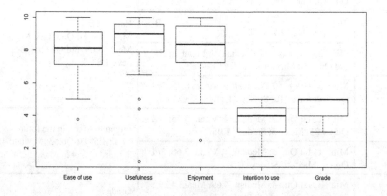

Figure 2 and Figure 3 reveal that the students generally evaluated the ease of use, usefulness, and enjoyment of the teaching approach with high average scores, while their intention to use the approach in the future was evaluated with lower average scores (from 1 to 5). A possible reason for lower scores of students' intention to use the technology in the future could be in the fact that simulation modeling is still rarely used in Croatian companies. The technology is yet to be widely incorporated in business practice, and it will be interesting to observe the results of this survey with future generations of students.

Histograms of relative frequencies and estimated density function presented in Figure 4 imply that assumption of normality is disturbed, while p-values of the Shapiro-Wilk test of normality indicate that the null hypothesis about normality should be rejected for usefulness, enjoyment, intention to use, and grades (see Table 2). Thus, the nonparametric measure of correlation as well as nonparametric statistical tests were used to analyze the relationships among variables.

Due to the absence of normality distribution, Spearman's rank order coefficient (Sheskin, 1997) as a nonparametric measure of correlation was calculated. The one-sided test of significance of positive correlation was conducted for each pair of construct variables except for "intention to use" and "grades," for which the one-sided test of significance of negative correlation was conducted. The used level of significance was 0.05. Values are shown in Table 3.

As Table 3 shows, correlations between ease of use and usefulness, ease of use and enjoyment, usefulness and enjoyment, usefulness and intention to use, as well

Figure 4. Histograms of relative frequencies and estimate of density function

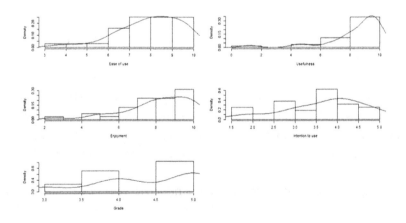

*Table 2. p-values of the Shapiro-Wilk test of normality, * - significant on 0.05 level*

Variable	Ease of use	Usefulness	Enjoyment	Intention to use	Grade
p-value	0.07471	7.201e-06*	0.002262*	0.0168*	7.565e-06*

*Table 3. Spearman's rank order correlation coefficients and p-values of one-sided test of significance, *significant at 0.05 level*

	Ease of use	Usefulness	Enjoyment	Intention to use	Grade
Ease of use	1				
Usefulness	0.58* (p-value = 0.0002391)	1			
Enjoyment	0.67* (p-value = 1.333e-05)	0.76* (p-value = 2.669e-07)	1		
Intention to use	0.29 (p-value = 0.05248)	0.52* (p-value = 0.001045)	0.42* (p-value = 0.007832)	1	
Grade	0.17 (p-value = 0.1635)	0.11 (p-value = 0.2629)	0.15 (p-value = 0.1949)	-0.06 (p-value = 0.3817)	1

as between enjoyment and intention to use are statistically significant, indicating a monotonically increasing relationship between those pairs of variables. In other words, higher ease of use is related to higher enjoyment, while higher enjoyment is related to higher usefulness of the teaching approach used. In addition, the students who assess their enjoyment higher also evaluate higher their intention to use the technology in the future.

Ease of Use and Enjoyment in Relation to the Usefulness

The main focus of this research was to investigate how ease of use and enjoyment are related to the usefulness, i.e., to learning outcomes. The conducted correlation tests show that both ease of use and enjoyment are significantly positively associated with usefulness, an important finding that teachers can use. Furthermore, it is possible to examine whether there is a significant difference between the medians of each pair of the construct variables: usefulness and ease of use, as well as usefulness and enjoyment. For that purpose, the nonparametric two-sided Mann-Whitney-Wilcoxon test (Sheskin, 1997) was conducted and Table 4 shows the results. The null hypothesis about equality of medians was not rejected in both cases, meaning that the median values of the two construct variables (ease of use and enjoyment) are not significantly different from the median values of usefulness.

Table 4. p-values of two-sided Mann-Whitney-Wilcoxon test, *significant at 0.05 level

	Ease of use	Enjoyment
Usefulness	p-value = 0.05362	p-value = 0.3764

Ease of Use, Usefulness and Enjoyment in Relation to the Intention to Use

The second research question was whether students' ease of use, usefulness, and enjoyment of using computer simulation tools combined with gathering knowledge in the field would affect their acceptance of this technology and intention to use it in the future. The results show that usefulness and enjoyment have a significant increased relationship with intention to use. Such findings can be beneficial information for the teachers and motivate them to make more efforts to enable a pleasant experience for students during the course, as well as putting a greater focus on learning outcomes. This is also a guideline for designers of computer-simulation tools to make the tools as interesting and user-friendly as possible, since the enjoyment and ease of use highly influence the perceived usefulness and acceptance of simulation tools.

Figure 2 also makes apparent that although students assigned relatively high values to ease of use, enjoyment, and usefulness, there is still a low intention to use computer-simulation tools in the future. That is also confirmed by the one-sided Mann-Whitney-Wilcoxon test showing that the medians of ease of use, enjoyment, and usefulness are significantly greater than the median of intention to use (see Table 5). Such results emphasize the need to improve the segments of teaching that are positively correlated with students' intention to use the tools in the future.

For a more advanced statistical analysis, a larger sample would be necessary and is planned for future research, after more cohorts of students complete the course using the LOSI method. In that second stage, the methodology of the research could be expanded by using the TAM model in combination with the SEM methodology (Hair et al., 2010) to explain the causal effects among the multiple variables within the model.

Table 5. p-values of one-sided Mann-Whitney-Wilcoxon test, *significant on 0.05 level

	Ease of use	Enjoyment	Usefulness
Intention to use	p-value = 1.968e-11*	p-value = 1.375e-10*	p-value = 6.107e-11*

SOLUTIONS AND RECOMMENDATIONS

The suggested LOSI approach and the subsequent survey that tested its efficiency revealed some important findings. The students positively evaluated their experience with the new teaching method of business-simulation modeling. They enjoyed the course more, it was easy and enjoyable for them to embrace the simulation tools and field teaching, and they found it very useful. It is worth mentioning that this approach is an extension of known theories about observational learning with the addition of a simulation. It coincides with the previous research that there is a positive relationship among ease of use of scenario-based simulation games and its usefulness and enjoyment, and between usefulness and enjoyment with intention to use them in the future. Therefore, the TAM model was an appropriate framework to test the efficiency of the LOSI approach.

Preparation and Field-Teaching Phase

After the preparation phase in which students were introduced to the theory on simulation methodology, the next step was the field teaching to gather knowledge on the real-life business processes.

Simulation-Modeling Phase

As the result of the field-teaching phase, students suggested creating eight simulation models that describe processes in companies visited during field teaching, but which can also, with some modifications, apply to companies with similar economic activities. The discrete-event simulation models that were created at the course included:

- Simulation of the natural-gas-supply application;
- Simulation of the wine-production processes in the winery;
- Simulation of the pizza-production processes in the food-production company;
- Simulation of the cheese-pie-production processes in the food-production company;
- Simulation of sales processes in the food-production company;
- Simulation of the process of solving customer complaints;
- Simulation of the credit-application processes;
- Simulation of the investment-application processes.

In the simulation-modeling phase, the Arena Simulation was used to create discrete-event simulation models of those processes. Students were working in teams of four, first designing a conceptual framework of the simulation model, then creating the model graphical diagram using the Arena Simulation tool, setting up the simulation parameters, running the model, and observing the results. Figure 5 shows one of the simulation diagrams that students created in that phase.

The model in Figure 5 shows that the whole process of applying for natural-gas supply (by a consumer) consists of eight main subprocesses that are mutually connected. The entry block shows a customer who submits an application for gas supply, connected to the process of the initial application screening. If the application is formally correct, the process of determining the location for connecting the customer to the gas-supply pipeline network is performed, followed by the process of selecting an authorized contractor for the pipeline connection. The rest of the processes include field work such as digging, connecting the pipes, controlling the connection (quality assurance), technical approval, and, if the connection is approved, the customer signing the contract with the supplier for natural-gas supply.

The model parameters, such as the dynamic of entities (customers' requests for gas supply) entering the system, the resources (workers, machines, tools) needed for each process, the duration of each process (in minutes or hours or days), the percentage of accepted requests, the percentage of connections that pass the quality-assurance tests, are estimated based on the field trip to the main natural-gas supplier in the region (HEP Plin). After discussing the estimated duration of each subprocess, students used the triangle distribution function to generate the duration time of each subprocess in each iteration of the simulation (with estimated minimum, maximum,

Figure 5. Simulation model diagram for the process of natural gas supply application
Source: Lefler, Kožnjak, Iličić & Ramljak, 2018

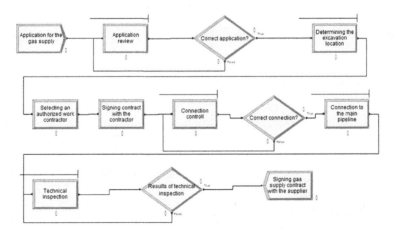

and most likely duration of process based on interviewing the managers during the field teaching). After running the simulation model five times to observe the whole process in a one-month period, reports were generated and students analyzed the results of the simulation. Figure 6 shows a report of the simulation model of a natural-gas-supply application, namely the costs per entity and accumulated cost for the simulated processes.

Students analyzed the reports of the simulation processes by taking into account the following output variables: value-added (VA) time per entity (average, minimum, and maximum), wait time per entity, total time per entity, size of the queue (average, minimum, and maximum number of entities in the queue), the utilization of resources (the percentage of time each resource was busy and idle, respectively), as well as the cost of each process, each resource involved and the total cost.

Figure 6. The report of results of the simulation model of natural gas supply application

Process

Cost per Entity

Total Cost Per Entity	Average	Half Width	Minimum Average	Maximum Average	Minimum Value	Maximum Value
Application review	4.1916	0.07	4.1449	4.2811	2.2095	6.0360
Connection controll	11.7593	0.09	11.6477	11.8427	4.3783	18.4004
Connection to the main pipeline	6.2794	0.06	6.2431	6.3512	4.2935	8.1937
Determining the excavation location	12.4814	0.37	12.1115	12.8853	8.5042	16.3270
Selecting an authorized work contractor	0.00	0.00	0.00	0.00	0.00	0.00
Signing contract with the contractor	0.00	0.00	0.00	0.00	0.00	0.00
Technical inspection	26.1231	0.44	25.5937	26.4684	17.7458	34.6327

Accumulated Cost

Accum VA Cost	Average	Half Width	Minimum Average	Maximum Average
Application review	398.71	104.35	294.62	481.34
Connection controll	1090.52	270.64	789.21	1278.16
Connection to the main pipeline	576.49	148.35	416.14	685.93
Determining the excavation location	1141.80	266.05	850.43	1325.98
Selecting an authorized work contractor	0.00	0.00	0.00	0.00
Signing contract with the contractor	0.00	0.00	0.00	0.00
Technical inspection	2446.68	645.38	1746.30	2907.08

Improvements to Business Processes

After analyzing the results of the simulation, students were asked to suggest improvements by detecting weak points in the simulation process, and to create a different simulation scenario where some improvements in the weak points were made, such as introducing extra workers or machines, technology improvements, some reductions of workers, or organizational changes. For example, the model above shows that the average cost per entity was the largest for the process of technical inspection (26.123). To reduce that cost which mainly refers to the cost of traveling of the technical inspector and his expertise in controlling, students proposed the engagement of technical inspectors that have their business located closer to the location of investors. Also, when the value-added time was analyzed, it was shown that the selection of an authorized contractor was 15.33 hours. The students identified that weak point in the model and proposed a technology improvement—development of a web application that would gather information on all available authorized contractors in the region and enable a quick selection of the available one for the job. Also, the process of determining the location for excavation was found to take a long time (14.32 hours in average). To overcome this problem, students suggested the outsourced engagement of workers who could shorten this process. The new scenario with suggested improvements was run, and the results were observed and compared to the first scenario results. Students were also required to explain the adequacy and justification for such changes in the business process.

In that regard, the improvements-suggestion phase is an important part of the LOSI teaching approach. Benefits emerge for both students and companies that were included in field teaching. This phase enforces students' critical thinking on business processes, creativity, and problem-solving skills. It also brings companies new ideas and technology-supported suggestions for improvements from objective observers. It stimulates companies to use computer simulations to re-estimate their efficiency, to improve productivity, and to decrease costs.

This model is the illustration of various models that students created during that phase of the course. The best student project assignments were selected and sent to the managers of the companies included in the field teaching, and the feedback was very positive. The companies were surprised by the number of suggestions they received from students, and they are willing to continue the collaboration with the institution of higher education in the future. This phase therefore contributes to the process of leading organizations with the help of computer simulations.

FUTURE RESEARCH DIRECTIONS

The LOSI teaching approach discussed in this research shows a way of improving teaching, learning, and leading with computer simulations. The course instructors alone could not provide such deep insight into business processes; their collaboration with business practitioners, however, significantly improved student motivation to use computer-simulation modeling. The LOSI approach has been used so far with one cohort of students. The survey results show that students find the approach highly enjoyable and very useful. Further testing of mutually causal relationships between the construct variables that determine the acceptance of the suggested teaching technology could occur if several future cohorts of students were included in the research, thus enabling the usage of the Structural Equation Modeling (SEM) method, which enables further validation of this approach and its positive effects. In addition, future research will include the investigation of efforts that lead to a higher level of student intention to use the computer-simulation tools in the future, since that is still the weak point of teaching computer simulations in higher-education institutions. Computer-simulation software producers should embrace emerging trends in information technology, such as customization of software, cloud platforms, and Big Data concepts, to increase student intentions to use the tools in their future education and work.

CONCLUSION

The chapter describes a new approach to teaching computer simulations, which includes four components: (1) learning about simulation modeling and computer-simulation tools, (2) observing the business processes through field teaching, (3) simulating business processes using a discrete-event simulation tool, and (4) suggesting improvements for business processes (LOSI approach). The approach was conducted at a business school in a higher education institution in Croatia. Three companies were visited by the instructors and the students, and students were able to actively observe and even try some business processes. As the project assignment of the course, students designed simulation models, estimated the parameters, ran the simulation and analyzed the results, in terms of value-added time, wait time, the size of the queues, utilization of resources, and costs. As the last step, students suggested improvements to business processes and tested them in different simulation scenarios. The suggestions and the simulation models were sent to companies involved, and the collaboration was mutually beneficial. A survey conducted on the first cohort of students, based on the Technology Acceptance Model (TAM), showed that students find such teaching technology easy to use, useful in achieving their learning outcomes, and highly enjoyable. According to research results, students perceive that the usage of computer-simulation tools in combination with field teaching improves learning outcomes of the course, such as the adoption of basic terms in simulations, describing the basic steps in the simulation-modeling process, choosing the appropriate methods for simulation modeling of a business process, creating a simulation model and explaining the results, and understanding how to apply simulation modeling in practice, were highly rated by the students. In addition, it was found that the ease of use and enjoyment is positively associated with usefulness; therefore, the efforts in making computer-simulation software easy to use and fun contributes to their learning outcomes. The results reveal that students embrace the suggested teaching approach of integrating computer simulations with field teaching, while their suggestions for improving business processes indicate that this approach can help make them better managers and leaders in the future.

ACKNOWLEDGMENT

This research was supported by the Croatian Science Foundation [grant number IP-2016-06-8350].

REFERENCES

Ajzen, I., & Fishbein, M. (1980). *Understanding attitudes and predicting social behavior*. Englewood Cliffs, NJ: Prentice-Hall.

Borshchev, A., & Filippov, A. (2004, July). *From system dynamics and discrete event to practical agent based modeling: reasons, techniques, tools*. Retrieved from https://www.systemdynamics.org/assets/conferences/2004/SDS_2004/PAPERS/381BORSH.pdf

Chapman, K. J., & Sorge, C. L. (1999). Can a simulation help achieve course objectives? An exploratory study investigating differences among instructional tools. *Journal of Education for Business, 74*(4), 225–230. doi:10.1080/08832329909601689

Greasley, A. (2017). *Simulation modelling for business*. London, UK: Routledge. doi:10.4324/9781315243085

Grusec, J. E. (1992). Social learning theory and developmental psychology: The legacies of Robert Sears and Albert Bandura. *Developmental Psychology, 28*(5), 776–786. doi:10.1037/0012-1649.28.5.776

Hair, J. F., Black, W. C., Babin, B. J., & Anderson, R. E. (2010). *Multivariate data analysis*. Englewood Cliffs, NJ: Prentice-Hall.

Jadrić, M., Ćukušić, M., & Bralić, A. (2014). Comparison of discrete event simulation tools in an academic environment. *Croatian Operational Research Review, 5*(2), 203–219. doi:10.17535/crorr.2014.0008

Law, A. M., Kelton, W. D., & Kelton, W. D. (1991). *Simulation modeling and analysis* (Vol. 2). New York, NY: McGraw-Hill.

Lefler, V., Kožnjak, T., Iličić, M., & Ramljak, H. (2018). *Simulacija poslovnog procesa uvođenja plinskog priključka u poduzeću Plin Vtc (Unpublished seminar)*. Osijek: Faculty of Economics in Osijek.

Legris, P., Ingham, J., & Collerette, P. (2003). Why do people use information technology? A critical review of the technology acceptance model. *Information & Management, 40*(3), 191–204. doi:10.1016/S0378-7206(01)00143-4

Majić, A., Has, A., & Zekić-Sušac, M. (2015). Discrete-event simulation model of customer support service in telecommunications. *Proceedings of the 13th International Symposium on Operational Research SOR'15 in Slovenia*, 514-519.

Park, S. Y. (2009). An analysis of the technology acceptance model in understanding university students' behavioral intention to use e-learning. *Journal of Educational Technology & Society, 12*(3), 150–162.

Pasin, F., & Giroux, H. (2011). The impact of a simulation game on operations management education. *Computers & Education, 57*(1), 1240–1254. doi:10.1016/j.compedu.2010.12.006

Pereira, G., Dias, L., Vik, P., & Oliveira, J. A. (2011). Discrete simulation tools ranking: A commercial software packages comparison based on popularity. *International Journal of Production Economics, 111*, 229–243.

Qian, Y. (2016). Computer simulations in higher education: Affordances, opportunities and outcomes. In P. Vu, S. Fredrickson, & C. Moore (Eds.), *Handbook of research on innovative pedagogies and technologies for online learning in higher education* (pp. 236–262). Hershey, PA: IGI Global.

Sheskin, D. J. (1997). *Handbook of Parametric and Nonparametric Statistical Procedures.* Washington, DC: CRC Press.

Tao, Y. H., & Cheng, C. J., & Sun, S.Y. (2012). Alignment of teacher and student perceptions on the continued use of business simulation games. *Journal of Educational Technology & Society*, *15*(3), 177–189.

Tao, Y. H., Cheng, C. J., & Sun, S. Y. (2009). What influences college students to continue using business simulation games? The Taiwan experience. *Computers & Education*, *53*(3), 929–939. doi:10.1016/j.compedu.2009.05.009

Tiwari, S. R., Nafees, L., & Krishnan, O. (2014). Simulation as a pedagogical tool: Measurement of impact on perceived effective learning. *International Journal of Management Education*, *12*(3), 260–270. doi:10.1016/j.ijme.2014.06.006

van der Aalst, W. M. (2010). Business process simulation revisited. *Enterprise and Organizational Modeling and Simulation*, 1-14.

van der Heijden, H. (2004). User acceptance of hedonic information systems. *Management Information Systems Quarterly*, *28*(4), 695–704. doi:10.2307/25148660

Zeigler, B. P., Praehofer, H., & Kim, T. G. (1976). *Theory of modelling and simulation* (Vol. 7). New York, NY: Wiley.

ADDITIONAL READING

Balog, A., & Pribeanu, C. (2018). An extended acceptance model for augmented reality educational applications. In M. Khosrow-Pour (Ed.), *Virtual and augmented reality: Concepts, methodologies, tools, and applications* (pp. 424–441). Hershey, PA: IGI Global. doi:10.4018/978-1-5225-5469-1.ch020

Burkle, M., & Magee, M. (2018). Virtual learning: Videogames and virtual reality in education. In M. Khosrow-Pour (Ed.), *Virtual and augmented reality: Concepts, methodologies, tools, and applications* (pp. 1067–1087). Hershey, PA: IGI Global. doi:10.4018/978-1-5225-5469-1.ch050

Fregola, C. (2011). Simulation games and emotive, affective and social issues. In C. Fregola (Ed.), *Simulation and gaming for mathematical education: Epistemology and teaching strategies* (pp. 57–64). Hershey, PA: IGI Global. doi:10.4018/978-1-60566-930-4.ch005

Martens, A. (2011). Simulation in teaching and training. In M. Khosrow-Pour (Ed.), *Gaming and simulations: Concepts, methodologies, tools and applications* (pp. 248–255). Hershey, PA: IGI Global. doi:10.4018/978-1-60960-195-9.ch115

Piu, A. (2011). Simulation games for the learning and teaching of mathematics. In C. Fregola (Ed.), *Simulation and gaming for mathematicel Education: Epistemology and teaching strategies* (pp. 47–56). Hershey, PA: IGI Global. doi:10.4018/978-1-60566-930-4.ch004

KEY TERMS AND DEFINITIONS

Business Process: A set of linked activities and tasks that aim to accomplish an organizational goal, such as the delivery of a product or service to a client. It can be modeled as a flowchart of a sequence of activities with interleaving decision points or as a process matrix of a sequence of activities with relevance rules based on data in the process.

Computer: Simulation: A way of experimenting with a model of an organizational system in the attempt to understand its behavior under several scenarios using computer.

Discrete-Event Simulation: Modeling of a system as it evolves over time by a representation in which the state variables change instantaneously at separate points in time.

Field Teaching: Teaching students outside of the classroom, typically as field trips to a company or other institution where students can observe and experience real processes with the aim to enhance their understanding and confidence.

LOSI Approach: Learning by observing, simulating, and improving—a teaching approach that integrates observational learning through field teaching and simulation tools in order to increase students' acceptance of computer-simulation technology and learning outcomes.

Simulation Model: A set of rules that describe how the system being modeled will change in the future, given its present state.

Chapter 7

Designing a Minecraft Simulation Game for Learning a Language Through Knowledge Co-Construction

Joeun Baek
Boise State University, USA

Hyekyeong Park
Sancheong Middle School, South Korea

Ellen Min
Timberline High School, USA

ABSTRACT

The purpose of this chapter is to design a Minecraft simulation game where players can learn a language by communicating and negotiating meaning with other players. To achieve this, Gagné's events of instruction and Schmitt's strategic experience modules were adopted as a theoretical lens for simulation building. After the simulation game was designed, it was implemented to test its feasibility. The result shows that the simulation game has both the intended features of knowledge co-construction and the negotiation of meaning, as well as enjoyment of the game. The test result, however, also suggests that the simulation game needs more conditionals and loops in order for players to repeat their simulation game at any place and time.

DOI: 10.4018/978-1-7998-0004-0.ch007

Copyright © 2020, IGI Global. Copying or distributing in print or electronic forms without written permission of IGI Global is prohibited.

INTRODUCTION

Minecraft is no longer a new tool in game-based learning. Teachers have been experimenting with different ways to use it in the classroom for some time. Some teachers use it to teach mathematic concepts like ratios and proportions, to experiment with science phenomena, and to experience cultural differences in society, while others adopt it to support student creativity and collaboration. Minecraft also can be integrated indirectly to stimulate creativity, imagination, and collaboration in learning languages. For example, Marcon (2013) used Minecraft to get students to describe in writing the unique features of their characters. Uusi-Mäkelä (2014) included it for students write journal entries during game play, while Lorence (2015) had students write in-game books that could be loaned out to one another. As noted by Kuhn and Stevens (2017), Minecraft seems to be an ideal fit for language learning.

This chapter aims to show how one might design a Minecraft simulation where players can communicate and negotiate meaning during game play, as well as construct knowledge with other players. Additionally, the chapter will explore how to boost students' interests in learning a language through simulation game features, and essential expressions are introduced to help students become more fluent in everyday conversations. In Minecraft there are four real-life based themes that players experience through the simulation game play: Landmarks in the World, Having Fun in an Amusement Park, Attending a Party at a Friend's House, and Designing a Share House. While playing the simulation game and completing the various quests, players are encouraged to negotiate unfamiliar words or phrases and co-construct new knowledge by carrying out their individual or collaborative tasks. Since the four themes in the simulation game are related to real-life situations that players may have experience with, the players are led to learn essential expressions in natural and motivating ways. In order to meet the objectives of using Minecraft as described in this chapter, various learning theories related to role playing, and research on Minecraft use in the classroom, are explored. Gagné's (1992) instructional design model and Schmitt's (1999) Strategic Experience Modules are reviewed as the basis for building the simulation. After the simulation was designed, it was implemented to test its feasibility. Many non-English speakers have difficulty in learning English since they learn the language as an academic object rather than a communication tool. Moreover, they are often taught English expressions in fragmented and decontextualized ways. As a result, even though non-native English speakers may experience years and years of English education, they can be afraid of having conversations in English. The contribution of this simulation game in conjunction with language classes is to help language learners recognize English as a communication tool, acquire essential English expressions meaningfully and holistically in context, and apply what they have learned outside of the classroom by communicating fluently with other English speakers.

REVIEW OF RELATED LITERATURE

In this section, the basis for the main topic of this study, co-construction of knowledge, will be briefly introduced before looking at its theoretical background in the next section. First, a brief definition of co-construction of knowledge will be discussed and followed by how game play interactions are beneficial for learning in general or learning languages in particular. Then, how the features of knowledge co-construction are implemented within a designed Minecraft simulation game will be described.

Co-Construction of Knowledge in Language Learning

With a constant flood of information, it is impossible for people to store huge amounts of information in memory without some of it becoming meaningless. As a result, society does not look for polymaths, but rather for people who can create new information by sharing and understanding pre-existing knowledge through collaborative interaction. Co-construction of knowledge, which is the essential part of this information trend, can be defined in a variety of ways, as there are various common characteristics among the myriad of definition. Roschelle (1992) describes the co-construction of knowledge as the process people use to arrive at a shared meaning and description. This definition is theoretically supported by Ludvigsen (2009), who maintains that individuals make new meanings by employing or organizing their existing knowledge through actions and social interaction. This means that knowledge is newly formed when learners are interdependent and interact with each other during learning process (Säljö, 2010). To explain how co-construction of knowledge can be activated in learning activities, Vygotsky defined the Zone of Proximal Development as "the distance between the actual developmental level as determined by independent problem solving and the level of potential development as determined through problem solving under adult guidance or in collaboration with more capable peers" (Vygotsky, 1978, p. 86) to explain how co-construction of knowledge can be activated in learning activities. Tudge (1990) explains that this interaction with more competent peers can lead to highly effective cognitive development. The co-construction of knowledge can also encourage fostering added value, such as, the diverse perspectives that individuals can bring to a group process (Dillenbourge, 1999; Donato, 2004). Since learner interaction also occurs through revision and feedback, language learners can identify the strengths and weakness in their own language production, which results in language skill development (Dippold, 2009). Moreover, when collaborative activities are combined with games, they can improve learners' participation in learning activities and social skills (Fenstermacher, Olympia, & Sheridan, 2006).

The designed Minecraft simulation games basically motivate students to collaborate with each other through quests which are challenging or too difficult to complete alone. When players engage in the theme "The Landmarks in the World," they need to understand the information associated with each landmark in order to progressively take quizzes. The amount of information to memorize for each quiz might be overwhelming for one student, however, so students are asked to keep one piece of information in mind. Later, when students take quizzes collaboratively to complete the game quest, they share what they have memorized together in order to finish the game quiz. Additionally, learners in the game are encouraged to share their own understanding of the theme to complete the given quests successfully. For instance, in the beginning of the game "Designing a Share House," players enter a big empty room to figure out which materials they can use for decoration. Players will discuss the various items and determine which items they can utilize appropriately and share good items with other players so that they can build a better share house as a group.

Learning by Role-Playing in Minecraft

In this section, a sense of role playing will be briefly introduced, followed by features of the technique. Next, how role-playing produces positive effect on language learning and how the designed Minecraft simulation game has implemented features of role-playing (and its expected results in language learning) will be explained. Then the chapter will conclude with the use of Minecraft simulation games in classrooms and the role that teachers should have in mind.

Learning by Role-Playing

Although role playing as a learning strategy has been actively utilized in language learning classrooms, the application of massive multiplayer online role-playing games (MMORPGs) is controversial since many people are quick to think of the negative influence of games on learning rather than advantageous ones. Role playing in language learning basically has learners take the role of a particular person or character and act it out as if they were the real person or character. As Liu and Ding (2009) insist, role playing has many positive effects, especially on language learning, since the technique can animate the learning atmosphere and foster interest in learning the language and making its acquisition impressive. Dorathy and Mahalakshmi (2011) explain that role-playing does not only help learners deal with real-life situations and the use of daily expressions, but it also encourages learners to work together in order to understand each other. Furthermore, since role-playing can be organized around a particular student interest or need, the technique increases learner responsibility in learning and motivation. MMORPGs, which are the combination of role-playing and games, help learners participate in language learning in a meaningful way. As Peterson (2010) suggests, the features of MMORPGs have potential advantages in second language learning. For example, Role Playing Simulation games are able to provide network-based real-time text and voice chat. These functions help learners experience multiple communication channels with real-time feedback on the target language. Moreover, these functions facilitate learner-centered interactions, encourage active game participation, and enhance cross-cultural knowledge. Since simulation games give learners the chance to represent themselves with personal avatars, learners are likely to take more risks and have reduced inhibition regarding language use because they regard the avatar as a separate identity from their own in reality.

The designed simulation Minecraft game also contains not only the features of MMORPGs but has comparable effects on language learning as do other MMORPGs. Since Minecraft provides a real-time chatting function, players can communicate with each other to figure out the meaning of novel expressions. Furthermore, when players' breakdowns in communication occur while playing the simulation game, players can provide immediate feedback on language errors. Consequently, players not only learn new language items throughout the course of the game, but also have the chance to develop their English accuracy skills based on the linguistic feedback. Players can play the simulation game with minimal teacher instruction and are ultimately led to learner-centered interactions and active participation in the simulation game.

Minecraft in the Classrooms and Teachers' Role

Teachers have already been using Minecraft in a variety of subject areas. Students have created objects or built maps in Minecraft and kept journals about math and writing (Herold, 2015; Uusi-Mäkelä, 2014). Karsenti, Bugmann, and Gros (2017) observed social skill development, and Balnaves (2018) used Minecraft to build a world for students to play with that enabled global participation and increased intercultural competencies. Educators who have integrated Minecraft in their lessons have found successful results. Teachers have noticed that students were more motivated to do work and developed communicative and social skills (Petrov, 2014). Another key point to mention about Minecraft is that students were often engaged in unexpected ways. Aside from increased rates of assignment completion, for example, students who normally did not actively take a leading role in class were able to act as leaders within the game (Hulstrand, 2015). One main factor in ensuring the helpfulness of Minecraft is peer-to-peer collaboration, as more experienced gamers can use their skills to enable a smoother integration of the simulation game with all students (Hewett, 2016). However, varying levels of student experience—which, understandably, may be a point of concern—did not detract from learning. Players who were beginners at the simulation game, with some instruction, could follow along with the lesson relatively well (Callaghan, 2016).

Possible concerns, such as issues of time management or distractions, had little impact in a study of 168 middle school students. Students completed their objectives and tasks on time (Callaghan, 2016). Interestingly, one study noted that less content may be better in Minecraft; too much information can be overwhelming. It could be more effective to present a narrow range of topics but delve into the material more deeply (Steinbeiß, 2017). Although Minecraft facilitates more self-regulation and student-driven learning, the guiding role of the teacher should not be overlooked. That is, teachers' roles are ever more important in such an environment. Teachers are the main guiding figure in Minecraft learning, and players are eager to complete their tasks and show results to their teachers (Callaghan, 2016).

Not only are teachers paramount in enabling an effective use of the simulation game in learning, they are also crucial in getting such a program started in their classrooms. For maximum success, teachers should be fully supportive of the idea, and their teaching styles should be compatible with a student-centered approach (Petrov, 2014). Teachers should also be familiar with the simulation game and with knowledge of how social interactions and spaces within the simulation game function. However, many teachers are reluctant to use Minecraft in their curriculum, and part of this may stem from the gap between students' and teachers' video simulation game literacies (Kuhn, 2017). Many teachers have started projects to help bridge this gap. One group of teachers made an online space called TESOL (Teaching English to Speakers of Other Languages) EVO (Electronic Village Online), and another developed a 5-week MOOC (Massive Online Open Course) to help teachers become familiar with the simulation game (Kuhn, 2017).

Minecraft is viewed as an effective tool in multiple learning circumstances. It upholds principles crucial to effective learning by providing motivation, improving social and communication skills, and encouraging critical and creative thinking. Further research on how Minecraft benefits players, as well as on how to make it more suitable to teachers and learners, is promising.

Lessons from Minecraft Studies

The use of Minecraft in classroom environments has been explored in a variety of studies. Researchers have suggested various ways to integrate the game into curriculum, have offered insight into some of the benefits and drawbacks of doing so, and have proposed additional potential applications (Callaghan, 2016; Kuhn, 2017; Mail, 2015; Petrov, 2014; Steinbeiß, 2017). This research lends evidence to the theory that Minecraft is meaningfully contributive to language acquisition within real life situations.

Beneficial Qualities for Learning

Studies illustrate that teachers who play Minecraft generally view it as being a useful learning platform (Mail, 2015). Considering the unique advantages of Minecraft, it is not difficult to see why. Minecraft possesses the five principles that should be included in game-based learning: intrinsic motivation, learning through enjoyment and fun, authenticity, self-reliance and autonomy, and experiential learning (Petrov, 2014). Through these characteristics, Minecraft allows students to have a sense of control, provides motivation for success, and sets clear boundaries while simultaneously allowing exploration and creative thinking (Callaghan, 2016). Additionally, video games model real-life experiences instead of simply providing written or visual descriptions of them, which makes for a more hands-on approach than traditional classroom tools such as textbooks and worksheets (Bogost, 2011). Experiential learning meshes especially well with the "open and fluid nature of language learning"—in fact, Minecraft appears to be an "ideal fit for language learning" (Kuhn & Stevens 2017).

Minecraft, as a learning platform, is ultimately a blend of many conditions and/or characteristics that are necessary for proper learning, including entertainment, social skills, and creativity. Together, they make Minecraft an apt game to use in the classroom (Petrov, 2014).

Suggested Ways to Successfully Introduce Minecraft into Curricula

One way of introducing Minecraft to aid learning is to prompt where students play the game normally but with intermittent interruptions during which they must answer questions correctly to continue. Another way is to utilize in-game quests where tasks are given and accomplished within the Minecraft world (Mail, 2015).

Prompting can be used in a fashion similar to flashcards which is most effective for asking trivia or relatively simple questions in order to practice knowledge recall, whereas in-game quests provide a more interactive, embedded approach to game-based learning (Mail, 2015).

Minecraft also has two modes of play to choose from: creative mode, which gives the player unlimited material and no danger of dying within the game, or survival mode, in which the player must gather material and defend themselves against possible threats in the game. Within the game, numerous "Modes" - or add-ons to the standard version of Minecraft - can be used to change the game as needed in terms of rules, content, design, or to fit to teachers' individual needs (Steinbeg, 2017). Furthermore, Minecraft allows educators to quickly and effectively design, modify, create, or delete experiments, and its capacity to have multiplayer modes and individual servers make it easy to collaborate and share content among teachers (Nebel et al, 2016). As we can see from the variety of ways that Minecraft can be implemented in educational programs, it is a flexible simulation game that can adapt to fit many different subjects and classes.

DESIGN METHODS

How the activities of gaming in Minecraft could be arranged for language learning is a question of identifying, selecting, arranging, and sequencing learning experiences for players. Gagné, Briggs, and Wager (1992) provide a robust framework for designing learning events and Bernd Schmitt's (1999) Strategic Experience Modules (SEMs) are good guidelines for players to have an optimal learning experience when playing Minecraft. Below are explanations of how the target simulation game follows their ideas and suggestions.

The Implementation of Gagné's Nine Events of Instruction

How Minecraft gaming activities can be arranged for language learning is a question of identifying, selecting, arranging, and sequencing the learning experience for players. Gagné, Briggs, and Wager (1992) provide a framework for designing learning. They developed a framework of nine general events that should take place during learning. This process is called Gagné's 9 Events of Instruction. The first event is gaining the attention of players with a stimulus that engages their minds. A good way to accomplish this is to present something that piques the players' curiosity such as a thought-provoking question. The second is informing players of the objectives. This gives players the motivation to learn by setting the level of expectations. The third is stimulating recall of prior learning. Players can then build upon their prior knowledge with the new material. The fourth is presenting the content. It is important to deliver the information in organized chunks through explanations and demonstrations using a variety of modes of media, such as combination of videos, texts, and images. The fifth is providing learning guidance through additional examples and other supportive materials. The sixth is eliciting performance or practicing. By practicing the new skill, learners solidify their understanding of the material and are more likely to retain the knowledge. The seventh is providing feedback. Players should receive immediate and specific feedback, but at this stage, the feedback should not be used to formally score the players. The eighth event is assessing performance. Players are given a final test or assessment, which should be completed without any help from the instructor. Mastery is generally considered to be achieved when the student gets 80% to 90% of the questions correct. The ninth, and final, event of the process is enhancing retention and transferring skills and learning for future application. Repetition and rephrasing of concepts are examples of content retention strategies.

To Gain Attention and Inform Objectives

In the amusement park, a Non-Playable Character (NPC) asks players a question, "Have you ever been to an amusement park?" Since most players are curious enough to visit the amusement park, this question not only helps players pay attention to the simulation game but also makes them more curious about the day's activities. The NPC introduces players to what they are going to do in the simulation game after getting their attention with the question "Have you ever been to an amusement park?" For example, the NPC says, "Today, you guys will have a great time in an amusement park going on fun rides, having food, and looking around the zoo." Through this interaction, players can understand what tasks they are required to do and how they are going to complete the objectives.

To Stimulate Recall of Prior Learning

In a friendly party, stimulating recall of prior learning naturally occurs when players are informed about the daily objectives. When players visit a friend's house, they can recall their personal experience of the same situation. This helps players understand the new information that they are gaining by relating the information to their own pre-existing knowledge.

To Present Contents and Provide Learning Guidance

In the Landmarks theme, players visit various famous places in the world. In each location, players will meet an NPC tour guide. The tour guide briefly explains where the landmark is and what additional information players should find out. After the briefing, players will figure out what to do to complete the quest based on some ideas from the NPC in terms of effective strategies for the simulation game. Guidance is offered to players such as following signs to get the required information easily. For instance, when players look around to gather information in Machu Picchu, they can find signs on the ground. Following the signs, players can easily get to other spots where they can find out more information about the landmark. Additionally, players can get some help if they do not understand some aspect of the landmark. All these devices provide instructional support for players' needs.

To Elicit Performance

In the Landmarks theme, activities are designed for players to look around and gather several pieces of information related to the landmark. By moving around the environment and reading information presented in signs, players can not only understand the landmark better, but they can also internalize new English expressions during the activities.

In the Share House theme, players' performance is elicited by letting them discuss how to decorate the house and delegate who decorates which parts. While discussing the design of the house and assigning a role to each player, players can internalize knowledge or English expressions related to the specific situation.

To Provide Feedback

In the Amusement Park theme, many chances are presented to players to communicate using the target language (English), and it also provides players with appropriate feedback regarding their activities and language use. For instance, players converse in English with the cashier when ordering some food to eat. While ordering food, players might experience a communication breakdown. In this case, through meaning negotiation or with the help of other players' linguistic feedback, players can successfully order the food they would love to have. This enables players to not only respond to the given request, but also improve their language skills through peer feedback.

To Assess Performance

Quiz stages are provided at landmarks in order to provide feedback and access players' performance. For example, after looking around Machu Picchu, players are led to a maze. There, they need to take quizzes related to Machu Picchu. With the quizzes, players can self-assess their understanding of Machu Picchu, and teachers can assess players' performance through their quiz scores.

Design for Players' Strategic Experience

Schmitt (1999) proposes five different types of strategic experience modules (SEMs) for learners. These modules can yield new insight into how to design learning experiences for game players.

The first type of experience is "Sense" the product (or game in this context) engages one or more of the customer's five senses: sight, sound, scent, taste, and touch. The second is "Feel": the product or service should elicit positive feelings from the customer in order to be successful. The third is "Think". Marketers should encourage customers to think creatively, which could potentially lead to a shift of their opinions on the company or product. The fourth is "Act". The marketing encourages customers to change their behaviors to incorporate the product in their daily lives. The fifth is "Relate," which allows customers to feel connected to a certain message presented in the company's marketing.

Experiential marketing is a methodology and concept that moves beyond the traditional ''features-and-benefits'' marketing. Experiential marketing connects consumers with brands in personally relevant and memorable ways. Schmitt (1999) proposed the strategic experiential modules (SEMs) as the assessment items of customer experience (Sheu, Su, & Chu, 2009).

Managers can use the different SEMs to create different types of customers. The term module has been borrowed from research in cognitive science and the philosophy of mind, referring to circumscribed functional domains of the mind. Modules have distinct structures and functions. The experiential modules in experiential marketing include sensory experiences, affective experiences, creative cognitive experiences, physical experiences, behaviors, and lifestyles, and social-identity experiences that result from relating to a reference group or culture. Each SEM has its own objectives, internal structure, and principles (Schmitt, 2015).

To create different experiences and achieve marketing goals, Schmitt proposed five Strategic Experiential Modules (SEMs): sensory experiences (Sense), feel experience (Feel), think experience (Think), act experience (Act), and relate experience (Relate). The definitions of strategic experiential modules are described as follows:

Module of Sense Experience (Sense)

This type of experience primarily derives from the five senses (sight, hearing, smell, taste, and touch). These senses can be exploited to affect the behavior of the customer. For example, pleasant music or delicious food elevates the value of an experience or product as perceived by the customer, increasing their interest in, and knowledge/usage of the product or service (Schmitt, 2012).

In the Minecraft theme "The Landmarks in the World," we constructed some iconic structures such as the Eiffel Tower and the Sphinx. We closely recreated the designs in order to provide student players with a sense experience. As a result, students can see a Minecraft version of the landmarks that resembles the original's distinctive features. These visual simulations make students feel more excited within the game, which can lead to higher motivation in learning during game play. In the map of "Attending a Party at a Friend's House," the game provides sensory inputs through various scenes in the game. Student players in the simulation game experience a variety of situations related to their daily lives. For instance, students visit a supermarket to buy some groceries for a party. Students will look for many items they need and can easily find in the supermarket, and these visual cues enhance students' motivation on the game. In "Designing a Share House," to enable a visually stimulating sense experience, the game begins in front of a share house that students need to decorate. The exterior of the building is decorative, and the elaborate exterior can make students feel excited since they will soon go inside the house. Moreover, since the exterior of the building is visually appealing, students will be motivated to decorate the interior in a commensurate fashion. In this way, the simulation game provides students with visual cues that enhance students' motivations to both play the game and learn. Lastly, in the theme "Having Fun in an Amusement Park," student players can experience many types of senses while playing the game. For instance, students can find rides similar to the actual rides in an amusement park such as roller coaster or merry-go-round. In addition to inspiring visual scenes, the game stimulates players with background music fitting to each activity. Through these visual and auditory cues, students will feel a great satisfaction in the game.

Module of Feel Experience (Feel)

This type of experience primarily stimulates the inner feelings and emotions of the customer. The presentation of experiential text, music, and images establishes a strong connection between customers and service/product providers, causing customers to resonate with the brand or product and have positive emotional responses (Kim & Perdue 2013).

In the map of the Minecraft game "The Landmarks in the World," the simulation game makes students feel satisfied by providing indirect experiences of visiting famous landmarks throughout the world.

Since the representations of the landmarks in the game are quite similar to the real structures, students will feel like they are traveling around the world. This exciting experience not only makes students motivated to learn, but also helps with a longer retention of language items used in the game. In "Attending a Party at a Friend's House," the game helps students feel satisfied by giving them several quests to complete. Before reaching the party host's house, students need to complete some tasks such as borrowing a DVD to watch and buying some food at a supermarket. When students reach the friend's house after the tasks are complete, the sense of achievement gives student players satisfaction in addition to confidence regarding their English skills. In the theme "Designing a Share House," the simulation game helps students experience happiness by letting them decorate the house based on their own preferences. After decorating the living room together, each student is given their own room to decorate individually. Since students can think about the interior of their own room and realize it by themselves, this will give them high satisfaction within the game and learning English through the game. In 'Having Fun in an Amusement Park', to provoke student players' inner feelings and emotions, the game offers students many opportunities to decide by themselves through discussion. For instance, in the beginning of the game students can negotiate which rides to go on, and after taking 3 rides, they will decide what to eat for lunch. Since students have many chances to employ their autonomy within the simulation game, their satisfaction and motivation on learning will be more advanced.

Module of Think Experience (Think)

Think experiences appeal to the intellect-oriented brand positioning and focus on action at awareness and knowledge level of consumer response by taking into account personal experiences, which help people connect with a brand and to make intelligent and informed purchasing decisions (Kailani & Ciobotar, 2015).

In the theme "The Landmarks in the World," to appeal to student players' intelligence, we have students take quizzes at the end of some landmarks such as the Sphinx and Machu Picchu. For example, after student players look around the Sphinx and collect information related to the place, students need to solve a riddle to move on to other landmarks. Since the riddle provides students with a slight intellectual challenge, students will feel intellectual satisfaction after solving it. In the theme "Attending a Party at a Friend's House," the game provides students with an intellectual challenge by letting them find the party host's house using spatial clues. For instance, student players get direction to the house from an NPC through dialogues. "Once you are out of the supermarket, you could find the bank. Keep walking straight ahead for 3 blocks. After you pass the library you have to turn left."

Using the clues students have to find the various locations, such as the library, and finally the party host's house. Therefore, this serves as an intellectual challenge for students furthering their satisfaction.

In "Designing a Share House," the map itself motivates players by letting them complete the tasks in their own creative ways. For instance, when students are to decorate the living room, they are given some conditions they need to carry on such as making a big screen to watch movies, a sofa to rest on, and a refrigerator to store food. Since the student roles and means of achieving these tasks are not directed, student players should think hard to complete the tasks, resulting in students' sense of achievement after finishing the work.

Module of Act Experience (Act)

This type of experience integrates numerous behavioral options, such as physical activities, living patterns, and interaction. Behavioral activities in the daily lives of a user leave a lasting impression or become a subconscious direct response (Chen & Lin, 2014).

We implemented "Module of Act Experience" in our Minecraft game as follows. In the map of "The Landmarks in the World," the game induces students' action by giving them quests to complete. Whenever students visit a landmark, they need to collect five pieces of information related to the place. That means, students are not passively given the information, but rather they must actively find it by moving around the virtual world. These activities help students learn better the information and related language expressions used in the simulation game, resulting in a more meaningful game and learning.

In "Designing a Share House," this map requires students to utilize the most autonomous actions compared to other themes in the game. Unlike the other themes where students perform activities within a ready-made-map, this theme provides students with an almost empty house. Therefore, students need to decorate the house based on their own decisions. Since students themselves are the ones who design and finish the map, students can feel a greater sense of achievement and satisfaction when they complete the quest.

Module of Relate Experience (Relate)

Relational experience marketing incorporates each of the other four experiences to integrate the product into social culture. It surpasses individual marketing, individual personalities, and emotions to connect the consumer to an ideal self, social culture, and to influence potential members of a social group (Sheu, Chu, & Wang, 2017).

Considering the Module of Relate Experience, our Minecraft game is designed as follows. In the map of "The Landmarks in the World," we implemented a famous landmark in Korea, Gyeongbokgung (a royal palace), for Korean players in addition to the landmarks elsewhere in the world. This custom landmark helps Korean students connect their local identity to the game. While looking at landmarks around the world, students feel like tourists. However, when they explore Gyeongbokgung, they will feel like local Koreans and feel proud of how beautiful the construction is, and how wonderful the traditional architecture is. This kind of localized experience makes playing the game more meaningful. In the theme "Attending a Party at a Friend's House," the simulation game helps students connect the game to their real lives, making them feel more excited and motivated to learn English and play the game. For instance, picking up a DVD to watch together and buying some food to share frequently occur in students' daily lives. Consequently, students feel learning English through the simulation game is more meaningful and valuable since it is possible for them to experience similar situations (i.e., hanging out with international friends and communicating in English) in the future. In "Designing a Share House," we devised for students to relate their personal experiences to the game by making them decorate their own room. Most students dream of their own places or houses. Students can realize their dream house through this theme, so this makes them feel happier within learning English through this simulation game.

A VILLAGE IN MINECRAFT FOR LANGUAGE LEARNING

Based on the reviews of theories related to language learning and the design of educational simulation games, a Minecraft simulation was designed and is presented below.

Getting Started with Landmarks

In the Landmarks, players are expected to learn about various landmarks in the world. While playing the simulation games, they will visit several famous landmarks. By looking around the landmarks, they will read and collect pieces of information related to each landmark. From the perspective of language learning, players should be able to negotiate the meanings of unfamiliar words they encounter and construct new knowledge in groups. Figure 1 shows the activity flow in Landmarks.

In the simulation game, the co-construction of knowledge including meaning negotiation occurs as follows. While looking around the Eiffel Tower and playing the simulation game, players are asked to keep in mind facts about the Eiffel Tower for quizzes later in the game. Then, players will delegate who memorizes which information. This encourages players to communicate and interact with each other more actively, and by having a specific role, players will be more responsible for completing the task and the simulation game overall.

Although each student has their own role to memorize a piece of specific information, players will help each other when they encounter challenging expressions such as "be named after" and "81-storey building" because they need to collaborate to complete the whole simulation game. To understand the meaning of difficult words, players will guess the meanings and share their ideas with the other players. By doing so, players can develop an understanding of the meaning of the challenging words, and they will naturally co-construct knowledge about the Eiffel Tower (See Figure 2). Similar to the previous stages, players will assign a role to each group member and help each other to understand facts about the landmarks. While negotiating the meaning of incomprehensible words such as "emperor" and "plunder", players will use their own background knowledge or guess. If they cannot figure out the meaning, they can ask for help to a teacher or a teacher's avatar in the simulation game. In this case, the teacher decides whether the challenging words are key words students must understand. If so, the teacher gives hints so that players can figure out the meaning

Figure 1. Activity flow in "Landmarks in the World"

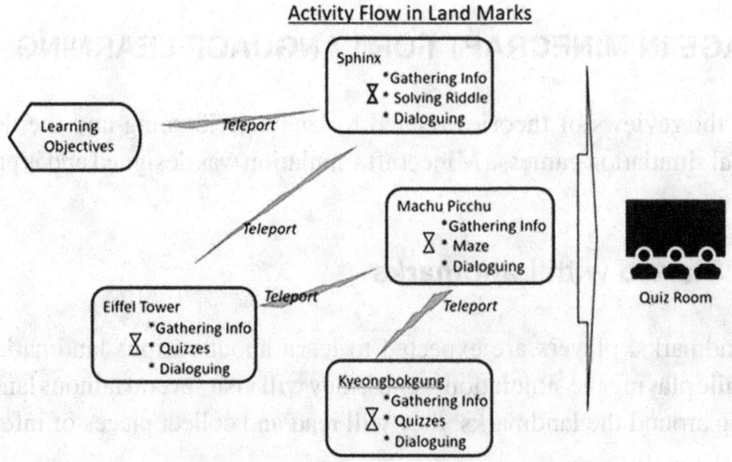

Activity Flow in Land Marks

196

of the words by themselves. By doing so, players can learn the words' meaning, which is the result of negotiation of meaning and co-construction of knowledge.

Having Fun in an Amusement Park

In the Amusement Park, players are expected to complete the given quests in an amusement park and zoo. While playing the simulation game, players will experience some typical situations they are likely to encounter when they visit a real amusement park or zoo. In the beginning of the simulation game, players will buy tickets for the ride. Also, they will order food in a cafeteria, and look around the zoo for certain animals. Since all of these situations based on experiences in their real lives, players will be more motivated to play the simulation game and learn new expressions in English. Figure 2 shows activity flow in the Amusement Park.

Players will be able to negotiate meaning and co-construct new knowledge in groups. In the simulation game, players will experience a variety of meaning negotiation and knowledge co-construction situations. For instance, players will discuss choosing a ride (See Figure 4). They also have chances to read the safety

Figure 2. The overview of "Landmarks in the World"

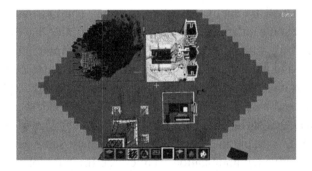

Figure 3. Activity flow in "Having Fun in the Amusement Park"

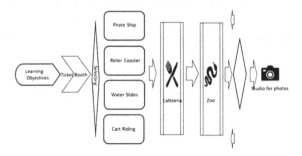

Figure 4. The overview of "Having Fun in the Amusement Park"

instruction before going on rides. If they do not understand some difficult words, they will negotiate the meaning by sharing each other's background knowledge. By completing quests, players will learn which expressions to use in each situation, resulting in co-construction of knowledge about the respective situations and the appropriate expressions in English.

In the theme, numerous events for players require meaning negotiation and knowledge co-construction. Specifically, after being told about today's simulation goals, players move to a ticket box to buy tickets for rides. In the ticket booth, players will have a conversation with an NPC or a teacher's avatar about "buying tickets." The conversation will be about the cost, discounts, coupons, and so on. When players encounter some unfamiliar words or expressions, they have to negotiate the meaning of the words with other players or the teacher's avatar, and they will learn new expressions and understand the situation better. This interaction leads to co-construction of knowledge related to "buying tickets in the public places" such as amusement park and museums. When players go on three rides successfully, they will move to a cafeteria for lunch. There, players will discuss what to eat after reading the menu. While discussing the menu, players will learn some new words related to food through active communication. While ordering food, players are asked to talk about their food preferences, such as "What kinds of sauce do you like for your French fries?" When players need more explanation about the food, they can ask the clerk, and this naturally facilitates the negotiation of meaning. Through this series of activities, players will be aware of what to say in English when ordering food, which indicates construction of knowledge about "ordering food in a restaurant."

Attending a Party at a Friend's House

In the Amusement Park, players should be able to complete the tasks required to visit a friend's house. In the beginning of the simulation game, players are invited to a house party hosted by a friend. On the way to the friend's house, players stop by a DVD shop and supermarket. To complete the tasks, players need to use appropriate simulation game strategies and have conversations in English with other characters. Figure 5 shows activity flow to attend a party at a friend's house.

In this simulation game, players are exposed to various situations which have them negotiate meaning and co-construct knowledge. For instance, once players enter the supermarket, they walk around to find the items they need to buy. Some of the ingredients such as "beetroot" and "salmon" are unfamiliar to them. To figure out the meaning of the words, they negotiate the meaning with each other or they can get help from pictures.

In addition, players can choose one item they want to buy for the party as shown in Figure 6. To determine which item to purchase, players share ideas, which leads to active interaction and authentic communication. Throughout this whole process, players will negotiate the meaning of unfamiliar words and co-construct knowledge

Figure 5. Activity flow in "Having a Party at a Friend's House"

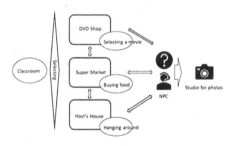

Figure 6. A supermarket scene in "Having a Party at a Friend's House"

about "the name of some ingredient" or "expressions related to grocery shopping." Similar interactions may occur in the DVD shop where players can choose film titles to take to the friend's house.

Designing a Share House

As the activities in "Designing a Share House" mostly depend on players' personal preference and creativity, they provide a variety of opportunities to negotiate meaning and co-construct knowledge. In detail, players in the beginning enter a basement room to figure out what materials they can use to decorate the house. Figure 7 shows activity flow in a Share house.

There, players will help each other understand what each item is and how it can be used to decorate the house (see Figure 8). During this process, players naturally have conversations regarding the items and when a student does not understand the exact usage of the item, other players can explain it in simpler terms by repeating the key words or using easier words. After figuring out the items to use, players move to the living room. Then they share ideas on how to decorate the house. For example,

Figure 7. Activity flow in "Designing a Share House"

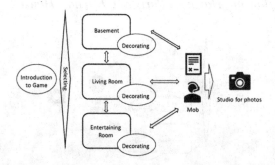

Figure 8. A living room scene in "Designing a Share House"

players assign which part each student will decorate and what type of items or materials they will use for the decoration. Players might have some misunderstanding due to some players' asymmetrical language competency.

In this case, players will help each other overcome any misunderstanding or miscommunication by giving feedback or using a simpler lexicon, all of which includes the negotiation of meaning. Since players will learn the name of items and how to use them for house decoration in addition to other new English expressions, they will co-construct the knowledge related to the given topic.

IMPLEMENTATION AS A PILOT TEST

After the simulation game was designed, two technology teachers and eleven students at elementary schools played the simulation game. They were told about the simulation game in advance and how it was developed. In addition, the objective of the simulation game was explained and the students were asked to play it and report any errors they found, and to make suggestions for the simulation game for learning a language.

Collection of Reviews

In order to collect review data, video was recorded during their gameplay and interviews with all participants were performed after their gameplay. Three research assistants who were trained in video recording participated in pilot game play to record gameplays of the participants. Researchers performed interviews with two teachers and eleven students. They played the simulation game for about sixty minutes. Interviews were also video recorded for analysis. Questions such as "how did you play the simulation game?" "were there any errors?" and "what recommendations do you have to revise it?" were asked. For teachers' interviews, a question about its effectiveness for language learning was added.

Analysis of the Data

The videos recorded during the participants' gameplay were analyzed and evaluated by researchers using the criteria in Table 1 below. Special attention was given to activities in navigating, communicating and gaming actions. The researchers observed the gameplay of participants and took notes when any notable actions of participants were found. The researchers discussed and summarized all observations.

Table 1. Criteria for evaluating gameplay video

Navigation	Communication	Gaming actions
Teleporting to	Talking to	Gathering information
Teleporting from	Asking	Decorating
Moving forward	Answering	Crafting
Moving backward	Negotiating	Buying
Turning left	Interacting with others	Selecting
Turning right		Dialoguing
Walking/Jumping		Quizzing
Running/Flying		Hanging around

The interview data was analyzed by researchers using questioning criteria in Table 2 below. Questions were created around how the simulation can help to learn a language, any errors found, and any recommendations for revising the simulation game. The answers were recorded, transcribed and summarized by researchers.

Results from the Pilot Implementation

In the interviews, students reported that the intended features could be easily found in the designed Minecraft simulation game. Results from interviews and video observations are summarized as follows. Overall, players in the designed simulation game are encouraged to interact with each other through chat rooms for a variety of purposes. In the theme "Designing a Share House," players could have discussion time about how to decorate their shared house. In the discussion, players could assign a role to each other to decorate the whole house and talk about how to achieve the

Table 2. Interview points in questioning

Contribution to Language learning	Errors	Revisions
Easy to learn languages?	Typing	Navigation
Active interaction in target language	Questioning	Interacting with colleagues
Real life situation	Answering	Gaming actions
Meaningful learning	Interacting with colleagues	Quizzes
Low affective filter	Interacting with objects	Maps
Long retention		Language learning
Reflecting English skills by interacting with others		Suggestions

given quests, such as which material they are using and what furniture they have chosen. This interaction provided learners not only with a chance to communicate in the target language but also the opportunity for exchanging linguistic feedback or negotiating meanings when they did not understand each other. Moreover, every theme of the Minecraft simulation games had clear goals for players to complete. In the case of "The Landmarks in the World," players were asked to look around some landmarks in the world such as Machu Picchu and the Sphinx, and take quizzes after exploring the landmarks. Since the level of difficulty of the quizzes was slightly difficult for one player to handle alone, players were naturally required to collaborate with each other by assigning a role and helping others to understand unfamiliar words or phrases in the simulation games. Lastly, like typical RPGs, players in Minecraft also could have their own avatars. When playing with avatars, learners were less afraid of making mistakes since the avatar was not identified to their actual identity in reality (Chin, Oppezzo, & Schwartz, 2009). Consequently, this reduced inhibition allowed players to participate in the learning process more actively, leading to the enhancement of skills. Two technology teachers also reported that the simulation game should have more conditionals and loops so that players can repeat their simulation game at any place and time.

Implications and Revisions

Findings from the pilot implementation identified a few areas for improvement. There should be clear objectives for the simulation game presented *inside* of Minecraft. These could be hidden in the simulation or manifested overtly somewhere at the beginning of the simulation. If this simulation is used in conjunction with classroom teaching, teachers should consider allotting more time to each map inside the simulation. Lastly, interactions among players in terms of language learning should be more elaborately devised based on each map's purpose.

The designed simulation game has been revised as a result of the findings from the pilot implementation. In addition, some minor cosmetic revisions were made in regard to its appearance in color, arrangement of objects, and location of each map. Additionally, built-in dialogues were revised so that they were more visually appealing and could stimulate players' language learning.

CONCLUSION AND NEXT STEPS

A simulation is a goal-driven activity which occurs in a clearly described, realistic setting. As such, students in a simulation are given various tasks to complete, or problems to solve either alone or together. The information needed to complete the tasks and solve the problems is embedded strategically in the environment. To learn a language, a simulation can be a good tool where learners both play roles as characters, and themselves (Hyland, 1993). The authors wanted to stimulate language learning of learners by simulating the negotiation of meaning and knowledge co-construction in Minecraft. By adopting the 9 events of instruction from Gagné et al. (1992) and the strategic experience modules from Schmitt (1999), the authors designed a language learning simulation in Minecraft. These principles are expected to give learners an optimal experience and environment to play and communicate with others in a target language.

The designed simulation game was able to allow learners to practice a target language by constructing knowledge and negotiating meanings through game play. Based on the findings from the pilot, the simulation game was revised with more focus on language learning interactions. Researchers will start to collect more data when more students begin playing the simulation game. In addition, the simulation game will be tested to see if it is effective for language learning, and what can be done to iterate and revise the design in order to enhance players' language learning.

At the very least, the designed simulation game allows learners to develop experience in specific situations that also require them to apply the target language. However, the key to this simulation game is that it is a dynamic rather than fixed experience. The scenario can constantly be changed realistically as a result of player actions, and players must then also adapt to those changes. Thus, the simulation might work best with skilled speakers or trained instructors because the simulation game is a mechanism for learners to obtain real-time feedback on their actions. The inclusion of a qualified language speaker might be a future challenge in this simulation game.

REFERENCES

Balnaves, K. (2018). World building for children's global participation in Minecraft. In M. Ciussi (Ed.), *Proceedings of the 12th European Conference on Game Based Learning* (pp. 858-862). Reading, UK: Academic Conferences and Publishing International Limited.

Bogost, I. (2011). *How to do things with videogames*. Minneapolis, MN: University of Minnesota Press. doi:10.5749/minnesota/9780816676460.001.0001

Callaghan, N. (2016). Investigating the role of Minecraft in educational learning environments. *Educational Media International*, *53*(4), 244–260. doi:10.1080/09523987.2016.1254877

Chen, S.-C., & Lin, C.-P. (2014). The impact of customer experience and perceived value on sustainable social relationship in blogs: An empirical study. *Technological Forecasting and Social Change, 96*, 40–50. doi:10.1016/j.techfore.2014.11.011

Chin, D. B., Oppezzo, M. A., & Schwartz, D. L. (2009). Teachable agents and the protégé effect: Increasing the effort towards learning. *Journal of Science Education and Technology, 18*(4), 334–352. doi:10.100710956-009-9180-4

Dillenbourg, P. (1999). What do you mean by collaborative learning? In P. Dillenbourg (Ed.), *Collaborative learning: Cognitive and computational approaches* (pp. 1–19). Oxford, UK: Elsevier.

Ding, Y. (2009). Perspectives on social tagging. *Journal of the Association for Information Science and Technology, 60*(12), 2388–2401. doi:10.1002/asi.21190

Dippold, D. (2009). Peer feedback through blogs: Student and teacher perceptions in an advanced German class. *ReCALL, 21*(1), 18–36. doi:10.1017/S095834400900010X

Donato, R. (2004). Aspects of collaboration in pedagogical discourse. *Annual Review of Applied Linguistics, 24*, 284–302. doi:10.1017/S026719050400011X

Dorathy, A. A., & Mahalakshmi, S. N. (2011). Second language acquisition through task based approach – role-play in English language teaching. *English for Specific Purposes World, 33*(11), 1–7.

Fenstermacher, K., Olympia, D., & Sheridan, S. M. (2006). Effectiveness of a computer-facilitated interactive social skills training program for boys with attention deficit hyperactivity disorder. *School Psychology Quarterly, 21*(2), 197–224. doi:10.1521cpq.2006.21.2.197

Gagné, R. M., Briggs, L. J., & Wager, W. W. (1992). *Principles of instructional design* (4th ed.). Fort Worth, TX: Harcourt Brace Jovanovich College Publishers.

Herold, B. (2015). Minecraft fueling creative ideas, analytical thinking. *Education Week, 35*(01), 12. Retrieved from https://www.edweek.org/ew/articles/2015/08/19/minecraft-fueling-creative-ideas-analytical-thinking-in.html

Hewett, K. J. E. (2016). *The Minecraft project: Predictors for academic success and 21st century skills gamers are learning through video game experiences* (Doctoral dissertation). Texas A&M University-Corpus Christi, College Station, TX.

Hyland, K. (1993). Language learning simulations: A practical guide. *English Teaching Forum, 31*(4), 16-22.

Jarvenoja, H., & Jarvela, S. (2009). Emotion control in collaborative learning situations: Do students regulate emotions evoked by social challenges? *The British Journal of Educational Psychology, 79*(3), 463–481. doi:10.1348/000709909X402811

Kailani, C., & Ciobotar, N. (2015). Experiential marketing: An efficient tool to leverage marketing communication impact on consumer behavior. *International Conference on Marketing and Business Development Journal, 1*(1), 281-287.

Karsenti, T., Bugmann, J., & Gros, P. P. (2017). *Transforming education with Minecraft? Results of an exploratory study conducted with 118 elementary-school students*. Montréal, Canada: CRIFPE.

Kim, D., & Perdue, R. R. (2013). The effects of cognitive, affective, and sensory attributes on hotel choice. *International Journal of Hospitality Management, 35*, 246–257. doi:10.1016/j.ijhm.2013.05.012

Kuhn, J., & Stevens, V. (2017). Participatory culture as professional development: Preparing teachers to use Minecraft in the classroom. *TESOL Journal, 8*(4), 753–767. doi:10.1002/tesj.359

Liu, F., & Ding, Y. (2009). Role-play in English language teaching. *Asian Social Science, 5*(10), 140–143. doi:10.5539/ass.v5n10p140

Lorence, M. (2015). School of Minecraft. *School Library Journal*. Retrieved from https://www.slj.com/?detailStory=minecraftedu-takes-hold-in-schools

Ludvigsen, S. R. (2009). Sociogenesis and cognition: The struggle between social and cognitive activities. In B. Schwarz, T. Dreyfus, & R. Herskowitz (Eds.), *Transformation of knowledge through classroom interaction* (pp. 302–317). New York, NY: Routledge.

Mail, T. M. (2015). In-game Minecraft quests for elementary education. *International Journal for Innovation Education and Research, 3*(8), 164–174.

Marcon, N. (2013). Minecraft as a powerful literacy prompt in the secondary English classroom. *Idiom, 49*(2), 35–37.

Nebel, S., Schneider, S., & Rey, G. D. (2016). Mining learning and crafting scientific experiments: A literature review on the use of Minecraft in education and research. *Journal of Educational Technology & Society, 19*(2), 355–366.

Peterson, M. (2010). Massively multiplayer online role-playing games as arenas for second language learning. *Computer Assisted Language Learning, 23*(5), 429–439. doi:10.1080/09588221.2010.520673

Petrov, A. (2014). *Using Minecraft in education: A qualitative study on benefits and challenges of game-based education* (Unpublished master's thesis). University of Toronto, Ontario, Canada.

Pusey, M., & Pusey, G. (2015). Using Minecraft in the science classroom. *International Journal of Innovation in Science and Mathematics Education, 23*(3), 22–34.

Roschelle, J. (1992). Learning by collaborating: Convergent conceptual change. *Journal of the Learning Sciences, 2*(3), 235–276. doi:10.120715327809jls0203_1

Säljö, R. (2010). Learning and technologies, people and tools in coordinated activities. *International Journal of Educational Research, 41*(6), 489–494. doi:10.1016/j.ijer.2005.08.013

Scarcella, R. C., & Oxford, R. L. (1992). *The tapestry of language learning: The individual in the communicative classroom.* Boston, MA: Heinle & Heinle.

Schmitt, B. (1999). Experiential marketing. *Journal of Marketing Management, 15*(1-3), 53–67. doi:10.1362/026725799784870496

Schmitt, B. (2012). The consumer psychology of brands. *Journal of Consumer Psychology, 22*(1), 7–17. doi:10.1016/j.jcps.2011.09.005

Schmitt, B. (2015). Experiential Marketing: A new framework for design and communications. *DMI 40th Anniversary Issue 2015, 25*(4), 19-26. doi:10.1111/drev.10298

Sheu, J.-J., Chu, K.-T., & Wang, S.-M. (2017). The associate impact of individual internal experiences and reference groups on buying behavior: A case study of animations, comics, and games consumers. *Telematics and Informatics, 34*(4), 314–325. doi:10.1016/j.tele.2016.08.013

Sheu, J.-J., Su, Y.-H., & Chu, K.-T. (2009). Segmenting online game customers – The perspective of experiential marketing. *Expert Systems with Applications, 36*(4), 8487–8495. doi:10.1016/j.eswa.2008.10.039

Steinbeiß, G. (2017). *Minecraft as a learning and teaching tool - Designing integrated game experiences for formal and informal learning activities* (Unpublished master's thesis). University of Oulu, Oulu, Finland.

Tudge, J. (1990). Vygotsky, the zone of proximal development, and peer collaboration: Implications for classroom practice. In L. Moll (Ed.), *Vygotsky and education: Instructional implications and applications of sociohistorical psychology* (pp. 155–172). Cambridge, UK: Cambridge University Press. doi:10.1017/CBO9781139173674.008

Uusi-Mäkelä, M. (2014). Immersive language learning with games: Finding flow in MinecraftEdu. In *Proceedings of ED-MEDIA 2014: World Conference on Educational Multimedia, Hypermedia & Telecommunications*. Chesapeake, VA: AACE.

Vygotsky, L. (1978). *Mind in society*. Cambridge, MA: Harvard University Press.

Woolfe, R. (1992). Experiential learning in workshops. In T. Hobbs (Ed.), *Experiential training: Practical guidelines* (pp. 1–13). London, UK: Tavistock/Roudledge.

KEY TERMS AND DEFINITIONS

Gagne's Events of Instruction: In 1992, Robert Gagné and his colleagues developed a nine-step instructional process that includes (1) gaining attention, (2) informing learners of objectives, (3) stimulating recall of prior learning, (4) presenting the stimulus, (5) providing learning guidance, (6) eliciting performance, (7) providing feedback, (8) assessing performance, and (9) enhancing retention and transfer.

Knowledge Co-Construction: A premise that learners can learn and grow from social interaction.

MMORPG (Massively Multiplayer Online Role-Playing Game): An online game-playing environment where a large number of people can participate simultaneously.

Negotiation of Meaning: A process that people go through to reach a clear understanding of each other. In second language acquisition, it is defined as an attempt to overcome comprehension problems.

Role Play: The act of imitating the character and behavior of someone who is different from oneself.

Schmitt's Strategic Experiential Modules: A framework for enhancing participants' experiences, including sensory experiences (SENSE), affective experiences (FEEL), creative cognitive experiences (THINK), physical experiences, behaviors and lifestyles (ACT), and social-identity experiences that result from relating to a reference group or culture (RELATE).

Simulation Game: Computer games in which players are provided with a simulated environment. Such games contain a mixture of skills, chances, and strategies to simulate an aspect of reality.

Chapter 8

Using a 3D Simulation for Teaching Functional Skills to Students with Learning, Attentional, Behavioral, and Emotional Disabilities

Maria-Ioanna Chronopoulou
University of the Aegean, Greece

Emmanuel Fokides
iD https://orcid.org/0000-0003-3962-0314
University of the Aegean, Greece

ABSTRACT

The study presents results from the use of a 3D simulation for teaching functional skills to students with learning, attentional, behavioral, and emotional disabilities, attending regular schools. An A-B single-subject study design was applied. The participating students (eight eight-to-nine years old) explored the simulation (a virtual school), encountered situations in which they observed how they are expected to behave, and had to demonstrate what they have learned. Each student attended a total of four two-hour sessions. Data were collected by means of observations and semi-structured interviews. All students demonstrated improved functional skills both in terms of the number of behaviors they acquired and in terms of those that were retained and manifested in the real school environment. On the basis of the results, it can be argued that 3D simulations are a promising tool for teaching functional skills to students with disabilities.

DOI: 10.4018/978-1-7998-0004-0.ch008

Copyright © 2020, IGI Global. Copying or distributing in print or electronic forms without written permission of IGI Global is prohibited.

INTRODUCTION

The Salamanca Statement paved the way for the inclusion of children with special needs in regular schools (Unesco, 1994). The fundamental goal of inclusion is to avoid social discrimination by offering opportunities for students with disabilities to learn together with their non-disabled peers in typical classrooms. Students with special needs studying at regular primary schools represent a variety of disabilities, including -but not limited to- learning difficulties, social, emotional, and communication deficits, physical and mental disabilities (Espelage, Rose, & Polanin, 2016; O'Brennan, Waasdorp, Pas, & Bradsow, 2015). As a result, the idea of inclusion is not free of problems. For example, the disadvantaged students find it difficult to communicate with others and engage in a debate, while their interpersonal relationships constitute a stress factor. Their imagination may be limited and their participation in games is passive or dysfunctional. Their academic progress is inconsistent with that of their peers and quite often they exhibit severe weakness, for example, in mathematics or spelling (Wagner, 1995). Their emotional immaturity, their inability to be aware of or understand the emotions of others, leads to non-functional social relationships, isolation, outbursts of anger, and, in general, problems in understanding everyday situations (Nye, Gardner, Hansford Edwards, Hayes, & Ford, 2016; Vlachou, Stavrousi & Didaskalou, 2016). Finally, their deficits in focusing attention on a given task or situation and the neglect of the self, are factors that increase the likelihood of being victimized or manifesting undesirable/ unacceptable behaviors (Thompson, Whitney, & Smith, 1994).

In order to improve students' well-being, additional help is provided through structured school programs, aiming to support their academic performance and improve their everyday functional skills, both within and outside the school environment (Rose, Shevlin, Winter, & O' Raw, 2015). Such programs try to enhance their emotional (e.g., Domitrovich, Cortes, & Greenberg, 2007), behavioral (e.g., Espelage et al., 2016) and communication skills (e.g., Blandon, Calkins, Grimm, Keane, & O'Brien, 2010). Despite the fact that such programs exist and as far as students with mild disabilities (with learning difficulties, attentional, behavioral, and emotional disabilities) are concerned, it seems that the emphasis often lies in structuring the environment to accommodate their academic needs, while issues regarding their social adjustment are neglected (Office of Special Education and Rehabilitative Services, 2015). What is more, the relevant literature suggests that there is a need for intervention studies examining strategies for enhancing their social skills (Garrote, Dessemontet, & Opitz, 2017).

Needless to say, educational technology plays an important role in the above interventions. One such technology is 3D simulations, which is an umbrella term for a family of technologies such as virtual reality and extended reality. 3D simulations are realistic representations of a situation through the computer and users interact with the virtual objects in a lifelike way (Freina & Ott, 2015). Moreover, users can get emotionally involved as they feel the senses of presence and immersion (Portman, Natapov, & Fisher-Gewirtzman, 2015). In general, 3D simulations are considered effective teaching tools (Merchant, Goetz, Cifuentes, Keeney-Kennycutt, & Davis, 2014), because they offer safe and controllable environments as well as the context in which knowledge is applied (Marshall, 2014). In addition, users can practice their social skills (Didehbani, Allen, Kandalaft, Krawczyk, & Chapman, 2016), skills of self-care and self-protection (Kalyvioti & Mikropoulos, 2014), and also express their emotions (Lorenzo, Lledo, Pomares, & Roig, 2016). Due to the above, simulations can be used to teach students with special educational needs new skills, reduce unacceptable behaviors, and prepare them to manifest the appropriate behaviors in real life.

Taking into account that: (a) more studies are needed in order to establish effective strategies for enhancing the social skills of students with learning, attentional, behavioral, and emotional disabilities and (b) 3D simulations can be an effective teaching tool, a short research project was designed and implemented in order to study exactly this. The skills/behaviors were related to how students are expected to function in the school environment. The rationale, methodology, and the results of the project are presented and analyzed in the coming sections.

BACKGROUND

Several studies have used simulations for teaching functional living skills to students with special educational needs such as learning and mental disabilities, developmental disorders, psychological or emotional disorders, and motor or sensory impairments (Lanyi, Geiszt, Karolyi, Tilinger, & Magyar, 2006). For example, Wuang, Chiang, Su, and Wang (2011) tried to improve the motor skills of children with Down Syndrome. Language skills were the objective in another study (Lan, Hsiao, & Shih, 2018). On the other hand, it seems that most of the research targets students with autism spectrum disorders (ASD). The core problem in students with ASD is the impairment of social communication and social relations (Ames, McMorris, Alli, & Bebko, 2016). Given that, Stichter, Laffey, Galyen, and Herzog (2014) tried to improve the social performance of students with ASD through a virtual environment. Wang, Laffey, Xing, Galyen, and Stichter (2017) used a 3D multi-user simulation with the same objective. In another study, researchers implemented an intervention using Opensimulator with the objective to advance the problem-solving skills of students with ASD (Volioti, Tsiatsos, Mavropoulou, & Karagiannidis, 2014). Researchers also tried to teach social and emotional skills to children with ASD, through problematic situations presented in a virtual world (Craig, Brown, Upright, & DeRosier, 2016).

Students with ASD are also confronted with severe difficulties in everyday school life (Vasquez, Marino, Donehower, & Koch, 2017). As a result, simulations of school environments have been (effectively) used for enhancing skills like social perception, interaction, and communication (e.g., Cheng & Ye, 2010; Ke & Im, 2013; Ke & Moon, 2018; Stichter et al., 2014). Cheng, Huang, and Yang (2015) tried to teach students with ASD social understanding through an immersive virtual environment that included two conditions: in a bus and in the classroom. Didehbani et al. (2016) used Second Life for presenting different settings like a classroom, a school dining room, and a schoolyard, in order to teach students with ASD how to make friends, confront someone who harasses them, deal with social dilemmas, and advise a friend. Teaching interaction and communication skills to students with ASD was the goal in another study; it was implemented during school time and regualr students participated as well (Parsons, 2015).

Far fewer studies targeted students with other (milder) disorders, such as attention-deficit/hyperactivity disorder (ADHD) and tried to improve skills like socializing, problem-solving and self-protection (e.g., Didehbani et al., 2016). The use of a virtual environment also significantly improved the social problems and psychosomatic behavior of children with ADHD (Shema-Shiratzky et al., 2018). With respect to difficulties in working memory, executive function, and attention in children with ADHD, the findings of other studies indicated that simulations can be very helpful to assess and improve these conditions (e.g., Rose, Brooks, & Rizzo, 2005; Schwebel, Gaines, & Severson, 2008). As simulations facilitate action-based answers, they can be used for reducing the behavioral symptoms and problems of children with ADHD (e.g., Dehn, 2011; Wang & Reid, 2011). Other studies indicated that 3D virtual environments can improve memory functionality, sensory processing, and attention, in individuals with ADHD (e.g., Schwebel et al., 2008). Then again, none of the above studies was conducted in the school environment nor did the applications they used simulate a school environment. Thus, it can be concluded that even though there are studies that used simulations, targeted students with mild disorders, and tried to teach or train them in life functional skills (e.g., social, communicational, and emotional skills), few illustrated specific and plain behaviors that are anticipated in school conditions, for example, during lessons, breaks, or a school event.

DEVELOPMENT AND EVALUATION OF THE 3D SIMULATION

On the basis of what was presented in the preceding section, it was considered worth examining if a 3D simulation can help students with mild disorders (i.e., learning, attentional, behavioral, and emotional disabilities) to understand how they are expected to function in the school environment. The study employed a single-subject design with a baseline and a treatment phase (A-B design). In this type of research, participants serve as their own controls. Data are collected multiple times during the baseline phase (A phase) until stability is reached. The treatment is introduced during the intervention phase (B phase) and data are, once again, collected for multiple times. The researcher then seeks for changes in level or trend in the dependent variable (i.e., behaviors/performances before the intervention are contrasted with those that occurred during or after the intervention) (Engel & Schutt, 2012; Wong, 2010).

This type of research design is commonly employed in the field of special education as an alternative to group designs and constitutes the most feasible type of experimental design for individuals with disabilities (Engel & Schutt, 2012; Parker, Grimmett, & Summers, 2008). In special education, a significant problem is that large sample sizes are, most of the times, not achievable. An advantage of the single-subject design is that research can be conducted with just one, or, typically, with three to eight participants (Horner, Swaminathan, Sugai, & Smolkowski, 2012). It has to be noted that a withdrawal design (A-B-A) was also considered but could not be implemented, as the study involved skills and behaviors which are impossible to un-learn (Ledford & Gast, 2009).

As the study sought to examine the impact of simulations on students' behavior in the school environment, one has to consider what constitutes a school environment. In essence, a student has to function properly in the classroom (i.e., during lessons), in the schoolyard (i.e., during breaks and when playing), and when all students are gathered for an event (i.e., during a school play, a speech, and a ceremony). The above conditions, which require certain skills/behaviors, provided the basis for the design of the simulation and also for the formulation and testing of the study's research hypothesis, namely: 3D simulations can help primary school students with learning, attentional, behavioral, and emotional disabilities, attending regular schools, to understand how to function/behave in the school environment, during lessons, breaks, or a school event.

Participants and Sample Size

As the study's target group was primary school students with learning, attentional, behavioral, and emotional disabilities, a major problem was the proper selection of participants, because the terms "learning, attentional, behavioral, and emotional disabilities" are used for describing a wide range of conditions and there is always the chance that the sample may not be homogeneous. Thus, a set of selection criteria was applied, in order to avoid selecting extreme cases or cases that differed significantly. Following three months of observations of students with learning, attentional, behavioral, and emotional disabilities attending typical classes in a number of public schools in Athens, Greece, eight students were recruited (five boys and three girls, aged between eight and nine). All (i) were Greeks, (ii) had a similar social and family background, (iii) did not have sensory-motor disabilities, (iv) their mental abilities were normal as assessed by the Greek version of Wechsler Intelligence Scale for Children, (v) their disorders were formally diagnosed by a public assessing institution and fall into the "learning, attentional, behavioral, and emotional disabilities" category, (vi) they attended regional public regular schools, and (vii) were supported, on a daily basis, by a special education teacher, each according to their diagnosis needs. More importantly, all had problems (to a varying extent) in their functional skills regarding the school environment. Detailed data for the extent of these deficits are presented in the "Results" section. The participants' profiles were as follows:

- XS (boy, 8y 2m). Diagnosed with ADHD and learning disabilities. He is often distracted to the point of not remembering the correct order of simple instructions. Because of this lack of functional attentional focus, he does not manifest appropriate or expected social behaviors.
- NF (boy, 9y 2m). Diagnosed with social-emotional and learning disabilities (SELD). He hardly focuses on lessons. The lack of concentration leads to an apparent indifference to social conventions or sometimes ignorance of the expected acceptable behaviors.
- LR (boy, 8y 6m). Diagnosed with ADHD and behavioral problems. He has trouble following rules; often gets involved in fights with his classmates; he is indifferent to social conventions; refuses to respect and follow commonly accepted rules; and often breaks out in bouts of anger.
- DA (boy, 8y 6m). Diagnosed with SELD. He faces severe concentration difficulties and often has outbursts of anger and denial. He also refuses to comply with rules or engages in socially unacceptable activities. He is usually the leader of a team or a group; however, his aim is to negatively influence the decisions and actions of the team.

- KB (boy, 8y 11m). Diagnosed with SELD and ADHD. He is intensely hyperactive and impulsive. His actions are careless and he often engages in inappropriate behaviors. Because he does not process or make sense of the social stimuli, he is unable to choose the correct behavior. The non-functional focus of his attention prevents him from manifesting the desired behaviors.
- DB (girl, 8y 10m). Diagnosed with ADHD and learning disabilities. She has a limited repertoire of attitudes and skills, she is highly introvert, and has a generalized weakness in social interactions. Her poor mnemonic skills allow the manifestation of inappropriate behaviors.
- MG (girl, 8y 10m). Diagnosed with ADHD and learning disabilities. She appears not to be able to revoke and use the desired behaviors in the appropriate contexts. She is also easily distracted and disorganized.
- AL (girl, 8y 11m). Diagnosed with SELD. She is highly introvert, has low self-esteem, intense insecurities, and introspective behavior. She is often isolated. Depending on the circumstances, she hesitates or avoids to manifest the required behaviors.

It has to be noted that since minors were the study's target group, approval from the University's ethical committee was granted prior to the beginning of the project. Moreover, since it was necessary to have access to students' school performance, psychological evaluations, and diagnoses, their parents were contacted and their written consent was obtained. The schools' headmasters and teachers were also informed of the study's objectives and procedures.

Materials

The simulation was developed by the researcher using OpenSimulator (http://opensimulator.org/) and represented a school complex with classrooms, an assembly hall, and a schoolyard (Figure 1). Around fifty hours were required for its development. It was then installed in laptops, as a stand-alone, single-user application, as there was no need for multiple users to be simultaneously present at the same simulation. Programming scripts implemented basic interactions (e.g., controls for opening or closing doors) and all areas could be visited without any restrictions. While the virtual environment was pretty minimalistic in its design, it was populated with non-playable characters (NPCs) who acted (i) as students and (ii) as guides/teachers. The latter were placed at the entrance of the classrooms, the schoolyard, and the assembly hall. When students entered these areas, they were

Figure 1. Screenshots from the simulation

greeted by the teacher-NPCs who made a brief presentation of what behaviors are expected in the given area. Following that, both teacher- and student-NPCs, using a combination of pre-defined paths and animations, demonstrated how students were expected to behave. In addition, media screens in each area provided further details regarding the desired behaviors (using videos, texts, and images). All NPCs' actions could be re-run for as many times as the students/participants liked. In addition, by controlling their avatars, they could intervene and either follow the NPCs or block their actions (e.g., block their paths and push them around). If the latter was the case, as the NPCs were not programmed to avoid obstacles or correct their paths, students could cause havoc to the simulation; in essence, they could see the consequences of "inappropriate" behavior.

Procedure

The single-variable rule in A-B designs recommends that, following the baseline phase, only one variable/treatment can be introduced and studied during the intervention phase. After this cycle is complete, another variable can be introduced (McMillan, 2004). Consequently, the project was organized as follows: (i) for establishing the baseline, the participating students were observed for a period of two weeks (two observation sessions per week, each observation lasting for the whole duration of the school day), (ii) students used the simulation and one of the three conditions was introduced to them (i.e., how to behave during lessons, during breaks, and during a school event), and (iii) intervention observations were conducted, again, for a period of two weeks. The above procedure was repeated three times as there were three conditions. It has to be noted that there was an introductory session, prior to the beginning of the project, in which the participating students familiarized themselves with the simulation and how to control their avatars.

Each condition was introduced during a two-hour session on an individualized basis (one session per student). Video-modelling is an instructional technique commonly used in special education, in which the modeled behaviors/skills are presented in a video clip and then the child practices them (Miltenberger & Charlop, 2015). The principles of video-modeling, as well as other teaching guidelines frequently applied in special education, provided the basis for the study's instructional method (Ashman & Conway, 2017; Norwich & Lewis, 2001): (i) the objectives were explicitly stated, (ii) the learning material was broken into small and understandable segments and presented gradually, (iii) the teacher oversaw the whole process and draw student's attention on what was relevant, and (iv) the teacher encouraged the display of the desired skills/behaviors. In detail, the teaching method was as follows:

- At the beginning of the session, the researcher welcomed the student, and through discussion tried to establish what he/she already knew for the given condition and the behaviors/skills he/she was supposed to exhibit.
- Using a laptop, the student entered the simulation's area in which the given condition was presented. He/she could follow the teacher-NPC, watch the NPCs interact, and read, at will, the media screens. As already mentioned, the student could also intervene in such a way so that the NPCs stop functioning properly. When this was the case, the simulation was reset and rerun.
- After the simulation was explored for at least fifteen minutes, the researcher and the student engaged in a discussion, in order for the former to develop an outline of what the latter understood. Also, the NPCs behavior when they were "derailed" and the consequences provided a good starting point for a discussion. The researcher then summarized key-points and drew the student's attention to them. These key-points are presented in the "Instruments" section.
- Following that, the simulation was explored for a second time. During this part, either the researcher or the student could stop exploring the simulation and discuss the key-points established in the previous step.
- A final round of discussions followed. This time, a "What will you do if…" game was played. The researcher presented hypothetical situations (related to the condition that was the session's theme). For example, the

researcher presented a situation in which another student sitting right behind the participating student was constantly annoying/harassing him/her. The participating student was then asked to "act" how he/she would behave or what would his/her responses might be. The student was also encouraged to visit the area of the simulation in which a similar situation was presented and elaborated even further on the reasoning behind his/her course of actions.

- The last two steps were repeated if the teacher deemed it necessary.

Instruments

Data were collected using an observation protocol and semi-structured interviews. As already mentioned, there was a three-month period during which students with learning, attentional, behavioral, and emotional disabilities attending various public schools were observed. During this period, twelve behaviors/functional skills were detected, four for each condition, in which students faced significant problems:

- Functional skills/behaviors during lessons. I enter the classroom and sit down calmly; I take my books out and I wait for the lesson to begin; I raise my hand if I want to participate or if I want to answer a question; and I wait for my turn before I speak.
- Functional skills/behaviors during breaks. I walk calmly in the schoolyard; I play with my schoolmates following the rules of our game; if I have a disagreement with my classmates, I talk to them about it; and if I can't find a solution to the disagreement I ask for the teacher's help.
- Functional skills/behaviors during a school event (e.g., during a school play, a speech, and a ceremony). I enter the assembly hall before the event starts and I sit down; during the event I watch/listen carefully, during the event I try to be quiet; and at the end of the event I clap or cheer; and I leave the assembly hall calmly.

The above conditions and target behaviors/skills formed the observation protocol. Observational data (the number of times the desired behavior was evident) were collected simultaneously by two teachers in both the study's baseline and intervention phases. Both were trained prior to the beginning of the project (by observing the behavior of normal students) and during the baseline phase. An interrater reliability analysis using Cohen's kappa coefficient was performed to determine the consistency among raters. The interrater reliability was found to be $\kappa = .90$ ($p < .001$), 95% CI.88, and .92), which was considered very good (Landis & Koch, 1977).

In addition, semi-structured interviews were used on three occasions: at the beginning of each session, at the end of each session, and at the end of the project. Their objective was to examine what students knew, learned, and retained of the desired behaviors and skills.

Results

To test the study's research hypothesis, two instruments were used: semi-structured interviews and observations. The semi-structured interviews recorded students' knowledge regarding the desired skills and behaviors prior to the intervention, after the intervention, and at the end of the project. The interviews were transcribed verbatim on paper, viewed and re-viewed by the two raters, and the correct responses were summed. Table 1 and Figure 2 present the results of this procedure and clearly illustrate that, in terms of knowledge acquisition, there was a significant change in all participants. More importantly, all were able to retain a considerable portion of this knowledge at least until the end of the project.

A prerequisite of A-B designs is to achieve stability of the results during the baseline phase, before proceeding to the intervention phase. The observations' results, as presented in Table 2 and Figure 3, indicate that this requirement was met. Thus, any changes in the intervention phase can be attributed to the intervention per se. Indeed, as data indicate, there was a considerable positive change in all students' behavior and in all three conditions. In detail and taking into account the results of all students: (i) on average, there were 39.67 correct behaviors during the baseline phase for the "during breaks" condition and after the intervention there were 74.75

Table 1. Participants' knowledge of the desired behaviors and skills

Condition		During break			During lesson			During an event		
		Prior	After	Retention	Prior	After	Retention	Prior	After	Retention
Participant	XS	2	5	4	4	7	4	1	5	3
	NF	1	4	3	3	6	3	1	3	2
	LR	4	7	5	5	8	6	0	4	3
	DA	0	4	3	0	4	4	0	4	3
	KB	1	4	3	2	6	5	1	3	2
	DB	3	7	6	2	6	6	2	3	3
	MG	2	6	7	3	7	7	2	4	3
	AL	3	7	6	3	7	7	2	4	2

Note: Although the desired skills and behaviors which were examined were 4 for each condition (12 in total), in a number of occasions, students were able to name more.

Figure 2. Number of correct answers for all conditions per participant

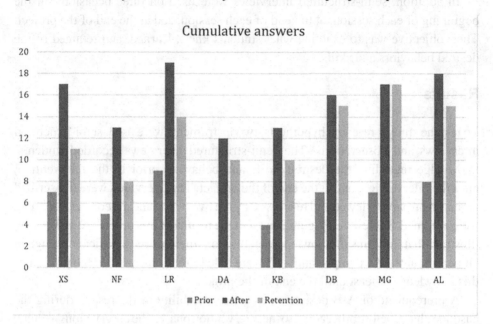

correct ones (88.45% change), (ii) for the "during lessons" condition the averages were 38.67 and 80.17 respectively (107.33% change), and (iii) for the "during a school event" condition the averages were 45.00 and 88.67 respectively (97.04% change).

Given that the data indicate a significant change both in knowledge acquisition and behaviors, the study's hypothesis can be accepted. It seems that 3D simulations do help primary school students with learning, attentional, behavioral, and emotional disabilities, attending regular schools, to understand how to function/behave in the school environment.

SOLUTIONS AND RECOMMENDATIONS

The purpose of the study was to examine whether simulations can help students with mild special educational needs (i.e., with learning, attentional, behavioral, and emotional disabilities) to learn and manifest functional living skills common in the school environment. Twelve such behaviors/skills were selected, falling into three conditions, namely, during lessons, during breaks, and during a school event. Four

Table 2. Number of correct behaviors per observation session and per participant

Subject	Condition	Observation session								
		Baseline phase					Intervention phase			
		1	2	3	4		5	6	7	8
XS	A	4.33	6.33	6.00	6.00		8.67	8.33	6.67	8.33
	B	4.33	3.33	4.00	4.33		8.33	8.67	8.33	7.33
	C	5.33	5.33	5.33	5.33		10.33	10.00	10.33	9.33
NF	A	4.00	3.67	3.67	3.33		10.00	9.67	8.67	9.00
	B	2.67	2.67	2.67	2.67		9.67	9.00	9.33	9.33
	C	3.00	3.00	3.00	3.00		10.00	9.67	9.67	9.33
LR	A	4.33	4.33	4.33	4.33		7.67	7.67	7.67	7.67
	B	6.67	6.33	5.67	5.33		10.67	10.00	8.00	7.33
	C	8.67	8.00	7.00	5.67		11.33	11.00	11.33	10.33
DA	A	7.33	7.33	7.33	7.33		9.67	9.00	8.00	8.00
	B	5.00	5.00	4.33	4.33		8.67	7.67	8.00	7.67
	C	4.33	4.33	4.33	4.33		12.33	11.67	12.00	12.00
KB	A	3.33	3.33	3.33	3.33		7.67	8.00	8.33	8.00
	B	2.67	2.67	2.67	2.67		10.67	10.33	8.33	9.33
	C	4.33	4.33	4.33	4.33		10.67	10.33	10.00	10.33
DB	A	5.33	5.00	5.33	5.67		10.00	9.67	9.67	8.00
	B	5.00	6.00	5.67	6.00		11.00	11.67	11.33	11.33
	C	7.33	6.67	7.33	8.00		12.67	12.00	11.33	12.00
MG	A	5.00	5.00	6.00	6.67		12.67	13.33	13.00	13.00
	B	5.33	5.33	6.00	6.00		13.00	12.33	12.67	12.67
	C	5.00	6.00	6.33	6.67		12.00	11.67	11.33	13.00
AL	A	4.00	4.33	4.33	4.67		11.00	10.67	9.67	11.67
	B	6.67	7.00	7.67	8.00		11.67	11.33	12.67	12.33
	C	6.33	8.33	7.67	7.00		12.67	11.00	11.33	11.67

Notes: The numbers in cells are the average of the two raters' number of observations; Condition A = during breaks; Condition B = during lessons; Condition C = during a school event

two-hour sessions were conducted with eight participating students. The teaching method was formulated in accordance with the pedagogical guidelines frequently applied to special education: (i) the objectives to be explicitly stated, (ii) the learning

Figure 3. Cumulative number of correct behaviors per observation session

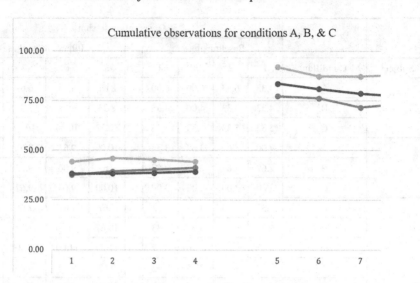

material to be gradually presented in small and understandable steps, (iii) the teacher to oversee the whole process, ensuring that students focus their attention on what is relevant, and (iv) the teacher to encourage the display of the desired skills/behaviors (Ashman & Conway, 2017; Norwich & Lewis, 2001).

Each of the participating students had a different starting level, though all had severe or, at least, noteworthy problems in knowing, understanding, and exhibiting behaviors that would allow them to function properly in the school environment. The results, as presented in the preceding section, demonstrated that, at the end of the project, all students had a significant positive change both in terms of the knowledge they acquired and of the behaviors/skills they were able to display in real school conditions (see Tables 1 & 2). In this respect, the study's results are in line with previous research. Indeed, according to the existing literature, in the context of special education, 3D simulations are considered ideal for life functional skills' training (Wilson, Foreman, & Stanton, 1997). Moreover, relevant research suggested that simulations do contribute to the improvement of behaviors/skills related to the school environment (e.g., Cheng & Ye, 2010; Didehbani et al., 2016; Ke & Im, 2013; Ke & Moon, 2018; Lan et al., 2018; Stichter et al., 2014; Wang et al., 2017), although most of these studies involved children with ASD.

A number of reasons related to the use of a simulation and the teaching method might have contributed to the study's positive outcomes. First, simulations provide students with special needs a controlled, realistic, secure, and rich environment, in which they have no fear of failing (Raskind, Smedley, & Higgins, 2005) and, at the same time, it is easier to transfer the behaviors they have learned in the virtual environment to real life situations (Blume, Hudak, Dresler, Ehlis, Kühnhausen, Renner, & Gawrilow, 2017; Freina & Ott, 2015; Vasquez et al., 2017). Second, it is suggested that the skills/behaviors to be taught through simulations have to be linked with skills/behaviors that are part of situations individuals experience in their daily life and with ones that they can be practiced relatively promptly and regularly (Gregg & Tarrier, 2007; Rizzo et al., 2011). This also applies to interventions in special education; the tool has to be related to real conditions and to allow students to learn how to manifest and adapt their behaviors. Furthermore, students have to be given the chance to test this new knowledge in the (real) situations it applies, to further practice it, and, ideally, to generalize it in similar circumstances (Blume et al., 2017; Freina & Ott, 2015; Vasque, et al., 2017). The above guidelines were followed in the present study. While exploring the simulation, the participants faced plausible/ realistic conditions in which they recognized elements from their daily school life. They were able to see how they are expected to function and they were encouraged to focus their attention on NPCs' actions and the relevant material presented to them. They were then asked to apply and demonstrate the target behaviors/skills, and, also, to further elaborate on the matter with their teacher.

The literature also suggested that 3D simulations are effective because they motivate students with special educational needs to be actively involved in the learning process, resulting in better understanding and knowledge gains (Blume et al., 2017; Didehbani et al., 2016; Freina & Ott, 2015; Ramachandiran, Jomhari, Thiyagaraja, & Mahmud, 2015; Vasque et al., 2017). This, in turn, gives them a sense of fulfillment and satisfaction (Rix, Hall, Nind, Sheehy, & Wearmouth, 2009). In addition, by seeing that they can master skills important to their social, emotional, and behavioral status in school life, their self-esteem and self-image are improved and they also gain more confidence (Craig et al., 2016; Sakiz, Sart, Börkan, Korkmaz, & Babür, 2015). As they become more confident, they feel that they can be more independent, which encourages them to manifest even more behaviors that are acceptable by others (Lan et al., 2018).

The above chain of knowledge-behavior transformations can be confirmed through the study's results. From Table 1 and Figure 2, it can be inferred that almost all participants had limited initial knowledge regarding all conditions. Right after each intervention, there was a peak in the results, indicating significant knowledge gains. Although at the end of the project there was a decline in the results, the retention of knowledge was still significant. Moreover, from Table 2 and Figure 3, it can be inferred that during the baseline phase the limited knowledge of correct behaviors was not the most crucial problem; students manifested a limited number of acceptable behaviors as well (again in all conditions). As the results in the intervention phase indicate that the number of correct behaviors was almost doubled, it can be concluded that knowledge was "transformed" into actual skills/behaviors. More importantly, as data were recorded not in a single point in time but multiple times during a span of two weeks, this indicates that students mastered these skills/behaviors and that they became more confident.

Finally, an issue that has to be addressed is whether it is feasible to integrate 3D simulations in special education, given that the availability of such applications is limited and they are not that easy to develop. As already mentioned, although the simulation was rather simplistic, it took the researcher around fifty hours to develop. Moreover, the researcher was, by no means, an expert programmer. The reason for this approach was to test whether a special education teacher can undertake such a task. One might argue that because the application was "amateurish", it was ineffective, and, quite possibly, its weaknesses had a negative impact on the results. Then again, it is questionable whether a large number of such applications can be professionally developed. That is because students with special educational needs present a great number of diverse problems and disabilities; thus, an application suitable for a set of problems, quite possibly, is not suitable for another set. In addition, Stichter et al. (2014) argued that applications developed by the special education teachers are better aligned with the needs of their students, as they are developed for their specific needs. It seems that the issue cannot be easily resolved as both sides present equally valid arguments. A plausible solution is to develop software tools that make the whole process of developing simulations much more efficient and appealing to non-experts (Scacchi, 2012).

FUTURE DIRECTIONS

While the results were interesting, there are limitations to the study that should be acknowledged but that also provide several avenues for future research. The sample size, although acceptable for a single case study with a baseline and intervention phase, raises concerns regarding the generalizability of the results. This is a weakness of all studies dealing with individuals with special educational needs. Also, due to restrictions imposed by the schools' timetables, there was a limited number of interventions and the number of observations was also limited (although within the suggested number of observations for a baseline and an intervention phase). Thus, one might question whether they were enough either for the establishment of behavioral changes or their accurate recording. The long-term retention of knowledge and skills is also unknown. In future research, the target group can encompass students from different age groups and with other special needs and compare the results. More observations and interviews will allow an in-depth understanding of the impact of simulations. Professionally developed applications can also be used to examine whether there is a significant variation in the results. Finally, an interesting research path is to use multiuser simulations, the target group to be both regular and special needs students and examine if and how inclusion works in virtual environments.

CONCLUSION

In sum, despite the aforementioned limitations, the study provided an idea about how 3D simulations might prove useful to students with mild disabilities. What is more, it contributes to the relevant literature by providing evidence that, through 3D simulations, students with learning, attentional, behavioral, and emotional disabilities can: (i) learn and retain knowledge related to how they are expected to function in the school environment and (ii) apply this knowledge and significantly change their behavior in real-life conditions. In conclusion, the study's findings might prove useful to researchers and teachers in understanding and effectively utilizing 3D simulations in special education.

REFERENCES

Ames, M. E., McMorris, C. A., Alli, L. N., & Bebko, J. M. (2016). Overview and evaluation of a mentorship program for university students with ASD. *Focus on Autism and Other Developmental Disabilities*, *31*(1), 27–36. doi:10.1177/1088357615583465

Ashman, A. F., & Conway, R. N. (2017). *Using cognitive methods in the classroom*. London, UK: Routledge; doi:10.4324/9781315271019

Blandon, A. Y., Calkins, S. D., Grimm, K. J., Keane, S. P., & O'Brien, M. (2010). Testing a developmental cascade model of emotional and social competence and early peer acceptance. *Development and Psychopathology*, *22*(4), 737–748. doi:10.1017/S0954579410000428

Blume, F., Hudak, J., Dresler, T., Ehlis, A. C., Kühnhausen, J., Renner, T. J., & Gawrilow, C. (2017). NIRS-based neurofeedback training in a virtual reality classroom for children with attention-deficit/hyperactivity disorder: Study protocol for a randomized controlled trial. *Trials*, *18*(1), 41. doi:10.118613063-016-1769-3

Cheng, Y., Huang, C. L., & Yang, C. S. (2015). Using a 3D immersive virtual environment system to enhance social understanding and social skills for children with autism spectrum disorders. *Focus on Autism and Other Developmental Disabilities*, *30*(4), 222–236. doi:10.1177/1088357615583473

Cheng, Y., & Ye, J. (2010). Exploring the social competence of students with autism spectrum conditions in a collaborative virtual learning environment-The pilot study. *Computers & Education*, *54*(4), 1068–1077. doi:10.1016/j.compedu.2009.10.011

Craig, A. B., Brown, E. R., Upright, J., & DeRosier, M. E. (2016). Enhancing children's social emotional functioning through virtual game-based delivery of social skills training. *Journal of Child and Family Studies*, *25*(3), 959–968. doi:10.100710826-015-0274-8

Dehn, M. J. (2011). *Working memory and academic learning: Assessment and intervention*. Hoboken, NJ: John Wiley & Sons.

Didehbani, N., Allen, T., Kandalaft, M., Krawczyk, D., & Chapman, S. (2016). Virtual reality social cognition training for children with high functioning autism. *Computers in Human Behavior*, *62*, 703–711. doi:10.1016/j.chb.2016.04.033

Domitrovich, C. E., Cortes, R. C., & Greenberg, M. T. (2007). Improving young children's social and emotional competence: A randomized trial of the preschool "PATHS" curriculum. *The Journal of Primary Prevention*, *28*(2), 67–91. doi:10.100710935-007-0081-0

Engel, R. J., & Schutt, R. K. (2012). *The practice of research in social work*. Thousand Oaks, CA: Sage.

Espelage, D. L., Rose, C. A., & Polanin, J. R. (2016). Social-emotional learning program to promote prosocial and academic skills among middle school students with disabilities. *Remedial and Special Education*, *37*(6), 323–332. doi:10.1177/0741932515627475

Freina, L., & Ott, M. (2015). A literature review on Immersive Virtual Reality in education: State of the art and perspectives. *eLearning & Software for Education*, 1.

Garrote, A., Dessemontet, R. S., & Opitz, E. M. (2017). Facilitating the social participation of pupils with special educational needs in mainstream schools: A review of school-based interventions. *Educational Research Review*, *20*, 12–23. doi:10.1016/j.edurev.2016.11.001

Gregg, L., & Tarrier, N. (2007). Virtual reality in mental health. *Social Psychiatry and Psychiatric Epidemiology*, *42*(5), 343–354. doi:10.100700127-007-0173-4

Horner, R. H., Swaminathan, H., Sugai, G., & Smolkowski, K. (2012). Considerations for the systematic analysis and use of single-case research. *Education & Treatment of Children*, *35*(2), 269–290. doi:10.1353/etc.2012.0011

Kalyvioti, K., & Mikropoulos, T. A. (2014). Virtual environments and dyslexia: A literature review. *Procedia Computer Science*, *27*, 138–147. doi:10.1016/j.procs.2014.02.017

Ke, F., & Im, T. (2013). Virtual-reality-based social interaction training for children with high-functioning autism. *The Journal of Educational Research*, *106*(6), 441–461. doi:10.1080/00220671.2013.832999

Ke, F., & Moon, J. (2018). Virtual collaborative gaming as social skills training for high-functioning autistic children. *British Journal of Educational Technology*, *49*(4), 728–741. doi:10.1111/bjet.12626

Lan, Y. J., Hsiao, I. Y., & Shih, M. F. (2018). Effective learning design of game-based 3D virtual language learning environments for special education students. *Journal of Educational Technology & Society*, *21*(3), 213–227.

Landis, J. R., & Koch, G. G. (1977). The measurement of observer agreement for categorical data. *Biometrics*, *33*(1), 159–174. doi:10.2307/2529310

Lányi, C. S., Geiszt, Z., Károlyi, P., Tilinger, Á., & Magyar, V. (2006). Virtual reality in special needs early education. *The International Journal of Virtual Reality*, *5*(4), 55–68.

Ledford, J. R., & Gast, D. L. (2009). *Single Subject research methodology in behavioral sciences: Applications in special education and behavioral sciences*. London, UK: Routledge; doi:10.4324/9780203877937

Lorenzo, G., Lledó, A., Pomares, J., Roig, R., & Arnaiz, P. (2016). Bibliometric indicators in the study of Asperger syndrome between 1990 and 2014. *Scientometrics*, *109*(1), 377–388. doi:10.100711192-016-1975-5

Marshall, A. (2014). Sensemaking in Second Life. *Procedia Technology, 13*, 107–111. doi:10.1016/j.protcy.2014.02.014

McMillan, J. H. (2004). *Educational research: Fundamentals for the consumer* (4th ed.). Boston, MA: Allyn and Bacon.

Merchant, Z., Goetz, E. T., Cifuentes, L., Keeney-Kennicutt, W., & Davis, T. J. (2014). Effectiveness of virtual reality-based instruction on students' learning outcomes in K-12 and higher education: A meta-analysis. *Computers & Education, 70*, 29–40. doi:10.1016/j.compedu.2013.07.033

Miltenberger, C. A., & Charlop, M. H. (2015). The comparative effectiveness of portable video modeling vs. traditional video modeling interventions with children with autism spectrum disorders. *Journal of Developmental and Physical Disabilities, 27*(3), 341–358. doi:10.100710882-014-9416-y

Norwich, B., & Lewis, A. (2001). Mapping a pedagogy for special educational needs. *British Educational Research Journal, 27*(3), 313–329. doi:10.1080/01411920120048322

Nye, E., Gardner, F., Hansford, L., Edwards, V., Hayes, R., & Ford, T. (2016). Classroom behaviour management strategies in response to problematic behaviours of primary school children with special educational needs: Views of special educational needs coordinators. *Emotional & Behavioural Difficulties, 21*(1), 43–60. doi:10.1 080/13632752.2015.1120048

O'Brennan, L. M., Waasdorp, T. E., Pas, E. T., & Bradshaw, C. P. (2015). Peer victimization and social-emotional functioning: A longitudinal comparison of students in general and special education. *Remedial and Special Education, 36*(5), 275–285. doi:10.1177/0741932515575615

Office of Special Education and Rehabilitative Services (ED). (2015). *37th annual report to Congress on the implementation of the" Individuals with Disabilities Education Act*. ERIC Clearinghouse.

Parker, A. T., Grimmett, E. S., & Summers, S. (2008). Evidence-based communication practices for children with visual impairments and additional disabilities: An examination of single-subject design studies. *Journal of Visual Impairment & Blindness, 102*(9), 540–552. doi:10.1177/0145482X0810200904

Parsons, S. (2015). Learning to work together: Designing a multi-user virtual reality game for social collaboration and perspective-taking for children with autism. *International Journal of Child-Computer Interaction, 6*, 28–38. doi:10.1016/j. ijcci.2015.12.002

Portman, M. E., Natapov, A., & Fisher-Gewirtzman, D. (2015). To go where no man has gone before: Virtual reality in architecture, landscape architecture and environmental planning. *Computers, Environment and Urban Systems, 54*, 376–384. doi:10.1016/j.compenvurbsys.2015.05.001

Ramachandiran, C. R., Jomhari, N., Thiyagaraja, S., & Mahmud, M. M. (2015). Virtual reality based behavioural learning for autistic children. *The Electronic Journal of e-Learning, 13*(5), 357-365.

Raskind, M., Smedley, T. M., & Higgins, K. (2005). Virtual technology: Bringing the world into the special education classroom. *Intervention in School and Clinic, 41*(2), 114–119. doi:10.1177/10534512050410020201

Rix, J., Hall, K., Nind, M., Sheehy, K., & Wearmouth, J. (2009). What pedagogical approaches can effectively include children with special educational needs in mainstream classrooms? A systematic literature review. *Support for Learning, 24*(2), 86–94. doi:10.1111/j.1467-9604.2009.01404.x

Rizzo, A., Parsons, T. D., Lange, B., Kenny, P., Buckwalter, J. G., Rothbaum, B., ... Reger, G. (2011). Virtual reality goes to war: A brief review of the future of military behavioral healthcare. *Journal of Clinical Psychology in Medical Settings, 18*(2), 176–187. doi:10.100710880-011-9247-2

Rose, F. D., Brooks, B. M., & Rizzo, A. A. (2005). Virtual reality in brain damage rehabilitation. *Cyberpsychology & Behavior, 8*(3), 241–262. doi:10.1089/cpb.2005.8.241

Rose, R., Shevlin, M., Winter, E., & O'Raw, P. (2015). *Project IRIS, inclusive research in Irish schools. A longitudinal study of the experiences of and outcomes for pupils with special educational needs (SEN) in Irish schools. Trim (Meath)*. National Council for Special Education.

Sakiz, H., Sart, Z. H., Börkan, B., Korkmaz, B., & Babür, N. (2015). Quality of life of children with learning disabilities: A comparison of self-reports and proxy reports. *Learning Disabilities Research & Practice, 30*(3), 114–126. doi:10.1111/ldrp.12060

Scacchi, W. (2012). *The future of research in computer games and virtual world environments*. Irvine, CA: Institute for Software Research, University of California.

Schwebel, D. C., Gaines, J., & Severson, J. (2008). Validation of virtual reality as a tool to understand and prevent child pedestrian injury. *Accident; Analysis and Prevention, 40*(4), 1394–1400. doi:10.1016/j.aap.2008.03.005

Shema-Shiratzky, S., Brozgol, M., Cornejo-Thumm, P., Geva-Dayan, K., Rotstein, M., Leitner, Y., ... Mirelman, A. (2018). Virtual reality training to enhance behavior and cognitive function among children with attention-deficit/hyperactivity disorder: Brief report. *Developmental Neurorehabilitation*, 1–6. doi:10.1080/17518423.2018.1476602

Stichter, J. P., Laffey, J., Galyen, K., & Herzog, M. (2014). iSocial: Delivering the social competence intervention for adolescents (SCI-A) in a 3D virtual learning environment for youth with high functioning autism. *Journal of Autism and Developmental Disorders, 44*(2), 417–430. doi:10.100710803-013-1881-0

Thompson, D., Whitney, I., & Smith, P. K. (1994). Bullying of children with special needs in mainstream schools. *Support for Learning, 9*(3), 103–106. doi:10.1111/j.1467-9604.1994.tb00168.x

United Nations Educational, Scientific and Cultural Organization (UNESCO). (1994). *The Salamanca statement and framework for action on special needs education*. Retrieved from http://unesdoc.unesco.org/images/0009/000984/098427eo.pdf

Vasquez, E. III, Marino, M. T., Donehower, C., & Koch, A. (2017). Functional analysis in virtual environments. *Rural Special Education Quarterly, 36*(1), 17–24. doi:10.1177/8756870517703405

Vlachou, A., Stavroussi, P., & Didaskalou, E. (2016). Special teachers' educational responses in supporting students with special educational needs (SEN) in the domain of social skills development. *International Journal of Disability Development and Education, 63*(1), 79–97. doi:10.1080/1034912X.2015.1111305

Volioti, C., Tsiatsos, T., Mavropoulou, S., & Karagiannidis, C. (2014, July). VLSS-Virtual Learning and Social Stories for Children with Autism. In *Proceedings of the 2014 IEEE 14th International Conference on Advanced Learning Technologies* (pp. 606-610). Athens, Greece: IEEE. 10.1109/ICALT.2014.177

Wagner, M. M. (1995). Outcomes for youths with serious emotional disturbance in secondary school and early adulthood. *The Future of Children, 5*(2), 90–112. doi:10.2307/1602359

Wang, M., & Reid, D. (2011). Virtual reality in pediatric neurorehabilitation: Attention deficit hyperactivity disorder, autism and cerebral palsy. *Neuroepidemiology, 36*(1), 2–18. doi:10.1159/000320847

Wang, X., Laffey, J., Xing, W., Galyen, K., & Stichter, J. (2017). Fostering verbal and non-verbal social interactions in a 3D collaborative virtual learning environment: A case study of youth with Autism Spectrum Disorders learning social competence in iSocial. *Educational Technology Research and Development, 65*(4), 1015–1039. doi:10.100711423-017-9512-7

Wilson, P. N., Foreman, N., & Stanton, D. (1997). Virtual reality, disability and rehabilitation. *Disability and Rehabilitation, 19*(6), 213–220. doi:10.3109/09638289709166530

Wong, S. E. (2010). Single-case evaluation designs for practitioners. *Journal of Social Service Research, 36*(3), 248–259. doi:10.1080/01488371003707654

Wuang, Y. P., Chiang, C. S., Su, C. Y., & Wang, C. C. (2011). Effectiveness of virtual reality using Wii gaming technology in children with Down syndrome. *Research in Developmental Disabilities, 32*(1), 312–321. doi:10.1016/j.ridd.2010.10.002

ADDITIONAL READING

Baker, B. L., Brightman, A. J., Blacher, J. B., Heifetz, L. J., Hinshaw, S. R., & Murphy, D. M. (2004). *Steps to independence: Teaching everyday skills to children with special needs*. Baltimore, MD: Brookes.

Danckaerts, M., Sonuga-Barke, E. J., Banaschewski, T., Buitelaar, J., Döpfner, M., Hollis, C., ... Taylor, E. (2010). The quality of life of children with attention deficit/hyperactivity disorder: A systematic review. *European Child & Adolescent Psychiatry, 19*(2), 83–105. doi:10.100700787-009-0046-3

DuPaul, G. J., Weyandt, L. L., & Janusis, G. M. (2011). ADHD in the classroom: Effective intervention strategies. *Theory into Practice, 50*(1), 35–42. doi:10.1080/00405841.2011.534935

Einfeld, S. L., Beaumont, R., Clark, T., Clarke, K. S., Costley, D., Gray, K. M., ... Taffe, J. R. (2018). School-based social skills training for young people with autism spectrum disorders. *Journal of Intellectual & Developmental Disability*, *43*(1), 29–39. doi:10.3109/13668250.2017.1326587

Florian, L., & Linklater, H. (2010). Preparing teachers for inclusive education: Using inclusive pedagogy to enhance teaching and learning for all. *Cambridge Journal of Education*, *40*(4), 369–386. doi:10.1080/0305764X.2010.526588

Hodkinson, A. (2015). Key issues in special educational needs and inclusion. *Sage (Atlanta, Ga.)*.

Ip, H. H., Wong, S. W., Chan, D. F., Byrne, J., Li, C., Yuan, V. S., ... Wong, J. Y. (2018). Enhance emotional and social adaptation skills for children with autism spectrum disorder: A virtual reality enabled approach. *Computers & Education*, *117*, 1–15. doi:10.1016/j.compedu.2017.09.010

Lee, F. L. M., Yeung, A. S., Tracey, D., & Barker, K. (2015). Inclusion of children with special needs in early childhood education: What teacher characteristics matter. *Topics in Early Childhood Special Education*, *35*(2), 79–88. doi:10.1177/0271121414566014

Liu, G. Z., Wu, N. W., & Chen, Y. W. (2013). Identifying emerging trends for implementing learning technology in special education: A state-of-the-art review of selected articles published in 2008–2012. *Research in Developmental Disabilities*, *34*(10), 3618–3628. doi:10.1016/j.ridd.2013.07.007

Standen, P. J., & Brown, D. J. (2005). Virtual reality in the rehabilitation of people with intellectual disabilities. *Cyberpsychology & Behavior*, *8*(3), 272–282. doi:10.1089/cpb.2005.8.272

KEY TERMS AND DEFINITIONS

3D Simulation: A three-dimensional computer-generated imitation of a real-world process or environment.

Attention-Deficit/Hyperactivity Disorder (ADHD): A brain disorder marked by an ongoing pattern of inattention and/or hyperactivity that interferes with normal functioning or development.

Autism Spectrum Disorder (ASD): A developmental disorder affecting communication and behavior. Symptoms generally appear in the first two years of life.

Learning Disabilities: Neurologically-based processing problems interfering with learning basic skills (e.g., reading, writing, and math) and/or higher-level skills (e.g., abstract reasoning, long-/short--term memory, and attention).

Non-Playable Character (NPC): Any character in a game not controlled by a player.

OpenSimulator: An open-source server platform for hosting virtual worlds.

Single-Subject Design (A-B design): A two part or phase research design composed of a baseline (A phase) with no changes, and a treatment or intervention (B phase). If changes are found, then the treatment had an effect.

Chapter 9
Teaching About Terrorism Through Simulations

Mat Hardy
Deakin University, Australia

Sally Totman
Deakin University, Australia

ABSTRACT

Creating positive learning outcomes regarding terrorism can be challenging. The nature of the topic offers several obstacles to learner understanding, not least of which is how to enable students to transcend their own cultural perspectives and develop deeper and more objective insights regarding the groups and causes that foster terrorism. Following an exploration of the growth in terrorism as an academic subject and the challenges posed to teaching in this area, this chapter presents a possible solution by describing an online role play exercise that has proven learning results over more than 25 years of usage. This tool, grounded in an experiential learning approach, can assist in easing some of the stresses faced by teachers and institutions, while also offering deeper and more insightful discoveries for participants.

DOI: 10.4018/978-1-7998-0004-0.ch009

Copyright © 2020, IGI Global. Copying or distributing in print or electronic forms without written permission of IGI Global is prohibited.

INTRODUCTION

The burgeoning growth of radical groups and ideologies around the world has seen a related expansion of terrorism as a 'subject' to be delivered in an educational context. The 9/11 attacks and the subsequent War on Terror spurred rapid development in higher education courses that either focus wholly on terrorism or include component modules on the topic. Today the need for students and teachers to grasp this phenomenon has not abated and educational providers are increasingly required to offer learning aimed at preparing graduates for careers in security and counter-terrorism.

Despite all this activity and demand, creating effective learning outcomes regarding terrorism can be challenging (Pinar Alakoc, 2018). The nature of the topic offers several obstacles to learner understanding, not least of which is how to enable students to transcend their own cultural perspectives and develop deeper and more objective insights regarding the groups and causes that foster terrorism. Achieving such comprehension by climbing the dry mountain of scholarly literature on terrorism is not likely, yet neither can traditional 'hands-on' experiences such as field trips be offered. At the same time, the emotive aspects of terrorism can be challenging for teachers to deal with, particularly in a political and legal environment that reacts strongly and punitively to perceived 'sympathy' for terrorists.

How then can educators best impart a multifaceted understanding of terrorism as a form of political violence? Following an exploration of the growth in terrorism as an academic subject and the challenges posed to teaching in this area, this chapter presents a possible solution by describing an online role play exercise that has learning results proven over more than 25 years of usage. This tool, grounded in an experiential learning approach, can assist in easing some of the stresses faced by teachers and institutions, while also offering deeper and more insightful discoveries for participants.

The growth in scholarly publication on terrorism after 9/11 is staggering. An audit of book titles available via *Amazon* carried out by Silke (2009) noted that prior to the attacks 1,310 non-fiction works had been published containing the world 'terrorism' in their title. But within the subsequent seven years, another 2,281 titles had been added. Dolnik (2015) reports that a new book on terrorism is released roughly every six hours! Similar studies on journal outputs covering terrorism offer comparable results: within four or five years after 9/11, the volume of scholarly articles produced on terrorism had exceeded the entire number produced in all the decades prior. Whole new journals devoted to terrorism studies were created and existing journals in the topic area increased their publishing frequency and article counts. To illustrate the physical extent of this slew of material, Dexter and Guittet (2014) describe their compilation of a 'scroll' by connecting printed pages of all the references they could find to books and articles on terrorism. The resulting list rolls out to over 120 metres.

This increase in words is paralleled by an increase in study options for those interested in terrorism, either intellectually or in terms of career progression. Degree courses offering majors in terrorism, counter-terrorism and related areas of political violence and security have blossomed, often on the back of post-9/11 funding avenues that saw universities around the world establish new research institutes, think tanks or outreach programs (Jackson, 2012). Existing degrees in areas such as International Relations, Political Science, Criminology and Sociology began to include modules and options that examined terrorism and/or political violence generally or in specific regions. For example, according to its archived handbooks, in 2002 Australia's Monash University offered only a single undergraduate module that dealt with security (in this case arms control).[1] They also offered just one unit dealing with the Middle East and none at all that mentioned terrorism in the title. By 2007, however, there were nine undergraduate units that had the words 'terrorism' or 'violence' in their titles, including ones that allowed for writing extended research projects on terrorism and security. There were also now three units specifically on the Middle East and another on 'Political Islam'. The same university had also opened a Global Terrorism Research Centre in 2006, which had emerged from a group called the Global Terrorism Research Unit, which was quickly put together in 2002. Such a growth in course offerings and dedicated research centres would be a common narrative around the world.

The growth and routine presence of academic studies of terrorism is in one way laudable and in another manner of concern. Whilst discussion and investigation of this topic help to improve understanding, satisfy intellectual curiosity and, hopefully, help us ameliorate the causes and effects of terrorism, the obstacles to *successfully* teaching in this area are significant (Miller, Mills, & Harkins, 2011). There are several reasons for this.

OBSTACLES TO SUCCESSFUL TEACHING ON TERRORISM

The initial challenge is posed by the sheer volume of published material. As noted above, literature and commentary on terrorism is overwhelming in quantity and the variety of themes pursued. Dolnik (2015) argues that over the last decade no other branch of the Humanities and Social Sciences has seen such a growth in output as that of terrorism studies. Not only is there the standard approach in looking at terrorism as a form of political violence, there are also troves of research on aspects such as the economics of terrorism, the psychology of terrorism, the history of specific groups or conflicts, legal remedies, counter-terrorism, media depiction and so on. For teachers or students, trying to distil some core readings or lines of enquiry into terrorism can therefore be daunting. Added to this is the Sisyphean nature of the task. The emergence of new terrorist groups, amalgamations of existing movements, name changes, state failures, tactical adaptions, counter offensives ...... all of these happen at such a rapid pace that what is written and published one year will likely be redundant the following. The slow pace of academic investigation and publishing will never succeed in catching up to the rapid evolution of this topic. This increases the difficulty for teachers in trying to deliver relevant material on terrorism and can deter students with a seemingly hopeless undertaking.

On top of this volume of scholarly attention is the extensive and sensational media coverage that results in an exaggeration of terrorism's reach and power. This can affect the preconceptions with which students approach the topic (Alakoc, 2018). Dramatic attacks such as those that took place on 9/11, or in Manchester, Boston or Paris, capture a great deal of notice and analysis in comparison to the more regular outrages that occur in states such as Afghanistan and Iraq. This raises the fear level of Western citizens disproportionately high in relation to the actual threat. Students may not be aware that the majority of casualties caused by terrorism do not happen in the West, do not target non-Muslims and tend to go largely unreported. This leads to a skewed and geo-centric perspective on the nature of terror, not to mention being infused with racial stereotypes and prejudices. Moreover, the depiction of terrorism and counter-terrorism in popular culture also serves to create a more fantastic impression of the topic, replete with nefarious masterminds, dashing heroes and climactic outcomes of choreographed violence. Terrorists have become a "popular and generic enemy" and thus a bankable ingredient in film, television and video game production for decades (Dexter & Guittet, 2014). As these romantic plotlines deliberately mirror some of the discourse and events surrounding the War on Terror and world events, a confused reality that merges fact and fiction becomes an accepted wisdom (Van Veeren, 2009). A focus on the tactical is also inevitable. The imagined abilities of terrorists and those who fight against them therefore become increasingly hyperbolic and divorced from the more mundane realities. Cutting through this blurred truth is therefore challenging for teachers, since their students' foundation for understanding terrorism and the campaign against it may be skewed from the outset.

An additional encumbrance encountered when teaching about terrorism is attracting criticism from those who see such analysis as a form of appeasement or encouraging of sympathy with extremists (Gereluk, 2012). Depending on the region and cause being studied, this can lead to accusations of national treachery, anti-Semitism and other vitriol. Poorly planned teaching activities can lead to media scrutiny and public outrage, such as in the case of an Australian high school teacher who asked her class to plan a fictitious mass casualty attack upon the country (Associated Press, 2010). Furthermore, concerns around the radicalisation of 'home-grown' terrorists at universities can exert pressure on academics to curtail their speech or teaching material on terrorism, either through fear of bad publicity or because of anti-terror laws (Dexter & Guittet, 2014). The 2008 case at the University of Nottingham highlights this paranoia. A pair of students were arrested for possessing an 'al-Qaeda training document' after nervous staff noticed it saved on a shared computer. The fact that one of the men was preparing a PhD proposal on militant Islam, that he had downloaded the document from the US Department of Justice website and that the so-called training manual was also available on *Amazon,* were not taken into account before police were contacted. Furthermore, the University of Nottingham subsequently instituted a peer review system, whereby the teaching material and reading lists of academics presenting classes on terrorism were scrutinised by a "module review committee" (Miller et al., 2011).

It is to be noted that there need not be an overt set of regulations proscribing the presentation of terrorism in university classes in order for academics to be nervous about their offerings. Instead the prevailing political climate combined with the realities of the 21st century higher education workplace can place an *implicit* gag on teachers. Factors such as the erosion of tenure, the growing reliance on corporate funding, enhanced cyber surveillance, risk-averse (and often non-academic) senior management and increasingly strident populist rhetoric in the media: all of these can exert a pressure on teachers to 'keep their heads down' (Gerstmann, 2006). In such an atmosphere it is likely that the teaching and study of terrorism may become shallow and generic, or at least limited to 'dates and names' type exposition.

This fear of becoming too close to the terrorist cause is related to a final challenge: how to impart understanding in a topic area that is often dichotomised into a simplistic contest between good and evil.[2] Moreover, that evil side of the equation is often swiftly dismissed not only as wicked, but also as irrational, perverse and un-representative of the demographic it purports to represent. Even those who avoid such moral judgement still tend to express a binary belief system encapsulated by the hackneyed adage of "One man's terrorist is another man's freedom fighter". Whilst having the intent of relativism, this dodge has very little to do with some of the ideological (rather than secessionist) terror movements of today and all the gradations in between. Conclusions that simplify terrorism would seem at odds with the time, money and commentary that are devoted to the issue.

Expanding the breadth and depth of terrorism teaching coverage is therefore necessary. As outlined above, there is no shortage of academic material on the topic, but dumping volumes of text on students is not an efficient tactic. Given that a teacher will have, at most, a few dozen hours to facilitate student learning on terrorism, much more than 'chalk and talk' is required. This is where computer simulations can help.

CHALKING IT UP TO EXPERIENCE

The strength of simulations is that they can offer the opportunity for experiential learning. At its simplest, experiential learning involves 'learning by doing'; the natural ability of human beings to gain knowledge and insight from having experienced or undertaken something (Beard & Wilson, 2006). Stehno (quoted in Itin, 1999) elaborates further, describing experiential learning as

- action that creates an experience
- reflection on the action and experience
- abstractions drawn from the reflection
- application of the abstraction to a new experience or action.

The reflective stage is critical and stems from the scholarship of Schön (1983), Kolb (1984) and Boud et al. (1985). The defining outcome is the transformation of that which is experienced into new knowledge or perspectives which can then be re-applied or adapted to future experience. Without this reflection and assimilation, experiences just remain experiences; effective learning does not occur. A graphical representation of this process is furnished by Kolb's model, which describes how new knowledge can be created through the transformation of experience. Under this process, the opportunity to reflect upon experience, analyse the components and concepts involved and then test them in new situations, cycles back to provide new experiences and learning.

Well established as this model is, fulfilling the cycle through *literal* experience in terrorism is an obviously absurd proposition for countless reasons. The need is for students to learn about and understand terrorism, not be involved in it. Indeed,

Figure 1. Kolb's (1984) description of the reflective learning cycle

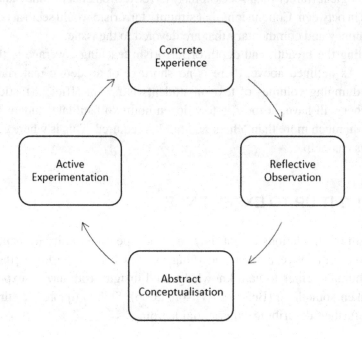

this quandary reflects many of the same challenges inherent to studying other, even non-violent areas of Political Science: how to give students practical experience? Concepts such as international co-operation, non-state violence, compromise and choosing between two wrong decisions; these are all difficult to experience and apply in a classroom setting. "Like card games and sports, politics is something that makes the most sense if it is actually played, not just talked about" (Grant, 2004, p. vii). The same would be true for understanding terrorism and global responses to it.

Naturally someone studying terrorism cannot just become a real politician or leader of a dissident group just for experiential learning purposes. It is necessary to pretend and for this reason, the use of role plays and simulations offer substantial benefits for those engaged with political and security studies.[3,4] Simulations allow students to experiment with variables and hypotheses in a safe environment. These can operate in a variety of formats, including face-to-face, via computer, in class, out of class and so on. They may be quite short or build up over weeks. They can be assessed or form the basis for further tasks such as reports or essays. There may be only a handful of teams or students or potentially hundreds. Whatever their configuration, these exercises allow examination of political topics, such as terrorism, in an experiential learning format that can unlock improved levels of understanding.

Even a cursory examination of Political Science pedagogical literature will offer many examples of in-class or face-to-face simulations being used to teach political topics. This includes the use of video conferencing or other technological means to facilitate synchronous negotiations where students are not co-located. However, there are fewer examples where a dedicated online environment is utilised and the emphasis in these studies is often on technology as a supplementary means of supporting or providing background for some sort of climactic *live* negotiation. This preliminary online communication may also be 'out of character' and mainly involve intra-team planning of their approach to the final event. Simulations that take place entirely online and entirely in-character are less apparent in the literature.

Whilst there is nothing problematic with using technology to plan or facilitate face-to-face simulation events there is further benefit to be found in removing the live factor and utilising a dedicated online interface, especially where the true identity of the student is hidden. Wills et al. (2010), emphasise the anonymity and asynchronicity provided by such online environments encourages the journey from passive learner to active contributor. When online roles remain anonymous participants can feel more liberated in their engagement with the exercise and in the adoption of their character. Their performance is less likely to be fettered by external, real-life factors such as power relationships, gender, reputation, cultural restraints or language ability. For example, it may be less credible, more uncomfortable and more likely to result in a stereotypical performance if a very masculine student is required to play a female role in front of his classroom peers, compared to him being able to do it anonymously. Likewise, the student well known for their strong left-wing and humanitarian views may also seem less plausible when trying to *publicly* play an ultra-conservative politician. Yet such examination of contrary viewpoints is a rewarding and encouraging possibility with role plays.

Beyond these practicalities, though, Wills et al. (2010) suggest that asynchronicity generates a greater depth of research, reflection and learning. Participants are not so much 'on the spot' as they are in live role play and can therefore put more thought into their words and actions, both before and after their 'turn'.

Furthermore, using an online role play can eliminate many of the temporal-spatial limitations of face-to-face role play. Depending on how the exercise is designed, asynchronous and remote participation are possible, meaning that off-campus students are much more able to take part (Hardy & Totman, 2013; Lloyd, 2004). Given the burgeoning numbers of remotely located students enrolled in higher education this is a significant advantage. Student cohorts that may be geographically dispersed, part-time and with significant commitments to paid work and family, can be accommodated more easily in an online format.

For the purposes of fostering experiential learning as well as addressing many of the realities of teaching the topic of terrorism today, online models of role play therefore seem to offer the best overall format option. A case study of a long-running example that deals with terrorism and political crisis will now be explored.

SIMULATING THE MIDDLE EAST

The Middle East Politics Simulation (MEPS) runs twice yearly at Deakin University, Australia.[5] Operating through a custom-built web browser interface, this email-driven simulation of diplomatic activity has been used for teaching Middle East studies content since the late 1980s, and has even moved between different universities. At around 30 years of age, it is possibly the oldest continually running online political role play and certainly one of the largest (in player numbers) and most complex examples used in the Political Science discipline.[6] In any iteration of the MEPS around 100-150 students will fill 50-70 roles comprising state and non-state actors concerned with the Middle East. The role play lasts 12 days and activity can take place 24/7 during that period. Over the last two decades thousands of students have taken part in at least one occurrence of the MEPS (Hardy & Totman, 2017a).

The MEPS uses a simple HTML interface (originally designed by a Computer Science student as an Honors project) to provide an imitation webmail environment that has no connectivity outside the simulation's walled garden. Students log in as their role (e.g., Whitehouse Press Secretary) and then have access to an email account with that alias. The appearance of the interface is very similar to a basic webmail client. A chat and tweeting function are also included. The basis of the exercise involves these students then playing the role they have been assigned by communicating through these various forms of text. The use of the team email identities is an important component of the simulation's realism, since emails received will have the role's name as the sender rather than a student's. This helps to hide the identity of the student, assisting role adoption and promoting credible in-character performance.

From the start the teams are expected to adopt their role and communicate with each other in character. The simulation relies upon the participants themselves to drive the narrative and act according to the goals, duties or views of the role they are playing. There is no specific goal or winning criteria beyond this need to act in character. There is no fundamental problem to solve or treasure to locate. Peace is not expected to break out. This is in contrast to other political roleplays, such as a Model UN or single-issue negotiation, that usually revolve around concluding with a particular output, like the wording of a resolution or a treaty that satisfies all stakeholders.

The simulation begins with a series of about 20 invented news stories (always based on real events). Every role will be a stakeholder in more than one of these stories and so have a natural opportunity to react. For example, there may be a story about the King of Jordan wanting to host a regional summit on terrorism. This obviously includes the King as a stakeholder, but also those teams playing his neighbouring states, perhaps some American cabinet members and so on. The students performing as the King of Jordan could then begin their simulation by planning the summit, sending out invitations, developing an agenda and so on. They would probably use the interface's chat function to hold the summit. Their job might be complicated by factors such as the Israeli government wanting to attend, which might then cause recrimination from Arab states, and so on. As the simulation progresses, these original news stories will usually fade from relevance because the actions and reactions of the teams provide their own self-sustaining plotlines.

Teams devising acts of violence, military intervention and so forth must first ask permission from the in-game referees, providing a plan, a rationale and some expected consequences. These will then be judged as to their viability, including whether other teams have taken specific counter-measures, as well as whether the act is 'in character'. Usually some form of negotiation between students and referee then occurs, where the original plan and its outcomes are adjusted before being approved.

The intended learning outcome for the MEPS is for students to gain a deeper understanding of the Middle East political system. This includes exploring the use, misuse, and limitations of violence as a political tool. Whilst not focussed solely on terrorism, the MEPS necessarily incorporates coverage of this tactic. This occurs through the inclusion of terror groups as roles in the simulation, as well as the roles of the state leaders and institutions that deal with terrorism and its effects. For example, at one time or another the exercise has included some of the following roles directly classed as terrorists:

- Islamic State
- Al-Qaeda in the Arabian Peninsula
- Al-Qaeda in the Islamic Maghreb
- Hamas
- Hezbollah
- The PKK

In addition to these groups the leadership of every state from Morocco to Iran is also represented, as well as the USA, Russia, China, UK and France. In some cases these national groupings will also incorporate cabinet roles, such as foreign and defence ministers, intelligence agencies and so on. International institutions such as the UN, UNHCR, EU, mass media and peak aid and development NGOs are also included.

Of significant difference to many one-off political simulations is that students can participate repeatedly in the MEPS. As the exercise is used in three Middle Eastern Studies modules offered in the major, some students will have the chance to undertake up to three MEPS iterations during the course of their degree, typically over a two-year period. These repeats will always be in different roles. This repetition not only assists in their own learning, but it provides a scaffold of peer exemplars to the first-timers on how to play the game, since in any run of the MEPS around half the participants will have one or two previous simulations under their belts. This ameliorates the very daunting first day or two of the MEPS where the rookies will have a limited idea of how to proceed. The repeat students then become the 'locomotives' that pull the neophytes along until they build up their own speed. By the time students have completed their third MEPS, the most successful will have developed a great deal of subject expertise, often being called upon by their peers and their teachers to share knowledge and opinions in class on the topics they have dealt with (Hardy & Totman, 2012).

The amount of work that students invest in the 12 days the MEPS runs is significant. Over six years of collecting data on the exercise, the average student reports around 4.5 hours a day as their involvement, far more time than they would probably spend on a task such as an essay (Hardy & Totman, 2017a). This leads to great depth and breadth of knowledge, not just regarding the role they are playing, but those other roles and issues that they will interact with. As a complex storyline emerges and students become more immersed in their roles, Kolb's reflective learning cycle accelerates. The simplistic actions and responses of the first days will become more nuanced, better researched and exhibit a growing depth of understanding.

Evidence of the learning journey in the MEPS is offered by long-term studies of the cohorts that have undertaken it. Students in each of the two runs per year are invited to take place in an anonymous feedback survey at the conclusion of the exercise (and prior to receiving their grade).[7] This survey has now been running across eight years and has attracted 986 responses. Although neither the MEPS nor the survey are targeted at terrorism learning specifically, one of the open-ended questions asks *"What did you learn about terrorism as a political tactic during the simulation?"* Some of the responses from that survey are included in the discussion of learning presented below.

THE SOLUTIONS OFFERED BY THE MEPS

A better understanding of the roots of terrorism is a principal gain for most participants in the MEPS. The two-week period allows multiple revolutions of the experiential learning cycle and a consequent evolution of attitudes and understanding. Whilst saying that the students 'learn more' could be seen as a nebulous claim, the gains made can be better exemplified by addressing them in the context of the challenges regarding teaching terrorism outlined above and in relation to Kolb's reflective learning cycle.

Developing Deeper Thinking

The phenomenon of seeing terrorism as a global omnipresence and/or having a media driven and exaggerated vision of it can be ameliorated by the MEPS. In the first two or three days of the exercise there is certainly a tendency for those 'popular culture' visions of terrorism to be apparent. The terrorist teams begin their experimentation by proposing repeated and simplistic schemes of bombings and other mass casualty attacks to the referees. These often pay little regard to the realities of their group's strength and location, what the repercussions might be and with scant thought as to what other goals their group may have aside from killing innocents. The estimates of what the result of such attacks might be in terms of casualties or damage are often vastly over-estimated by the students, as is the frequency with which a given group could undertake large and very complex attacks away from their core geography. For these students at the start of the simulation, the prevailing idea is that terrorist groups should be killing almost as a *raison d'être*: it's what they do, isn't it? Beyond this violence, the understanding of what a radical group might want to achieve politically or in the longer term is less obvious.

When such requests for violence are made to the MEPS referees they are usually met with gentle refusal and a suggestion to do more research. This would include asking the students what their group would hope to gain from such an act besides some vague 'statement', as well as asking them to investigate what their groups have tended to do historically and with what outcomes. Likewise, the anti-terror teams tend to have a Hollywood or video game understanding of how to respond to violent deeds, which is always focussed on the kinetic. Fanciful schemes of SEAL team raids, fleet movements, drone strikes and somehow finding all the terrorists by 'listening in' on their communications are the norm. Dramatic hostage rescues by Special Forces seem to be a particularly attractive fantasy. Again the predicted results of such acts are misjudged, with students making the assumption that a sufficient increase in airstrikes or troop deployments will somehow solve the problems posed by a terrorist insurgency. Teams proposing such plans are also urged to do more research as to the realities of their resources and the likely outcomes (including the low success rate of armed hostage rescues in the real world).

These negative responses from the referees/teachers form the 'concrete experience' end of the learning cycle; something was proposed and experimented with but did not have the expected outcome. It is now the task of the students to reflect as to why and conceptualise new or amended ideas.

Some students will struggle with this next step. As with any cohort there are a range of abilities and work ethics on display and those who have not done enough initial research on their role will find it difficult to put aside their preconceptions. It is not unusual to have students playing an insurgent group feeling deeply frustrated by the half-way point of the MEPS because they have no idea what else to do besides setting off bombs. Similarly some state-based teams will be clueless as to what else they can do to combat terror apart from *drop* bombs. An associated irritation will arise from the belief that organisations such as the CIA or Israeli military intelligence are omnipotent and it is *just not fair* that the referees are refusing to let them find the location of the hostages or where an attack is being planned.

This is where the simulation's long duration and asynchronous nature offer the chance for further reflection, though some further guidance from the teachers can be offered. This might be posed as a set of questions: Have you read your group's manifesto or mission statement? Based on this, what do you want to achieve? What are your major grievances and with whom? Who funds you? Who else could you approach for support? What geographies are you strong in? What type of actions has this group undertaken before and what were the results? Since the objective of the MEPS is to communicate in character and deepen one's understanding of the region, having a terrorist team write an updated manifesto or pen a reasoned plea to a sympathetic government for more political support is demonstratively more important for student learning than fixating on a tactical outcome such as suicide bombing. Likewise, for the Jordanian team to participate in a virtual summit on regional terror with their Arab neighbours is more valuable for all concerned than just asking "Can we send more planes to bomb ISIS?" This sort of experiential learning is also of greater worth than writing a standard academic essay on such topics.[8]

As the exercise progresses and the learning circle turns again and again, the teams inevitably advance their understanding of terrorism and the way that it operates in the Middle East and North African region. Plans become more considered and for the terrorist groups, questions of ideological, political and financial support come to the fore. Students begin to appreciate that killing a handful of people with a car bomb is limited as to its long-term impact. A sense of why some groups resort to the use of terror also emerges, expressed as an identification rather than an endorsement.[9] This is an important outcome since for students who aspire to working in fields where they may have to deal with the security and political consequences of terrorism, an awareness of the 'why' is more important than the 'how'. Examples of this deepening understanding are provided by comments taken from the student feedback that is gathered after each MEPS:[10]

- *Whilst I don't condone terrorism you can see why some people resort to extremism. You see people's lack of opportunity, disenfranchisement, the human rights abuses they face (often at the hands of their own government) and you can understand on a personal level how this would change someone.*

- *I do not think that terrorism is a valid form of resistance at all. I think that its use only gives your enemies a moral standpoint from which to attack you and your organisation's beliefs further. Each time a terrorist group attacks, the rest of the world unites around the victims of that cause (although observably less so if you're Iraqi and not French). I understand the effectiveness of terrorism as a tactic, however I believe it to be short term and is not suitable as a catalyst for any real political change.*

- *I think terrorism is a lot more complicated than I anticipated; it's a lot more than blowing up something. For some groups it is their only valid method of standing up to an oppressor or making a point about something. I think its deeply entrenched in the region's political history and that makes it almost inescapable, as so many people turn to it because it is the political norm.* (By participating in the MEPS) *I never expected to understand terrorism the way I did.*

- *I think the* (MEPS) *changed my views on terrorism in that I understand why certain groups may be inclined to use terrorism as a tactic. I definitely saw the strengths and weaknesses in terrorism - it definitely helps achieve certain goals but it comes at a cost, usually through the response of the international community. I feel that I view terrorism as more complex now. Terrorists are not necessarily out to shed blood for the sake of it but have 'legitimate' reasons for feeling the way they do and are often pushed into seeking alternative ways to achieve their goals and terrorism happens to be a semi effective way of doing so.*

A more measured contemplation of the way that governments can use the threat of terrorism as a rallying point or excuse for further repression is another conclusion for some students. This includes addressing the reality of whether terrorism really is as potent a force as they previously believed:

- *Terrorism didn't seem like a hugely successful tactic and only seemed to draw countries closer in the Middle East and the West.*
- *You can move an agenda when acts of terrorism occur. Enacting a closed border policy is simple when you cause terrorism to justify your response.*
- *What I get from it is that a terrorist organization can become a common enemy for feuding countries to fight together against.*
- *What we did find was that people have many different ideas when it comes to tackling it. Terrorism seemed to be more of a shadow, and not anything physical yet it was all anyone talked about.*
- *The sim shows how much impact a terrorist organisation can have. The unpredictability of attacks exacerbates people's fear.*
- *It's amazing how such an isolated event can cause such wide spread ramifications. A murder is a murder and is worth maybe a two second mention. But call it a terrorist attack and everyone thinks they are going to die for no apparent reason.*

Understanding of specific debates or examples of terrorism can also arise. Among those teams playing Palestinian actors a vigorous debate inevitably ensues over the use of terrorism, with some wanting to take a peaceful stance of negotiation while others want to lash out in any way possible. In the pro-peace camp, a fear of how acts of terror can affect the image of the Palestinian cause is paramount, yet this is tempered with some acceptance that other options are disappearing. Even the violent factions will understand that their acts are ultimately self-defeating, but they will also become conscious that acts of militancy are important in building prestige both with domestic audiences and those in non-Western states.

- *Trying to work alongside Hamas who continuously resorted to violence instead of negotiating with Israel identified how short term terrorism is. They were fighting a losing battle by resorting to violence and it was extremely difficult to negotiate with that thorn in our side.*
- *As Hamas, I learned that when the media ignore or misconstrue your perspective, when everyone refuses to acknowledge your diplomatic efforts and when it really feels like you're caught between a rock and a hard place,*

sometimes acts of resistance seem like the only way to not get trampled on, even if it means being branded a terror organization. However, we always gained more sympathy and support when we tried to buck that trend and make our enemies look worse than we did. I think violent resistance is always going to make a message heard more effectively, but probably not in the way that's going to provide the best outcome. It is a valid form of resistance but one that is going to have significant draw backs.

To facilitate even wider reflection, the MEPS convenors encourage (but never force) students to play a role that has a diametrically opposing viewpoint to their own, real-world sympathies. For example, asking students with strong Zionist views to play Palestinian roles, or those with strident anti-American sentiments to play US government roles. The aim here is not to 'convert' people, but merely temper them through a deeper understanding of the other perspective. In the context of researching this role, this can also push them towards sources and scholarship that they would not have ordinarily been exposed to. For those students who will play the MEPS three times during the course of their studies, the convenors will guide them to play quite different roles each time in order to ensure a broad spread of learning.

Cutting Through the Volume of Scholarship

Having learning outcomes driven by the students themselves provides a solution to another of the challenges noted at the start of this chapter: dealing with the vast volume of scholarship on terrorism. The MEPS helps to reduce this because the required reading and scholarship for any one student becomes more focussed around their particular role. This makes the mountain of literature less daunting and gives a natural entry to the topic as a whole. The typical reported journey shows a progression through levels of reference material. As with any student these days, the MEPS participant will most likely start with a *Wikipedia* article on their assigned group or leader. From there they will progress to relevant books, news articles and primary sources. The simulation therefore flips most Political Science teaching: the students start with a case study and this then acts as the key for unlocking reflection on wider issues. For example, rather than the typical approach of students wading through literature and debate on the definition of terrorism, the MEPS team members will begin with a belief system on terrorism dictated by the role they are playing. They then have to test this against the values of the other parties in the simulation. By the end of the MEPS they will have experienced all sorts of definitions of what is and is not terrorism and responses to it. This equips them to engage in sustained discussion on the 'bigger picture' of the topic outside of the simulation without that initial inundation of reading.

A Dangerous Topic

The student-driven approach also goes some way to alleviating another of the tensions described earlier: the implied pressures felt by teachers regarding what they present on terrorism and how this might be construed as supportive of radical causes. The students in a role play will need to research their own roles, removing the need for the teacher to 'lecture' about the topic and have this material ascribed to them. The experiential learning cycle also offers a deeper level of insight than a standard lecture approach can and allows students to form their own opinions.

With regard to awakening 'terrorist sympathies' in students, the likelihood of someone becoming radicalised *solely* due to participating in a simulation seems remote. As with any approach to the topic, there may be a tiny chance of someone *already* on the brink of radical activity having their beliefs further substantiated by a simulation.[11] There is no antidote for this besides not teaching anything at all about terrorism and discouraging any exploration of the phenomenon. Of course, this could have the exact opposite outcome, with the resulting ignorance leading to a more romanticised vision of radical groups.

Caution is still required when running simulations dealing with terrorism, particularly in the way the content or intention may be misconstrued by security agencies and the public accidentally encountering this activity. This is the reasoning behind making the MEPS a fully closed system where emails cannot leave the interface. To avoid misunderstandings, students are also forbidden from contacting each other on simulation business outside of the system (e.g. via Facebook or messaging apps) and warned about discussing things in public places where they may be overheard and, understandably, cause alarm. The convenors of the MEPS also counsel students about accessing, downloading and distributing what might be considered illegal content in Australia; such as the magazines and manuals produced by groups such as al-Qaeda or Islamic State. Finally, the Australian intelligence authorities are notified prior to each running of the MEPS to avoid any confusion. Being conscious of this intersection between state security sensitivities and education will always be something that needs to be considered in any planning of such a simulation and firm learning objectives should always be kept in mind.

CONCLUSION

The challenges posed by teaching about terrorism are a consequence of its centrality to world political discourse since 2001. This has created a great market demand for academic analysis but also formed sensitivities on the topic and an overwhelming volume of scholarly material and popular culture treatment. All of these can combine to hinder effective learning outcomes for students seeking to understand terrorism. However, online role plays such as the MEPS can address these difficulties.

Based on decades of experience with the MEPS, a common realisation regarding terrorism is a greater understanding of the underlying causes of radicalisation and what drives individuals and groups to adopt terror as a tactic. However, an awareness of the ultimate futility of this approach is also gained, along with the limitations of the military solutions often used to counter terrorism. Students emerge with thoughts along the lines of 'I can see *why* they do it, *but* I don't agree that it is the right path. More needs to be done to address the roots of these grievances.' This sort of sophisticated learning outcome is a direct result of that chance afforded by simulations to play the role rather than read the book or write the essay.

REFERENCES

Al-Rawi, A. (2018). Video games, terrorism, and ISIS's Jihad 3.0. *Terrorism and Political Violence*, *30*(4), 740–760. doi:10.1080/09546553.2016.1207633

Asal, V. (2005). Playing games with international relations. *International Studies Perspectives*, *6*(3), 359–373. doi:10.1111/j.1528-3577.2005.00213.x

Associated Press. (2010). *Teacher's assignment to HS students: Plan a deadly terror attack*. Retrieved from https://warisboring.com/stealth-bombers-blast-libya-14c7566558ee#.yrukq66o1

Beard, C., & Wilson, J. P. (2006). *Experiential learning: A best practice handbook for educators and trainers*. London, UK: Kogan Page.

Ben-Yehuda, H., & Zohar, G. (2018). Fanaticism through the looking glass of simulations. *Journal of Political Science Education*, *14*(2), 197–221. doi:10.1080/15512169.2017.1418367

Boud, D., Keogh, R., & Walker, D. (1985). What is reflection in learning? In D. Boud, R. Keogh, & D. Walker (Eds.), *Reflection: Turning Experience into Learning* (pp. 7–17). London: Kogan Page.

Boyer, M. A., Trumbore, E., & Frick, D. E. (2006). Teaching theories of international political economy from the Pit: A simple in-class simulation. *International Studies Perspectives*, *7*(1), 67–76. doi:10.1111/j.1528-3577.2006.00231.x

Chasek, P. S. (2005). Power politics, diplomacy and role playing: Simulating the UN security council's response to terrorism. *International Studies Perspectives*, *6*(1), 1–19. doi:10.1111/j.1528-3577.2005.00190.x

Dexter, H., & Guittet, E.-P. (2014). Teaching (something about) terrorism: Ethical and methodological problems, pedagogical suggestions. *International Studies Perspectives*, *15*(4), 374–393. doi:10.1111/j.1528-3585.2012.00507.x

Dolnik, A. (2015). Conducting field research on terrorism. In C. Kennedy-Pipe, G. Clubb, & S. Mabon (Eds.), Terrorism and Political Violence (pp. 288-296). London: SAGE. doi:10.4135/9781473917248.n21

Dougherty, B. K. (2003). Byzantine politics: Using simulations to make sense of the Middle East. *PS, Political Science & Politics*, *36*(02), 239–244. doi:10.1017/S1049096503002154

Gereluk, D. (2012). *Education, extremism and terrorism. [electronic resource]: What should be taught in citizenship education and why*. New York: *Continuum*.

Gerstmann, E. (2006). The century ahead: A brief survey of potential threats to freedom of speech, thought, and inquiry at American universities. In E. Gerstmann & M. J. Streb (Eds.), *Academic freedom at the dawn of a new century* (pp. 175–186). Stanford, CA: Stanford University Press.

Hardy, M., & Totman, S. (2012). From dictatorship to democracy: Simulating the politics of the Middle East. In C. Nygaard, N. Courtney, & E. Leigh (Eds.), *Transforming university teaching into learning via games, simulations and role-plays* (pp. 189–206). Faringdon, UK: Libri Publishing.

Hardy, M., & Totman, S. (2013). Using an online simulation to address equity issues for off-campus students. In J. Willems, B. Tynan, & R. James (Eds.), *Outlooks and opportunities in blended and distance learning* (pp. 139–153). Hershey, PA: IGI Global. doi:10.4018/978-1-4666-4205-8.ch011

Hardy, M., & Totman, S. (2017a). The long game: Five years of simulating the Middle East. *Australasian Journal of Educational Technology*, *33*(4), 38–52. doi:10.14742/ajet.2696

Hardy, M., & Totman, S. (2017b). Teaching an old game new tricks: Long-term feedback on a re-designed online role play. *British Journal of Educational Technology*, *48*(6), 1260–1272. doi:10.1111/bjet.12498

Hintjens, H. M. (2008). *Through the looking glass? Learning from simulating Rwanda.* Paper presented at the World Conference on E-Learning in Corporate, Government, Healthcare, and Higher Education 2008, Las Vegas, NV.

Itin, C. M. (1999). Reasserting the philosophy of experiential education as a vehicle for change in the 21st century. *Journal of Experiential Education, 22*(2), 91–98. doi:10.1177/105382599902200206

Jackson, R. (2012). The study of terrorism 10 years after 9/11: Successes, issues, challenges. *International Relations / Uluslararasi Iliskiler, 9*(33), 1-16.

Kolb, D. (1984). *Experiential Learning: Experience as the Source of Learning and Development.* Upper Saddle River, NJ: Prentice-Hall.

Lloyd, K. (2004). *Playing games with conflict: The Ha Long Bay e-Sim.* Paper presented at the International Conference on Computers in Education 2004, Melbourne, Australia. Retrieved from http://plum.yuntech.edu.tw/icce2004/Theme1/022_Lloyd.pdf

McCarthy, J. P., & Anderson, L. (2000). Active learning techniques versus traditional teaching styles: Two experiments from history and political science. *Innovative Higher Education, 24*(4), 279–294. doi:10.1023/B:IHIE.0000047415.48495.05

Miller, D., Mills, T., & Harkins, S. (2011). Teaching about terrorism in the United Kingdom: How it is done and what problems it causes. *Critical Studies on Terrorism, 4*(3), 405–420. doi:10.1080/17539153.2011.623416

Pinar Alakoc, B. (2018). Terror in the classroom: Teaching terrorism without terrorizing. *Journal of Political Science Education*, 1–19. doi:10.1080/15512169.2018.1470002

Sasley, B. E. (2010). Teaching students how to fail: Simulations as tools of explanation. *International Studies Perspectives, 11*(1), 61–74. doi:10.1111/j.1528-3585.2009.00393.x

Schon, D. (1983). *The reflective practitioner.* New York, NY: Basic Books.

Silke, A. (2009). Critical terrorism studies: A new research agenda. In J. Gunning, R. Jackson, & M. Smyth (Eds.), *Routledge critical terrorism studies* (pp. 34–48). New York, NY: Routledge.

Simpson, A. W., & Kaussler, B. (2009). IR teaching reloaded: Using films and simulations in the teaching of international relations. *International Studies Perspectives*, *10*(4), 413–427. doi:10.1111/j.1528-3585.2009.00386.x

Tobin Grant, J. (2004). *Playing politics*. New York, NY: W.W. Norton & Company.

Van Veeren, E. (2009). Interrogating 24: Making sense of US counter-terrorism in the global war on terrorism. *New Political Science*, *31*(3), 361–384. doi:10.1080/07393140903105991

KEY TERMS AND DEFINITIONS

Experiential Learning: Learning through experience and reflection upon those experiences. The process involves the student progressing through their own learning journey and can incorporate experience gained in non-classroom settings too.

Middle East: A geographical and political term used to define an area of the world incorporating parts of West Asia and North Africa. This is approximate to the Arab-speaking states, plus Israel, Turkey and Iran.

Political Science: A discipline within the Social Sciences that analyses political behavior, governance, and philosophies of leadership and communal activity. Comprised of numerous sub-fields.

Reflective Learning: Taking learned experiences and transforming those into new knowledge or perspectives which can then be re-applied or adapted to inform future experience. Part of the Experiential Learning cycle.

Role Play: Acting the part of another person or entity or a framework for doing so. In an educational context this includes adopting the behaviors and priorities of a real-world person or group and interacting with other players who will have their own competing agendas.

Simulation: A role-playing framework that seeks to imitate genuine scenarios or parameters in order for participants to undertake an experiential learning process through their interactions.

Terrorism: A form of politically or ideologically motivated violence intended to invoke fear and change among a wider population via indiscriminate attacks or threats against civilians.

ENDNOTES

1   For a list of archived handbooks at this university, see www.monash.edu.au/pubs/handbooks/archive.html .

2   For example, see Baylouny, Anne Marie. 2009. "Seeing Other Sides: Nongame Simulations and Alternative Perspectives of Middle East Conflict." *Journal of Political Science Education* 5 (3):214-232; Stover, William James. 2005. "Teaching and Learning Empathy: An Interactive, Online Diplomatic Simulation of Middle East Conflict." *Journal of Political Science Education* 1 (2):207-219; Hardy, Mat, and Sally Totman. 2012. "From Dictatorship to Democracy: Simulating the Politics of the Middle East." In *Simulations, Ganes and Role Play in University Education*, edited by Claus Nygaard, Nigel Courtney and Elyssebeth Leigh, 189-206. Faringdon, UK: Libri Publishing.

3   The term 'role play' does not in itself equate to simulation and nor does every simulation involve role play. However, role play may be an element of a game or simulation, particularly those focussed on 'social processes'. For example, simulating the diplomacy prior to a UN Security Council meeting may involve students playing the roles of delegates. For purposes of this chapter, though, the terms 'simulation' and 'role play' will be used interchangeably.

4   For a broad range of coverage on this topic, see Asal, V. (2005); Boyer, M.A., E. Trumbore, and D.E. Frick. (2006) 2006; Chasek, P.S. (2005); Hintjens, H.M. (2008); Simpson, A.W., and B. Kaussler (2009); Dougherty, B. K. (2003); McCarthy, J. P., and L. Anderson (2000); Sasley, B.E. (2010).

5   For a fuller description of the task and its assessment practices, see Hardy & Totman (2012, 2013, 2017a). For a discussion of how the game has evolved technologically over time, including student feedback to changes in the interface, see Hardy and Totman, 2017b.

6   The University of Maryland's ICONS Project has a similar timeline as an online political simulation tool. However, it is not one single simulation but rather a platform for facilitating multiple examples, both off-the-shelf and tailor-made.

7   For data presented after the five-year mark on how students have evaluated their learning experience of the MEPS see (Hardy & Totman, 2017a).

8   In the five-year study (Hardy & Totman, 2017a), an average of 94% of respondents (n=609) rated the MEPS exercise as 'better' or 'much better' than a traditional written assignment, despite the fact that it is much more work for them.

9   See also Ben-Yehuda and Zohar (2018) for a good exploration of identification versus empathy in simulations of fanaticism.

10   All the student responses utilised in this chapter are from a cohort that undertook the MEPS and completed the feedback survey on September 2016.

11   For example, unknown supporters of Islamic State released a video game in 2014 called "Salil al-Sawarem" (*The Clanging of the Swords*) in an attempt to glamorize the group's battlefield actions and draw attention from a demographic *already sympathetic* to the IS ideology (Al-Rawi, 2018).

Chapter 10
Shaping an Evaluation Framework for Simulations:
A Marriage Proposal

Wendi M. Kappers
https://orcid.org/0000-0002-7491-5276
Embry-Riddle Aeronautical University, USA

ABSTRACT

This chapter presents a hypothesized evaluation framework for measuring the effectiveness of simulations for learning, while indirectly providing an instructional design framework. The proposed framework was formulated using course design concepts, a newly emerged purpose-based simulation taxonomy, and a frame using Kolb's Experiential Learning Theory. To examine the untested taxonomy, which posited an alignment between purpose-based simulation categories to that of Bloom, an analysis reviewing literature within the last decade identified 80 articles. Correlation analysis indicated the area of application when compared to that of a modeling-based simulation type presented the strongest relationship. A summary section includes various domain examples to demonstrate an initial examination for fit to the newly proposed framework.

DOI: 10.4018/978-1-7998-0004-0.ch010

Copyright © 2020, IGI Global. Copying or distributing in print or electronic forms without written permission of IGI Global is prohibited.

INTRODUCTION

As this chapter is one of several within our book "Teaching, Learning, and Leading with Computer Simulations" that explores some aspect of using simulations for learning, the intent of this particular chapter is to provide a new evaluation framework for measuring effectiveness of simulations for learning, while indirectly providing an instructional design framework in which to build courses containing simulations. To support this goal, a discussion will unfold that begins by discussing the importance of simulations to the educational field. Since gaps in teaching and design of learning activity support were identified within the literature, both challenges and opportunities will be presented that showcase the need for such an evaluation framework. An extended discussion will include the more predominate happenings in the field of working with educational simulations. The chapter will explore the more popularized forms of examination techniques and theories currently being used in the field that explore simulation effectiveness for learning. The focus of the chapter, however, will shift midway to review issues found that led to the conception of said framework. They include: (a) missing implementation guidelines, (b) missing instructional design support, and (c) the lack of cross-domain investigations in which data could be generalized. To address these concerns, it is posited that a uniquely hypothesized framework be considered. This particular evaluation framework was formulated using course design concepts, a newly emerged simulation taxonomy, and a frame based lens using Kolb's Experiential Learning Theory (ELT). Taken from previous systematic literature reviews and literature reviewed within the last decade, 80 articles were located in support of this research goal to better investigate one of the three framework components, which is a newly proposed purpose-based taxonomy for the classification of simulation types per learning activity. To this end, a "marriage of the ages" is suggested for the purpose of embedding this taxonomy into a Kolb-based course investigation to posit how these elements can work in tandem in order to begin to address these gaps of support for the field. While some may say this is a lofty goal to address such a great issue using only a suggested framework, discussed in a small chapter of a book, it is hoped that this chapter will spark a greater discussion, and exhibit an acceptable resource for educators alike. Therefore, let's begin and consider how to better provide much need support to tackle these profound issues.

Definition of Computer Simulation

When reviewing the historical literature, a major discrepancy of constant complaint is the many confounded definitions for the term simulation. Therefore, without consistency, comparative analyses can become hard to complete due to the varying measures used to evaluate one type of simulation over the next. Oren (2011) made great strides to correct this error by undertaking a project to create a Body of Knowledge index to address these many differences. In his exploration, the author uncovered over 400 representations of the term alone. Oddly, the author delineated the works discovered between the areas of "defense-related" and "civilian" resources, clearly indicating a military background and viewpoint, which may have hindered the overall project by using a limited structural system. Nevertheless, the author found a total of nine ways in which to classify four decades-worth of research.

For the sake of this chapter, a more current and acceptable definition posited by Qian (2016) will be used: a "computer-based instructional program that is designed to reproduce a real life entity, phenomenon, activity, situation, process, or system, the purpose of which is to provide a real-life or close-to-real-life learning environment," (p. 265). Simulations after all are seen as a mechanism for the sake of this discussion.

Importance of (Learning) Simulations

In these times of technology expansion within our daily lives, information literacy is no longer a topic for simple discussion. It has become a much needed skill in order to ascertain the truth behind the information gathered to ensure reliability is found (Kappers, 2017). We live in a society that is no longer based upon an "expert to pupil" pyramid (Berragan, 2011). It is a society in which information is gathered through many sources and persons, and somewhat a quest or personal learning experience all in its own right. This learning experience can be shaped by personal experience, previous knowledge, influenced by those around us, or at least, this is what the many theories indicate. Yet, it has been found that this type of learning is, well, natural. Similarly, simulations often draw upon the learner experience and concurrently allow for personalized experiences in which to build new learning and understanding in a critical manner due to the immediate feedback a simulation can provide. This lack of educator intervention being replaced by an informal simulator is important to the field. This shift is seen as providing an opportunity for students to draw upon reflective techniques to best quantify a condition rather than focusing upon the overall "how" of the concept (Lee-Kelley, 2018).

There are many important reasons behind the use of simulations in the learning experience as well. Simulations can represent real-aspects of the given scenario, have the ability to conceptualize in a simple format, and can best explain otherwise "complex theories, rules of the situation, or the phenomena itself" (Qian, 2016, p. 7). Guise, Chambers, and Valimaki (2012) express the numerous benefits that can be realized when using simulations in the learning process as these tools provide methods to create: (a) standardized practices, (b) hands-on practice in high-stakes arenas, (c) the possibility of immediate feedback, and (d) in some situations, in which there are ethical concerns (p. 411). Additionally, important was the correlation between the momentums of simulation adoption to that of computer power of the time causing some to ask why. Moore's Law is an easy answer. Moore's law describes that the doubling of transistors translates exponentially to the doubling of computing power. This law then explains as computing power was slow to grow so was the investigation for using simulations for learning. This correlation slowed changes made to the type of technology used for teaching within the curriculum.

However, many believe the implementation of simulation in the science curriculum community was very profound no matter the limitations or slow pace of growth (Greca, Seoane, & Arriassecq, 2014). Simulations have greatly changed the landscape by providing new insight and guidance otherwise not afforded. Historically, the implementation of simulations for learning was a multifaceted introduction, one that changed the methods for investigation but also introduced a new tool for learning at the same time (Greca et al., 2014). Thus, some believe this implementation to be a revolution of sorts and have compared this paradigm shift as powerful as the implementation of the microscope or telescope (Greca et al., 2014).

Challenges Found

Challenges for using simulations span domains ranging from real-life representation issues to that of fidelity concerns within areas outside of the medical field, a domain in which fidelity is of high importance. Berragan (2011) commented about the inadvertent "theoretical vacuum" that simulated conditions may create. Simulations do tend to lend themselves to isolated working conditions since many aspects are of discrete processes rather than a combined event or one that is specifically created to meet the challenges required for social exploration possibilities. One might even suggest that this vacuum simply exists as simulations cannot truly create a genuine environment unless the simulation is the exact replica of the tool used. Also, simulations cannot be the event itself containing all normal conditions as they present themselves in an active situation. Prensky (2001) disagrees indicating the military does very well to present "'physically' correct as possible, at whatever level of detail is appropriate" (p. 213) conditions as to manage expectations prior to entry in active situations. However, this support is of a very unique learning environment and domain in which much funding and technology are available. Thus, this domain may have the ability to remove larger implementation barriers experienced in academia.

Further, some argue for the need for better representation of affective domain needs, such as communication or positive reinforcement conditions that only human-to-human interaction can create (Guise et al., 2012). While these statements appeared to be stated in a matter-of-fact notion within the literature, one must acknowledge that even Artificial Intelligence (AI) hasn't even risen to the expected plateau, nor are AI tools able to eliminate the prejudice of speaking with a computer. Conditions of this nature can cause one to become bored with the training event and create conditions in which learning is no longer perpetuated (Prensky, 2001). Conversely, Eckhardt, Urhahne, Conrad, and Harms (2013) indicate that automated, yet positive simulated feedback, attributes aside, will always have need for self-regulation. Simulation utilization in a self-regulated environment "implies that learners can acquire new contents in an autonomous and meaningful way" (p. 108). This may not always be the case. "True hands-on activities may not exist or be available for all types of industries, such as within healthcare and core engineering sciences fields due to cost, access, or ethical obligations" (Kappers & Cutler, 2016, p. 66).

Lastly, larger areas of concern, that of trainer preparation (Greca et al., 2014), missing modular design, and implementation guidance, appeared. Moule (2011) indicated that simulation implementation presents a double-edged sword in so far as the need for those who employ these types of tools for learning must be equally trained in order manage the learning environment to maximize the potential of use. Furthermore, if time to learn to use a particular simulation is difficult to situate, content design may also suffer and be haphazardly implemented presenting students with incorrect instructions for utilization. This condition culminates in the possibility of a failed learning event. To support this view, Guise, Chambers, and Valimaki (2012) confirmed there is a true lack of guidance when deploying simulations for learning making this a primary concern for trainer preparation or when seeking answers to questions of effectiveness and existence of achievement increases. This injection creates a double-conundrum that may affect one's selection to include a simulation in a process. On one hand, there is a tool that should be used to its maximum potential in the classroom setting, yet, there are many parameters or considerations that need to be defined and implemented in order to have goals and learning outcomes realized. Thus, accepting that these learning events must be properly constructed and designed in order to maximize the expected outcome(s), guidance and unified evaluation methods must be provided and this is the primary challenge in which to focus.

Opportunities Realized

As with any challenges there will always be positives to balance the equation. The same can be said for the many opportunities provided by simulations when used as training tools within a learning event. Many of the opportunities showcased within the field mention the importance of technological improvements (de Jong, 2019) for creating said changes. In specific, much reflection can be seen concerning updates to software now available, which has the ability to create more realistic learning environments. The most compelling opportunity afforded by the literature concerned trial and error settings and the creation of safer training environments in which to explore medical conditions (Smetana & Bell, 2012), such as those provided by Virtual Operating Rooms (Palter & Grantcharov, 2010). McCaughey and Traynor (2010) praised the many opportunities for patient protection that high-fidelity simulations create. Whereas, low-fidelity simulations are seen to only provide improved didactic moments. This view is sometimes referred to as Concept Analysis training. High-fidelity simulations strongly support the practice of gaining understanding of general principles or experiences in such situations when details are simply too overwhelming for a novice to process (Prensky, 2001).

While technological advances may be seen by some as a hindrance as having to continually update hardware and software elements, those in the healthcare domain are embracing the greater benefit and the many affordances realized due to improvements in technology. For example, Barragan (2011) was extremely supportive of the changes in manikin technology in comparison to those devices from past decades. While an obvious condition, improvement in fields of engineering and psychology directly contributed to the improved realistic qualities of said manikins and working with simulated patients. These upgrades have the ability to surpass expected outcomes and create unrealized opportunities that can be uncovered during future investigations. Exposure to environments otherwise inaccessible for ecological experimentation has also seen great strides, such as those examining the disposal of hazardous materials (Chung, Harmon, & Baker, 2001). Furthermore, the Physical Sciences domain, specifically Chemistry, has seen opportunities to create safer learning environments, much like those found in the medical field.

The most profound opportunity afforded by the literature is that simulated environments have been found to be more effective than traditional modes (Plass et al., 2012). To further demonstrate these benefits, Xie, Scimpf, Chao, Nourian, and Massicotte (2018) provided a heat transfer example. This example demonstrated heat transfer theory as it applies to a zero-energy building scenario using the invisible conceptual element. As the authors explained, the heat transfer is unseen to the naked eye, yet is a highly important consideration within zero-energy design concepts. In turn, the simulation is able to demonstrate the escaping heat. In total, the visualization provides support for students to make informed decisions that equate to rationale and understanding of the cognitive topic. Therefore, due to the expansive and flexible nature of simulations, many industries can be served by implementing simulations as learning tools (Sanko, 2017). To this end, the appeal of simulation usage can be directly aligned with the ability to expose learners to real-life conditions but provide a safe environment (Moule, 2011).

In conclusion, learners are simply now able to examine properties otherwise off limits when situated within face-to-face laboratories or when working with conditions otherwise unheard of due to the overwhelming safety concerns in which in-lab realities may create hazardous or unsafe conditions. Alas, simulations are still tools built upon ever-changing advancements in technology. Therefore, these tools must be continually evaluated and their implementation must be properly designed, framed, and provide templates to educators to ensure the implementation approach is administered correctly to maximize the many opportunities for learning. With so many positive affirmations, it only stands to further investigate areas to improve the design and implementation of simulated environments. This can be done via following instructional design best practices created using theories, taxonomies, and solid frameworks for investigation and reporting.

RESEARCH QUESTION

While the literature presents the various conditions in which to examine simulation inclusion, not all simulations are equal in nature, nor is their implementation, which can vary per discipline/domain (Berragan, 2011; Qian, 2016; Rutten, van Joolingen, & van der Veen, J. T, 2012). The larger problem then becomes the situational exploration when presented with ever-changing technological advances spanning multiple domains without guidance of process. In a seminal study conducted by Cant and Cooper (2017) that examined simulation impact upon the nursing field when simulations were implemented, positive findings were noted regarding knowledge acquisition. Missing within this systematic review, at no fault of the authors, was the mention of modular course design, classifications of tasks per domain, or specific simulation implementation guidance. Thus, the review solely addressed and outlined the many study designs, self-efficacy results, and skill development outcomes. However, their concluding remarks highly suggested a need for identical conditions at both the procedural and evaluation levels in conducting future investigations of this type. Sometimes these conditions will never be identical due to domain restrictions. However, the tools are. Therefore, the need to evaluate and design across domains is being heralded, and new tools for these tasks, no matter the method, tool, or domain, are needed.

The remainder of the chapter will focus upon the creation of a hypothesized evaluation framework to satisfy this lack of support of both design and evaluation of simulations for learning as gleaned from the field. This problem appears unique to this field and is the impetus for the research question expressed within this chapter. The suggested framework intends to solidify evaluation needs of learning events otherwise missing from within the current literature. It should be noted, the framework was conceptualized using a taxonomy presented by Qian (2016), which has yet to be validated.

The purpose of this chapter is, therefore, to examine if current literature found within the last decade support a simulation purpose-based taxonomy that aligns to Bloom's cognitive levels when simulations are used for learning.

FRAMEWORK FROM THEORY TO PRACTICE: THE HEART OF THE MATTER

Theories, Taxonomies, Frameworks, and Methods

As seen in the literature, there is a large focus upon the medical field mainly stemming from the need for hands-on skill acquisition in 'high-stakes' conditions. These skills were once believed to only be able to be taught effectively in real-time conditions. However, with improvement in technology and simulation training tools in general, this perception has changed in recent decades since real benefits for using simulations have now been realized. However, over time a new condition emerged, one referred to as the Theory-Practice Gap. This gap refers to the lack of implementing research into teaching and real practice. To combat this gap, researchers at many levels (Ferrara, 2010; Hanberg & Brown, 2006) suggest the utilization of Evidence-Based Practice (EBP) to demonstrate true learning. EBP is considered a method rather than a theory as it suggests using a facilitator to create an environment that makes the learner active within the overall experience and construct an output. This "method" is closely aligned to other theories used in studies in which gaps were identified in similar conditions. Others have suggested gaps between classification of task, method, and theory. Thus, limiting skill-learning measurements. Many theories are discussed within the literature to combat this lack, the most notable were (a) Contextual Learning Theory (CLT), (b) Vygotsky's Social Development Theory (SDT), and (c) Kolb's Experiential Learning Theory (ELT). While these theories will be briefly explained shortly, to better conceptualize their application within the field, one must first understand the basic concepts, meaning, and purpose between theories, taxonomies, frameworks, and methods as they apply to the overall research process.

Theories only attempt to explain the settings, conditions, or explain the many aspects found in the natural world. However, they do not test these settings, nor provide guidance for implementation or best practices. Then, we must organize the knowledge surrounding a topic for application and interpretation, create a hypothesis and test. This testing environment needs a frame in which to support the overall investigation and the ideas these theories suggest, whereas taxonomies provide a classification system in which to sort elements within an event or activity. A framework is a structure that can support a theory's examination that may lead to validation, provide a guide to continually evaluate a theory's effectiveness, and can demonstrate the relationship between the elements under investigation. Lastly, methods are those tasks undertaken to complete the activity of investigation.

Central Theories Surrounding Simulations for Learning: From Contextual Learning to Experiential Learning

Contextual Learning Theory

A topic of high importance when working with simulations is that of context of the simulated environment (Guise et al., 2012; Plass et al., 2012; Qian, 2016; Weller, Nestel, Marshall, Brooks, & Conn, 2012). In some instances, authors specifically referenced Contextual Learning Theory (CLT) (Qian, 2016) and argue when learners process new information, and the context is perceived as authentic, true learning takes place. CLT is a constructivist theory that posits learners will use their own experiences to create meaning. When using context as a frame for investigation, relationships become the meaning. In contrast, while still in support of this theory, Berragan (2011) further indicates that these conditions must go beyond perception and must reflect the true realities of the context otherwise the experience will be limited.

Vygotsky's Social Development Theory

Vygotsky's Social Development Theory (SDT) of 1978 was introduced to the western world in 1962, much later after his death (David, 2014). As the title indicates, the theory frames the social and collaborative aspects, along with play (Kappers, 2009), for the attainment of learning expansion. When speaking of Vygotsky's (1978) theory, it should be noted it is held in direct contrast to that of Piaget in-so-much as the primary process begins with social interaction in comparison to Piaget's notion that development is paramount prior to learning. "In moving towards individual problem-solving the student moves from the intermental to the intramental dimension through what Vygotsky termed "the zone of proximal development" (ZPD)" (Berragan, 2011, p. 662). Therefore, zones are considered the process and potential for learning when under select conditions. Berragan (2011) indicates this is an acceptable theory when investigating simulations for learning specifically to the field of nursing since nurses must transverse between social to individual understanding over time as they learn.

Kolb's Experiential Learning Theory

Developed in 1984, Kolb's Experiential Learning Theory (ELT) focuses upon four main phases of knowledge acquisition during a learning activity and examines how the learner moves from one phase to another until a phase of construction is complete. It is expected that learners will metamorphose using a personal perspective recognizing a learning event is taking place to construct a new model of understanding built upon the experience (Abdulwahed & Nagy, 2009). The learning process can be a single event that includes knowledge gathering and transformation, examining perspectives, and new experiences gained (Kappers & Cutler, 2016). Many studies, however, have argued that there is a true need to consider one's prior knowledge and experience in order to create formidable learning settings (Lee-Kelley, 2018) which is not explicitly addressed within Kolb's theory. However, experience after all creates prior knowledge, and thus prior knowledge is simply implied. ELT, as described by Abdulwahed and Nagy (2009), consists of four ability phases in which to examine a learning activity: Concrete Experience (CE), (b) Reflective Observation (RO), (c) Abstract Conceptualization (AC), and (d) Active Experimentation (AE) (p. 284). It should be noted that EBP (Evidence-based Practice) is highly similar to that of Kolb by suggesting a reflective event with knowledge construction as demonstration. EBP is only a method and unlike Kolb must contain a facilitator.

A New Taxonomy Emerges

A Purpose-Based Taxonomy for Simulations

While Qian (2016) and others (Berragan, 2011; Bluestone et al., 2013; Palter & Grantcharov, 2010; Weller et al., 2012; Yuan, Williams, & Fang, 2012) believe that simulations should represent real life and contain a degree of fidelity, there is also a conceptual model that needs to be considered when they are implemented. Qian argues that a conceptual model that explores the exact relationships differentiates simulations from other technologies making simulations distinctive if you will. Models then extend research through manipulation of the setting to gain information about localized activities. Moreover, simulation applications must consider the types of simulations and interactions made that result in a meaningful learning activity. Qian suggests taking this simulation-based analysis a step further by creating a "categorization system linking cognitive levels, learning outcomes, and distinctive attributes" (p. 244) alike. This posit suggests an extension of Bloom's learning outcome identification within an analysis framework condition. Therefore, built using the Bloom's Classification Taxonomy to showcase cognitive levels, Qian suggests a new three-category learning outcome-based classification system for consideration that examines linkages between technology, learning, and the activity outcomes expected.

Bloom's Taxonomy

Bloom's Taxonomy is a well-known taxonomy used to identify and establish equal areas of measurement for learning outcomes. Those areas include: (a) knowledge, (b) comprehension, (c) application, (d) analysis, (e) synthesis, and (f) evaluation. Also well-known is the fact that Bloom's original 1956 Cognitive Theory was revised in 2001 by his former student, Lorin Anderson, and fellow researcher, David Krathwoh (Armstrong, n.d.). This embodiment of action created a new vision of the original taxonomy entitled A Taxonomy for Teaching, Learning, and Assessment, sometimes referred to as Bloom's Revised Version, Blooms V2. When this new version emerged, terms were made active (e.g., Application = Apply), others reordered (e.g., Create was now the pinnacle of the overall model), and a new focus was placed upon the embodiment of knowledge of the process (e.g., subcomponents of Knowledge now included: (a) Factual, (b) Conceptual, (c) Procedural, and (d) Metacognitive area (para. 1).

Hence, Qian in essences suggests a taxonomy that is specific to that of the three main simulation purposes, or types, of simulations that are able to be linked to a cognitive level as indicated by Bloom: (a) Modeling = Memorization/Comprehension (b) Task/Skills = Application, and (c) Problem-solving/Decision-making = Analysis/Evaluation/Synthesis

An Evaluation Framework: A Marriage Proposal

Kolb's ELT Simply Can Transverse Domains

In answering the call to create better guidance for simulation selection, implementation, and evaluation of learning events when simulations are implemented as instruments within the process, a taxonomy alone cannot fully support this need. Nor does a classification tool alone appear to have the ability to fully evaluate the learning events as suggested by the extensive literature reviewed. While this chapter highlighted only three of the more popularized theories found within the extensive literature, the mere suggestion of "popularized" is indicative of the need for a theoretical inclusion within any effectiveness examination. Based upon the contextual reliance of the CLT theory, it could be rejected as a framework due to the many high-stakes learning conditions in which simulations are used for training to prevent grave errors (e.g., military/aviation/life-saving measures). While simulated environments do attempt to mirror real-life conditions, the context simply cannot be fully replicated for all conditions. Thus, limitations cannot be avoided. However, Vygotsky's theory relies heavily upon social interaction. Social aspects, while may be present in limited commodities as a reflective group event, are typically not found in a simulated environment, which is typically both personalized and highly individualized. Thus, a perfect fit could not be realized. However, when Kolb's theory is invoked, the examination focuses upon the injection of the simulation and the transformational affects upon the cognitive experience to produce new learning independent of a facilitator. This event may or may not contain social conditions nor be facilitated during the learning event, yet it must include moments for reflective conditions.

The very structure of ELT "provides an excellent theoretical framework to explore the course design structure and to assess student learning that will inform and guide the course design process" (Kappers & Cutler, 2016, p. 66). Kolb's theory is also a widely accepted framework when examining simulations in attainment of learning (Lee-Kelley, 2018; Qian, 2016). The alignment to that of Kolb's theory appears to mirror the majority of thoughts and affordances of simulations and their evaluation within the learning community. Thus, the selection of Kolb's theory would be only natural. As discussed earlier, there are many frameworks that are specific to particular domains when using simulations, such as the National League for Nursing. ELT does not present domain limitations. ELT is able to transverse all domains as it contains four main phases for learning construction found in all. Specifically, two of the elements look to the individual to construct new knowledge, and the ELT framework showcases a linkage to Bloom in-so-much that at each ELT intersection a concept can be applied, reevaluated, or observed based upon learning outcome.

Therefore, an alignment with a learning outcome-based categorization tool with that of a highly accepted learning evaluation theory appears worthy of suggestion and investigation. If a taxonomy is embedded within a systematic evaluation process based upon a highly accepted theory of examination, such an ELT, it appears this marriage would provide a tool to satisfy elements labeled as missing within the majority of simulation studies when the learning events are evaluated. Additionally, if selecting a taxonomy that can transverse domains as also suggested since it was conceived using a Bloom's structure used throughout the educational field, with that of a framework that also appears to have the same acceptance, true instructional design support and measure for those implementing simulations for learning will be realized.

A Marriage for the Ages

Courses, when created, include modules, expected outcomes, content, activities/tasks, and assessment. It should be a holistic process of creation with an intended design that supports the achievement of the expected outcomes. No matter the domain being measured, such as the cognitive domain, there are specific challenges and opportunities unique to the domain, as well as preferred techniques in which to measure success. These preferences can come in the form of theoretical applications, classification systems, or accepted tools for learning. Due to the wide variety of outcomes in conjunction to the many domains in which simulation implementation may exist and are measured, the designer needs to be specific in their course design to achieve course learning goals. These are shared concerns within any learning environment but of particular interest with regard to cognitive load which can be problematic when using simulations for learning.

Qian's (2016) original literature review analysis revealed specific conditions unique to each type of simulation procedure. For example, modeling-based simulations appeared to be supportive of discipline-specific studies, and conceptually supported Bloom's level of *understanding*. This unique situation reoccurred during the same analysis of both task/skills-based and problem/decision-making based simulation types. Since ELT is best to frame simulation analysis, and in acknowledging the three types of simulations available within today's learning market, a proposed marriage between the newly posited taxonomy with that of ELT is suggested.

Figure 1 displays a theoretical graphic depicting the location in which the posited taxonomy should be embedded within the ELT theoretical model for course design and learning outcome analysis when implementing simulations as solutions to meet learning objectives.

Therefore, to answer the intended research question, and discuss applicability of this suggested marriage, the chapter is divided into the following sections: (a) Method,

Figure 1. Learning outcome-based taxonomy embedding within ELT

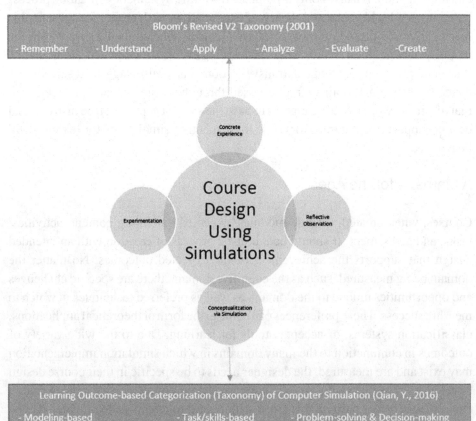

(b) Results, (c) Sample Comparison for Review and Application, (c) Solutions and Recommendations: Future Research Considerations, and (d) Conclusion.

METHOD

Due to the nature of wanting to posit an evaluation framework marriage between an untested taxonomy and learning theory used for evaluation, it was decided to conduct a two-phased research collection and examination approach.

Phase 1 intended to locate research to investigate the correlation between that of domain, Bloom's cognitive levels, and the posited purpose-based taxonomy. Using ProQuest, which focuses upon journals specific to computing, was used to collect studies using the following keywords, whether alone or in combination: (a) computer simulation, (b) education, (c) learning, and (d) teaching. This allowed for a more high-level inclusion in case definition or term disagreement that existed. Literature parameters were intentionally left unrestrictive at the onset. 62,598 articles were identified [Business 4107; Chemistry 2831; Computer Science 6415; Economics 2721; Education 20668; Engineering 7427; History/Archaeology 1030; Languages/Literature 1125; Law 1709; Library/Information Sciences 1092; Mathematics 1756; Medical/Nursing 4402; Physics 1055; Psychology 3368; Sciences 1878; Social Sciences 1014]. Noted were possibilities in the fields of Cyber Security and Data Science, two trending topics found in the literature due to the state and need of data protection. Security of, and not implementation, was the focus. Thus, those articles were removed. Articles containing systematic literature reviews, as suggested by Cant and Cooper (2017), became a larger focus to ensure a broad collection of work was examined. Study abstracts, methods, citation popularity, and those containing projects within the last decade (2000-2018) were all considered.

While too numerous to summate, additional restrictions were implemented. Using Cant and Cooper's (2017) article review selection process, which implemented gateways for article exclusion (identification, screening, and eligibility), abstracts were reviewed, additional keywords applied, duplicates removed, and references written outside the decade were withdrawn, identifying 96. If eligibility was unclear, a full document retrieval was necessary. Articles that introduced a new simulation for field testing, those in which a true cognitive domain could not be realized, or those providing an "evaluative" narrative of simulations in general rather than analyzing for situational effects upon learning outcomes, were omitted. Sixteen of the 96 presented only literature reviews or reviews not applicable to the historical or theoretical elements of this chapter. Eighty articles remained.

Phase 2 then sought to classify these investigations as to support the views of the proposed purpose-based taxonomy; thus, this identification phase specifically examined each for elements of (a) modeling-based, (b) task/skills-based, and (c) problem-based/decision-making activities. This classification is seen in Table 1 with Table 2 presenting correlation results.

RESULTS

To explore the plausibility of such a marriage between the framework and taxonomy for the sake of providing a guide for instructional designers and educators alike when considering the inclusion of a simulation for learning, the following section examines a few highlights gleaned from the systematic review of the literature to demonstrate the initial framework analysis in practice.

Table 1 contains curriculum identification, the three simulation types used within an in-class activity, and Bloom's cognitive expectations of the learning activity. Summaries compared projects, interventions, and findings. Sixteen of the original 96 articles included provided only literature or theoretical reviews and those findings were only referenced within the introductory elements of this chapter and not used as references for analysis collected under the Samples section of this chapter.

Table 1. Marriage categorization analysis between subject, bloom's classification levels, and purposed-based simulation taxonomy (n=80)

	Modeling	Tasks/ Skills	Problem- Solving	Remember	Understand	Apply	Analyze	Evaluate	Create
Chemistry	1	1			1	1			
Communication		1				1			
Electrical	2				1			1	
Engineering	1		3			1	2	1	
Environmental Science	1		1				1	1	
Geologists		1			1				
Hospitality		1		1					
Industrial	1						1		
Literature/ Model/ Theory	(n=16)								
Management			1		1				
Mechanics	1				1				
Medical (All)	3	7	1		5	4	2		
Network		2			2				
Physics	1	1			1		1		
Robotics	1							1	
Science	1	1	3		3	1	1		
SIM Design		1					1		
Technology		2			2				

Table 2. Taxonomy correlation between Bloom's and purpose-based simulation types

	Model	Tasks	Problem
Remember	n/a	n/a	n/a
Understand	0.714286	0.875155	0
Apply	1	1	-1
Analyze	0.632456	1	0
Evaluate	n/a	n/a	n/a
Create	n/a	n/a	n/a

Note: R^2 values not displayed in table

The narrative that follows the data portion of this section, under the heading *Sample Comparison for Review and Application*, referred to as "samples" moving forward, provides annotated summary details from select studies that represent some of the more popular domains that utilized simulations for learning, for example, engineering. To set the stage of organization between the proposed taxonomy and ELT, the remaining 80 articles included within the chapter's overall discussion were further analyzed by categories to demonstrate the applicability of this type of marriage and embedded analysis. Each comparison displays the study's sample, subject area, expected learning outcome(s), and project/activity completed – all of which are components that would be elements for analysis and inclusion if applying the proposed framework.

Studies selected as "samples" contained, in this author's opinion, well-grounded research projects, and presented rich detail as to the environment, settings, conditions, tasks, learning outcomes, and results. The "samples" dialogue is meant to provide a reflective setting, as suggested by Kolb's theory, while not prescribing how the framework should be applied as to leave that determination and discretion of the user. Nevertheless, by identifying these unique characteristics in a multi-discipline showcase, it is meant to demonstrate the identification process for utilizing the suggested embedded taxonomy in action. Lastly, the "samples" portion of the chapter is meant to provide examples for others to investigate while providing a brief overview of exploratory cases spread across various domains for practitioners in which to mirror, dissect, or use as guidance when considering the implementation of a tool for the purpose of learning.

Using Excel, a brief correlation analysis was conducted. Table 2 displays the results of this analysis. The area of *Apply* when compared to that of a *Modeling-based* simulation type presented the strongest relationship, both positive and negative (1, -1), whereas *Understand* to *Modeling-based* simulation type (.71, R^2=.51), *Understand* to *Task/Skills-based* simulation type (.88, R^2=.77), and *Analyze* to *Modeling-based* simulation type (.63, R^2=.40), all indicated positive relationships, thus one area, Task/Skill-based, explained 77% (R^2=.77) of the variation.

Sample Comparison for Review and Application

The following literary sample was selected to represent the broad variety of disciplines showcased in the literature. These studies were selected as "samples" as they contained rich detail as to the environment, settings, conditions, tasks, learning outcomes, and results in comparison to the others not included for display. These studies also represent the more popular domains identified within the literature in which learning simulations were utilized. Therefore, at least one randomly selected study from each of the following domains (a) engineering, (b) healthcare and medical disciplines, and (c) physical sciences is represented.

Keeping in mind ELT and following the guidance of Kappers and Cutler's (Kappers & Cutler, 2016) course analysis for applying ELT guidance, examples showcased within this section presented all elements contained within the ELT "loop of learning" from *Experience* to *Exploration*, whether intentionally or unintentionally constructed. Each sample identifies the purpose-based classification area as well. It should be noted that for this analysis one ELT stage does not denote the beginning element of a study loop, since it was assumed that none of the following studies was created with the Kolb framework in mind unless otherwise noted. Furthermore, rather than examining passive learning settings, the select works demonstrate true active learning situations in which simulations were utilized and outcomes of success measured. Findings are not included within the summaries as this was not the focus of this showcase. The intention was to provide an additional reflective moment as it may relate to personal implementation or design concerns by you, the reader.

Each entry will therefore be proceeded by the following categorization structure:
OVERVIEW: Sample // Discipline // Cognitive Outcome // Purpose-based Classification

Categories

Engineering

Carey (2017)

OVERVIEW: Sample n=10 (fresh water ecology) – n=40 (freshwater ecology): Environmental Science (Biology), Ecosystem Understanding for Improvement, Modeling

This is a topic that is rarely taught according to the authors. However, it is a topic of high importance as it pertains to climate change. There is an ever-growing requirement for those in the field to not only conduct environmental research, but to be fluent in the way of data analysis, especially with regard to large datasets. While not a conflicting request, dataset analysis has created a change in the skillset need for those in this field, who now need to become data analysts of sorts in order to make use of the available data stored and collected to make informed decisions. Analysis and modeling, with the skill of interpretation, are now in high demand. Advanced skills are needed in the areas of reasoning and data manipulation at all levels. To address these issues, the Environmental Data-Driven Inquiry and Exploration (EDDIE) collaborative established a team to create a module specifically to address the skill gap. Using modeling in this nature, students were exposed to several technologies for this unified purpose within the proposed module. This aspect is greatly different from a normal science classroom setting in which technology is not the focus. Modeling simply equates to that of the practice itself. The Kolb alignment included an Introductory PowerPoint containing general information, exploration of modeling software, hypothesis creation, analysis of data after input, presentation of findings, ending in a recap of findings and a secondary analysis of new data where needed. Findings from the overall study indicated students increased knowledge in their understanding of climate change effects.

Chung (2001)

OVERVIEW: Sample n=28, Civil and Environmental Engineering, Hazardous Waste, Soil and Contaminant Transport Analysis, Problem/Decision-making

The authors introduce a new software package entitled Interactive Site Investigation Software (ISIS) for use to explore the environmental conditions and the particulars of contaminant transport of Hazardous Waste, in particular locations such as at an abandoned airfield. Virtual data collection and analysis was required using the simulation tool. Students were expected to utilize the same tasks within the field of drilling, sample collection, analysis, and field tests as normally expected within a true investigation. Pre and post analysis were conducted and knowledge mapping supported visualization of understanding of the conditions and processes. Findings supported positive results concerning knowledge from pre to post surveys.

Xie, Schimpf, Chao, Nourian, & Massicotte (2018)

OVERVIEW: Sample (Pilot) n=37 (15 girls/10 boys), Engineering, Solar Power Exploration via Solarized House Project, Modeling

The authors describe the findings from a pilot project in which "Solarization" of a home was the focus. Within this case study, students are requested to create a 3D mock-up of a solarized home. The project required students to calculate output levels and then compare the values for efficiency. This case is of high importance since solar power has been on the forefront of many design projects to support changing environmental needs. However, the beauty in this project is that students are the consultants with their parents acting as the client. Pre/Post surveys were conducted alongside reflection design journals. While self-reported elements were included within evaluation mechanisms, the authors critiqued final design models and administered a final exit survey to gain insight. Paired t-test results revealed significant gains for learning.

Healthcare and Medical disciplines

Silvennoinen, Helfenstein, Ruoranen, & Saariluoma (2012)

OVERVIEW: Sample n=13, Medical (Surgical Skills), Laparoscopy Demonstration, Task-Skills-based

Using a real-life simulator, LAP Mentor ™, which is a training tool that contains real surgical instruments, laparoscopy skill levels were tested and documented in a pre-post manner over a four-month period of time. Students of various levels were tasked to complete various quests, such as locator quests, with task completion times logged. The authors identified two areas of concern when using the simulator: (a) the unique style of the performer, and (b) successes, or lack thereof, seen during the training session. While the study did not boast significant findings, the authors indicated camera movement reduction needs, completion time reports, and correct hits that support a positive outcome in relation to the requirements set forth, such as understanding. However, immediate feedback appeared to be lacking and presented a slight hindrance within the examination.

Physical Science

Khan (2011)

OVERVIEW: Sample n=33, Chemistry (science and non-science majors), Heat Calorimetry, Mass/Type/Weight Plotting Exercise for Analysis, Problem/Decision-making

The key activities expressed were those of "teacher" interaction with the students, thus presenting a highly supportive project for Kolb analysis. Rather than identifying Kolb's theory, the researchers referred to the process of "generate-evaluate-modify" to teach chemistry. Students utilized the simulation to analyze the temperature change over time. The teacher's role became an embedded transformational event working as an intermediary within the overall flow from concept to experimentation. At each stage, the teacher's involvement within the process helped to fortify the next stage of the learning process. The teacher requested information in order to highlight the relationships of the concept. Secondary requests for information explicated the concepts found in order to present evaluation and reflective moments. The final interaction requested modifications be made to their original design to make ready for evaluation. Transversely, the students' intermediary activities closed the learning loop once the modifications were analyzed. Student surveys indicated positive results concerning predictive activities.

Horiguchi, Imai, Toumoto, & Hirashimna (2014)

OVERVIEW: Sample n=84, (n=54 assigned to Error-Based Simulations (EBS) & n=30 Normal Operating Course (NOC)), Mechanics, Formulation, Problem/Decision-making

The authors hypothesized when a simulation activity is careful in its design and can provide instant feedback during training sessions, simulation were supportive to easily understand abstract concepts. Additionally, the authors posited, if simulation are sequentially well-aligned, students are not only able to find the solution to a problem but also formulate a scheme of understanding to address knowledge in a natural progression. Authors indicated error-simulation events are unnatural, almost as if viewing a double-negative. After simulation activities were completed authors indicated a reduced level of confusion when operating in said unnatural conditions. Having the opportunity to override normal constraints via simulation without the normal precautionary warnings – referred to as unnatural phenomena – allowed for a clearer examination. Authors were able to remove the distractions which would normally lend to uninterested students rather than those motivated by the adventure to find a solution. Positive findings with regard to simulations used for the training were reported and it was noted that students became more aware of the relationship between the topic and concept. This study was defined, however, as a simple case study, one that should be tested within other domains.

SOLUTIONS AND RECOMMENDATIONS: FUTURE RESEARCH CONSIDERATIONS

Based upon the many suggestions seen within the literature, the future of simulation research has the potential to become highly active. Opportunities for diversity exploration (Smetana & Bell, 2012), authentic workspaces (Bluestone et al., 2013), and instructional design needs (Qian, 2016) have all been mentioned as being on the forefront of immediate requests. While true costs of simulation implementation studies need to be placed on the list of "things to do" (Moule, 2011), "planned studies across nursing training programs that utilize identical clinical simulation procedures and the same evaluation tools could provide strong experimental evidence of the effect[s] of simulation on clinical knowledge" (Cant & Cooper, 2017, p. 70.). Inadvertently, studies of this nature could provide insight into simulation training costs as well. Thus, with many options for investigation spanning multiple domains, an evaluation framework to measure learning achievement across domains could provide comparative answers between different domains rather than focusing upon a single domain. Findings could be generalized across the field of learning when using simulations.

Furthermore, team-based simulation utilization studies, which can be viewed under the umbrella of accreditation requirements, may be considered as imperative needs for future research consideration as simulations continue to be seen as positive learning influences in the classroom, in which real hands-on skills are needed. Yet, there are simply few to no investigations that support research studies of this nature. Paradigm shifts can be seen via theory selection and application that support social versus individual learning opportunities when using simulations (Bluestone et al., 2013) with some presenting themselves in a very domain specific fashion. Again, using a unified evaluation framework would be highly supportive.

Lastly, practitioners and educators alike need guidance for simulation implementation and learning outcome alignment via instructional design models (Qian, 2016). Firm statements existed within the literature, as seen throughout this chapter that indicate a lack of formal implementation structures and unified evaluation tools in which to follow or use. By exploring the possibilities of applying true instructional design approaches, such as when using a framework to begin course development when using simulations for learning, this may spawn an entire branch of investigation that can produce new and improved learning theories solely unique to these tools rather than those limited to a specific domain.

CONCLUSION

Positive views were overwhelmingly reported when using simulations in educational settings as found within the literature. This chapter provided a firm lens via an evaluation framework to support comparative investigations of simulations when used as learning mechanisms outside of domain constraints. While historical aspects of simulations showed an implementation reliance upon technological improvements, the research supported a paradigm shift of acceptance that spanned approximately four decades no matter the technological growth. Furthermore, the "samples" provided showcased an ever-active area of research that must further be explored for design and implementation guidance. Thus, using a unified evaluation framework would aid to produce results that could span multiple domains.

Furthermore, elements were confirmed in which simulation training arenas create safer environments in which to explore the benefits found within each domain of investigation. Yet again, a true comparison across domains cannot be made without the use of a comparative tool that has the possibility to break down the walls between domains. Simulations for learning have been found to be tools that provide safe havens for individuals, yet have the ability to create personalized learning environments in which students could explore content and topics at their convenience and within their comfort level with little to no overly overt effort. As seen via Kolb's analysis for learning, one can also gain a true appreciation for hands-on activities that are supported via simulated tasks or those activities that culminate in a reflective moment, as both best scaffold learning. Thus, creating these types of supportive and holistic events and conditions in which to situate positive learning experiences is simply requested if not a requirement. Thus, evidence from such types of learning events that could allow for a larger comparison across domains would be truly effective in creating change. This possibility can also be realized if utilizing an agreed upon evaluation framework with this framework providing support to close the aforementioned design gap.

While much research is still needed in the area of simulation implementation for learning, if we begin with the end in mind by utilizing an evaluation framework built upon learning domains created by theory, married within an evaluation framework containing a purposed-based classification system, we greatly support best instructional design practices at the onset of a learning event. Additionally, researchers can provide findings that can best enhance the greater impact as all research should be expected to ensure. In conclusion, the simple suggestion of making changes in the way we view the instructional environments via a newly posited taxonomy and framework expansion, shows promise and appreciation for the type of opportunities simulations can provide.

REFERENCES

Abdulwahed, M., & Nagy, Z. K. (2009). Applying Kolb's experiential learning cycle for laboratory education. *Journal of Engineering Education*, *98*(3), 283–294. doi:10.1002/j.2168-9830.2009.tb01025.x

Armstrong, P. (n.d.). *Bloom's taxonomy*. Retrieved from https://wp0.vanderbilt.edu/cft/guides-sub-pages/blooms-taxonomy/#2001

Berragan, L. (2011). Simulation: An effective pedagogical approach for nursing? *Nurse Education Today*, *31*(7), 660–663. doi:10.1016/j.nedt.2011.01.019 PMID:21334797

Bluestone, J., Johnson, P., Fullerton, J., Carr, C., Alderman, J., & BonTempo, J. (2013). Effective in-service training design and delivery: Evidence from an integrative literature review. *Human Resources for Health*, *11*(1), 51. doi:10.1186/1478-4491-11-51 PMID:24083659

Cant, R. P., & Cooper, S. J. (2017). Use of simulation-based learning in undergraduate nurse education: An umbrella systematic review. *Nurse Education Today*, *49*, 63–71. doi:10.1016/j.nedt.2016.11.015 PMID:27902949

Carey, C. C., & Gougis, R. D. (2017). Simulation modeling of lakes in undergraduate and graduate classrooms increases comprehension of climate change concepts and experience with computational tools. *Journal of Science Education and Technology*, *26*(1), 1–11. doi:10.100710956-016-9644-2

Chung, G. K. W. K., Harmon, T. C., & Baker, E. L. (2001). The impact of a simulation-based learning design project on student learning. *IEEE Transactions on Education*, *44*(4), 390–398. doi:10.1109/13.965789

David, L. (2014). *Social development theory (Vygotsky) in learning theories*. Retrieved from https://www.learning-theories.com/vygotskys-social-learning-theory.html

de Jong, T. (2019). Technological advances in inquiry learning. *Science*, *312*(5773), 532–533. doi:10.1126cience.1127750 PMID:16645080

Eckhardt, M., Urhahne, D., Conrad, O., & Harms, U. (2013). How effective is instructional support for learning with computer simulations? *Instructional Science*, *41*(1), 105–124. doi:10.100711251-012-9220-y

Ferrara, L. R. (2010). Integrating evidence-based practice with educational theory in clinical practice for nurse practitioners: Bridging the theory practice gap. *Research and Theory for Nursing Practice*, 24(4), 213–216. doi:10.1891/1541-6577.24.4.213 PMID:21197916

Greca, I. M., Seoane, E., & Arriassecq, I. (2014). Epistemological issues concerning computer simulations in science and their implications for science education. *Science & Education*, 23(4), 897–921. doi:10.100711191-013-9673-7

Guise, V., Chambers, M., & Valimaki, M. (2012). What can virtual patient simulation offer mental health nursing education? *Journal of Psychiatric and Mental Health Nursing*, 19(5), 410–418. doi:10.1111/j.1365-2850.2011.01797.x PMID:22070549

Hanberg, A., & Brown, S. C. (2006). Bridging the Theory–Practice gap with evidence-based practice. *Journal of Continuing Education in Nursing*, 37(6), 248–249. doi:10.3928/00220124-20061101-07 PMID:17144113

Horiguchi, T., Imai, I., Toumoto, T., & Hirashima, T. (2014). Error-based simulation for error-awareness in learning mechanics: An evaluation. *Journal of Educational Technology & Society*, 17(3), 1–13.

Kappers, W. M. (2009). *Educational video game effects upon mathematics achievement and motivation scores: An experimental study examining differences between the sexes.* Unpublished manuscript.

Kappers, W. M. (2017). Through the lens of the reviewer: Information literacy, an LMS, and peer review. *Computers in Education Journal*, 8(2), 83–96.

Kappers, W. M., & Cutler, S. L. (2016). Simulation to application. The use of computer simulations to improve real-world application of learning. *Computers in Education Journal*, 64–74.

Khan, S. (2011). New pedagogies on teaching science with computer simulations. *Journal of Science Education and Technology*, 20(3), 215–232. doi:10.100710956-010-9247-2

Lee-Kelley, L. (2018). When 'knowing what' is not enough: Role of organised simulations for developing effective practice. *International Journal of Project Management*, 36(1), 198–207. doi:10.1016/j.ijproman.2017.08.003

McCaughey, C. S., & Traynor, M. K. (2010). The role of simulation in nurse education. *Nurse Education Today*, *30*(8), 827–832. doi:10.1016/j.nedt.2010.03.005 PMID:20483188

Moule, P. (2011). Simulation in nurse education: Past, present and future. *Nurse Education Today, 31*(7), 645-646. doi-org.ezproxy.libproxy.db.erau.edu/10.1016/j.nedt.2011.04.005

Oren, T. (2011, April). The many facets of simulation through a collection of about 100 definitions. *SCS M&S Magazine,* 82. Retrieved from https://www.researchgate.net/publication/228939089_The_Many_Facets_of_Simulation_through_a_Collection_of_about_100_Definitions

Palter, V. N., & Grantcharov, T. P. (2010). Simulation in surgical education. *CMAJ: Canadian Medical Association Journal = Journal De L'Association Medicale Canadienne, 182*(11), 1191-1196. doi:10.1503/cmaj.091743

Plass, J. L., Milne, C., Homer, B. D., Schwartz, R. N., Hayward, E. O., Jordan, T., ... Barrientos, J. (2012). Investigating the effectiveness of computer simulations for chemistry learning. *Journal of Research in Science Teaching*, *49*(3), 394–419. doi:10.1002/tea.21008

Prensky, M. (2001). *Digital game-based learning*. New York, NY: McGraw-Hill.

Qian, Y. (2016). Computer simulation in higher education: Affordances, opportunities, and outcomes. In P. Vu, S. Fredrickson, & C. Moore (Eds.), *Handbook of research on innovative pedagogies and technologies for online learning in higher education* (pp. 236–262). Hershey, PA: IGI Global.

Rutten, N., van Joolingen, W. R., & van der Veen, J. T. (2012). The learning effects of computer simulations in science education. *Computers & Education*, *58*(1), 136–153. doi:10.1016/j.compedu.2011.07.017

Sanko, J. S. (2017). Simulation as a teaching technology: A brief history of its use in nursing education. *Quarterly Review of Distance Education*, *18*(2), 77–103.

Silvennoinen, M., Helfenstein, S., Ruoranen, M., & Saariluoma, P. (2012). Learning basic surgical skills through simulator training. *Instructional Science*, *40*(5), 769–783. doi:10.100711251-012-9217-6

Smetana, L. K., & Bell, R. L. (2012). Computer simulations to support science instruction and learning: A critical review of the literature. *International Journal of Science Education, 34*(9), 1337–1370. doi:10.1080/09500693.2011.605182

Vygotsky, L. S. (1978). *Mind in society: The development of higher psychological processes*. Cambridge, MA: Harvard University Press.

Weller, J. M., Nestel, D., Marshall, S. D., Brooks, P. M., & Conn, J. J. (2012). Simulation in clinical teaching and learning. *The Medical Journal of Australia, 196*(9), 594–599. doi:10.5694/mja10.11474 PMID:22621154

Xie, C., Schimpf, C., Chao, J., Nourian, S., & Massicotte, J. (2018). Learning and teaching engineering design through modeling and simulation on a CAD platform. *Computer Applications in Engineering Education, 26*(4), 824–840. doi:10.1002/cae.21920

Yuan, H. B., Williams, B. A., & Fang, J. B. (2012). The contribution of high-fidelity simulation to nursing students' confidence and competence: A systematic review. *International Nursing Review, 59*(1), 26–33. doi:10.1111/j.1466-7657.2011.00964.x

KEY TERMS AND DEFINITIONS

Computer Simulation: Hypothetical situation taking place on a computer to allow a user to observe a relationship.

Fidelity: The degree of realism of a computer simulation.

Framework: Conceptual structure.

Modeling-Based Simulation: A program that displays a static model of real life.

Problem-Solving and Decision-Making Simulation: A program in which learners must solve a real-life problem.

Task/Skill-Based Simulation: A program that allows a user to demonstrate a real-life task for skill mastery.

Compilation of References

Abdul-Muhsin, H. M., & Humphreys, M. R. (2016). Advances in laparoscopic urologic surgery techniques. *F1000Res, 21*(5), 716. doi:10.12688/f1000research.7660.1

Abdulwahed, M., & Nagy, Z. K. (2009). Applying Kolb's experiential learning cycle for laboratory education. *Journal of Engineering Education, 98*(3), 283–294. doi:10.1002/j.2168-9830.2009.tb01025.x

Aebersold, M., Voepel-Lewis, T., Cherara, L., Weber, M., Khouri, C., Levine, R., & Tait, A. R. (2018). Interactive anatomy-augmented virtual simulation training. *Clinical Simulation in Nursing, 15*, 34–41. doi:10.1016/j.ecns.2017.09.008 PMID:29861797

Aguilera, A., Fúquene, C. A., & Ríos, W. F. (2014). Aprende jugando: El uso de técnicas de gamificación en entornos de aprendizaje. *IM-Pertinente, 2*(1), 125–143.

Ahlqvist, J. B., Nilsson, T. A., Hedman, L. R., Desser, T. S., Dev, P., Johansson, M., ... Gold, G. E. (2013). A randomized controlled trial on 2 simulation-based training methods in radiology: Effects on radiologic technology student skill in assessing image quality. *Simulation in Healthcare, 8*(6), 382–387. doi:10.1097/SIH.0b013e3182a60a48 PMID:24096919

Aichert, A., Wein, W., Ladikos, A., Reichl, T., & Navab, N. (2012). Image-based tracking of the teeth for orthodontic augmented reality. *Medical image computing and computer-assisted intervention: MICCAI 2012 International Conference on Medical Image Computing and Computer-Assisted Intervention, 15*(2), 601-8.

Ajzen, I., & Fishbein, M. (1980). *Understanding attitudes and predicting social behavior.* Englewood Cliffs, NJ: Prentice-Hall.

Al Hamdan, E. M., Tulbah, H. I., Al Duhayan, G. A., & Al Bedaiwi, L. S. (2016). Preferences of dental students towards teaching strategies in two major dental colleges in Riyadh, Saudi Arabia. *Education Research International, 2016*, 1–9. doi:10.1155/2016/4178471

Compilation of References

Albright, G., Bryan, C., Adam, C., McMillan, J., & Shockley, K. (2018). Using virtual patient simulations to prepare primary health care professionals to conduct substance use and mental health screening and brief intervention. *Journal of the American Psychiatric Nurses Association, 24*(3), 247–259. doi:10.1177/1078390317719321 PMID:28754067

Aldrich, C. (n.d.). *Six criteria of an educational simulation.* Retrieved from https://goo.gl/LoUFrU

Aldrich, C. (2002). *A field guide to educational simulations.* Alexandria, VA: ASTD.

Aldrich, C. (2004). *Simulations and the future of learning: An innovative (and perhaps revolutionary) approach to e-Learning.* San Francisco, CA: Pfeiffer.

Aleksandrova, M. (2018). *Augmented reality in education: The hottest EdTech trend 2018 and how to apply it to your business.* Eastern Peak 2019. Retrieved from https://easternpeak.com/blog/augmented-reality-in-education-the-hottest-edtech-trend-2018-and-how-to-apply-it-to-your-business

Alexander, L., Sheen, J., Rinehart, N., Hay, M., & Boyd, L. (2018). Mental health simulation with student nurses: A qualitative review. *Clinical Simulation in Nursing, 14,* 8–14. doi:10.1016/j.ecns.2017.09.003

Alqahtani, N. D., Al-Jewair, T., AL-Moammar, K., Albarakati, S. F., & ALkofide, E. A. (2015). Live demonstration versus procedural video: A comparison of two methods for teaching an orthodontic laboratory procedure. *BMC Medical Education, 15*(1), 199. doi:10.118612909-015-0479-y PMID:26537393

Al-Rawi, A. (2018). Video games, terrorism, and ISIS's Jihad 3.0. *Terrorism and Political Violence, 30*(4), 740–760. doi:10.1080/09546553.2016.1207633

Aly, M., Willems, G., Carels, C., & Elen, J. (2003). Instructional multimedia programs for self-directed learning in undergraduate and postgraduate training in orthodontics. *European Journal of Dental Education, 7*(1), 20–26. doi:10.1034/j.1600-0579.2003.00263.x PMID:12542685

Ames, M. E., McMorris, C. A., Alli, L. N., & Bebko, J. M. (2016). Overview and evaluation of a mentorship program for university students with ASD. *Focus on Autism and Other Developmental Disabilities, 31*(1), 27–36. doi:10.1177/1088357615583465

Anatomage. (2018). Retrieved from https://www.anatomage.com/anatomage-dental

Anderson, P. H., & Lawton, L. (1988). Assessing student performance on a business simulation exercise. *Developments in Business Simulation & Experiential Exercises, 15,* 241–245.

Anderson, T., & Dron, J. (2011). Three generations of distance education pedagogy. *International Review of Research in Open and Distance Learning, 12*(3), 80–97. doi:10.19173/irrodl.v12i3.890

Armstrong, P. (n.d.). *Bloom's taxonomy*. Retrieved from https://wp0.vanderbilt.edu/cft/guides-sub-pages/blooms-taxonomy/#2001

ARRT. (2016). *2017 radiography didactic and clinical competency requirements*. Retrieved from https://www.arrt.org/docs/default-source/discipline-documents/radiography/rad-competency-requirements.pdf?sfvrsn=20

Asal, V. (2005). Playing games with international relations. *International Studies Perspectives*, *6*(3), 359–373. doi:10.1111/j.1528-3577.2005.00213.x

Ashman, A. F., & Conway, R. N. (2017). *Using cognitive methods in the classroom*. London, UK: Routledge; doi:10.4324/9781315271019

ASPiH. (2016). *ASPiH Standards for Simulation-Based Education*. Retrieved from https://aspih.org.uk/standards-framework-for-sbe

Assis, G. A., Corrêa, A. G., Martins, M. B., Pedrozo, W. G., & Lopes Rde, D. (2016). An augmented reality system for upper-limb post-stroke motor rehabilitation: A feasibility study. *Disability and Rehabilitation. Assistive Technology*, *11*(6), 521–528. PMID:25367103

Associated Press. (2010). *Teacher's assignment to HS students: Plan a deadly terror attack*. Retrieved from https://warisboring.com/stealth-bombers-blast-libya-14c7566558ee#.yrukq66o1

Augmented Reality in Medical Education - Harmony Studios. (2017). Retrieved from https://www.youtube.com/watch?v=9XGsebK0TPI

Azuma, R., Baillot, Y., Behringer, R., Feiner, S., Julier, S., & MacIntyre, B. (2001). Recent advances in augmented reality. *IEEE Computer Graphics and Applications*, *21*(6), 34–47. doi:10.1109/38.963459

Bacca, J., Baldiris, S., Fabregat, R., & Graf, S., & Kinshuk. (2014). Augmented reality trends in Education: A systematic review of research and applications. *Journal of Educational Technology & Society*, *17*(4), 133–149.

Badial, G., Ferrari, V., Cutolo, F., Freschi, C., Caramella, D., Bianchi, A., & Marchetti, C. (2014). Augmented reality as an aid in maxillofacial surgery: Validation of a wearable system allowing maxillary repositioning. *Journal of Cranio-Maxillo-Facial Surgery*, *42*(8), 1970–1976. doi:10.1016/j.jcms.2014.09.001 PMID:25441867

Ball, J., Kumar Gunda, R., Awoseyila, A., & Sharma, A. (2014). Nuneosim survey - A triple blind study of nursing perception to simulation training in a tertiary neonatal intensive care setting. *BMJ Simulation*, *1*(1). doi:10.1136/bmjstel-2014-000002.162

Balnaves, K. (2018). World building for children's global participation in Minecraft. In M. Ciussi (Ed.), *Proceedings of the 12th European Conference on Game Based Learning* (pp. 858-862). Reading, UK: Academic Conferences and Publishing International Limited.

Barab, S. A., Hay, K. E., Barnett, M. G., & Squire, K. (2001). Constructing virtual worlds: Tracing the historical development of learner practices/understandings. *Cognition and Instruction, 19*(1), 47–94. doi:10.1207/S1532690XCI1901_2

Bauman, E. B., & Ralston-Berg, P. (2015). Virtual simulation. In J. Palagapas, J. Maxworthy, C. Epps, & M. Mancini (Eds.), *Defining excellence in simulation programs* (pp. 241–251). Philadelphia, PA: Lippincott Williams & Wilkins.

Bazarov, S. E., Kholodilin, I. Y., Nesterov, A. S., & Sokhina, A. V. (2017). Applying augmented reality in practical classes for engineering students. *IOP Conference Series: Earth and Environmental Science, 87*. Retrieved from https://iopscience.iop.org/article/10.1088/1755-1315/87/3/032004/pdf

Beard, C., & Wilson, J. P. (2006). *Experiential learning: A best practice handbook for educators and trainers*. London, UK: Kogan Page.

Bednar, E. D., Hannum, W. M., Firestone, A., Silveira, A. M., Cox, T. D., & Proffit, W. R. (2007). Application of distance learning to interactive seminar instruction in orthodontic residency programs. *American Journal of Orthodontics and Dentofacial Orthopedics, 132*(5), 586–594. doi:10.1016/j.ajodo.2007.06.008 PMID:18005831

Ben-Gal, G., Katorza, L., Weiss, E. I., & Ziv, A. (2017). Testing motor learning curves among dental students. *Journal of Dental Education, 81*(10), 1171–1178. doi:10.21815/JDE.017.076 PMID:28966181

Ben-Yehuda, H., & Zohar, G. (2018). Fanaticism through the looking glass of simulations. *Journal of Political Science Education, 14*(2), 197–221. doi:10.1080/15512169.2017.1418367

Ben-Zvi, T. (2010). The efficacy of business simulation games in creating decision support systems: An experimental investigation. *Decision Support Systems, 49*(1), 61–69. doi:10.1016/j.dss.2010.01.002

Berge, Z., & Collins, M. (1995). *Computer-mediated communication and the online classroom in distance learning*. Retrieved from https://www.december.com/cmc/mag/1995/apr/berge.html

Bergeron, B., & Cline, A. (2011). An adaptive signal-processing approach to online adaptive tutoring. *Studies in Health Technology and Informatics, 163*, 60–64. PMID:21335759

Bernie M. G., Joseph, A., & Cathryn, J. (2018). Using mobile augmented reality to enhance health professional practice education. *Current Issues in Emerging eLearning, 4*(1), 224-247.

Berragan, L. (2011). Simulation: An effective pedagogical approach for nursing? *Nurse Education Today, 37*(7), 660–663. doi:10.1016/j.nedt.2011.01.019 PMID:21334797

Berry, M., Lystig, T., Beard, J., Klingestierna, H., Reznick, R., & Lohn, L. (2007). Porcine transfer study: Virtual reality simulator training compared with porcine training in endovascular novices. *Cardiovascular and Interventional Radiology, 30*(3), 455–461. doi:10.100700270-006-0161-1 PMID:17225971

Biggs, J. B., & Collis, K. F. (1982). *Evaluating the quality of learning – the SOLO taxonomy.* New York, NY: Academic Press.

Biggs, J., & Tang, C. (Eds.). (2007). *Teaching for quality learning at university.* Belkshire, UK: Open University Press.

Birknerová, Z. (2010). The use of simulation business games in university education. *Bulgarian Journal of Science and Education Policy, 4*(2), 202–215.

Bizelli, M. H., Fiscarelli, P. E., & Fiscarelli, S. H. (2013). Interactive simulations to physics teaching: A case study in Brazilian high school. *International Journal of Learning and Teaching, 5*(1), 18–23.

Blandon, A. Y., Calkins, S. D., Grimm, K. J., Keane, S. P., & O'Brien, M. (2010). Testing a developmental cascade model of emotional and social competence and early peer acceptance. *Development and Psychopathology, 22*(4), 737–748. doi:10.1017/S0954579410000428

Bloom, B. S. (1984). *Taxonomy of educational objectives: The classification of educational goals.* New York, NY: Longman.

Bluestone, J., Johnson, P., Fullerton, J., Carr, C., Alderman, J., & BonTempo, J. (2013). Effective in-service training design and delivery: Evidence from an integrative literature review. *Human Resources for Health, 11*(1), 51. doi:10.1186/1478-4491-11-51 PMID:24083659

Blume, F., Hudak, J., Dresler, T., Ehlis, A. C., Kühnhausen, J., Renner, T. J., & Gawrilow, C. (2017). NIRS-based neurofeedback training in a virtual reality classroom for children with attention-deficit/hyperactivity disorder: Study protocol for a randomized controlled trial. *Trials, 18*(1), 41. doi:10.118613063-016-1769-3

Boger-Mehall, S. R. (1996). Cognitive flexibility theory: Implications for teaching and teacher education. In *Proceedings of Society for Information Technology & Teacher Education International Conference 1996* (pp. 991-993). Chesapeake, VA: Association for the Advancement of Computing in Education (AACE).

Bogers, M., & Sproedt, H. (2012). Playful collaboration (or not): Using a game to grasp the social dynamics of open innovation in innovation and business education. *Journal of Teaching in International Business, 23*(2), 1–32. doi:10.1080/08975930.2012.718702

Bogost, I. (2011). *How to do things with videogames.* Minneapolis, MN: University of Minnesota Press. doi:10.5749/minnesota/9780816676460.001.0001

Booth, R., Sinclair, B., McMurray, J., Strudwick, G., Watson, G., Ladak, H., & Brennan, L. (2018). Evaluating a serious gaming electronic medication administration record system among nursing students: Protocol for a pragmatic randomized controlled trial. *JMIR Research Protocols, 7*(5), 138. doi:10.2196/resprot.9601 PMID:29807885

Borshchev, A., & Filippov, A. (2004, July). *From system dynamics and discrete event to practical agent based modeling: reasons, techniques, tools.* Retrieved from https://www.systemdynamics.org/assets/conferences/2004/SDS_2004/PAPERS/381BORSH.pdf

Bosse, H. M., Nickel, M., Huwendiek, S., Schultz, J. H., & Nikendei, C. (2015). Cost-effectiveness of peer role play and standardized patients in undergraduate communication training. *BMC Medical Education, 15*(1), 183. doi:10.118612909-015-0468-1 PMID:26498479

Boud, D., Keogh, R., & Walker, D. (1985). What is reflection in learning? In D. Boud, R. Keogh, & D. Walker (Eds.), *Reflection: Turning Experience into Learning* (pp. 7–17). London: Kogan Page.

Boyer, M. A., Trumbore, E., & Frick, D. E. (2006). Teaching theories of international political economy from the Pit: A simple in-class simulation. *International Studies Perspectives, 7*(1), 67–76. doi:10.1111/j.1528-3577.2006.00231.x

Breymier, T. L., Rutherford-Hemming, T., Horsley, T. L., Atz, T., Smith, L. G., Badowski, D., & Connor, K. (2015). Substitution of clinical experience with simulation in prelicensure nursing programs: A national survey in the United States. *Clinical Simulation in Nursing, 11*(11), 472–478. doi:10.1016/j.ecns.2015.09.004

Bridge, P., Appleyard, R. M., Ward, J. W., Phillips, R., & Beavis, A. W. (2007). The development and evaluation of a virtual radiotherapy treatment machine using an immersive visualization environment. *Computers & Education, 49*(2), 481–494. doi:10.1016/j.compedu.2005.10.006

Bridge, P., Crowe, S. B., Gibson, G., Ellemor, N. J., Hargrave, C., & Carmichael, M. A. (2016). A virtual radiation therapy workflow training simulation. *Radiography, 22*(1), e59–e63. doi:10.1016/j.radi.2015.08.001

Brown, J. (2008). Applications of simulation technology in psychiatric mental health nursing education. *Journal of Psychiatric and Mental Health Nursing, 15*(8), 638–644. doi:10.1111/j.1365-2850.2008.001281.x PMID:18803737

Brownstein, S. A., Murad, A., & Hunt, R. J. (2015). Implementation of new technologies in U.S. dental school curricula. *Journal of Dental Education, 79*(3), 259–264. PMID:25729019

Brudvig, T., Mattson, D., & Guarino, A. (2015). Critical thinking skills and learning styles in physical therapists trained in India enrolled in a master's program. *Journal, Physical Therapy Education, 29*(4), 5–13. doi:10.1097/00001416-201529040-00003

Brudvig, T., Mattson, D., & Guarino, A. (2016). Critical thinking skill and learning styles in entry-level doctor of physical therapy students. *Journal, Physical Therapy Education, 30*(4), 3–10. doi:10.1097/00001416-201630040-00002

Burden, C., Preschaw, J., White, P., Draycott, T. J., Grant, S., & Fox, R. (2012). Validation of virtual reality simulation for obstetric ultrasonography: A prospective cross-sectional study. *Simulation in Healthcare, 7*(5), 269–273. doi:10.1097/SIH.0b013e3182611844 PMID:22878584

Burgess, A., Bleasel, J., Haq, I., Roberts, C., Garsia, R., Robertson, T., & Mellis, C. (2017). Team-based learning (TBL) in the medical curriculum: Better than PBL? *BMC Medical Education*, *17*(1), 243. doi:10.118612909-017-1068-z PMID:29221459

Burke, B. (2012, November 5). *Gamification 2020: What is the future of gamification?* Retrieved from https://goo.gl/lQrJxo

Callaghan, N. (2016). Investigating the role of Minecraft in educational learning environments. *Educational Media International*, *53*(4), 244–260. doi:10.1080/09523987.2016.1254877

Cant, R. P., & Cooper, S. J. (2017). Use of simulation-based learning in undergraduate nurse education: An umbrella systematic review. *Nurse Education Today*, *49*, 63–71. doi:10.1016/j.nedt.2016.11.015 PMID:27902949

Carey, C. C., & Gougis, R. D. (2017). Simulation modeling of lakes in undergraduate and graduate classrooms increases comprehension of climate change concepts and experience with computational tools. *Journal of Science Education and Technology*, *26*(1), 1–11. doi:10.100710956-016-9644-2

Castillo, J., Caruana, C. J., & Wainwright, D. (2011). The changing concept of competence and categorisation of learning outcomes in Europe: Implications for the design of higher education radiography curricula at the European level. *Radiography*, *17*(3), 230–234. doi:10.1016/j.radi.2010.12.008

Cesim. (2014). *Manual del usuario*. Helsinki: Cesim Global Challenge.

Cesim. (n.d.). *Cesim global challenge introduction*. Helsinki: Cesim Global Challenge.

Chang, K.-E., Chang, C.-T., Hou, H.-T., Sung, Y.-T., Chao, H.-L., & Lee, C. M. (2014). Development and behavioral pattern analysis of a mobile guide system with augmented reality for painting appreciation instruction in an art museum. *Computers & Education*, *71*, 185–197. doi:10.1016/j.compedu.2013.09.022

Chapman, K. J., & Sorge, C. L. (1999). Can a simulation help achieve course objectives? An exploratory study investigating differences among instructional tools. *Journal of Education for Business*, *74*(4), 225–230. doi:10.1080/08832329909601689

Chasek, P. S. (2005). Power politics, diplomacy and role playing: Simulating the UN security council's response to terrorism. *International Studies Perspectives*, *6*(1), 1–19. doi:10.1111/j.1528-3577.2005.00190.x

Cheng, Y., Huang, C. L., & Yang, C. S. (2015). Using a 3D immersive virtual environment system to enhance social understanding and social skills for children with autism spectrum disorders. *Focus on Autism and Other Developmental Disabilities*, *30*(4), 222–236. doi:10.1177/1088357615583473

Cheng, Y., & Ye, J. (2010). Exploring the social competence of students with autism spectrum conditions in a collaborative virtual learning environment-The pilot study. *Computers & Education*, *54*(4), 1068–1077. doi:10.1016/j.compedu.2009.10.011

Chen, S.-C., & Lin, C.-P. (2014). The impact of customer experience and perceived value on sustainable social relationship in blogs: An empirical study. *Technological Forecasting and Social Change, 96*, 40–50. doi:10.1016/j.techfore.2014.11.011

Chetlen, A. L., Mendiratta-Lala, M., Probyn, L., Auffermann, W. F., DeBenedectis, C. M., Marko, J., ... Gettle, L. M. (2015). Conventional medical education and the history of simulation in radiology. *Academic Radiology, 22*(10), 1252–1267. doi:10.1016/j.acra.2015.07.003 PMID:26276167

CHFG. (2019). *What are clinical human factors?* Retrieved from https://chfg.org/what-are-clinical-human-factors

Chin, D. B., Oppezzo, M. A., & Schwartz, D. L. (2009). Teachable agents and the protégé effect: Increasing the effort towards learning. *Journal of Science Education and Technology, 18*(4), 334–352. doi:10.100710956-009-9180-4

Choi, I., & Lee, K. (2009). Designing and implementing a case-based learning environment for enhancing ill-structured problem solving: Classroom management problems for prospective teachers. *Educational Technology Research and Development, 57*(1), 99–129. doi:10.100711423-008-9089-2

Chou, C. H., & Liu, H. C. (2015). The effectiveness of web-based foreign exchange trading simulation in an international finance course. *Journal of Teaching in International Business, 24*(1), 4–20. doi:10.1080/08975930.2013.810047

Chung, G. K. W. K., Harmon, T. C., & Baker, E. L. (2001). The impact of a simulation-based learning design project on student learning. *IEEE Transactions on Education, 44*(4), 390–398. doi:10.1109/13.965789

Clarke, T., & Holmes, S. (2007). Fit for practice? An exploration of the development of newly qualified nurses using focus groups. *International Journal of Nursing Studies, 44*(7), 1210–1220. doi:10.1016/j.ijnurstu.2006.05.010 PMID:16872614

Clark, J. (2018). New methods of documenting health visiting practice. In R. Michael (Ed.), *Vision and value in health information* (pp. 121–142). London, UK: CRC Press. doi:10.1201/9781315375380-10

Coker, P. (2010). Effects of an experiential learning program on the clinical reasoning and critical thinking skill of occupational therapy students. *Journal of Allied Health, 39*(4), 281–286. PMID:21184024

Coline, C., Gihad, C., Philippe, B., & Yves, V. (2015). Randomized clinical trial of virtual reality simulation training for transvaginal gynecologic ultrasound skills. *Journal of Ultrasound in Medicine, 34*(9), 1663–1667. doi:10.7863/ultra.15.14.09063 PMID:26283753

Connolly, T., & Stansfield, M. (2006). Using games-based elearning technologies in overcoming difficulties in teaching information systems. *Journal of Information Technology Education, 5*(1), 450–476.

Cook, D. A., Brydges, R., Hamstra, S. J., Zendejas, B., Szostek, J. H., Wang, A. T., ... Hatala, R. (2012). Comparative effectiveness of technology-enhanced simulation versus other instructional methods: A systematic review and meta-analysis. *Simulation in Healthcare, 7*(5), 308–320. doi:10.1097/SIH.0b013e3182614f95 PMID:23032751

Cook, D. A., Hatala, R., Brydges, R., Zendejas, B., Szostek, J. H., Wang, A. T., ... Hamstra, S. J. (2011). Technology-enhanced simulation for health professions education: A systematic review and meta-analysis. *Journal of the American Medical Association, 306*(9), 978–988. doi:10.1001/jama.2011.1234 PMID:21900138

Cosson, P., & Willis, R. N. (2012a). *Comparison of student radiographers' performance in a real x-ray room after training with a screen based computer simulator*. Retrieved from Shaderware website: www.shaderware.com/distrib/etc/WhitePaper-ComparisonOfStudentRadiographersPerformanceInaRealXrayRoomAfterTrainingWithAScreenBasedComputerSimulator.pdf

Cosson, P., & Willis, R. N. (2012b). *Student radiographer perspectives on using a screen based computer simulator in diagnostic radiography*. Retrieved from Shaderware website: http://www.shaderware.com/distrib/etc/Whitepaper201211-StudentRadiographerPerspectivesOnUsingAScreenBasedComputerSimulatorInDiagnosticRadiography.pdf

Costello, E., Elrod, C., & Teppers, S. (2011). Clinical decision making in the acute care environment: A survey of practicing clinicians. *Journal of Acute Care Physical Therapy, 2*(2), 46–54. doi:10.1097/01592394-201102020-00001

Cowen, K. J., Hubbard, L. J., & Hancock, D. C. (2016). Concerns of nursing students beginning clinical courses: A descriptive study. *Nurse Education Today, 43*, 64–68. doi:10.1016/j.nedt.2016.05.001 PMID:27286947

CQC. (2018). *Opening the door to change. NHS safety culture and the need for transformation*. Retrieved from https://www.cqc.org.uk/sites/default/files/20181224_openingthedoor_report.pdf

Craig, A. B., Brown, E. R., Upright, J., & DeRosier, M. E. (2016). Enhancing children's social emotional functioning through virtual game-based delivery of social skills training. *Journal of Child and Family Studies, 25*(3), 959–968. doi:10.100710826-015-0274-8

Crewswell, J. (1994). *Qualitative inquiry and research design: Choosing among the five approaches*. Thousand Oaks, CA: SAGE.

Crookall, D., Oxford, R., & Saunders, D. (1987). Towards a reconceptualization of simulation: From representation to reality. *Simulation/Games for Learning, 17*(4), 147-171.

Cross, K. P. (1982). *Adults as learners.* San Francisco, CA: Josey-Bass.

Csikszentmihalyi, M. (1990). *Flow: The psychology of optimal experience.* New York, NY: Harper Collins.

Culp, M. (2015). Constructivist learning theory and global health education for the radiologic sciences. *Radiologic Science & Education, 20*(2), 21–27. Retrieved from https://www.researchgate. net/publication/301543463_Constructivist_Learning_Theory_and_Global_Health_Education_ for_the_Radiologic_Sciences

Cutolo, F., Meola, A., Carbone, M., Sinceri, S., Cagnazzo, F., Denaro, E., & Ferrari, V. (2017). A new head-mounted display-based augmented reality system in neurosurgical oncology: A study on phantom. *Computer Assisted Surgery, 22*(1), 39–53. doi:10.1080/24699322.2017.135 8400 PMID:28754068

Dangel, J. R., Guyton, E., & McIntyre, C. B. (2004). Constructivist pedagogy in primary classrooms: Learning from teachers and their classrooms. *Journal of Early Childhood Teacher Education, 24*(4), 237–245. doi:10.1080/1090102040240404

David, L. (2014). *Social development theory (Vygotsky) in learning theories.* Retrieved from https://www.learning-theories.com/vygotskys-social-learning-theory.html

Davis, S., Josephsen, J., & Macy, R. (2013). Implementation of mental health simulations: Challenges and lessons learned. *Clinical Simulation in Nursing, 9*(5), e157–e162. doi:10.1016/j. ecns.2011.11.011

de Jong, T. (2019). Technological advances in inquiry learning. *Science, 312*(5773), 532–533. doi:10.1126cience.1127750 PMID:16645080

Dean, E. (2009). Physical therapy in the 21st century (part II): Evidence-based practice within the context of evidence-informed practice. *Physiotherapy Theory and Practice, 25*(5), 354–368. doi:10.1080/09593980902813416 PMID:19842863

Dearsley, A. (2013). Using standardized patients in an undergraduate mental health simulation AU - Alexander, Louise. *International Journal of Mental Health, 42*(2-3), 149–164. doi:10.2753/ IMH0020-7411420209

Decker, S. D., Sportsman, S., Puetz, L., & Billings, L. (2008). The evolution of simulation and its contribution to competency. *Journal of Continuing Education in Nursing, 39*(2), 74–80. doi:10.3928/00220124-20080201-06 PMID:18323144

Dehn, M. J. (2011). *Working memory and academic learning: Assessment and intervention.* Hoboken, NJ: John Wiley & Sons.

Denis, G., & Jouvelot, P. (2005). Motivation-driven educational games design: Applying best practices to music education. In *Proceedings of the 2005 ACM SIGCHI international conference on advances in computer entertainment technology* (pp. 462-465). New York, NY: ACM. 10.1145/1178477.1178581

Densen, P. (2011). Challenges and opportunities facing medical education. *Transactions of the American Clinical and Climatological Association, 122*, 48–58. Retrieved from https://www.ncbi.nlm.nih.gov/pmc/articles/PMC3116346/ PMID:21686208

Deshmukh, A. (2018). *Summary of health education England regional simulation strategies.* Unpublished manuscript.

Desser, T. S., Ahlqvist, J., Dev, P., Hedman, L., Nilsson, T., & Gold, G. E. (2006, November). *Learning radiology in simulated environments: Development of a simulator for teaching cervical spine radiography.* Paper presented at the Ninety-second International Conference of the Radiological Society of North America, Chicago, IL. Retrieved from https://www.researchgate.net/publication/266124016_Learning_Radiology_in_Simulated_Environments_Development_of_a_Simulator_for_Teaching_Cervical_Spine_Radiography

Desser, T. S. (2007). Simulation-based training: The next revolution in radiology education? *Journal of the American College of Radiology, 4*(11), 816–824. doi:10.1016/j.jacr.2007.07.013 PMID:17964504

Dexter, H., & Guittet, E.-P. (2014). Teaching (something about) terrorism: Ethical and methodological problems, pedagogical suggestions. *International Studies Perspectives, 15*(4), 374–393. doi:10.1111/j.1528-3585.2012.00507.x

Dickinson, T., Hopton, J., & Pilling, M. (2016). An evaluation of nursing students' perceptions on the efficacy of high-fidelity clinical simulation to enhance their confidence, understanding and competence in managing psychiatric emergencies. *Journal of Clinical Nursing, 25*(9-10), 1476–1478. doi:10.1111/jocn.13211 PMID:27001411

Didehbani, N., Allen, T., Kandalaft, M., Krawczyk, D., & Chapman, S. (2016). Virtual reality social cognition training for children with high functioning autism. *Computers in Human Behavior, 62*, 703–711. doi:10.1016/j.chb.2016.04.033

Dikshit, A., Wu, D., Wu, C., & Zhao, W. (2005). An online interactive simulation system for medical imaging education. *Computerized Medical Imaging and Graphics, 29*(6), 395–404. doi:10.1016/j.compmedimag.2005.02.001 PMID:15996851

Dillenbourg, P. (1999). What do you mean by collaborative learning? In P. Dillenbourg (Ed.), *Collaborative learning: Cognitive and computational approaches* (pp. 1–19). Oxford, UK: Elsevier.

Ding, Y. (2009). Perspectives on social tagging. *Journal of the Association for Information Science and Technology, 60*(12), 2388–2401. doi:10.1002/asi.21190

Dippold, D. (2009). Peer feedback through blogs: Student and teacher perceptions in an advanced German class. *ReCALL*, *21*(1), 18–36. doi:10.1017/S095834400900010X

Dolnik, A. (2015). Conducting field research on terrorism. In C. Kennedy-Pipe, G. Clubb, & S. Mabon (Eds.), Terrorism and Political Violence (pp. 288-296). London: SAGE. doi:10.4135/9781473917248.n21

Dolphin. (2019). *Dolphin Ceph Tracing*. Retrieved from https://www.dolphinimaging.com/product/Imaging?Subcategory_OS_Safe_Name=Imaging_Plus#Ceph_Tracing

Domitrovich, C. E., Cortes, R. C., & Greenberg, M. T. (2007). Improving young children's social and emotional competence: A randomized trial of the preschool "PATHS" curriculum. *The Journal of Primary Prevention*, *28*(2), 67–91. doi:10.100710935-007-0081-0

Donato, R. (2004). Aspects of collaboration in pedagogical discourse. *Annual Review of Applied Linguistics*, *24*, 284–302. doi:10.1017/S026719050400011X

Dorathy, A. A., & Mahalakshmi, S. N. (2011). Second language acquisition through task based approach – role-play in English language teaching. *English for Specific Purposes World*, *33*(11), 1–7.

Dougherty, B. K. (2003). Byzantine politics: Using simulations to make sense of the Middle East. *PS, Political Science & Politics*, *36*(02), 239–244. doi:10.1017/S1049096503002154

Dragan, I. F., Dalessandri, D., Johnson, L. A., Tucker, A., & Walmsley, A. D. (2018). Impact of scientific and technological advances. *European Journal of Dental Education*, *22*(Suppl. 1), 17–20. doi:10.1111/eje.12342 PMID:29601675

Driscoll, M. P. (2000). *Psychology of learning for instruction* (2nd ed.). Needham Heights, MA: Allyn & Bacon.

Dudley, F. (2018). *The simulated patient handbook: A comprehensive guide for facilitators and simulated patients*. London: CRC Press. doi:10.1201/9781315383774

Dutã, M., Amariei, C. I., Bogdan, C. M., Popovici, D. M., Ionescu, N., & Nuca, C. I. (2011). An overview of virtual and augmented reality in dental education. *Oral Health and Dental Management*, *10*(1), 42–49.

Eckhardt, M., Urhahne, D., Conrad, O., & Harms, U. (2013). How effective is instructional support for learning with computer simulations? *Instructional Science*, *41*(1), 105–124. doi:10.100711251-012-9220-y

Efstathiou, I., Kyza, E. A., & Georgiou, Y. (2018). An inquiry based augmented reality mobile learning approach to fostering primary school students' historical reasoning in non-formal settings. *Interactive Learning Environments*, *26*(1), 22–41. doi:10.1080/10494820.2016.1276076

Eisenhardt, A., & Ninassi, S. B. (2016). The use of simulation and cases to teach real world decision making: Applied example for health care management graduate programs. *Journal of Learning in Higher Education, 12*(1), 71–75.

e-LfH. (2019). *Health Education England e-LfH Hub Learner Analytics.* Unpublished manuscript.

Eliades, T., & Athanasiou, A. E. (2015). *Orthodontic postgraduate education: A global perspective.* New York, NY: Thieme.

Engel, R. J., & Schutt, R. K. (2012). *The practice of research in social work.* Thousand Oaks, CA: Sage.

Eppich, W., & Cheng, A. (2015). Promoting excellence and reflective learning in simulation (PEARLS): Development and rationale for a blended approach to health care simulation debriefing. *Simulation in Healthcare, 10*(2), 106–115. doi:10.1097/SIH.0000000000000072 PMID:25710312

Ertmer, P. A., Stepich, D. A., Flanagan, S., Kocaman, A., Christian, R., Reyes, L., . . . Ushigusa, S. (2008). Ill-structured problem solving: Helping instructional design novices perform like experts. *Annual meeting of the American Educational Research Association.* Retrieved from http://ertmer_AERA2008_ExpertNovice.pdf

Espelage, D. L., Rose, C. A., & Polanin, J. R. (2016). Social-emotional learning program to promote prosocial and academic skills among middle school students with disabilities. *Remedial and Special Education, 37*(6), 323–332. doi:10.1177/0741932515627475

Fasli, M., & Michalakopoulos, M. (2006). Learning through game-like simulations. *Innovation in Teaching and Learning in Information and Computer Sciences, 5*(2), 1–11. doi:10.11120/ital.2006.05020005

Fenstermacher, K., Olympia, D., & Sheridan, S. M. (2006). Effectiveness of a computer-facilitated interactive social skills training program for boys with attention deficit hyperactivity disorder. *School Psychology Quarterly, 21*(2), 197–224. doi:10.1521cpq.2006.21.2.197

Fent, G., Blythe, J., Farooq, O., & Purva, M. (2015). In-situ simulation as a tool for patient safety: A systematic review identifying how it is used and its effectiveness. *BMJ Simulation and Technology Enhanced Learning, 1*(3), 103–110. doi:10.1136/bmjstel-2015-000065

Ferrara, L. R. (2010). Integrating evidence-based practice with educational theory in clinical practice for nurse practitioners: Bridging the theory practice gap. *Research and Theory for Nursing Practice, 24*(4), 213–216. doi:10.1891/1541-6577.24.4.213 PMID:21197916

Ferrazzi, K. (n.d.). *Getting virtual teams right.* Retrieved from https://goo.gl/byiOjF

Frederiksen, N. (1984). Implications of cognitive theory for instruction in problem solving. *Review of Educational Research, 54*(3), 363–407. doi:10.3102/00346543054003363

Freina, L., & Ott, M. (2015). A literature review on Immersive Virtual Reality in education: State of the art and perspectives. *eLearning & Software for Education*, 1.

Frey, S. H., & Gerry, V. E. (2006). Modulation of neural activity during observational learning of actions and their sequential orders. *The Journal of Neuroscience*, *26*(51), 13194–13201. doi:10.1523/JNEUROSCI.3914-06.2006 PMID:17182769

Fugill, M. (2013). Defining the purpose of phantom head. *European Journal of Dental Education*, *17*(1), 1–4. doi:10.1111/eje.12008 PMID:23279394

Furze, J., Black, L., Hoffman, J., Barr, J., Cochran, T., & Jensen, G. (2015). Exploration of students' clinical reasoning development in professional physical therapy education. *Journal, Physical Therapy Education*, *29*(3), 22–33. doi:10.1097/00001416-201529030-00005

Furze, J., Gale, J., Black, L., Cochran, T., & Jensen, M. (2015). Clinical reasoning: Development of a grading rubric for student assessment. *Journal, Physical Therapy Education*, *29*(3), 34–45. doi:10.1097/00001416-201529030-00006

Fushima, K., & Kobayashi, M. (2016). Mixed-reality simulation for orthognathic surgery. *Maxillofacial Plastic and Reconstructive Surgery*, *38*(1), 13. doi:10.118640902-016-0059-z PMID:27014664

Fu, W. (2015). Development of an innovative tool to assess student physical therapists' clinical reasoning competency. *Journal, Physical Therapy Education*, *29*(4), 14–26. doi:10.1097/00001416-201529040-00004

Gaba, D. M. (2004). The future vision of simulation in healthcare. *BMJ Quality & Safety*, *13*(suppl_1), 2–10. doi:10.1136/qshc.2004.009878

Gaca, A. M., Frush, D. P., Hohenhaus, S. M., Luo, X., Ancarana, A., & Frush, K. S. (2007). Enhancing pediatric safety: Using simulation to assess resident preparedness for anaphylaxis from intravenous contrast media. *Radiology*, *245*(1), 236–244. doi:10.1148/radiol.2451061381 PMID:17885191

Gagné, R. M., Briggs, L. J., & Wager, W. W. (1992). *Principles of instructional design* (4th ed.). Fort Worth, TX: Harcourt Brace Jovanovich College Publishers.

Gamble, A., Bearman, M., & Nestel, D. (2016). A systematic review: Children and adolescents as simulated patients in health professional education. *Advanced Simulation*, *1*(1), 1. doi:10.118641077-015-0003-9 PMID:29449970

Ganguli, S., Pedrosa, I., Yam, C. S., Appignani, B., Siewert, B., & Kressel, H. Y. (2006). Part I: Preparing first-year radiology residents and assessing their readiness for on-call responsibilities. *Academic Radiology*, *13*(6), 764–769. doi:10.1016/j.acra.2006.02.057 PMID:16679280

Garrison, D. R., & Vaughan, N. D. (2008). *Blended learning in higher education: Framework, principles, and guidelines*. San Francisco, CA: Jossey-Bass.

Garris, R., Ahlers, R., & Driskell, J. E. (2002). Games, motivation, and learning: A research and practice model. *Simulation & Gaming*, *3*(4), 441–467. doi:10.1177/1046878102238607

Garrote, A., Dessemontet, R. S., & Opitz, E. M. (2017). Facilitating the social participation of pupils with special educational needs in mainstream schools: A review of school-based interventions. *Educational Research Review*, *20*, 12–23. doi:10.1016/j.edurev.2016.11.001

Geis, G. L., Pio, B., Pendergrass, T. L., Moyer, M. R., & Patterson, M. D. (2011). Simulation to assess the safety of new healthcare teams and new facilities. *Simulation in Healthcare*, *6*(3), 125–133. doi:10.1097/SIH.0b013e31820dff30 PMID:21383646

Gelder, C. L., & Paterson-Brown, S. (2015). The role of anatomy in surgical training and the use of cadaveric training courses. *Bulletin of the Royal College of Surgeons of England*, *97*(3), 123–126. doi:10.1308/147363515X14134529301381

Gentry, J. W. (1990). What is experiential learning? In J. W. Gentry (Ed.), *Guide to business gaming and experiential learning* (pp. 9–20). Asbury, IA: Nichols Publishing.

Gereluk, D. (2012). *Education, extremism and terrorism. [electronic resource]: What should be taught in citizenship education and why*. New York: *Continuum*.

Gerstmann, E. (2006). The century ahead: A brief survey of potential threats to freedom of speech, thought, and inquiry at American universities. In E. Gerstmann & M. J. Streb (Eds.), *Academic freedom at the dawn of a new century* (pp. 175–186). Stanford, CA: Stanford University Press.

Ge, X., & Land, S. M. (2003). Scaffolding students' problem-solving processes in an ill-structured task using question prompts and peer interactions. *Educational Technology Research and Development*, *51*(1), 21–38. doi:10.1007/BF02504515

Ghanbarzadeh, R., Ghapanchi, A. H., Blumenstein, M., & Talaei-Khoei, A. (2014). A decade of research on the use of three-dimensional virtual worlds in health care: A systematic literature review. *Journal of Medical Internet Research*, *16*(2), e47. doi:10.2196/jmir.3097 PMID:24550130

Gibson, D., Aldrich, C., & Prensky, M. (Eds.). (2007). *Games and simulations in online learning: Research and development frameworks*. Hershey, PA: IGI Global. doi:10.4018/978-1-59904-304-3

Gibson, D., & Baek, Y. (Eds.). (2009). *Digital simulations for improving education: Learning through artificial learning environments*. Hershey, PA: IGI Global. doi:10.4018/978-1-60566-322-7

Gilbody, J., Prasthofer, A. W., Ho, K., & Costa, M. L. (2011). The use and effectiveness of cadaveric workshops in higher surgical training: A systematic review. *Bulletin of the Royal College of Surgeons of England*, *93*(5), 347–352. doi:10.1308/147870811X582954 PMID:21943455

Glaser, R. (1984). Education and thinking: The role of knowledge. *The American Psychologist*, *39*(2), 93–104. doi:10.1037/0003-066X.39.2.93

Godwin-Jones, R. (2016). Augmented reality and language learning: From annotated vocabulary to place-based mobile games. *Language Learning & Technology*, *20*(3), 9–19.

Golafshani, N. (2003). Understanding reliability and validity in qualitative research. *Qualitative Report*, *8*(4), 597–606. Retrieved from http://nsuworks.nova.edu/tqr/vol8/iss4/6

Goldsman, D., Nance, R. E., & Wilson, J. R. (2010). A brief history of simulation revisited. In B. Johansson, S. Jain, J. Montoya-Torres, J. Hugan, & E. Yücesan (Eds.), *Proceedings of the 2010 winter simulation conference* (pp. 567-574). Piscataway, NJ: IEEE. 10.1109/WSC.2010.5679129

Gordon, J., Oriol, N., & Cooper, J. (2004). Bringing good teaching cases "to life": A simulator-based medical education service. *Academic Medicine*, *79*(1), 23–27. doi:10.1097/00001888-200401000-00007 PMID:14690993

Greasley, A. (2017). *Simulation modelling for business*. London, UK: Routledge. doi:10.4324/9781315243085

Greca, I. M., Seoane, E., & Arriassecq, I. (2014). Epistemological issues concerning computer simulations in science and their implications for science education. *Science & Education*, *23*(4), 897–921. doi:10.100711191-013-9673-7

Greenblat, C. (1981). Teaching with simulation games: A review of claims and evidence. In R. E. Duke & C. Greenblat (Eds.), *Principles of practice of gaming-simulation* (pp. 62–83). London, UK: Sage.

Green, D., & Appleyard, R. (2011). The influence of VERT™ characteristics on the development of skills in skill apposition techniques. *Radiography*, *17*(3), 178–182. doi:10.1016/j.radi.2011.04.002

Gregg, L., & Tarrier, N. (2007). Virtual reality in mental health. *Social Psychiatry and Psychiatric Epidemiology*, *42*(5), 343–354. doi:10.100700127-007-0173-4

Grusec, J. E. (1992). Social learning theory and developmental psychology: The legacies of Robert Sears and Albert Bandura. *Developmental Psychology*, *28*(5), 776–786. doi:10.1037/0012-1649.28.5.776

Guba, E. G., & Lincoln, Y. S. (1994). Competing paradigms in qualitative research. In N. K. Denzin & Y. S. Lincoln (Eds.), *Handbook of qualitative research* (pp. 105–117). Thousand Oaks, CA: Sage.

Guise, V., Chambers, M., & Valimaki, M. (2012). What can virtual patient simulation offer mental health nursing education? *Journal of Psychiatric and Mental Health Nursing*, *19*(5), 410–418. doi:10.1111/j.1365-2850.2011.01797.x PMID:22070549

Gundala, R. R., & Singh, M. (2016). Role of simulations in student learning: A case study using marketing simulation. *Journal of Educational Research and Innovation*, *5*(2), 1–14.

Hair, J. F., Black, W. C., Babin, B. J., & Anderson, R. E. (2010). *Multivariate data analysis.* Englewood Cliffs, NJ: Prentice-Hall.

Hamstra, S. J., Dubrowski, A., & Backstein, D. (2006). Teaching technical skills to surgical residents: A survey of empirical research. *Clinical Orthopaedics and Related Research, 449*: 108–115. PMID:16760810

Hamza-Lup, F. G., Rolland, J. P., & Hughes, C. (2018). *A distributed augmented reality system for medical training and simulation.* Retrieved from https://www.researchgate.net/publication/329362500_A_Distributed_Augmented_Reality_System_for_Medical_Training_and_Simulation

Hanberg, A., & Brown, S. C. (2006). Bridging the Theory–Practice gap with evidence-based practice. *Journal of Continuing Education in Nursing, 37*(6), 248–249. doi:10.3928/00220124-20061101-07 PMID:17144113

Harder, N. (2018). The value of simulation in healthcare: The obvious, the tangential, and the obscure. *Clinical Simulation in Nursing, 15*, 73–74. doi:10.1016/j.ecns.2017.12.004

Hardy, M., & Totman, S. (2012). From dictatorship to democracy: Simulating the politics of the Middle East. In C. Nygaard, N. Courtney, & E. Leigh (Eds.), *Transforming university teaching into learning via games, simulations and role-plays* (pp. 189–206). Faringdon, UK: Libri Publishing.

Hardy, M., & Totman, S. (2013). Using an online simulation to address equity issues for off-campus students. In J. Willems, B. Tynan, & R. James (Eds.), *Outlooks and opportunities in blended and distance learning* (pp. 139–153). Hershey, PA: IGI Global. doi:10.4018/978-1-4666-4205-8.ch011

Hardy, M., & Totman, S. (2017a). The long game: Five years of simulating the Middle East. *Australasian Journal of Educational Technology, 33*(4), 38–52. doi:10.14742/ajet.2696

Hardy, M., & Totman, S. (2017b). Teaching an old game new tricks: Long-term feedback on a re-designed online role play. *British Journal of Educational Technology, 48*(6), 1260–1272. doi:10.1111/bjet.12498

Harrell, W. E. Jr, Hatcher, D. C., & Bolt, R. L. (2002). In search of anatomic truth: 3-dimensional digital modeling and the future of orthodontics. *American Journal of Orthodontics and Dentofacial Orthopedics, 122*(3), 325–330. doi:10.1067/mod.2002.126147 PMID:12226616

Hayashi, S., Munekazu, N., Shinichi, K., Ning, Q., Naoyuki, H., Shuichi, H., & Masahiro, I. (2016). History and future of human cadaver preservation for surgical training: From formalin to saturated salt solution method. *Anatomical Science, 91*(1), 1–7. doi:10.100712565-015-0299-5 PMID:26670696

HEE. (2016). *Enhancing UK core medical training through simulation-based education: An evidence-based approach. A report from the joint JRCPTB/HEE Expert Group on Simulation in Core Medical Training.* Retrieved from https://www.jrcptb.org.uk/sites/default/files/HEE_Report_FINAL.pdf

HEE. (2018a). *A Health and Care Digital Capabilities Framework*. Retrieved from https://www.hee.nhs.uk/sites/default/files/documents/Digital%20Literacy%20Capability%20Framework%202018.pdf

HEE. (2018b). *National Framework for Simulation-Based Education*. Retrieved from https://www.hee.nhs.uk/our-work/technology-enhanced-learning/simulation-immersive-technologies

HEE. (2019a). *The Topol Review*. Retrieved from https://topol.hee.nhs.uk

HEE. (2019b). *Technology Enhanced Learning*. Retrieved from https://www.hee.nhs.uk/our-work/technology-enhanced-learning

Hellaby, M., Wood, S., & Herbert, N. (1997). Safely moving a hospital. *The Human Connection*, 2, 18–19.

Helsper, E. J., & Eynon, R. (2010). Digital natives: Where is the evidence? *British Educational Research Journal*, *36*(3), 503–520. doi:10.1080/01411920902989227

Herold, B. (2015). Minecraft fueling creative ideas, analytical thinking. *Education Week*, *35*(01), 12. Retrieved from https://www.edweek.org/ew/articles/2015/08/19/minecraft-fueling-creative-ideas-analytical-thinking-in.html

Hewett, K. J. E. (2016). *The Minecraft project: Predictors for academic success and 21st century skills gamers are learning through video game experiences* (Doctoral dissertation). Texas A&M University-Corpus Christi, College Station, TX.

Hintjens, H. M. (2008). *Through the looking glass? Learning from simulating Rwanda*. Paper presented at the World Conference on E-Learning in Corporate, Government, Healthcare, and Higher Education 2008, Las Vegas, NV.

Hoadley, C. (2004). Learning and design: Why the learning sciences and instructional system need each other. *Educational Technology*, *44*(3), 6–12. Retrieved from https://www.scribd.com/document/346368309/Learning-and-DesignL-Why-the-Learning-and-Instructional-Sciences-Need-Each-Other

Holmström, A., & Ahonen, S.-M. (2016). Radiography students' learning: A literature review. *Radiologic Technology*, *87*(4), 371–379. Retrieved from http://www.radiologictechnology.org/content/87/4/371.full?sid=1a3efa4a-7651-43f5-8b7d-7bc217953a25 PMID:26952061

Honey, M. A., & Hilton, M. (2011). *Learning science through computer games and simulations*. Washington, DC: National Research Council.

Horiguchi, T., Imai, I., Toumoto, T., & Hirashima, T. (2014). Error-based simulation for error-awareness in learning mechanics: An evaluation. *Journal of Educational Technology & Society*, *17*(3), 1–13.

Horner, R. H., Swaminathan, H., Sugai, G., & Smolkowski, K. (2012). Considerations for the systematic analysis and use of single-case research. *Education & Treatment of Children, 35*(2), 269–290. doi:10.1353/etc.2012.0011

Horst, J. A., Clark, M. D., & Lee, A. H. (2009). Observation, assisting, apprenticeship: cycles of visual and kinesthetic learning in dental education. *Journal of Dental Education, 73*(8), 919–933. PMID:19648563

Houser, K. (2019, February 11). *Google is rolling out AR navigation for its map app*. Retrieved from https://futurism.com/the-byte/ar-navigation-google-maps-app

Howe, K. (1988). Against the quantitative-qualitative incompatibility thesis or dogmas die hard. *Education Research, 17*(8), 10-16.

Hsiao, H.-S., Chang, C.-S., Lin, C.-Y., & Wang, Y.-Z. (2016). Weather observers: A manipulative augmented reality system for weather simulations at home, in the classroom, and at a museum. *Interactive Learning Environments, 24*(1), 205–223. doi:10.1080/10494820.2013.834829

Huang, K. T., Ball, C., Francis, J., Ratan, R., Boumis, J., & Fordham, J. (2019). Augmented versus virtual reality in education: An exploratory study examining science knowledge retention when using augmented reality/virtual reality mobile applications. *Cyberpsychology, Behavior, and Social Networking, 22*(2), 105–110. doi:10.1089/cyber.2018.0150 PMID:30657334

Huang, T.-K., Yang, C.-H., Hsieh, Y.-H., Wang, J.-C., & Hung, C.-C. (2018). Augmented reality (AR) and virtual reality (VR) applied in dentistry. *The Kaohsiung Journal of Medical Sciences, 34*(4), 243–248. doi:10.1016/j.kjms.2018.01.009 PMID:29655414

Huffman, A. H., Whetten, J., & Huffman, W. H. (2013). Using technology in higher education: The influence of gender roles on technology self-efficacy. *Computers in Human Behavior, 29*(4), 1779–1786. doi:10.1016/j.chb.2013.02.012

Hughes, J. M., Fallis, D. W., Peel, J. L., & Murchison, D. F. (2009). Learning styles of orthodontic residents. *Journal of Dental Education, 73*(3), 309–327. PMID:19289721

Huizinga, J. (1950). *Homo ludens: A study of the play-element in culture*. Boston, MA: Beacon.

Hulse, S. F. (1992). Learning theories: Something for everyone. *Radiologic Technology, 63*(3), 198–202. PMID:1736320

Hunter, S., Pitt, V., Croce, N., & Roche, J. (2014). Critical thinking skills of undergraduate nursing students: Description and demographic predictors. *Nurse Education Today, 34*(5), 809–814. doi:10.1016/j.nedt.2013.08.005 PMID:24018356

Hyland, K. (1993). Language learning simulations: A practical guide. *English Teaching Forum, 31*(4), 16-22.

Iacopino, A. M. (2007). The influence of "new science" on dental education: Current concepts, trends, and models for the future. *Journal of Dental Education, 71*(4), 450–462. PMID:17468305

Inman, T. (1860). Foundation for a new theory and practice of medicine (book review). *Journal of Medical Science, 40*, 450–458.

Ireland, A. J., Smith, A. S. A., Alder, D. M., Sandy, J. R., & Chadwick, S. M. (2005). Building a learning community on-line: The first step towards a national virtual learning environment in orthodontics. *Journal of Orthodontics, 32*(3), 214–219. doi:10.1179/146531205225021141 PMID:16170064

Issenberg, S. B., McGaghie, W. C., Petrusa, E. R., Lee Gordon, D., & Scalese, R. J. (2005). Features and uses of high-fidelity medical simulations that lead to effective learning: A BEME systematic review. *Medical Teacher, 27*(1), 10–28. doi:10.1080/01421590500046924 PMID:16147767

Issenberg, S., & Scalese, R. (2008). Simulation in health care education. *Perspectives in Biology and Medicine, 51*(1), 31–46. doi:10.1353/pbm.2008.0004 PMID:18192764

Itin, C. M. (1999). Reasserting the philosophy of experiential education as a vehicle for change in the 21st century. *Journal of Experiential Education, 22*(2), 91–98. doi:10.1177/105382599902200206

Jackson, R. (2012). The study of terrorism 10 years after 9/11: Successes, issues, challenges. *International Relations / Uluslararasi Iliskiler, 9*(33), 1-16.

Jadrić, M., Ćukušić, M., & Bralić, A. (2014). Comparison of discrete event simulation tools in an academic environment. *Croatian Operational Research Review, 5*(2), 203–219. doi:10.17535/crorr.2014.0008

James, J., Maude, P., Sim, J., & McDonald, M. (2012). Using Second Life for health professional learning: Informing multidisciplinary understanding. *International Journal of Modern Education Forum, 1*(1), 24–30.

Jarvenoja, H., & Jarvela, S. (2009). Emotion control in collaborative learning situations: Do students regulate emotions evoked by social challenges? *The British Journal of Educational Psychology, 79*(3), 463–481. doi:10.1348/000709909X402811

Jasinevicius, T. R., Landers, M., Nelson, S., & Urbankova, A. (2004). An evaluation of two dental simulation systems: Virtual reality versus contemporary non-computer-assisted. *Journal of Dental Education, 68*(11), 1151–1162. PMID:15520234

Jeffries, P. (2005). A framework for designing, implementing, and evaluating: Simulations used as teaching strategies in nursing. *Nursing Education Perspectives, 26*(2), 96–103. PMID:15921126

Jeffries, P. R. (2012). *Simulation in nursing education: From conceptualization to evaluation.* Washington, DC: National League for Nursing.

Jonassen, D. (1997). Instructional design models for well-structured and ill-structured problem-solving learning outcomes. *Educational Technology Research and Development, 45*(1), 64–94. doi:10.1007/BF02299613

Jonassen, D. (2000). Toward a design theory of problem solving. *Educational Technology Research and Development, 48*(4), 63–85. doi:10.1007/BF02300500

Jonassen, D., Strobel, J., & Lee, C. (2006). Everyday problem solving in engineering: Lessons for engineering educators. *Journal of Engineering Education, 95*(2), 139–151. doi:10.1002/j.2168-9830.2006.tb00885.x

Jozwiak, J. (2004). Teaching problem-solving skills to adults. *MPAEA Journal of Adult Education, 33*(1), 19–34.

Juan, M. C., Alexandrescu, L., Folguera, F., & García-G, I. (2016). A mobile augmented reality system for the learning of dental morphology. *Digital Education Review, 30*, 234–247.

Jung, S., Lee, J., Biocca, F., & Kim, J. W. (2019). Augmented reality in the health domain: Projecting spatial augmented reality visualizations on a perceiver's body for health communication effects. *Cyberpsychology, Behavior, and Social Networking, 22*(2), 142–150. doi:10.1089/cyber.2018.0028 PMID:30668138

Kailani, C., & Ciobotar, N. (2015). Experiential marketing: An efficient tool to leverage marketing communication impact on consumer behavior. *International Conference on Marketing and Business Development Journal, 1*(1), 281-287.

Kalyvioti, K., & Mikropoulos, T. A. (2014). Virtual environments and dyslexia: A literature review. *Procedia Computer Science, 27*, 138–147. doi:10.1016/j.procs.2014.02.017

Kantar, L. (2014). Assessment and instruction to promote higher order thinking in nursing students. *Nurse Education Today, 34*(5), 789–794. doi:10.1016/j.nedt.2013.08.013 PMID:24035312

Kappers, W. M. (2009). *Educational video game effects upon mathematics achievement and motivation scores: An experimental study examining differences between the sexes.* Unpublished manuscript.

Kappers, W. M. (2017). Through the lens of the reviewer: Information literacy, an LMS, and peer review. *Computers in Education Journal, 8*(2), 83–96.

Kappers, W. M., & Cutler, S. L. (2016). Simulation to application. The use of computer simulations to improve real-world application of learning. *Computers in Education Journal*, 64–74.

Kapp, K. M. (2012). *The gamification of learning and instruction: Game-based methods and strategies for training and education.* San Francisco, CA: Pfeiffer.

Kapp, K. M., Blair, L., & Mesch, R. (2014). *The gamification of learning and instruction fieldbook: Ideas into practice.* San Francisco, CA: Wiley.

Karsenti, T., Bugmann, J., & Gros, P. P. (2017). *Transforming education with Minecraft? Results of an exploratory study conducted with 118 elementary-school students.* Montréal, Canada: CRIFPE.

Kasprzak, T. (2016). Technology and radiology education – Meeting the needs of millennial learners. *Academic Radiology, 23*(7), 844–847. doi:10.1016/j.acra.2016.03.003 PMID:27118526

Katic, D., Spengler, P., Bodenstedt, S., Castrillon-Oberndorfer, G., Seeberger, R., Hoffmann, J., & Speidel, S. (2015). A system for context-aware intraoperative augmented reality in dental implant surgery. *International Journal of Computer Assisted Radiology and Surgery, 10*(1), 101–108. doi:10.100711548-014-1005-0 PMID:24771315

Katoue, M. G., Iblagh, N., Somerville, S., & Ker, J. (2015). Introducing simulation-based education to healthcare professionals: Exploring the challenge of integrating theory into educational practice. *Scottish Medical Journal, 60*(4), 176–181. doi:10.1177/0036933015607272 PMID:26403571

Ke, F., & Im, T. (2013). Virtual-reality-based social interaction training for children with high-functioning autism. *The Journal of Educational Research, 106*(6), 441–461. doi:10.1080/0022 0671.2013.832999

Ke, F., & Moon, J. (2018). Virtual collaborative gaming as social skills training for high-functioning autistic children. *British Journal of Educational Technology, 49*(4), 728–741. doi:10.1111/bjet.12626

Khan, S. (2011). New pedagogies on teaching science with computer simulations. *Journal of Science Education and Technology, 20*(3), 215–232. doi:10.100710956-010-9247-2

Khan, T., Johnston, K., & Ophoff, J. (2019). The impact of an augmented reality application on learning motivation of students. *Advances in Human-Computer Interaction, 1*, 14. Retrieved from https://www.hindawi.com/journals/ahci/2019/7208494

Kikot, T., Fernandes, S., & Costa, G. (2014). Business simulators and lecturer's perception! The case of University of Algarve. In *ETHICOMP 2014* (pp. 1–12). Paris, France: University of Pierre and Marie Currie.

Kim, D., & Perdue, R. R. (2013). The effects of cognitive, affective, and sensory attributes on hotel choice. *International Journal of Hospitality Management, 35*, 246–257. doi:10.1016/j.ijhm.2013.05.012

Kim, Y., Kim, H., & Kim, Y. O. (2017). Virtual reality and augmented reality in plastic surgery: A review. *Archives of Plastic Surgery, 44*(3), 179–187. doi:10.5999/aps.2017.44.3.179 PMID:28573091

Kings Fund. (2017). *How is the NHS structured?* Retrieved from https://www.kingsfund.org.uk/audio-video/how-new-nhs-structured

Kirriemuir, J., & McFarlane, A. (2004). *Report 8: Literature review in games and learning.* Bristol: FutureLab.

Kirschner, P. A., Sweller, J., & Clark, R. (2006). Why minimal guidance during instruction does not work: An analysis of the failure of constructivist, discovery, problem-based, experiential, and inquiry based learning. *Educational Psychologist, 41*(2), 75–86. doi:10.120715326985ep4102_1

Klein, K. A., & Neal, C. H. (2016). Simulation in radiology education: Thinking outside the phantom. *Academic Radiology, 23*(7), 908–910. doi:10.1016/j.acra.2016.02.013 PMID:27052525

Klopfer, E., Osterweil, S., Groff, J., & Haas, J. (2009). The instructional power of: Digital games, social networking, simulations and how teachers can leverage them. *The Education Arcade, 1*(1), 1–20.

Kolb, D. (1984). *Experiential Learning: Experience as the Source of Learning and Development.* Upper Saddle River, NJ: Prentice-Hall.

Kolb, D. A. (1984). The process of experiential learning. In D. A. Kolb (Ed.), *Experiential learning* (pp. 20–38). Upper Saddle River, NJ: Prentice-Hall.

Koldner, J. L. (1992). An introduction to case-based reasoning. *Artificial Intelligence Review, 6*(1), 3–34. doi:10.1007/BF00155578

Kolivand, H., Rhalibi, A. E., Tajdini, M., Abdulazeez, S., & Praiwattana, P. (2018). *Cultural heritage in marker-less augmented reality: A survey.* Retrieved from https://www.intechopen.com/books/advanced-methods-and-new-materials-for-cultural-heritage-preservation/cultural-heritage-in-marker-less-augmented-reality-a-survey

Kolodner, J. L., Dorn, B., Thomas, J. O., & Guzdial, M. (2012). In D. Jonassen & S. Land (Eds.), *Theoretical foundations of learning environments* (pp. 142–170). New York, NY: Routledge.

Kong, A., Hodgson, Y., & Druva, R. (2015). The role of simulation in developing clinical knowledge and increasing clinical confidence in first-year radiography students. *Focus on Health Professional Education: A Multi-Disciplinary Journal, 16*(3), 29-44. doi:10.11157/fohpe.v16i3.83

Kroeker, K. (2010). Mainstreaming augmented reality. *Communications of the ACM, 53*(7), 19–21. doi:10.1145/1785414.1785422

Küçük, S., Kapakin, S., & Göktaş, Y. (2016). Learning anatomy via mobile augmented reality: Effects on achievement and cognitive load. *American Association of Anatomists, 9*(5), 411–421. doi:10.1002/ase.1603 PMID:26950521

Kuehn, B. M. (2018). Virtual and augmented reality put a twist on medical education. *Journal of the American Medical Association, 319*(8), 756–758. doi:10.1001/jama.2017.20800 PMID:29417140

Kuehster, C. R., & Hall, C. D. (2010). Simulation: Learning from mistakes while building communication and teamwork. *Journal for Nurses in Professional Development, 26*(3), 123–127. doi:10.1097/NND.0b013e3181993a95 PMID:20508427

Kuhn, J., & Stevens, V. (2017). Participatory culture as professional development: Preparing teachers to use Minecraft in the classroom. *TESOL Journal*, *8*(4), 753–767. doi:10.1002/tesj.359

Kumar, A. (2017). E-learning and blended learning in orthodontic education. *APOS Trends Orthod*, *7*(4), 188–198. doi:10.4103/apos.apos_49_17

Kwon, H. B., Park, Y. S., & Han, J. S. (2018). Augmented reality in dentistry: A current perspective. *Acta Odontologica Scandinavica*, *76*(7), 497–503. doi:10.1080/00016357.2018.1 441437 PMID:29465283

Kyle, R., & Murray, W. B. (2007). *Clinical simulation: Operations, engineering and management*. San Diego, CA: Elsevier Science & Technology.

Landis, J. R., & Koch, G. G. (1977). The measurement of observer agreement for categorical data. *Biometrics*, *33*(1), 159–174. doi:10.2307/2529310

Lan, Y. J., Hsiao, I. Y., & Shih, M. F. (2018). Effective learning design of game-based 3D virtual language learning environments for special education students. *Journal of Educational Technology & Society*, *21*(3), 213–227.

Lányi, C. S., Geiszt, Z., Károlyi, P., Tilinger, Á., & Magyar, V. (2006). Virtual reality in special needs early education. *The International Journal of Virtual Reality*, *5*(4), 55–68.

Lapkin, S., Fernandez, R., Levett-Jones, T., & Bellchambers, H. (2010). The effectiveness of using human patient simulation manikins in the teaching of clinical reasoning skills to undergraduate nursing students: A systematic review. *JBI Library of Systematic Reviews*, *21*(6), 661–694. PMID:27820553

Larson, B. E., Vaubel, C. J., & Grünheid, T. (2013). Effectiveness of computer-assisted orthodontic treatment technology to achieve predicted outcomes. *The Angle Orthodontist*, *83*(4), 557–562. doi:10.2319/080612-635.1 PMID:23181776

Lave, J., & Wenger, E. (1991). Legitimate peripheral participation. In J. Lave & E. Wenger (Eds.), *Situated learning: Legitimate peripheral participation* (pp. 27–44). Cambridge, UK: Cambridge University Press. doi:10.1017/CBO9780511815355.003

Law, A. M., Kelton, W. D., & Kelton, W. D. (1991). *Simulation modeling and analysis* (Vol. 2). New York, NY: McGraw-Hill.

Ledford, J. R., & Gast, D. L. (2009). *Single Subject research methodology in behavioral sciences: Applications in special education and behavioral sciences*. London, UK: Routledge; doi:10.4324/9780203877937

Lee-Kelley, L. (2018). When 'knowing what' is not enough: Role of organised simulations for developing effective practice. *International Journal of Project Management*, *36*(1), 198–207. doi:10.1016/j.ijproman.2017.08.003

Lefler, V., Kožnjak, T., Iličić, M., & Ramljak, H. (2018). *Simulacija poslovnog procesa uvođenja plinskog priključka u poduzeću Plin Vtc (Unpublished seminar)*. Osijek: Faculty of Economics in Osijek.

Legg, T. J., Adelman, D., & Levitt, C. (2009). Constructivist strategies in online distance education in nursing. *The Journal of Nursing Education*, *48*(2), 64–69. doi:10.3928/01484834-20090201-08 PMID:19260397

Legris, P., Ingham, J., & Collerette, P. (2003). Why do people use information technology? A critical review of the technology acceptance model. *Information & Management*, *40*(3), 191–204. doi:10.1016/S0378-7206(01)00143-4

Lemheney, A. J., Bond, W. F., Padon, J. C., Leclair, M. W., Miller, J. N., & Susko, M. T. (2016). Developing virtual reality simulations for office-based medical emergencies. *Journal of Virtual Worlds Research*, *9*(6), 1–18. doi:10.4101/jvwr.v9i1.7184

Lendahls, L., & Oscarsson, M. G. (2017). Midwifery students' experiences of simulation and skills training. *Nurse Education Today*, *50*, 12–16. doi:10.1016/j.nedt.2016.12.005 PMID:28006699

Limbu, B. H., Jarodzka, H., Klemke, R., & Specht, M. (2018). Using sensors and augmented reality to train apprentices using recorded expert performance: A systematic literature review. *Educational Research Review*, *25*, 1–22. doi:10.1016/j.edurev.2018.07.001

Linjawi, A. L., Hamdan, A. M., Perryer, D. G., Walmsley, A. D., & Hill, K. B. (2009). Students' attitudes towards an on-line orthodontic learning resource. *European Journal of Dental Education*, *13*(2), 87–92. doi:10.1111/j.1600-0579.2008.00545.x PMID:19368551

Liu, F., & Ding, Y. (2009). Role-play in English language teaching. *Asian Social Science*, *5*(10), 140–143. doi:10.5539/ass.v5n10p140

Livingston, M. A., Rosenblum, L. J., Brown, D. G., Schmidt, G. S., Julier, S. J., Baillot, Y., ... Maassel, P. (2011). Military applications of augmented reality. In B. Furht (Ed.), *Handbook of augmented reality*. New York, NY: Springer. doi:10.1007/978-1-4614-0064-6_31

Llena, C., Folguera, S., Forner, L., & Rodríguez-Lozano, F. J. (2018). Implementation of augmented reality in operative dentistry learning. *European Journal of Dental Education*, *22*(1), e122–e130. doi:10.1111/eje.12269 PMID:28370970

Lloyd, K. (2004). *Playing games with conflict: The Ha Long Bay e-Sim*. Paper presented at the International Conference on Computers in Education 2004, Melbourne, Australia. Retrieved from http://plum.yuntech.edu.tw/icce2004/Theme1/022_Lloyd.pdf

Lorence, M. (2015). School of Minecraft. *School Library Journal*. Retrieved from https://www.slj.com/?detailStory=minecraftedu-takes-hold-in-schools

Lorenzo, G., Lledó, A., Pomares, J., Roig, R., & Arnaiz, P. (2016). Bibliometric indicators in the study of Asperger syndrome between 1990 and 2014. *Scientometrics, 109*(1), 377–388. doi:10.100711192-016-1975-5

Lubbers, J., & Rossman, C. J. N. (2017). Satisfaction and self-confidence with nursing clinical simulation: Novice learners, medium-fidelity, and community settings. *Nurse Education Today, 48*, 140–144. doi:10.1016/j.nedt.2016.10.010 PMID:27810632

Ludvigsen, S. R. (2009). Sociogenesis and cognition: The struggle between social and cognitive activities. In B. Schwarz, T. Dreyfus, & R. Herskowitz (Eds.), *Transformation of knowledge through classroom interaction* (pp. 302–317). New York, NY: Routledge.

Ludwig, B., Bister, D., Schott, T. C., Lisson, J. A., & Hourfar, J. (2016). Assessment of two e-learning methods teaching undergraduate students cephalometry in orthodontics. *European Journal of Dental Education, 20*(1), 20–25. doi:10.1111/eje.12135 PMID:25560366

Lu, S.-J., & Liu, Y.-C. (2015). Integrating augmented reality technology to enhance children's learning in marine education. *Environmental Education Research, 21*(4), 525–541. doi:10.1080/13504622.2014.911247

Lyon, L. J., Hoover, T. E., Giusti, L., Booth, M. T., & Mahdavi, E. (2016). Teaching skill acquisition and development in dental education. *Journal of Dental Education, 80*(8), 983–993. PMID:27480710

MacDougall, R. D., Scherrer, B., & Don, S. (2018). Development of a tool to aid the radiologic technologist using augmented reality and computer vision. *Pediatric Radiology, 48*(1), 141–145. doi:10.100700247-017-3968-9 PMID:28866805

MacLean, S., Geddes, F., Kelly, M., & Della, P. (2018). Simulated patient training: Using inter-rater reliability to evaluate simulated patient consistency in nursing education. *Nurse Education Today, 62*, 85–90. doi:10.1016/j.nedt.2017.12.024 PMID:29306751

Mail, T. M. (2015). In-game Minecraft quests for elementary education. *International Journal for Innovation Education and Research, 3*(8), 164–174.

Majić, A., Has, A., & Zekić-Sušac, M. (2015). Discrete-event simulation model of customer support service in telecommunications. *Proceedings of the 13th International Symposium on Operational Research SOR'15 in Slovenia*, 514-519.

Makri, S., & Blandford, A. (2012). Coming across information serendipitously – part 2: A classification framework. *The Journal of Documentation, 68*(5), 706–724. doi:10.1108/00220411211256049

Ma, M., Fallavollita, P., Seelbach, I., Von Der Heide, A. M., Euler, E., Waschke, J., & Navab, N. (2016). Personalized augmented reality for anatomy education. *Clinical Anatomy (New York, N.Y.), 29*(4), 446–453. doi:10.1002/ca.22675 PMID:26646315

Ma, M., Jain, L. C., & Anderson, P. (2014). Future trends of virtual, augmented reality, and games for health. In *Virtual, Augmented Reality and Serious Games for Healthcare 1* (pp. 1–6). Heidelberg, Germany: Springer Berlin Heidelberg. doi:10.1007/978-3-642-54816-1_1

Ma, M., Oikonomou, A., & Jain, L. C. (2011). *Serious games and edutainment applications.* London, UK: Springer. doi:10.1007/978-1-4471-2161-9

Mantovani, F., Castelnuovo, G., Gaggioli, A., & Riva, G. (2003). Virtual reality training for health-care professionals. *Cyberpsychology & Behavior, 6*(4), 389–395. doi:10.1089/109493103322278772 PMID:14511451

Marcon, N. (2013). Minecraft as a powerful literacy prompt in the secondary English classroom. *Idiom, 49*(2), 35–37.

Marshall, A. (2014). Sensemaking in Second Life. *Procedia Technology, 13*, 107–111. doi:10.1016/j.protcy.2014.02.014

Marshall, G., & Harris, P. (2000). A study of the role of an objective structured clinical examination (OSCE) in assessing clinical competence in third year student radiographers. *Radiography, 6*(2), 117–122. doi:10.1053/radi.1999.0229

Mason, S. L. (2016). Radiography student perception of clinical stressors. *Radiologic Technology, 77*(6), 437–450. Retrieved from http://www.radiologictechnology.org/content/77/6/437.long PMID:16864623

McCarthy, J. P., & Anderson, L. (2000). Active learning techniques versus traditional teaching styles: Two experiments from history and political science. *Innovative Higher Education, 24*(4), 279–294. doi:10.1023/B:IHIE.0000047415.48495.05

McCaughey, C. S., & Traynor, M. K. (2010). The role of simulation in nurse education. *Nurse Education Today, 30*(8), 827–832. doi:10.1016/j.nedt.2010.03.005 PMID:20483188

McClarty, K., Orr, A., Frey, P., Dolan, R., Vassileva, V., & McVay, A. (2012). *A literature review of gaming in education.* Upper Saddle River, NJ: Pearson.

McGaghie, W. C., Issenberg, S. B., Cohen, E. R., Barsuk, J. H., & Wayne, D. B. (2011). Does simulation-based medical education with deliberate practice yield better results than traditional clinical education? A meta-analytic comparative review of the evidence. *Academic Medicine, 86*(6), 706–711. doi:10.1097/ACM.0b013e318217e119 PMID:21512370

McMillan, J. H. (2004). *Educational research: Fundamentals for the consumer* (4th ed.). Boston, MA: Allyn and Bacon.

Mendoza, F. D. (2017). Uso de simuladores de negocio como estrategia de aprendizaje adaptativo: Una experiencia en el aula. *Revista Virtu@lmente, 5*(2), 26-44.

Merchant, Z., Goetz, E. T., Cifuentes, L., Keeney-Kennicutt, W., & Davis, T. J. (2014). Effectiveness of virtual reality-based instruction on students' learning outcomes in K-12 and higher education: A meta-analysis. *Computers & Education*, *70*, 29–40. doi:10.1016/j.compedu.2013.07.033

Miller, D., Mills, T., & Harkins, S. (2011). Teaching about terrorism in the United Kingdom: How it is done and what problems it causes. *Critical Studies on Terrorism*, *4*(3), 405–420. doi:10.1080/17539153.2011.623416

Miller, K. T., Hannum, W. M., Morley, T., & Proffit, W. R. (2007). Use of recorded interactive seminars in orthodontic distance education. *American Journal of Orthodontics and Dentofacial Orthopedics*, *132*(3), 408–414. doi:10.1016/j.ajodo.2007.03.015 PMID:17826612

Milovanovic, J., Moreau, G., Siret, D., & Miguet, F. (2017). Virtual and augmented reality in architectural design and education: An immersive multimodal platform to support architectural pedagogy. *Proceedings from 17th International Conference, CAAD Futures*.

Miltenberger, C. A., & Charlop, M. H. (2015). The comparative effectiveness of portable video modeling vs. traditional video modeling interventions with children with autism spectrum disorders. *Journal of Developmental and Physical Disabilities*, *27*(3), 341–358. doi:10.100710882-014-9416-y

Mitchell, J. K., Gillies, R. A., & Mackert, R. (2017). Setting expectations about feedback in dental education. *MedEdPORTAL*, *13*, 10580. Retrieved from https://www.mededportal.org/publication/10580

Monachino, A. M., & Tuttle, S. A. (2015). Just-in-time training programs. In J. Palagapas, J. Maxworthy, C. Epps, & M. Mancini (Eds.), *Defining excellence in simulation programs* (pp. 127–134). Philadelphia, PA: Lippincott Williams & Wilkins.

Monsky, W. L., Levine, D., Mehta, T. S., Kane, R. A., Ziv, A., Kennedy, B., & Nisenbaum, H. (2002). Using a sonographic simulator to assess residents before overnight call. *AJR. American Journal of Roentgenology*, *178*(1), 35–39. doi:10.2214/ajr.178.1.1780035 PMID:11756082

Motola, I., Devine, L. A., Chung, H. S., Sullivan, J. E., & Issenberg, S. B. (2013). Simulation in healthcare education: A best evidence practical guide. AMEE Guide No. 82. *Medical Teacher*, *35*(10), e1511e–1530. doi:10.3109/0142159X.2013.818632 PMID:23941678

Moule, P. (2011). Simulation in nurse education: Past, present and future. *Nurse Education Today*, *31*(7), 645-646. doi-org.ezproxy.libproxy.db.erau.edu/10.1016/j.nedt.2011.04.005

Moustakas, C. (1994). *Phenomenological research methods*. Thousand Oaks, CA: SAGE. doi:10.4135/9781412995658

Murphy, R. J., Gray, S. A., Straja, S. R., & Bogert, M. C. (2004). Student learning preferences and teaching implications. *Journal of Dental Education*, *68*(8), 859–866. PMID:15286109

Nagy, P. (1990). *Modelling ill-structured problem solving with schema theory.* Paper presented at the annual conference of the Midwestern Educational Research Association, Chicago, IL.

Nara, N., Beppu, M., Tohda, S., & Suzuki, T. (2009). The introduction and effectiveness of simulation-based learning in medical education. *Internal Medicine (Tokyo, Japan), 48*(17), 1515–1519. doi:10.2169/internalmedicine.48.2373 PMID:19721295

Naser-ud-Din, S. (2015). Introducing Scenario Based Learning interactive to postgraduates in UQ Orthodontic Program. *European Journal of Dental Education, 19*(3), 169–176. doi:10.1111/eje.12118 PMID:25212808

Nebel, S., Schneider, S., & Rey, G. D. (2016). Mining learning and crafting scientific experiments: A literature review on the use of Minecraft in education and research. *Journal of Educational Technology & Society, 19*(2), 355–366.

Nguyen, P. K., Wasserman, S. M., Fann, J. I., & Giacomini, J. (2008). Successful lysis of an aortic prosthetic valve thrombosis with a dosing regimen for peripheral artery and bypass graft occlusions. *The Journal of Thoracic and Cardiovascular Surgery, 135*(3), 691–693. doi:10.1016/j.jtcvs.2007.11.012 PMID:18329497

NHS. (2016). *About the NHS.* Retrieved from https://www.nhs.uk/using-the-nhs/about-the-nhs/the-nhs

NHS. (2019). *The NHS Long Term Plan.* Retrieved from https://www.longtermplan.nhs.uk

Nifakos, S., Tomson, T., & Zary, N. (2014). *Combining physical and virtual contexts through augmented reality: Design and evaluation of a prototype using a drug box as a marker for antibiotic training.* Retrieved from https://peerj.com/articles/697

Nincarean, D., Alia, M. B., Halim, N. D. A., & Rahman, M. H. A. (2013). Mobile augmented reality: The potential for education. *Procedia: Social and Behavioral Sciences, 103*(26), 657–664. doi:10.1016/j.sbspro.2013.10.385

Nkenke, E., Vairaktaris, E., Bauersachs, A., Eitner, S., Budach, A., Knipfer, C., & Stelzle, F. (2012). Spaced education activates students in a theoretical radiological science course: A pilot study. *BMC Medical Education, 12*(1), 32. doi:10.1186/1472-6920-12-32 PMID:22621409

Noll, C., Häussermann, B., von Jan, U., Raap, U., & Albrecht, U. (2014). Mobile augmented reality in medical education: An application for dermatology. In *Proceedings of the 2014 workshop on Mobile augmented reality and robotic technology-based systems.* Bretton Woods, NH: ACM.

Noll, C., von Jan, U., Raap, U., & Albrecht, U. V. (2017). *Mobile augmented reality as a feature for self-oriented, blended learning in medicine: Randomized controlled trial.* Retrieved from https://www.ncbi.nlm.nih.gov/pubmed/28912113

Norcini, J. J., & McKinley, D. W. (2007). Assessment methods in medical education. *Teaching and Teacher Education, 23*(3), 239–250. doi:10.1016/j.tate.2006.12.021

Norwich, B., & Lewis, A. (2001). Mapping a pedagogy for special educational needs. *British Educational Research Journal*, *27*(3), 313–329. doi:10.1080/01411920120048322

Nye, E., Gardner, F., Hansford, L., Edwards, V., Hayes, R., & Ford, T. (2016). Classroom behaviour management strategies in response to problematic behaviours of primary school children with special educational needs: Views of special educational needs coordinators. *Emotional & Behavioural Difficulties*, *21*(1), 43–60. doi:10.1080/13632752.2015.1120048

O'Brennan, L. M., Waasdorp, T. E., Pas, E. T., & Bradshaw, C. P. (2015). Peer victimization and social-emotional functioning: A longitudinal comparison of students in general and special education. *Remedial and Special Education*, *36*(5), 275–285. doi:10.1177/0741932515575615

O'Brien, K., & Spencer, J. (2015). A viewpoint on the current status of UK orthodontic education and the challenges for the future. *British Dental Journal*, *218*(3), 181–183. doi:10.1038j.bdj.2015.50 PMID:25686440

O'Dell, B., Mai, J., Thiele, A., Priest, A., & Salamon, K. (2009). The hot seat: Challenging critical thinking and problem solving skills in physical therapist students. *The Internet Journal of Allied Health Sciences and Practice*, *7*(1), 1–10.

O'Neil, H. F., Baker, E. L., & Perez, R. S. (Eds.). (2016). *Using games and simulations for teaching and assessment: Key issues.* New York, NY: Routledge. doi:10.4324/9781315817767

Office of Special Education and Rehabilitative Services (ED). (2015). *37th annual report to Congress on the implementation of the" Individuals with Disabilities Education Act.* ERIC Clearinghouse.

Olsson, P., Nysjö, F., Hirsch, J.-M., & Carlbom, I. B. (2013). A haptics-assisted cranio-maxillofacial surgery planning system for restoring skeletal anatomy in complex trauma cases. *International Journal of Computer Assisted Radiology and Surgery*, *8*(6), 887–894. doi:10.100711548-013-0827-5 PMID:23605116

Olxaewski, A. E., & Wolbrink, T. A. (2017). Serious gaming in medical education: A proposed structured framework for game development. *Simulation in Healthcare*, *12*(4), 240–253. doi:10.1097/SIH.0000000000000212 PMID:28027076

Onofrei, G., & Stephens, S. (2014). Simulation games in operations management: The importance of immediate post game analysis. *Global Management Journal*, *6*(1-2), 61–64.

OnyxCeph. (n.d.). Retrieved from, http://www.onyxceph.de

Oren, T. (2011, April). The many facets of simulation through a collection of about 100 definitions. *SCS M&S Magazine,* 82. Retrieved from https://www.researchgate.net/publication/228939089_The_Many_Facets_of_Simulation_through_a_Collection_of_about_100_Definitions

Orsini, C., Binnie, V., Evans, P., Ledezma, P., Fuentes, F., & Villegas, M. J. (2015). Psychometric validation of the academic motivation scale in a dental student sample. *Journal of Dental Education*, *79*(8), 971–981. PMID:26246537

Ortiz, A. (2015). Staff technologist to clinical instructor: Using the Clinical Instructor Academy. *Radiologic Technology*, *87*(1), 112–113. Retrieved from http://www.radiologictechnology.org/content/87/1/112.full?sid=872cc3bc-eaea-4a8f-bdc4-1a55c7f75830 PMID:26377276

Osnes, C., & Keeling, A. (2017). Development of haptic caries simulation for dental education. *Journal of Surgical Simulation*, *4*, 29–34. doi:10.1102/2051-7726.2017.0006

Palter, V. N., & Grantcharov, T. P. (2010). Simulation in surgical education. *CMAJ: Canadian Medical Association Journal = Journal De L'Association Medicale Canadienne*, *182*(11), 1191-1196. doi:10.1503/cmaj.091743

Papamichail, D., Pantelis, E., Papagiannis, P., Karaiskos, P., & Georgiou, E. (2014). A web simulation of medical image reconstruction and processing as an educational tool. *Journal of Digital Imaging*, *28*(1), 24–31. doi:10.100710278-014-9689-9 PMID:25000920

Parhizkar, B., Obeidy, W. K., Chowdhury, S. A., Gebril, Z. M., Ngan, M. N. A., & Lashkari, A. H. (2012). *Android mobile augmented reality application based on different learning theories for primary school children*. Paper presented at 2012 International Conference on Multimedia Computing and Systems. 10.1109/ICMCS.2012.6320114

Parker, A. T., Grimmett, E. S., & Summers, S. (2008). Evidence-based communication practices for children with visual impairments and additional disabilities: An examination of single-subject design studies. *Journal of Visual Impairment & Blindness*, *102*(9), 540–552. doi:10.1177/0145482X0810200904

Park, S. Y. (2009). An analysis of the technology acceptance model in understanding university students' behavioral intention to use e-learning. *Journal of Educational Technology & Society*, *12*(3), 150–162.

Parsons, S. (2015). Learning to work together: Designing a multi-user virtual reality game for social collaboration and perspective-taking for children with autism. *International Journal of Child-Computer Interaction*, *6*, 28–38. doi:10.1016/j.ijcci.2015.12.002

Pasin, F., & Giroux, H. (2011). The impact of a simulation game on operations management education. *Computers & Education*, *57*(1), 1240–1254. doi:10.1016/j.compedu.2010.12.006

Patterson, C., Perlman, D., Taylor, E. K., Moxham, L., Brighton, R., & Rath, J. (2018). Mental health nursing placement: A comparative study of non-traditional and traditional placement. *Nurse Education in Practice*, *33*, 4–9. doi:10.1016/j.nepr.2018.08.010 PMID:30216804

Pereira, G., Dias, L., Vik, P., & Oliveira, J. A. (2011). Discrete simulation tools ranking: A commercial software packages comparison based on popularity. *International Journal of Production Economics, 111*, 229–243.

Peterková, J. (2014). Evaluation of managerial simulation games benefit in teaching process. In M. Zięba, & K. Zięba (Eds.), Innovative approaches to business education-selected issues (pp. 31- 42). Horsens.

Peterson, M. (2010). Massively multiplayer online role-playing games as arenas for second language learning. *Computer Assisted Language Learning, 23*(5), 429–439. doi:10.1080/0958 8221.2010.520673

Petrov, A. (2014). *Using Minecraft in education: A qualitative study on benefits and challenges of game-based education* (Unpublished master's thesis). University of Toronto, Ontario, Canada.

Piaget, J. (1977). *The development of thought: Equilibration of cognitive structures.* Oxford, UK: Viking Press.

Pinar Alakoc, B. (2018). Terror in the classroom: Teaching terrorism without terrorizing. *Journal of Political Science Education*, 1–19. doi:10.1080/15512169.2018.1470002

Pintrich, P. R., & Schrauben, B. (1992). Students' motivational beliefs and their cognitive engagement in classroom academic tasks. In D. H. Schunk & J. L. Meece (Eds.), *Student perceptions in the classroom* (pp. 149–183). Hillsdale, NJ: Lawrence Erlbaum Associates.

Pinz, A., Brandner, M., Ganster, H., Kusej, A., Lang, P., & Ribo, M (2002). Hybrid tracking for augmented reality. *ÖGAI Journal, 21*(1), 17-24.

Plack, M., & Wong, C. K. (2002). The evolution of the doctorate of physical therapy: Moving beyond the controversy. *Journal, Physical Therapy Education, 16*(1), 48–59. doi:10.1097/00001416-200201000-00008

Plass, J. L., Milne, C., Homer, B. D., Schwartz, R. N., Hayward, E. O., Jordan, T., ... Barrientos, J. (2012). Investigating the effectiveness of computer simulations for chemistry learning. *Journal of Research in Science Teaching, 49*(3), 394–419. doi:10.1002/tea.21008

Portman, M. E., Natapov, A., & Fisher-Gewirtzman, D. (2015). To go where no man has gone before: Virtual reality in architecture, landscape architecture and environmental planning. *Computers, Environment and Urban Systems, 54*, 376–384. doi:10.1016/j.compenvurbsys.2015.05.001

Prensky, M. (2001). *Digital game-based learning.* New York, NY: McGraw-Hill.

Pusey, M., & Pusey, G. (2015). Using Minecraft in the science classroom. *International Journal of Innovation in Science and Mathematics Education, 23*(3), 22–34.

Qian, Y. (2016). Computer simulation in higher education: Affordances, opportunities, and outcomes. In P. Vu, S. Fredrickson, & C. Moore (Eds.), *Handbook of research on innovative pedagogies and technologies for online learning in higher education* (pp. 236–262). Hershey, PA: IGI Global.

Qian, Y. (2016). Computer simulations in higher education: Affordances, opportunities and outcomes. In P. Vu, S. Fredrickson, & C. Moore (Eds.), *Handbook of research on innovative pedagogies and technologies for online learning in higher education* (pp. 236–262). Hershey, PA: IGI Global.

Qutieshat, A. S. (2018). Assessment of dental clinical simulation skills: Recommendations for implementation. *Journal of Dental Research and Review, 5*(116), 23. Retrieved from http://www.jdrr.org/text.asp?2018/5/4/116/250788

Ramachandiran, C. R., Jomhari, N., Thiyagaraja, S., & Mahmud, M. M. (2015). Virtual reality based behavioural learning for autistic children. *The Electronic Journal of e-Learning, 13*(5), 357-365.

Rao, G. K. L., Mokhtar, N. B., & Iskandar, Y. H. P. (2017). An integration of augmented reality technology for orthodontic education: Case of bracket positioning. *Proceedings of 2017 IEEE Conference on e-Learning, e-Management and e-Services (IC3e)*, 7-11.

Rao, G. K. L., Iskandar, Y. H. P., & Mokhtar, N. (2018a). A review of learning styles in orthodontic education. *Education in Medicine Journal, 10*(3), 1–13. doi:10.21315/eimj2018.10.3.1

Rao, G. K. L., Mokhtar, N., Iskandar, Y. H. P., & Srinivasa, A. C. (2018b). Learning orthodontic cephalometry through augmented reality: A conceptual machine learning validation approach. *Proceedings of 2018 International Conference on Electrical Engineering and Informatics (ICELTICs)*, 133-138.

Raskind, M., Smedley, T. M., & Higgins, K. (2005). Virtual technology: Bringing the world into the special education classroom. *Intervention in School and Clinic, 41*(2), 114–119. doi:10.1177/10534512050410020201

Reed, T., Pirotte, M., McHugh, M., Oh, L., Lovett, S., Hoyt, A. E., ... McGaghie, W. C. (2016). Simulation-based mastery learning improves medical student performance and retention of core clinical skills. *Simulation in Healthcare, 11*(3), 173–180. doi:10.1097/SIH.0000000000000154 PMID:27093509

Reiser, R. A. (2001). A history of instructional design and technology: Part II: A history of instructional design. *Educational Technology Research and Development, 49*(2), 57–67. doi:10.1007/BF02504928

Rhienmora, P., Gajananan, K., Haddawy, P., Dailey, M. N., & Suebnukarn, S. (2010). Augmented reality haptics system for dental surgical skills training. *Proceedings of the 17th ACM Symposium on Virtual Reality Software and Technology*, 97-98. 10.1145/1889863.1889883

Riley, R. A. Jr, Cadotte, E. E., Bonney, L., & MacGuire, C. (2013). Using a business simulation to enhance accounting education. *Issues in Accounting Education, 28*(4), 801–822. doi:10.2308/iace-50512

Rix, J., Hall, K., Nind, M., Sheehy, K., & Wearmouth, J. (2009). What pedagogical approaches can effectively include children with special educational needs in mainstream classrooms? A systematic literature review. *Support for Learning, 24*(2), 86–94. doi:10.1111/j.1467-9604.2009.01404.x

Rizzo, A., Parsons, T. D., Lange, B., Kenny, P., Buckwalter, J. G., Rothbaum, B., ... Reger, G. (2011). Virtual reality goes to war: A brief review of the future of military behavioral healthcare. *Journal of Clinical Psychology in Medical Settings, 18*(2), 176–187. doi:10.100710880-011-9247-2

Robertson, H. J. F., Paige, J. T., & Bok, L. R. (2012). *Simulation in radiology*. New York, NY: Oxford University Press. doi:10.1093/med/9780199764624.001.0001

Rodrigues, M. A. F., Silva, W. B., Neto, M. E. B., Gillies, D. F., & Ribeiro, I. M. M. P. (2007). An interactive simulation system for training and treatment planning in orthodontics. *Computers & Graphics, 31*(5), 688–697. doi:10.1016/j.cag.2007.04.010

Roschelle, J. (1992). Learning by collaborating: Convergent conceptual change. *Journal of the Learning Sciences, 2*(3), 235–276. doi:10.120715327809jls0203_1

Rose, F. D., Brooks, B. M., & Rizzo, A. A. (2005). Virtual reality in brain damage rehabilitation. *Cyberpsychology & Behavior, 8*(3), 241–262. doi:10.1089/cpb.2005.8.241

Rose, R., Shevlin, M., Winter, E., & O'Raw, P. (2015). *Project IRIS, inclusive research in Irish schools. A longitudinal study of the experiences of and outcomes for pupils with special educational needs (SEN) in Irish schools. Trim (Meath)*. National Council for Special Education.

Röss, D. (2011). *Learning and teaching mathematics using simulations: Plus 2000 examples from physics*. Berlin, Germany: De Gruyter. doi:10.1515/9783110250077

Rountree, J., & Adam, L. (2014). *BDS clinical tutor evaluation results*. Dunedin, New Zealand: University of Otago Faculty of Dentistry.

Rubinstein, R. Y., & Kroese, D. P. (2007). *Simulation and the Monte Carlo method* (2nd ed.). Hoboken, NJ: Wiley & Sons. doi:10.1002/9780470230381

Ruiz, C. R., Castiblanco, I. A., Cruz, J. P., Pedraza, L., & Londoño, D. C. (2018). Juegos de simulación en la enseñanza de la Ingeniería Industrial: Caso de estudio en la Escuela Colombiana de Ingeniería Julio Garavito. *Entre Ciencia e Ingenieria, 12*(23), 48–57. doi:10.31908/19098367.3702

Rumelhart, D. (1980). Schemata: The building blocks of cognition. In R. J. Spiro, B. C. Bruce, & W. F. Brewer (Eds.), *Theoretical issues in reading comprehension* (pp. 33–58). Hillsdale, NJ: Erlbaum.

Rutten, N., van Joolingen, W. R., & van der Veen, J. T. (2012). The learning effects of computer simulations in science education. *Computers & Education, 58*(1), 136–153. doi:10.1016/j.compedu.2011.07.017

Sabir, S. H., Aran, S., & Abujudeh, H. (2014). Simulation-based training in radiology. *Journal of the American College of Radiology, 11*(5), 512–517. doi:10.1016/j.jacr.2013.02.008 PMID:23770063

Sakiz, H., Sart, Z. H., Börkan, B., Korkmaz, B., & Babür, N. (2015). Quality of life of children with learning disabilities: A comparison of self-reports and proxy reports. *Learning Disabilities Research & Practice, 30*(3), 114–126. doi:10.1111/ldrp.12060

Säljö, R. (2010). Learning and technologies, people and tools in coordinated activities. *International Journal of Educational Research, 41*(6), 489–494. doi:10.1016/j.ijer.2005.08.013

Sánchez, C., Mota, D. R., Hernández, G., García, J. L., & Tlapa, D. A. (2016). Simulation software as a tool for supply chain analysis and improvement. *Computer Science and Information Systems, 13*(3), 983–998. doi:10.2298/CSIS160803039S

Sanders, C. W., Sadoski, M., van Walsum, K., Bramson, R., Wiprud, R., & Fossum, T. W. (2008). Learning basic surgical skills with mental imagery: Using the simulation centre in the mind. *Medical Education, 42*(6), 607–612. doi:10.1111/j.1365-2923.2007.02964.x PMID:18435713

Sanko, J. S. (2017). Simulation as a teaching technology: A brief history of its use in nursing education. *Quarterly Review of Distance Education, 18*(2), 77–103.

Santos, M. E. C., Lübke, A. W., Taketomi, T., Yamamoto, G., Rodrigo, Ma. M. T., Sandor, C., & Kato, H. (2016). Augmented reality as multimedia: the case for situated vocabulary learning. *Research and Practice in Technology Enhanced Learning, 11*(1), 4. Retrieved from https://www.ncbi.nlm.nih.gov/pubmed/30613237

Sasley, B. E. (2010). Teaching students how to fail: Simulations as tools of explanation. *International Studies Perspectives, 11*(1), 61–74. doi:10.1111/j.1528-3585.2009.00393.x

Scacchi, W. (2012). *The future of research in computer games and virtual world environments.* Irvine, CA: Institute for Software Research, University of California.

Scarcella, R. C., & Oxford, R. L. (1992). *The tapestry of language learning: The individual in the communicative classroom.* Boston, MA: Heinle & Heinle.

Scheckel, M. (2009). Nursing education: Past, present, future. In G. Roux & J. A. Halstead (Eds.), *Issues and Trends in Nursing: Essential Knowledge for Today and Tomorrow* (pp. 27–61). Burlington, MA: Jones & Bartlett Learning.

Schmitt, B. (2015). Experiential Marketing: A new framework for design and communications. *DMI 40th Anniversary Issue 2015, 25*(4), 19-26. doi:10.1111/drev.10298

Schmitt, B. (1999). Experiential marketing. *Journal of Marketing Management, 15*(1-3), 53–67. doi:10.1362/026725799784870496

Schmitt, B. (2012). The consumer psychology of brands. *Journal of Consumer Psychology, 22*(1), 7–17. doi:10.1016/j.jcps.2011.09.005

Scholz, J., & Smith, A. N. (2016). Augmented reality: Designing immersive experiences that maximize consumer engagement. *Business Horizons, 59*(2), 149–161. doi:10.1016/j.bushor.2015.10.003

Schon, D. (1983). *The reflective practitioner.* New York, NY: Basic Books.

Schönwetter, D. J., Reynolds, P. A., Eaton, K. A., & De Vries, J. (2010). Online learning in dentistry: An overview of the future direction for dental education. *Journal of Oral Rehabilitation, 37*(12), 927–940. doi:10.1111/j.1365-2842.2010.02122.x PMID:20726942

Schorn-Borgmann, S., Lippold, C., Wiechmann, D., & Stamm, T. (2015). The effect of e-learning on the quality of orthodontic appliances. *Advances in Medical Education and Practice, 6,* 545–552. PMID:26346485

Schreuder, H. W. R., van Dongen, K. W., Roeleveld, S. J., Schijven, M. P., & Broeders, I. A. M. J. (2009). Face and construct validity of virtual reality simulation of laparoscopic gynecologic surgery. *American Journal of Obstetrics and Gynecology, 200*(5), 540.e1–540.e8. doi:10.1016/j.ajog.2008.12.030 PMID:19285646

Schwebel, D. C., Gaines, J., & Severson, J. (2008). Validation of virtual reality as a tool to understand and prevent child pedestrian injury. *Accident; Analysis and Prevention, 40*(4), 1394–1400. doi:10.1016/j.aap.2008.03.005

Schweller, M., Ribeiro, D. L., Passeri, S. R., Wanderley, J. S., & Carvalho-Filho, M. A. (2018). Simulated medical consultations with standardized patients: In-depth debriefing based on dealing with emotions. *Journal Revista Brasileira de Educação Médica, 42*(1), 84–93. doi:10.1590/1981-52712018v42n1rb20160089

Sedden, M. L., & Clark, K. R. (2016). Motivating students in the 21st century. *Radiologic Technology, 87*(6), 609–616. Retrieved from http://www.radiologictechnology.org/content/87/6/609.full?sid=1a3efa4a-7651-43f5-8b7d-7bc217953a25 PMID:27390228

Seethamraju, R. (2006). Enhancing student learning of enterprise integration and business process orientation through an ERP business simulation game. *Journal of Information Systems Education, 22*(1), 19–29.

Selim, A. A., Ramadan, F. H., El-Gueneidy, M. M., & Gaafer, M. M. (2012). Using objective structured clinical examination (OSCE) in undergraduate psychiatric nursing education: Is it reliable and valid? *Nurse Education Today*, *32*(3), 283–288. doi:10.1016/j.nedt.2011.04.006 PMID:21555167

Serrano, C. M., Botelho, M. G., Wesselink, P. R., & Vervoorn, J. M. (2018). Challenges in the transition to clinical training in dentistry: An ADEE special interest group initial report. *European Journal of Dental Education*. Retrieved from https://onlinelibrary.wiley.com/doi/full/10.1111/eje.12324

Shanahan, M. (2016). Student perspective on using a virtual radiography simulation. *Radiography*, *22*(3), 217–222. doi:10.1016/j.radi.2016.02.004

Shannon, R. E. (1988). *Simulación de sistemas diseño, desarrollo e implementación*. Editorial Trillas.

Shea, T. P., Sherer, P. D., Quilling, R. D., & Blewett, C. N. (2011). Managing global virtual teams across classrooms, students, and faculty. *Journal of Teaching in International Business*, *22*(4), 300–313. doi:10.1080/08975930.2011.653911

Shema-Shiratzky, S., Brozgol, M., Cornejo-Thumm, P., Geva-Dayan, K., Rotstein, M., Leitner, Y., ... Mirelman, A. (2018). Virtual reality training to enhance behavior and cognitive function among children with attention-deficit/hyperactivity disorder: Brief report. *Developmental Neurorehabilitation*, 1–6. doi:10.1080/17518423.2018.1476602

Sheskin, D. J. (1997). *Handbook of Parametric and Nonparametric Statistical Procedures*. Washington, DC: CRC Press.

Sheu, J.-J., Chu, K.-T., & Wang, S.-M. (2017). The associate impact of individual internal experiences and reference groups on buying behavior: A case study of animations, comics, and games consumers. *Telematics and Informatics*, *34*(4), 314–325. doi:10.1016/j.tele.2016.08.013

Sheu, J.-J., Su, Y.-H., & Chu, K.-T. (2009). Segmenting online game customers – The perspective of experiential marketing. *Expert Systems with Applications*, *36*(4), 8487–8495. doi:10.1016/j.eswa.2008.10.039

Shin, N., Jonassen, D. H., & McGee, S. (2003). Predictors of well-structured and ill-structured problem solving in an astronomy simulation. *Journal of Research in Science Teaching*, *40*(1), 6–33. doi:10.1002/tea.10058

Shin, S., Park, J.-H., & Kim, J.-H. (2015). Effectiveness of patient simulation in nursing education: Meta-analysis. *Nurse Education Today*, *35*(1), 176–182. doi:10.1016/j.nedt.2014.09.009 PMID:25459172

Silke, A. (2009). Critical terrorism studies: A new research agenda. In J. Gunning, R. Jackson, & M. Smyth (Eds.), *Routledge critical terrorism studies* (pp. 34–48). New York, NY: Routledge.

Siltanen, S. (2017). Diminished reality for augmented reality interior design. *The Visual Computer*, *33*(2), 193–208. doi:10.100700371-015-1174-z

Silvennoinen, M., Helfenstein, S., Ruoranen, M., & Saariluoma, P. (2012). Learning basic surgical skills through simulator training. *Instructional Science*, *40*(5), 769–783. doi:10.100711251-012-9217-6

Simpson, A. W., & Kaussler, B. (2009). IR teaching reloaded: Using films and simulations in the teaching of international relations. *International Studies Perspectives*, *10*(4), 413–427. doi:10.1111/j.1528-3585.2009.00386.x

Slone, L. K., & Sandhofer, C. M. (2017). Consider the category: The effect of spacing depends on individual learning histories. *Journal of Experimental Child Psychology*, *159*, 34–49. doi:10.1016/j.jecp.2017.01.010 PMID:28266333

Smetana, L. K., & Bell, R. L. (2012). Computer simulations to support science instruction and learning: A critical review of the literature. *International Journal of Science Education*, *34*(9), 1337–1370. doi:10.1080/09500693.2011.605182

Society for Simulation in Healthcare. (n.d.) *What is simulation?* Retrieved from http://www.ssih.org/About-SSH/About-Simulation

Sousa Freire, V. E. C., Lopes, M. V. O., Keenan, G. M., & Dunn Lopez, K. (2018). Nursing students' diagnostic accuracy using a computer-based clinical scenario simulation. *Nurse Education Today*, *71*, 240–246. doi:10.1016/j.nedt.2018.10.001 PMID:30340106

Splitter, L. J. (2009). Authenticity and constructivism in education. *Studies in Philosophy and Education*, *28*(2), 135–151. doi:10.100711217-008-9105-3

St. John-Matthews, J., Gibbs, V., & Messer, S. (2013). Extending the role of technology enhanced learning within an undergraduate radiography programme. *Radiography*, *19*(1), 67–72. doi:10.1016/j.radi.2012.10.003

Statista, The Statistics Portal. (2018). *Statista dossier about Augmented Reality (AR)*. Retrieved from https://www.statista.com/study/38227/augmented-reality-ar-statista-dossier

Steinbeiß, G. (2017). *Minecraft as a learning and teaching tool - Designing integrated game experiences for formal and informal learning activities* (Unpublished master's thesis). University of Oulu, Oulu, Finland.

Stein-Wexler, R., Sanches, T., Roper, G. E., Wexler, A. S., Arieli, R. P., Ho, C., ... Soosman, S. K. (2010). An interactive teaching device simulating intussusception reduction. *Pediatric Radiology*, *40*(11), 1810–1815. doi:10.100700247-010-1764-x PMID:20652235

Stichter, J. P., Laffey, J., Galyen, K., & Herzog, M. (2014). iSocial: Delivering the social competence intervention for adolescents (SCI-A) in a 3D virtual learning environment for youth with high functioning autism. *Journal of Autism and Developmental Disorders, 44*(2), 417–430. doi:10.100710803-013-1881-0

Strickland, C. D., Lowry, P. A., Petersen, B. D., & Jesse, M. K. (2015). Introduction of a virtual workstation into radiology medical student education. *AJR. American Journal of Roentgenology, 204*(3), W289–W292. doi:10.2214/AJR.14.13180 PMID:25714314

Suenaga, H., Tran, H. H., Liao, H., Masamune, K., Dohi, T., Hoshi, K., & Takato, T. (2015). Vision-based markerless registration using stereo vision and an augmented reality surgical navigation system: A pilot study. *BMC Medical Imaging, 15*(1), 51. doi:10.118612880-015-0089-5 PMID:26525142

Suksudaj, N., Townsend, G. C., Kaidonis, J., Lekkas, D., & Winning, T. A. (2012). Acquiring psychomotor skills in operative dentistry: Do innate ability and motivation matter? *European Journal of Dental Education, 16*(1), e187–e194. doi:10.1111/j.1600-0579.2011.00696.x PMID:22251344

Sural, I. (2017). Mobile augmented reality applications in education. In G. Kurubacak & H. Altinpulluk (Eds.), *Mobile technologies and augmented reality in open education* (pp. 200–214). Hershey, PA: IGI Global. doi:10.4018/978-1-5225-2110-5.ch010

Tanner, J. R., Stewart, G., Totaro, M. W., & Hargrave, M. (2012). Business simulation games: Effective teaching tools or window dressing? *American Journal of Business Education, 5*(2), 115–128. doi:10.19030/ajbe.v5i2.6814

Tao, Y. H., & Cheng, C. J., & Sun, S.Y. (2012). Alignment of teacher and student perceptions on the continued use of business simulation games. *Journal of Educational Technology & Society, 15*(3), 177–189.

Tao, Y. H., Cheng, C. J., & Sun, S. Y. (2009). What influences college students to continue using business simulation games? The Taiwan experience. *Computers & Education, 53*(3), 929–939. doi:10.1016/j.compedu.2009.05.009

Tawfik, A. A., Rong, H., & Choit, I. (2015). Failure to learn: Towards a unified design approach for failure-based learning. *Educational Technology Research and Development, 63*(6), 975–994. doi:10.100711423-015-9399-0

Tennyson, R. D. (2011). Simulation technologies in global learning. In P. Ordoñez de Pablos, M. Lytras, W. Karwowski, & R. W. Lee (Eds.), *Electronic globalized business and sustainable development through IT management: Strategies and perspectives* (pp. 1–16). Hershey, PA: Business Science Reference. doi:10.4018/978-1-61520-623-0.ch001

Teo, T., Fan, X., & Du, J. (2015). Technology acceptance among pre-service teachers: Does gender matter? *Australasian Journal of Educational Technology, 31*(3), 235–251. doi:10.14742/ajet.1672

The University of Sydney School of Dentistry Overarching Strategic Goals and Objectives. 2018-22. (n.d.). Retrieved from, https://sydney.edu.au/content/dam/corporate/documents/faculty-of-medicine-and-health/dentistry/sydney-dental-school-strategic-plan.pdf

Thoirs, K., Giles, E., & Barber, W. (2011). The use and perceptions of simulation in medical radiation science education. *The Radiographer*, *58*(3), 5–11. doi:10.1002/j.2051-3909.2011.tb00149.x

Thompson, D., Whitney, I., & Smith, P. K. (1994). Bullying of children with special needs in mainstream schools. *Support for Learning*, *9*(3), 103–106. doi:10.1111/j.1467-9604.1994.tb00168.x

Thornton, G. C., & Cleveland, J. N. (1990). Developing managerial talent through simulation. *The American Psychologist*, *45*(2), 190–199. doi:10.1037/0003-066X.45.2.190

Tiwari, S. R., Nafees, L., & Krishnan, O. (2014). Simulation as a pedagogical tool: Measurement of impact on perceived effective learning. *International Journal of Management Education*, *12*(3), 260–270. doi:10.1016/j.ijme.2014.06.006

Tjiam, I. M., Berkers, C. H., Shout, B. M., Brinkman, W. M., Witjes, J. A., Scherpbier, A. J., ... Koldewijn, E. L. (2014). Evaluation of the educational value of a virtual reality TURP simulator according to a curriculum-based approach. *Simulation in Healthcare*, *9*(5), 288–294. doi:10.1097/SIH.0000000000000041 PMID:25275719

Tobin Grant, J. (2004). *Playing politics*. New York, NY: W.W. Norton & Company.

Towbin, A. J., Paterson, B. E., & Chang, P. J. (2008). Computer-based simulator for radiology: An educational tool. *Radiographics*, *28*(1), 309–316. doi:10.1148/rg.281075051 PMID:18203945

Tsai, F. H., Yu, K. C., & Hsiao, H. S. (2012). Exploring the factors influencing learning effectiveness in digital game-based learning. *Journal of Educational Technology & Society*, *15*(3), 240–250.

Tshibwabwa, E., Mallin, R., Fraser, M., Tshibwaba, M., Sanii, R., Rice, J., & Cannon, J. (2017). An integrated interactive–spaced education radiology curriculum for preclinical students. *Journal of Clinical Imaging Science*, *7*(1), 22. doi:10.4103/jcis.JCIS_1_17 PMID:28584689

Tudge, J. (1990). Vygotsky, the zone of proximal development, and peer collaboration: Implications for classroom practice. In L. Moll (Ed.), *Vygotsky and education: Instructional implications and applications of sociohistorical psychology* (pp. 155–172). Cambridge, UK: Cambridge University Press. doi:10.1017/CBO9781139173674.008

Tussyadiah, I. P., Jung, T. H., & tom Dieck, M. C. (2018). Embodiment of wearable augmented reality technology in tourism experiences. *Journal of Travel Research*, *57*(5), 597–611. doi:10.1177/0047287517709090

UK College of Dentistry Strategic Plan 2016-2020. (n.d.). Retrieved from https://dentistry.uky.edu/sites/default/files/UKCDStrategicPlan2016.pdf

United Nations Educational, Scientific and Cultural Organization (UNESCO). (1994). *The Salamanca statement and framework for action on special needs education.* Retrieved from http://unesdoc.unesco.org/images/0009/000984/098427eo.pdf

University of Florida College of Dentistry. Strategic Plan 2019-2024. (n.d.). Retrieved from https://cod-strategic-plan.sites.medinfo.ufl.edu/files/2018/07/18-UFCD-Strategic-Plan-FINAL.pdf

University of Iowa College of Dentistry Strategic Plan 2015-2020. (n.d.). Retrieved from https://www.dentistry.uiowa.edu/sites/default/files/docs/admin/COD_Strategic_Plan_2015-20.pdf

University of Louisville School of Dentistry (ULSD). Strategic Plan, 2017–2020. (n.d.). Retrieved from http://louisville.edu/dentistry/about/strategic-plan-2017-2020

University of Toronto. Achieving Impact through Excellence, Strategic Plan, 2014-2019. (n.d.). Retrieved from https://www.dentistry.utoronto.ca/sites/default/files/2016-06/strategic_plan_2014-2019.pdf

Uusi-Mäkelä, M. (2014). Immersive language learning with games: Finding flow in MinecraftEdu. In *Proceedings of ED-MEDIA 2014: World Conference on Educational Multimedia, Hypermedia & Telecommunications.* Chesapeake, VA: AACE.

van der Aalst, W. M. (2010). Business process simulation revisited. *Enterprise and Organizational Modeling and Simulation*, 1-14.

van der Heijden, H. (2004). User acceptance of hedonic information systems. *Management Information Systems Quarterly*, *28*(4), 695–704. doi:10.2307/25148660

Van der Merwe, N. (2013). An evaluation of an integrated case study and business simulation to develop professional skills in South African accountancy students. *International Business & Economics Research Journal*, *12*(10), 1137–1155.

Van Veeren, E. (2009). Interrogating 24: Making sense of US counter-terrorism in the global war on terrorism. *New Political Science*, *31*(3), 361–384. doi:10.1080/07393140903105991

Vanchiswaran, R. (2005). *Computer simulations in chemistry education.* Iowa, IL: Iowa State University Press.

Vasquez, E. III, Marino, M. T., Donehower, C., & Koch, A. (2017). Functional analysis in virtual environments. *Rural Special Education Quarterly*, *36*(1), 17–24. doi:10.1177/8756870517703405

Vávra, J. P., Zonča, R. P., Ihnát, P., Němec, M., Kumar, J., Habib, N., & Gendi, A. E. (2017). Recent development of augmented reality in surgery: A review. *Journal of Healthcare Engineering*, *9*. doi:10.1155/2017/4574172 PMID:29065604

Vendrely, A. (2005). Critical thinking skills during a physical therapist professional education program. *Journal, Physical Therapy Education*, *19*(1), 55–59. doi:10.1097/00001416-200501000-00007

Victoroff, K. Z., & Hogan, S. (2006). Students' perceptions of effective learning experiences in dental school: A qualitative study using a critical incident technique. *Journal of Dental Education, 70*(2), 124–132. PMID:16478926

Vlachou, A., Stavroussi, P., & Didaskalou, E. (2016). Special teachers' educational responses in supporting students with special educational needs (SEN) in the domain of social skills development. *International Journal of Disability Development and Education, 63*(1), 79–97. doi:10.1080/1034912X.2015.1111305

Volioti, C., Tsiatsos, T., Mavropoulou, S., & Karagiannidis, C. (2014, July). VLSS-Virtual Learning and Social Stories for Children with Autism. In *Proceedings of the 2014 IEEE 14th International Conference on Advanced Learning Technologies* (pp. 606-610). Athens, Greece: IEEE. 10.1109/ICALT.2014.177

Vos, L. (2015). Simulation games in business and marketing education: How educators assess student learning from simulations. *International Journal of Management Education, 13*(1), 57–74. doi:10.1016/j.ijme.2015.01.001

Vuchkova, J., Maybury, T. S., Camile, S., & Farah, C. S. (2011). Testing the educational potential of 3D visualization software in oral radiographic interpretation. *Journal of Dental Education, 75*(11), 1417–1425. PMID:22058390

Vygotsky, L. (1978). *Mind in society*. Cambridge, MA: Harvard University Press.

Vygotsky, L. S. (1978). *Mind in society: The development of higher psychological processes*. Cambridge, MA: Harvard University Press.

Wagner, J. B. (2017). Online simulation in an undergraduate radiologic technology program. *Proceedings of the University of North Texas College of Information Research Exchange Conference, USA*, 51-55.

Wagner, M. M. (1995). Outcomes for youths with serious emotional disturbance in secondary school and early adulthood. *The Future of Children, 5*(2), 90–112. doi:10.2307/1602359

Wang, J., Suenaga, H., Yang, L., Kobayashi, E., & Sakuma, I. (2017). Video see-through augmented reality for oral and maxillofacial surgery. *International Journal of Medical Robotics and Computer Assisted Surgery, 13*(2), e1754. doi:10.1002/rcs.1754 PMID:27283505

Wang, M., & Reid, D. (2011). Virtual reality in pediatric neurorehabilitation: Attention deficit hyperactivity disorder, autism and cerebral palsy. *Neuroepidemiology, 36*(1), 2–18. doi:10.1159/000320847

Wang, R., DeMaria, S. Jr, Goldberg, A., & Katz, D. (2016). A systematic review of serious games in training health care professionals. *Simulation in Healthcare, 11*(1), 41–51. doi:10.1097/SIH.0000000000000118 PMID:26536340

Wang, X., Laffey, J., Xing, W., Galyen, K., & Stichter, J. (2017). Fostering verbal and non-verbal social interactions in a 3D collaborative virtual learning environment: A case study of youth with Autism Spectrum Disorders learning social competence in iSocial. *Educational Technology Research and Development*, *65*(4), 1015–1039. doi:10.100711423-017-9512-7

Wawer, M., Milosz, M., Muryjas, P., & Rzemieniak, M. (2010). Business simulation games in forming of students' entrepreneurship. *International Journal of Euro-Mediterranean Studies*, *3*(1), 49–71.

Weller, J. M., Nestel, D., Marshall, S. D., Brooks, P. M., & Conn, J. J. (2012). Simulation in clinical teaching and learning. *The Medical Journal of Australia*, *196*(9), 594–599. doi:10.5694/mja10.11474 PMID:22621154

Wertz, C. I., Hobbs, D. L., & Mickelsen, W. (2013). Integrating technology into radiology science education. *Radiologic Technology*, *86*(1), 23–31. Retrieved from http://www.radiologictechnology.org/content/86/1/23.full PMID:25224084

Whicker, M. L., & Sigelman, L. (1991). *Computer simulation applications: An introduction.* Thousand Oaks, CA: SAGE.

Whitney, R. R. (2014). Differentiating instruction in postsecondary education. *Radiologic Technology*, *85*(4), 458–462. Retrieved from http://www.radiologictechnology.org/content/85/4/458.full?sid=1a50e948-f86a-4c41-b3a2-c17bdaa24ebb PMID:24614440

Williams, D. (2011). *Impact of business simulation games in enterprise education.* Paper Presented at *2010 University of Huddersfield Annual Learning and Teaching Conference*, University of Huddersfield.

Williams, P. L., & Berry, J. S. (1999). What is competence? A new model for diagnostic radiographers: Part 1. *Radiography*, *5*(4), 221–235. doi:10.1016/S1078-8174(99)90055-X

Willis, J., Hovey, L., & Hovey, K. (1987). *Computer simulations: A source book to learning in an electronic environment.* New York, NY: Garland.

Wilson, P. N., Foreman, N., & Stanton, D. (1997). Virtual reality, disability and rehabilitation. *Disability and Rehabilitation*, *19*(6), 213–220. doi:10.3109/09638289709166530

Winn, W. D. (1993). *A conceptual basis for educational applications of virtual reality. Human Interface Technology Laboratory Technical Report.* Seattle, WA: Human Interface Technology Laboratory. Retrieved from https://husily.ga/su1gsor63u.pdf

Wong, S. E. (2010). Single-case evaluation designs for practitioners. *Journal of Social Service Research*, *36*(3), 248–259. doi:10.1080/01488371003707654

Won, Y. J., & Kang, S. H. (2017). Application of augmented reality for inferior alveolar nerve block anesthesia: A technical note. *Journal of Dental Anesthesia and Pain Medicine*, *17*(2), 129–134. doi:10.17245/jdapm.2017.17.2.129 PMID:28879340

Wood, P. (1983). Inquiring systems and problem structure: Implication for cognitive development. *Human Development*, *26*(5), 249–265. doi:10.1159/000272887

Woolfe, R. (1992). Experiential learning in workshops. In T. Hobbs (Ed.), *Experiential training: Practical guidelines* (pp. 1–13). London, UK: Tavistock/Roudledge.

Woo, T., Kraeima, J., Kim, Y. O., Kim, Y. S., Roh, T. S., Lew, D. H., & Yun, I. S. (2015). Mandible reconstruction with 3D virtual planning. *Journal of International Society for Simulation Surgery*, *2*(2), 90–93. doi:10.18204/JISSiS.2015.2.2.090

Wright, S. W., Lindsell, C. J., Hinckley, W. R., Williams, A., Holland, C., Lewis, C. H., & Heimburger, G. (2006). High fidelity medical simulation in the difficult environment of a helicopter: Feasibility, self-efficacy and cost. *BMC Medical Education*, *6*(49), 1–9. doi:10.1186/1472-6920-6-49 PMID:17020624

Wuang, Y. P., Chiang, C. S., Su, C. Y., & Wang, C. C. (2011). Effectiveness of virtual reality using Wii gaming technology in children with Down syndrome. *Research in Developmental Disabilities*, *32*(1), 312–321. doi:10.1016/j.ridd.2010.10.002

Xie, C., Schimpf, C., Chao, J., Nourian, S., & Massicotte, J. (2018). Learning and teaching engineering design through modeling and simulation on a CAD platform. *Computer Applications in Engineering Education*, *26*(4), 824–840. doi:10.1002/cae.21920

Yang, C.-W., Ku, S.-C., Ma, M. H.-M., Chu, T.-S., & Chang, S.-C. (2018). Application of high-fidelity simulation in critical care residency training as an effective learning, assessment, and prediction tool for clinical performance. *Journal of the Formosan Medical Association*. doi:10.1016/j.jfma.2018.12.003

Yang, X., & Yi, Y. (2010). Student learning in business simulation: An empirical investigation. *Journal of Education for Business*, *85*(4), 223–228. doi:10.1080/08832320903449469

Yuan, H. B., Williams, B. A., & Fang, J. B. (2012). The contribution of high-fidelity simulation to nursing students' confidence and competence: A systematic review. *International Nursing Review*, *59*(1), 26–33. doi:10.1111/j.1466-7657.2011.00964.x

Zeigler, B. P., Praehofer, H., & Kim, T. G. (1976). *Theory of modelling and simulation* (Vol. 7). New York, NY: Wiley.

Zhao, M. Y., Ong, S. K., & Nee, A. Y. C. (2016). An augmented reality-assisted therapeutic healthcare exercise system based on bare-hand interaction. *International Journal of Human-Computer Interaction*, *32*(9), 708–721. doi:10.1080/10447318.2016.1191263

Zhou, F., Duh, H. B.-L., & Billinghurst, M. (2008). Trends in augmented reality tracking, interaction and display: A review of ten years of ISMAR. *IEEE International Symposium on Mixed and Augmented Reality 2008*, 193-202. 10.1109/ISMAR.2008.4637362

Zhu, E., Lilienthal, A., Shluzas, L. A., Masiello, I., & Zary, N. (2015). Design of mobile augmented reality in healthcare education: A theory-driven framework. *JMIR Medical Education*, *1*(2), e10. doi:10.2196/mededu.4443 PMID:27731839

Zichermann, G., & Cunningham, C. (2011). *Gamification by design: Implementing game mechanics in web and mobile apps*. Sebastopol, CA: O'Reilly Media.

Ziv, A., Wolpe, P. R., Small, S. D., & Glick, S. J. A. M. (2003). Simulation-based medical education: An ethical imperative. *Academic Medicine*, *78*(8), 783–788. doi:10.1097/00001888-200308000-00006 PMID:12915366

About the Contributors

Yufeng Qian currently serves as the faculty lead and program advisor of the Master of Arts in Education, Educational Technology Specialization program in the School of Education at Louisiana State University. Previously she was a doctoral faculty at Northeastern University and St. Thomas University respectively, where she directed over 50 doctoral research studies on a variety of topics in education and produced 32 doctorates. Dr. Qian's research interests include technology-enabled academic transformation, digital transformation, and models of online education and best practices in online teaching for active and deep learning. Focusing on emerging technology and technology leadership, her most recent publications include four edited books: "Integrating Multi-User Virtual Environments in Modern Classrooms," "Technology Leadership for Innovation in Higher Education," "Teaching, Learning, and Leading with Computer Simulations," and "Advancing Educational Research Through Emerging Technology."

* * *

Andrés Aguilera-Castillo is currently Associate Professor at Universidad EAN, with more than 8 years experience in the education sector. His research interests gravitate towards technology and business, business education, innovation and labor markets and, most recently, cybersecurity.

Joeun Baek has a Master in Education in English as a New Language at Boise State University. Her research interest is focused on game-based language learning. She has been in the field of language teaching for many years, in both face-to-face and online settings. She has publications on learning a foreign language through instant messenger programs and game-based language learning. Her recent research interests include language-focused mobile learning, gaming and second language teaching.

Maria-Ioanna Chronopoulou holds Master's degrees in Special Education and New Technologies in Education. She serves as a special education teacher in public Greek schools, focusing on enhancing students' social, emotional, academic, and everyday functional living skills. She is involved in research projects examining how various ICT tools can be integrated into special education curricula so as to enhance positive skills, and decrease nonfunctional or harmful behaviors of pupils with special needs.

Emmanuel Fokides is an Assistant Professor in the Department of Primary School Education, University of the Aegean, Greece. His courses focus on the educational uses of Virtual Reality, digital storytelling, Augmented Reality, and Serious Games. Since 1994, he has been involved in a number of research projects regarding distance and lifelong learning and the educational uses of Virtual and Augmented Reality. His work is published in several conference proceedings, international volumes, and journals. He is also the co-author of two books.

Mat Hardy is a Senior Lecturer in Middle East Studies at Deakin University, Australia. He divides his publication efforts between exploring the use of role play technologies in delivering Political Science teaching, and unpacking the way in which fantasy authors depict Middle Eastern cultures.

Adela Has works as a teaching and research assistant at Faculty of Economics in Osijek Josip Juraj Strossmayer University of Osijek. She is a doctoral student in the program Entrepreneurship and Innovativeness at University of Osijek. Her teaching activities are primarily related to organizing classes and giving lectures for courses: Informatics, Digital Economy, ICT in Banking, Business Simulations, Business Intelligence Systems, Intelligent Decision Support Systems and Development of Business Applications. Her research areas are business simulations, predictive analytics, data mining methods such as, neural networks, decision trees in business, education and artificial intelligence and its application. She is a member of Association of Information Systems (AIS) and Croatian Operational Research Society.

Yulita Hanum P. Iskandar who was originally trained in computing is a Senior Lecturer in Graduate School of Business, Universiti Sains Malaysia. She currently teaches Management Information Systems and Technology Management courses for postgraduates and specializes in research related to technological and innovation. She graduated from the Universiti Teknologi PETRONAS, with an Honours degree and MSc in Information Technology, and then PhD in Computer Science from

University of Southampton, UK. She was attached with Learning Societies Lab, and her PhD thesis investigated the design of effective feedback in the computer-based training. Yulita has been involved in technology-enhanced learning since 2004 and presented numerous papers in the top key conferences in learning technologies. She has also been a professional member of the IEEE and Association for Computing Machinery (ACM).

Benjamin Just, PT, MPT, is an Instructor of Clinical Education in the Doctor of Physical Therapy program at the University of Cincinnati and previously held the position of Clinical Lead for Cardiovascular Services at the University of Cincinnati Medical Center. He is currently pursuing a Ph.D. in Education with a focus in Instructional Design and Technology at the University of Cincinnati.

Wendi Kappers has a Ph.D. in Instructional Technology from the University of Central Florida. Her thesis work explored how educational video game effects upon mathematics achievement and motivation scores differed between the sexes. During her tenure at Seminole Community College working as a Professor and Program Manager of the Network Engineering Program, she was Co-PI of a NSF CSEMS grant that explored collaborative administration and industry mentorship planning used to increase enrollments of women and minorities with declared majors in the areas of Computer Science (CS), Engineering (E), Mathematics (M), and Science (S). Currently, Dr. Kappers is an Assistant Professor of the M.S. in Information Security & Assurance program within Embry-Riddle Aeronautical University's College of Business, Worldwide Campus. Additionally, she instructs RSCH 202 – Introduction to Research within the College of Arts and Sciences and CS120 – Introduction to Computing in Aviation in the College of Engineering. Both positions allow her to stay focused upon real-life educational and classroom issues while designing training that explores technology utilization that is based upon structured learning principles and practices. She is an experienced computer engineer and instructional designer, designing in Blackboard, WebCT, eCollege, and Canvas, and holds many industry-related certifications including the Microsoft Certified Systems Engineer (MCSE) and Trainer (MCT) certificates.

Marinela Knežević graduated from the Department of Mathematics, University of Osijek in 2018, with a major in Financial Mathematics and Statistics. She currently works in the Faculty of Economics in Osijek as an assistant for the "Young Researchers Career Development Project – Training of Doctoral Students." She is also a doctoral candidate working on a research project for the Croatian Science

Foundation entitled "Methodological Framework for Efficient Energy Management by Intelligent Data Analytics." She is currently enrolled in postgraduate doctoral study at the University of Zagreb in Varaždin in Information Science in the Faculty of Organization and Informatics. She is involved in teaching and research in the area of business simulations and data analytics.

Wendy Mickelsen, MHE, R.T.(R)(M), is clinical assistant professor and clinical coordinator for the Radiographic Science Program at Idaho State University in Pocatello, Idaho. She also works as a mammography technologist at Eastern Idaho Regional Medical Center.

Ellen Min is a student at Timberline High School in Boise, Idaho. Before moving to Boise, she lived in northern and southern California, New York, and Seoul, South Korea. Her first coding class in middle school sparked her interest in computer science. Since then, she has been learning and developing her skills in various programming languages, including Python, Java, and Swift. Her research interests are focused on computer science and its applications in different fields, including education and biomedical technology. In her free time, she enjoys playing piano, skiing, reading, and spending time with her family.

Norehan Mokhtar (Dr.) is the Deputy Director of Research & Networking and Consultant Orthodontist at the Advanced Medical and Dental Institute, Universiti Sains Malaysia. She completed her undergraduate degree in Dentistry (BDS) from Universiti of Malaya in 1995. She then undertook her specialist training in Manchester. In 2005, she was awarded a membership in Orthodontics from the Royal College of Surgeons of Edinburgh and obtained her Master in orthodontics from the University of Manchester in 2006. She was appointed as the Director of Advanced Medical and Dental Institute from 2016 to 2018 and the Head of Oral and Craniofacial Science Cluster and Acting Deputy Director of Academic from 2010 to 2011. Her research interests are cleft and craniofacial anomalies, orthodontics and biomaterials.

Hye-Kyeong Park is an English teacher at Sancheong middle school in South Korea, where she has been teaching since 2018. Before beginning her career as a teacher, she studied English education at Kyungnam University. With strong academic interest in game-based and social media-based learning, as well as classes focusing on the development of critical thinking skills, she creates learning activities that are relevant to students' daily lives. Currently, she is running a Minecraft club, where she encourages students to solve real-life problems using Minecraft Education edition.

Richard Price BSc (Hons) MSc CMALT, is the learning technologies advisor at Health Education England where he specialises in researching, developing and implementing learning and educational technologies, simulation, e-learning and information systems across health and care. He is responsible for improving the delivery of education and training with health and care organisations in the UK and works with UK international development agencies to support and improve access to healthcare education around the world.

Gururajaprasad Kaggal Lakshmana Rao holds a master in Orthodontics from Nizhny Novgorod State Medical Academy, Russia. He is currently pursuing his PhD studies at Universiti Sains Malaysia with a focus on smart learning environments. His research interests are centred around orthodontic education, clinical education and smart learning environments with special interests in augmented reality and its educational applications.

Kay Seo is a Professor of Instructional Design and Technology at the University of Cincinnati. Her research focuses on learner engagement and interaction in virtual worlds and social networking spaces.

Sukie Shinn is the project lead for the Simulation-Based Education (SBE) strategy that sits within the Simulation and Immersive Technologies workstream of the Technology Enhanced Learning (TEL) programme in Health education England (HEE). Previous projects at HEE include: The Quality Review, Lead Provider Review, and Implementation Project for the London and South East Regional (LaSE). Prior to this, Sukie worked as the Assessment Development Manager for the National Clinical Assessment Service (NCAS) - an arm's length body of the NHS.

Sally Totman is an Associate Professor in Middle East Studies at Deakin University, Australia. She is the author of "How Hollywood Projects Foreign Policy" (2009) and publishes on persona and the Middle East.

Jessyca Wagner R.T.(R) is an Assistant Professor of Radiologic Sciences at Midwestern State University. She received her AAS, BS, and MS degrees in radiologic sciences in 2007, 2010, and 2013 respectively from Midwestern State University and is currently completing a PhD in Learning Technologies at the University of North Texas with an anticipated graduation date of May 2019. She currently serves as the Vice President of the Association of Collegiate Educators in Radiologic Technology. She writes and presents on topics concerning online learning in higher education, artificial intelligence in radiology, and professional development for allied health educators.

Trevor Ward R.T.(R)(CT)(MR) received his MS in Radiologic Science Education in 2016 from Midwestern State University in Wichita Falls, Texas. He is currently an Assistant Professor in the Radiographic Science Program at Idaho State University in Pocatello, Idaho. He also serves as the President Elect of the Idaho Society of Radiologic Technologists and as a Chapter Delegate in Radiography for the American Society of Radiologic Technologists. His research interests focus on digital technology and enhancing student and technologist learning to improve patient care in Radiography.

Christopher Wertz R.T.(R) is the Program Director and an assistant professor for Radiographic Science at Idaho State University. He received his BSRS degree from Idaho State University in 2009, an MSRS degree from Midwestern State University in 2012 and is currently a doctoral candidate completing an EdD in Educational Technology at Boise State University. His research interests include emerging educational technologies in health education, digital assessment methods, and virtual simulation.

Marijana Zekić-Sušac is a full professor with tenure at Josip Juraj Strossmayer University, Faculty of Economics, in Osijek, Croatia. She earned her doctoral degree at the University of Zagreb, Faculty of Organization and Informatics, Varaždin, Croatia. Her research interests include business simulations, artificial intelligence, machine learning, and data mining in business, education, and medicine. She currently teaches ICT courses at undergraduate, graduate, and doctoral levels. She is a member of the International Neural Network Society, Croatian Operational Research Society, and Croatian Statistical Association. She was the editor in chief of the journal Croatian Operational Research Review (2012-2017) and is currently the associate editor of the Central European Journal of Operations Research. She leads a scientific project "Methodological framework for energy management using intelligent data analytics" supported by the Croatian Science Foundation.

Index

Purchase Print, E-Book, or Print + E-Book

IGI Global's reference books can now be purchased from three unique pricing formats:
Print Only, E-Book Only, or Print + E-Book.
Shipping fees may apply.

www.igi-global.com

Recommended Reference Books

ISBN: 978-1-5225-9348-5
© 2019; 454 pp.
List Price: $255

ISBN: 978-1-5225-7763-8
© 2019; 253 pp.
List Price: $175

ISBN: 978-1-5225-7531-3
© 2019; 324 pp.
List Price: $185

ISBN: 978-1-5225-7802-4
© 2019; 423 pp.
List Price: $195

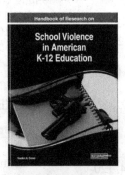

ISBN: 978-1-5225-6246-7
© 2019; 610 pp.
List Price: $275

ISBN: 978-1-5225-2998-9
© 2018; 352 pp.
List Price: $195

Looking for free content, product updates, news, and special offers?
Join IGI Global's mailing list today and start enjoying exclusive perks sent only to IGI Global members.
Add your name to the list at **www.igi-global.com/newsletters**.

Publisher of Peer-Reviewed, Timely, and Innovative Academic Research

IGI Global
DISSEMINATOR OF KNOWLEDGE

www.igi-global.com   Sign up at www.igi-global.com/newsletters   facebook.com/igiglobal   twitter.com/igiglobal

Ensure Quality Research is Introduced to the Academic Community

Become an IGI Global Reviewer for Authored Book Projects

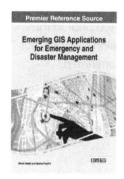

Premier Reference Source

Emerging GIS Applications for Emergency and Disaster Management

Premier Reference Source

Managerial Strategies and Green Solutions for Project Sustainability

Premier Reference Source

Comparative Approaches to Using R and Python for Statistical Data Analysis

Premier Reference Source

Solutions for High-Touch Communications in a High-Tech World

The overall success of an authored book project is dependent on quality and timely reviews.

In this competitive age of scholarly publishing, constructive and timely feedback significantly expedites the turnaround time of manuscripts from submission to acceptance, allowing the publication and discovery of forward-thinking research at a much more expeditious rate. Several IGI Global authored book projects are currently seeking highly-qualified experts in the field to fill vacancies on their respective editorial review boards:

Applications and Inquiries may be sent to:
development@igi-global.com

Applicants must have a doctorate (or an equivalent degree) as well as publishing and reviewing experience. Reviewers are asked to complete the open-ended evaluation questions with as much detail as possible in a timely, collegial, and constructive manner. All reviewers' tenures run for one-year terms on the editorial review boards and are expected to complete at least three reviews per term. Upon successful completion of this term, reviewers can be considered for an additional term.

If you have a colleague that may be interested in this opportunity, we encourage you to share this information with them.

IGI Global Proudly Partners With eContent Pro International

Receive a 25% Discount on all Editorial Services

Editorial Services

IGI Global expects all final manuscripts submitted for publication to be in their final form. This means they must be reviewed, revised, and professionally copy edited prior to their final submission. Not only does this support with accelerating the publication process, but it also ensures that the highest quality scholarly work can be disseminated.

English Language Copy Editing

Let eContent Pro International's expert copy editors perform edits on your manuscript to resolve spelling, punctuaion, grammar, syntax, flow, formatting issues and more.

Scientific and Scholarly Editing

Allow colleagues in your research area to examine the content of your manuscript and provide you with valuable feedback and suggestions before submission.

Figure, Table, Chart & Equation Conversions

Do you have poor quality figures? Do you need visual elements in your manuscript created or converted? A design expert can help!

Translation

Need your documjent translated into English? eContent Pro International's expert translators are fluent in English and more than 40 different languages.

Hear What Your Colleagues are Saying About Editorial Services Supported by IGI Global

"The service was very fast, very thorough, and very helpful in ensuring our chapter meets the criteria and requirements of the book's editors. I was quite impressed and happy with your service."

– Prof. Tom Brinthaupt,
Middle Tennessee State University, USA

"I found the work actually spectacular. The editing, formatting, and other checks were very thorough. The turnaround time was great as well. I will definitely use eContent Pro in the future."

– Nickanor Amwata, Lecturer,
University of Kurdistan Hawler, Iraq

"I was impressed that it was done timely, and wherever the content was not clear for the reader, the paper was improved with better readability for the audience."

– Prof. James Chilembwe,
Mzuzu University, Malawi

Email: customerservice@econtentpro.com   **www.igi-global.com/editorial-service-partners**

www.igi-global.com

Celebrating Over 30 Years of Scholarly
Knowledge Creation & Dissemination

InfoSci®-Books

A Database of Over 5,300+ Reference Books Containing Over 100,000+ Chapters Focusing on Emerging Research

GAIN ACCESS TO **THOUSANDS** OF REFERENCE BOOKS AT **A FRACTION** OF THEIR INDIVIDUAL LIST **PRICE**.

InfoSci®-Books Database

The **InfoSci®-Books** database is a collection of over 5,300+ IGI Global single and multi-volume reference books, handbooks of research, and encyclopedias, encompassing groundbreaking research from prominent experts worldwide that span over 350+ topics in 11 core subject areas including business, computer science, education, science and engineering, social sciences and more.

Open Access Fee Waiver (Offset Model) Initiative

For any library that invests in IGI Global's InfoSci-Journals and/or InfoSci-Books databases, IGI Global will match the library's investment with a fund of equal value to go toward **subsidizing the OA article processing charges (APCs) for their students, faculty, and staff** at that institution when their work is submitted and accepted under OA into an IGI Global journal.*

INFOSCI® PLATFORM FEATURES

* No DRM
* No Set-Up or Maintenance Fees
* A Guarantee of No More Than a 5% Annual Increase
* Full-Text HTML and PDF Viewing Options
* Downloadable MARC Records
* Unlimited Simultaneous Access
* COUNTER 5 Compliant Reports
* Formatted Citations With Ability to Export to RefWorks and EasyBib
* No Embargo of Content (Research is Available Months in Advance of the Print Release)

*The fund will be offered on an annual basis and expire at the end of the subscription period. The fund would renew as the subscription is renewed for each year thereafter. The open access fees will be waived after the student, faculty, or staff's paper has been vetted and accepted into an IGI Global journal and the fund can only be used toward publishing OA in an IGI Global journal. Libraries in developing countries will have the match on their investment doubled.

To Learn More or To Purchase This Database:
www.igi-global.com/infosci-books

eresources@igi-global.com • Toll Free: 1-866-342-6657 ext. 100 • Phone: 717-533-8845 x100

www.igi-global.com

Printed in the United States
By Bookmasters